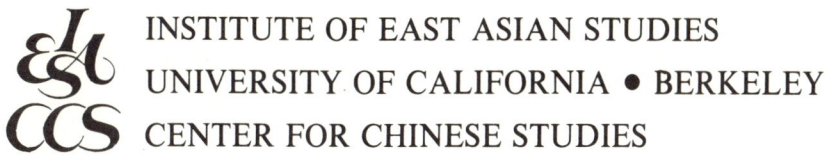
INSTITUTE OF EAST ASIAN STUDIES
UNIVERSITY OF CALIFORNIA • BERKELEY
CENTER FOR CHINESE STUDIES

Women in China

Bibliography of
Available English Language Materials

COMPILED BY
Lucie Cheng, Charlotte Furth, and Hon-ming Yip

HQ
1767
.C45
copy 2

Howard Wechsler Memorial Library

St. Olaf College Library

A publication of the
Institute of East Asian Studies
University of California
Berkeley, California 94720

Copyright © 1984 by the Regents of the University of California
ISBN 0-912966-72-6
Library of Congress Catalog Card Number 84-81228
Printed in the United States of America

Contents

Preface v
Sources Surveyed viii
Abbreviations xiv

Bibliographies and Serials 1

Education 1
    Education: Traditional China (to 1911) 1
    Education: The Chinese Republic (1911–1949) 1
    Education: The People's Republic of China (1949–) 2
    Education: Hong Kong, Taiwan, and Overseas China 3

Emancipation Movements: History and Ideology 3
    Emancipation Movements: General Surveys 3
    Women's Traditional Status 4
    The Issue of Emancipation Before 1911 5
    Emancipation Movements: The Chinese Republic (1911–1949) 5
    Emancipation Movements in the Communist Revolution, 1921–1949 7
    Emancipation Movements: The People's Republic of China (1949–) 9
    Emancipation Movements: Minorities 15
    Emancipation Movements: Hong Kong, Taiwan, and Overseas China 15

Health and Population 15
    Maternity and Child Care: Traditional and Republican China (to 1949) 15
    Maternity and Child Care: The People's Republic of China (1949–) 16
    Maternity and Child Care: Hong Kong, Taiwan, and Overseas China 16
    Health and Health Workers: Traditional and Republican China (to 1949) 17
    Health and Health Workers: The People's Republic of China (1949–) 17
    Footbinding and Infanticide 18
    Demographic Patterns and Population Policy 19
    Birth Control: General; Traditional and Republican China 20
    Birth Control: The People's Republic of China (1949–) 20
    Birth Control: Hong Kong, Taiwan, and Overseas China 22

Labor and Production 26
    Economic Development, General 26
    Urban and Industrial Labor: The Chinese Republic (1911–1949) 26
    Rural and Agricultural Labor: The Chinese Republic (1911–1949) 27
    Women in Production, General: The People's Republic of China (1949–) 27
    Urban and Industrial Labor: The People's Republic of China (1949–) 28
    Housewives and Production: The People's Republic of China (1949–) 30
    Rural and Agricultural Labor: The People's Republic of China (1949–) 31
    Xia Fang [Urban Youth in the Countryside]: The People's Republic of China (1949–) 34
    Social Welfare and the Socialization of Housework 34
    Consumer Affairs 35
    Slavery and Domestic Labor 35
    Prostitution 36
    Labor and Production in Minority Areas, the People's Republic of China (1949) 37
    Labor and Production in Hong Kong, Taiwan, and Overseas China 37

Literature, Art and Folklore 38
    Language and Linguistics 38
    Folklore and Folklore Studies 38
    Anthologies: Traditional Fiction, Poetry and Drama (to 1911) 39
    Traditional Fiction, Poetry and Drama: Through the Yuan Dynasty (to 1368) 40
    Traditional Fiction, Poetry and Drama: The Ming-Qing Dynasties (to 1911) 40
    Critical Studies: Traditional Literature 42
    Anthologies: Modern Short Stories (1911–present) 43

Republican Fiction, Poetry and Drama (1911-1949) 43
　　Critical Studies: Republican Literature 45
　The People's Republic of China: Fiction, Poetry and Drama (1949-) 46
　　Critical Studies: Literature of the People's Republic of China 48
　Women Writers and Artists 49
　　Chinese Women through Western Eyes: Literary Representations 50
　Hong Kong, Taiwan, and Overseas China: Fiction, Poetry and Drama 51
　　Critical Studies: Literature of Hong Kong, Taiwan, and Overseas China 52

Marriage and the Family 52
　Courtship, Marriage, Divorce and Widowhood: Traditional China (to 1911) 52
　Courtship, Marriage, Divorce and Widowhood: The Chinese Republic (1911-1949) 53
　Courtship, Marriage, Divorce and Widowhood: The People's Republic of China (1949-) 53
　Courtship, Marriage, Divorce, Widowhood and Celibacy: Hong Kong, Taiwan and Overseas China 56
　Sociology and Anthropology of the Family: General Works 57
　Clan and Lineage 58
　Family in Traditional China (to 1911) 59
　Family in Republican China (1911-1949) 60
　Family in the People's Republic of China (1949-) 60
　Marriage and the Family: Minorities 63
　Family in Hong Kong, Taiwan and Overseas China 64

Politics and the Law 66
　Family and Marriage Laws, Women's Legal Status: General and Comparative Surveys 66
　Family and Marriage Laws, Women's Legal Status: Traditional and Republican China (to 1949) ... 66
　Marriage and Family Laws in the People's Republic of China (1949-) 67
　Constitutional Law: The People's Republic of China (1949-) 68
　Marriage and Family Laws: Hong Kong, Taiwan and Overseas China 68
　Women in Politics: Traditional China (to 1911) 69
　Women in Politics: The Chinese Republic (1911-1949) 70
　Women in Politics; Cadres and Cadre Development: The People's Republic of China (1949-) 70
　Women in Politics: Minority Areas 75
　National and Regional Women's Organizations and Activities: The People's Republic
　　of China (1949-) 76
　International Women's Organizations and Activities: The People's Republic of China (1949-) 80
　Women's Organizations and Activities: Hong Kong, Taiwan and Overseas China 81

Psychology and Religion 82
　Psychology 82
　Sex and the Erotic 82
　Religion: Buddhism, Taoism, Confucianism and Folk Religions 83
　Religion: Christians and Christianity 83

Science, Technology and the Military 84
　Women and the Military: Traditional and Republican China (to 1949) 84
　Women and the Military: The People's Republic of China (1949-) 84
　Science and Scientists: The People's Republic of China (1949-) 85
　Science and Scientists: Hong Kong, Taiwan and Overseas China 86

Sport and Fashion 86
　Sports 86
　Fashion 89

Western Women in China 89
　Western Women (Other than Missionaries) in Traditional and Republican China (to 1949) 89
　Western Women (Other than Missionaries) in the People's Republic of China (1949-) 90
　Western Women Missionaries in China 90

Index of Authors *94*
Index of Chinese Women as Subjects *108*

Preface

This bibliography is designed to provide an introductory resource for the growing number of students and scholars in both East Asian area studies and women's studies who want access to research materials on the women of China. Interest in the historical circumstances and present status of Chinese women has been stimulated over the past decade by the coincidental development of the contemporary Anglo-American feminist movement and the emergence of the Chinese socialist revolution from a generation of isolation from the West. We hope that this sourcebook will contribute in a modest way to broadening and deepening our understanding of both women and China.

In gathering materials for the bibliography, we aimed to be comprehensive for all historical periods and all disciplines. In the interest of presenting as large a body of diverse source materials as possible, we have not personally examined every entry offered, and have provided only a limited number of annotations. Where entries have been unexamined, we have relied upon references from established, authoritative bibliographical sources such as the International Bibliography of the Social Sciences, the Library of Congress Catalog, or *Women's History Sources: A Guide to Archives and Manuscript Collections in the United States.* Archives noted in the text may be located through this latter work.

The bibliography is composed of approximately 4,100 entries, updated to the summer of 1981. Entries are classified under twelve general headings and a total of eighty-seven subheadings. Most of the important headings are subdivided into temporal periods and/or geographical areas. Generally, China proper is separate from minority areas and Hong Kong, Taiwan, and overseas China. Where there are no geographical or temporal indicators, the headings cover all periods and regions. There are some annotations: in particular, relevant chapters and sections are listed for entries where the work as a whole is not easily identified as being on the subject of women. An index of authors and an index of personal names of Chinese women are provided at the end. Journal references in the bibliography are generally in the form volume:number:pages. When the date is given, the number is usually omitted.

As a whole the bibliography reveals a typical pattern of existing Western social science research on the women of China. It shows that, as with the women of other more familiar cultures and societies, women of China have been explored most carefully when they appeared as an integral part of some other more established topic of research. The study of women in the family leads the bibliographer to anthropological research on China. The study of female health and reproduction draws attention to works on demography and on recent birth control programs. Women's labor becomes visible in the bibliographical record when women become an important part of China's infant industrial labor force in the early twentieth century. Historical studies on women have been rare among sinologists. The few we have are fleshed out bibliographically by the large body of reportage on Chinese life and customs that Western visitors and sojourners, missionary and otherwise, have been writing ever since the mid-nineteenth century for a public fascinated with "orientalism." Only in the past ten years do we see the first fruits of the new feminist research and of inquiry stimulated by the reopening of China to American contacts. This research overwhelmingly focuses on the issue of female emancipation and its relationship to China's socialist revolution. It constitutes the essential groundwork for serious scholarship of the future, which may be expected to go beyond its typically political and ideological orientation without losing its sense of commitment.

All of these patterns have governed the organization and selection of material presented here. We have brought together a selection of basic works on the anthropology of kinship, and on demography and birth control. We have surveyed the past century and a half's record of literature from missionaries and other "China hands." We have included titles not centrally about women where content analysis of the work in question shows that there is an identifiable section that is relevant. In dealing with reportage from China travelers and residents, we have found a substantial body of material that seems to require separate treatment. This includes bibliographical and autobiographical works by Western women sojourners in China and reports by recent visitors who discuss what they have learned about the contemporary status of Chinese women on the basis of the 1970s tourist experience. While the biographical works on Western women in China and the autobiographical works of Western women sojourners in China are placed under the heading "Western Women in China," reports on the women's liberation movement in China by Western women are grouped under "Emancipation Movements" and subdivided by time periods. As accurate presentations of Chinese life in China, such works are of varying quality. However, they reflect an historically valuable aspect of the changing relationship between China and the West, revealing the extent to which Western women offered a possibly distinctive dimension to our interpretations of China and showing how important China has been to contemporary Western feminists as a model of women's liberation.

In the bibliography original Western language sources have been complemented by titles of English language translations from the Chinese. Here there are two particularly important categories of material. The first is the growing body of important imaginative literature available in English language translation. Included here are approximately five hundred citations of stories, novels, poetry, and plays, divided by genre and period, together with a sampling of the most important relevant critical studies. For many entries brief annotations have been supplied by a specialist in Chinese literature. For the post-1911 period—the only one to have produced known women writers of fiction—female authors are identified by an asterisk. (For minor writers, such as those often published in the translation magazine *Chinese Literature,* the sex of the author has not always been possible to determine, since Chinese names in romanized form are not easily sex specific.) The value of such literature as a source should be obvious, both as an opening to the world of private experience where women have never been invisible and as a guide to the dominant cultural images of their roles.

The second important category of original Chinese materials rendered into English is that of news and opinion articles translated from the post-1950 Chinese press. Such translations have been produced in great numbers by U.S. government-sponsored services like Joint Publications Research Service or, until 1974, by the U.S. Consulate General in Hong Kong. This literature is basic for tracing the ebb and flow of political campaigns on women's emancipation in the People's Republic and for exploring how the Chinese have integrated women's issues into their strategies for socialist development. The translation literature collected by American sources is supplemented by that published by the Chinese themselves in such foreign language journals as *Peking Review* and *China Reconstructs* and by the longer and more scholarly translation series published by the International Arts and Sciences Press *(Chinese Studies in History, Chinese Studies in Sociology,* etc.). As a whole this literature can give the Western student a reasonably comprehensive overview of recent primary documentary sources available in Chinese.

In the bibliography, translation literature published by American government-sponsored services is not arranged by article title, but alphabetically by the abbreviated title of each translation series. The major ones are Joint Publications Research Service (JPRS), *Survey of China Mainland Press (SCMP), Selections from China Mainland Magazines (SCMM), Extracts from China Mainland Magazines (ECMM), Survey of People's Republic of China Press (SPRCP), Selections from People's Republic of China Magazines (SPRCM),* and *Current Background (CB).* Within each series entries are in chronological order by series number, as libraries and indexes record them. However, the date given for each title is the date of publication of the Chinese original. For this reason series numbers and article dates occasionally appear to be slightly out of sequence. For the best available analysis of these materials, readers should consult: Peter Berton and Eugene Wu, *Contemporary China: A Research Guide* (Stanford, 1967), chapter 20, "Translations and Monitoring Services."

Chinese authors' names in the bibliography and authors index appear as they are romanized on the title pages of their works. However, pinyin romanization is used in annotations. The reader is confronted not only with the variation between the Wade-Giles system and the pinyin system, but also with a bewildering array of personal styles of romanization adopted by older Chinese authors. Where a name appears in more than one form, cross references are supplied in square brackets. Pseudonyms are also cross referenced. We have attempted to provide a cross index of all the variant forms of cited personal names to assist the user.

The island of Taiwan (or the Republic of China) was the object of especially intensive American research inquiry during the years between 1950 and 1972, when the mainland was closed off from the United States. All Taiwan-based studies are treated as geographically distinct. Whether in any given instance the results hold true for "China" is left up to the reader's judgment. Hong Kong and minority areas are also treated as geographically and socially distinct "Chinas." Most of the entries under "Overseas China" deal with Chinese women in America because of our association with the UCLA Asian American Studies Center and the fact that this bibliography is published in the United States. Nevertheless, this should not delude readers into thinking that the bibliography is comprehensive for Chinese America or for the many other overseas "Chinas."

This bibliography is a work of collective authorship. It began in 1975 as a project undertaken by the students in Lucie Cheng's UCLA graduate seminar on the sociology of Chinese women. Over the succeeding months and years the compiling was carried on by Aleen Holly, Carol Iu, Jessica Kao, Hon-ming Yip, and Suellen Cheng. These researchers were supported by funds made available through the Academic Senate and the Asian American Studies Center at UCLA. The Committee on the Status of Women of the Association for Asian Studies supplied several small grants, a portion of which were used to engage the able services of Ying-ho Chiang in compiling the section on imaginative literature. Linda Pomerantz assisted in annotations. While Lucie Cheng initiated and organized the project, Charlotte Furth assumed major responsibility for editing and developing the classification scheme, and Hon-ming Yip was responsible for arranging the final typescript. While the manuscript was being prepared, Carol Sakala and Maureen Patterson made available their enormously helpful professional advice accumulated from working on Sakala's bibliography *Women of South Asia*. We are grateful to Susan Stone for her painstaking work as press technical editor. We are also grateful to the anonymous reviewers of our preliminary manuscript for their very helpful comments.

Each one of these people and others contributed to the project time and effort far beyond the value of the modest paychecks some of them received. Their reward will be to have helped create a useful tool for feminist scholarship.

Lucie Cheng
Department of Sociology
 and
Asian American Studies Center
UCLA

Charlotte Furth
Department of History
California State University
 at Long Beach

Hon-ming Yip
Department of History
UCLA

April 1982, Los Angeles

Sources Surveyed

Bibliographies

Abstracts in Anthropology. Westport, Conn.: Greenwood Periodicals. V. 1–, Feb., 1970–.

The American Humanities Index. N.Y.: Whitston Publishing Co. V. 1–, 1975–.

Berton, Peter; Menquez, Alexander; and Wu, Eugene. *Contemporary China: A Research Guide.* Stanford: Hoover Institution on War, Revolution and Peace, 1967.

Bibliography—Index to Current U.S. JPRS Translations: China and Asia Exclusive of Near East. N.Y., etc.: Research & Microfilm Publications, CCM Information Corp., etc. V. 3–, July 1964/June 1965–.

Bibliography of Asian Studies. Ann Arbor, etc.: Association for Asian Studies. 1941–.

Books in Print. N.Y.: R.R. Bowker Co. 1972–.

Cordier, Henri. *Bibliotheca Sinica,* 2nd ed., rev. Paris: E. E. Guilmoto, 1904–1908; Supplément et index. Paris: P. Genthner, 1922–1924.

Current Background [CB]. Hong Kong: U.S. Consulate General. No. 1–, June 13, 1950–.

Dissertation Abstracts. Ann Arbor: University Microfilms. V. 1–, 1938–.

Doctoral Dissertations on Asia. Ann Arbor: Association for Asian Studies, etc. V. 1–, Winter 1975–.

Extracts from China Mainland Magazine [ECMM]. Hong Kong: U.S. Consulate General. No. 1–212, Aug. 1, 1955–May 23, 1960. Succeeded by *Selections from China Mainland Magazines.*

Fraser, Steward Erskine and Hsu, Kuang-liang. *Chinese Education and Society: A Bibliographic Guide; the Cultural Revolution and Its Aftermath.* White Plains, N.Y.: International Arts & Sciences Press, 1972. Also published as *Chinese Education* 5:3/4 (Fall/Winter 1972–1973).

Fujimoto, Isao, et al. *Asian in America: A Selected Annotated Bibliography.* Davis, Ca., 1971.

Gibbs, Donald A. *Subject and Author Index to Chinese Literature Monthly, 1951–1976.* New Haven: Yale University Far Eastern Publications, 1978.

Gibbs, Donald and Li, Yun-chen. *A Bibliography of Studies and Translations of Modern Chinese Literature, 1918–1942.* Cambridge, Mass.: East Asian Research Center, Harvard University, 1975.

Gordon, Leonard, H. D. and Shulman, Frank J. *Doctoral Dissertations on China: A Bibliography of Studies in Western Languages, 1945–1970.* Seattle: University of Washington Press, 1972.

Hansen, Gladys C., et al. *The Chinese in California: A Brief Bibliographic History.* Portland: Richard Abel & Co., 1970.

Hinding, Andrea; Bower, Ames, Sheldon; Chambers, Clarke A.; and Moody, Suzanna. *Women's History Sources: A Guide to Archives and Manuscript Collections in the United States,* V. 1: Collections; V. 2: Index. N.Y. & London: R.R. Bowker Co., 1979.

Hoover Institution on War, Revolution, and Peace. *The Library Catalog of the Hoover Institution on War, Revolution, and Peace, Stanford University; Catalog of the Western Language Collections.* Boston: G.K. Hall, 1969.

Hucker, Charles O. *China: A Critical Bibliography.* Tucson: University of Arizona Press, 1962.

Humanities Index. Bronx, N.Y. V. 1–, June 1974–.

Index to People's Republic of China Press, Selections from People's Republic of China Magazines, and Current Background. Hong Kong: U.S. Consulate General. July/Sept. 1973–Oct./Dec. 1973; Jan./Mar. 1974–July/Sept. 1977. Continuation of *Index to Survey of China Mainland Press, Selections from China Mainland Magazines, and Current Background.*

Index to Survey of China Mainland Press. Hong Kong. Nov. 1950–Dec. 1952.

Index to Survey of China Mainland Press, Extracts from China Mainland Magazines, and Current Background, 1950–1960. Hong Kong: U.S. Consulate General, 1956–1960.

Index to Survey of China Mainland Press, Selections from China Mainland Magazines, and Current Background. Aug. 12, 1960–Jan./Mar. 1973. Hong Kong: U.S. Consulate General, 1960–1973. Continuation of *Index to Survey of China Mainland Press, Extracts from China Mainland Magazines, and Current Background, 1950–1960.*

International Bibliography of Economics. Paris: UNESCO. V. 1–, 1952–.

International Bibliography of Political Science. Paris: UNESCO. V. 1–, 1953–.

International Bibliography of Social and Cultural Anthropology. Paris: UNESCO. V. 1–, 1958–.

International Bibliography of Sociology. Paris: UNESCO. V. 1–, 1951–.

Kyōto daigaku jimbun kagaku kenkyūjo. *Tōyōshi kenkyū bunken ruimoku, 1946/50–1960.* (Annual Bibliography of Oriental Studies, 1946–60); *Tōyōgaku kenkyū bunken ruimoku* (Annual Bibliography of Oriental Studies, English and Japanese, 1961–62); *Tōyōgaku kenkyū bunken ruimoku* (Annual Bibliography of Oriental Studies, Japanese and English, 1963–). Kyoto, 1952–.

Kyriak, Theodore E. *China, a Bibliography.* Annapolis: Research and Microfilms. V. 1, No. 1, 3–V. 2; July–Sept. 1962–1963/64.

Library, University of California, Berkeley. *Author-Title Catalog.* Boston: G.K. Hall & Co., 1963.

Library of Congress and National Union Catalog. *Author List, 1942–62: A Master Cumulation.* Detroit: Gale Research Co., 1971.

The Library of Congress Catalogs. *The National Union Catalog, 1963–67.* Ann Arbor: J.W. Edwards Publisher, Inc., 1969.

The Library of Congress Catalogs. *The National Union Catalog (Author List), 1968–72.* Ann Arbor: J.W. Edwards Publisher, Inc., 1973.

Library of Congress Catalogs. *National Union Catalog, 1973–77.* Totowa, N.J.: Rewman & Littlefield, 1978.

Library of Congress Catalogs. *National Union Catalog, 1978.* Washington, D.C.: Library of Congress, 1979.

Library of Congress Catalogs. *National Union Catalog, 1979.* Washington, D.C.: Library of Congress, 1980.

Library of Congress Catalogs. *National Union Catalog, 1980.* Washington, D.C.: Library of Congress, 1981.

Library of Congress Catalogs. *National Union Catalog, 1981.* Washington, D.C.: Library of Congress, 1981.

Liu, Kwang-ching. *American and Chinese: A Historical Essay and a Bibliography.* Cambridge, Mass.: Harvard University Press, 1963.

London Bibliography of the Social Sciences. London, 1931–. V. 1–, 1929–.

Lum, William Wong and the Asian American Research Project, University of California, Davis. *Asians in America: A Bibliography.* Davis, Ca.: University Library, 1969.

Lum, William Wong and the Asian American Research Project, University of California, Davis, comp. *Asians in America: A Bibliography of Master's Theses and Doctoral Dissertations.* Davis, Ca., 1970.

Lust, John. *Index Sinicus: A Catalogue of Articles Relating to China in Periodicals and Other Collective Publications, 1920-1955.* Cambridge, England: W. Heffer, 1964.

New York Missionary Research Library. *Dictionary Catalog of the Missionary Research Library.* N.Y., Boston: G.K. Hall, 1968.

Nunn, Godfrey Raymand. *East Asia: A Bibliography of Bibliographies.* Honolulu: East West Center Library, 1967.

Ong, Paul M., et al., comps. *Theses and Dissertations on Asians in the United States, with Selected References to Other Overseas Asians.* Davis, Ca.: Asian American Studies, Department of Applied Behavioral Sciences, University of California, 1974.

Psychological Abstracts. Lancaster, Pa.: American Psychological Association. V. 1-, Jan., 1927-.

Reader's Guide to Periodical Literature. N.Y.: H.W. Wilson Co., 1915-. V. 1, 1900/04-.

Rosenberg, Marie Barovic; Bergstrom, Len V.; and Een, JoAnn Delores. *Women and Society: A Critical Review of the Literature with a Selected Annotated Bibliography.* 2 vols. Beverly Hills: Sage Publications Inc., 1975, 1978.

Selections from China Mainland Magazines [SCMM]. Hong Kong: U.S. Consulate. No. 1-760, Aug. 15, 1955-Oct. 1, 1973.

Selections from People's Republic of China Magazines [SPRCM] Hong Kong: U.S. Consulate. No. 761/762-943, Oct. 29, 1973-Sept. 26, 1977.

Shulman, Frank Joseph, ed. *Doctoral Dissertations on China, 1971-1975: A Bibliography of Studies in Western Languages.* Seattle: University of Washington Press, 1978.

Skinner, George William, et al. *Modern Chinese Society: An Analytical Bibliography,* V. 1: Publications in Western Languages, 1644-1972. Stanford: Stanford University Press, 1973.

Social Sciences and Humanities Index. N.Y., etc.: H.W. Wilson Co. V. 1-27, 1907/15-1973/74.

Social Sciences Citation Index. Philadelphia: Institute for Scientific Information. 1966/70-.

Social Sciences Index. Bronx, N.Y. V. 1-, June 1974-.

Sorich, Richard, ed. *Contemporary China: A Bibliography of Reports on China Published by the United States Joint Publications Research Service.* N.Y., 1961.

Survey of China Mainland Press [SCMP]. Hong Kong: U.S. Consulate General. No. 1-5469, Nov. 1, 1950-Oct. 5, 1973.

Survey of People's Republic of China Press [SPRCP]. Hong Kong: U.S. Consulate General. No. 5470-6434, Oct. 9, 1973-Sept. 30, 1977. Continuation of *SCMP.*

Tong, Te-kong and Wu, Robert. *The Third Americans: A Select Bibliography on Asians in America with Annotations.* Oak Park, Ill.: CHCUS, 1980.

Transdex: Bibliography and Index to the U.S. Joint Publications Research Service (JPRS) Translations. N.Y.: CCM Information Corp. V. 1, 1963?-.

Tsai, Meishi. *Contemporary Chinese Novels and Short Stories, 1949-1972: An Annotated Bibliography.* Draft, 1974.

United States. Joint Publications Research Service [JPRS]. Arlington, Va. V. 1-, July 3, 1957-.

University of California. *Union Catalog, 1963-67.* Berkeley: University of California, Berkeley, Institute of Library Research, 1972.

University of California, Los Angeles. Card catalog.

University of California, Los Angeles. *Dictionary Catalog of the University Library, 1919-62.* Boston: G.K. Hall & Co., 1963.

Yang, Winston L.Y.; Li, Peter; and Mao, Nathan K. *Classical Chinese Fiction: A Guide to Its Study and Appreciation, Essays and Bibliographies.* Boston: G.K. Hall & Co., 1978.

Yuan, Tung-li. *China in Western Literature: A Continuation of Cordier's Bibliotheca Sinica.* New Haven: Yale University, 1958.

Journals

Acta Asiatica: Bulletin of the Institute of Eastern Culture. Tokyo: Tōhō gakkai. No. 1-, 1960-.

Acta Psychologica Taiwanica. Taibei: Guoli Taiwan daxue, Lixue yuan, Xinlixue xi (National Taiwan University, College of Science, Dept. of Psychology). No. 1-, Nov. 1958-. Bilingual: articles in English or Chinese. Chinese title: *Guoli Taiwan daxue, Lixue yuan, Xinlixue xi yanjiu baogao.*

Acta Sociologica: Scandinavian Review of Sociology. Copenhagen, 1955-.

Amerasia J. Los Angeles. V. 1-, Mar. 1971-.

America: A Catholic Review of the Week. N.Y.: America Press. V. 1-, Apr. 17, 1909-.

Amer. Anthropologist. Washington, D.C.: Anthropological Society of Washington. After 1903, Lancaster, Pa.; Menasha, Wisc.; Washington, D.C.: American Anthropological Association and affiliated societies. V. 1, no. 1-v. 11, no. 1, Jan. 1888-Dec. 1898; new (2nd) series, v. 1, no. 1-, Jan. 1899-.

Amer. Ethnologist. Washington, D.C. V. 1-, Feb. 1974-.

Amer. Homes. Garden City, N.Y.: Doubleday, Doran & Co., Inc., 1928-. V. 1, Oct. 1928-.

Amer. J. of Comparative Law. Baltimore: American Association for the Comparative Study of Law. V. 1, no. 1-, Winter-Spring 1952-.

Amer. J. of Public Health. Boston, etc.: American Public Health Association. V. 1, no. 1-, Jan. 1911-.

Amer. J. of Sociology. Chicago: American Sinological Society; University of Chicago. V. 1, no. 1, July 1895-.

Amer. Scholar. N.Y.: Scribner Press, 1932-. V. 1-, Jan. 1932-.

Amer. Universities Field Staff Reports. East Asian series. N.Y.: American Universities Field Staff. V. 1, no. 1-, Aug. 15, 1952-.

Annals of Human Genetics. London: Cambridge University Press. V. 19-, July 1954-.

Annals of the Amer. Academy of Political and Social Science. Philadelphia. V. 1-, July 1890-.

The ASA Gray Bulletin. Ann Arbor. New series, v. 1-3, Jan. 1952-Spring 1961.

Asia. N.Y.: Asia Society. No. 1-, Spring 1964-.

Asia: J. of the Amer. Asiatic Association. N.Y.: American Asiatic Association; East and West Association. V. 17, no. 1-v. 46, no. 12, Mar. 1917-Dec. 1946. Title varies: V. 42, no. 11 to end issued as *Asia and the Americas.*

Asia and the Americas: see *Asia; J. of the Amer. Asiatic Association.*

Asia Major. Leipzig; London. V. 1-10, 1924-1935; neue (2.) Folge, v. 1, no. 1, 1944; new (3rd) series, v. 1-, 1949-.

Asian Affairs. N.Y. V. 1-, Sept./Oct. 1973-.

Asian Affairs: J. of the Royal Central Asian Society. London. V. 57-61, Feb. 1970-1974.

Asian American Women. Stanford. May 1976.

Asian Forum: A Quarterly J. of Asian Affairs. Washington, D.C.: Pan-Asia Foundation. V. 1, no. 1-, Jan.-Feb. 1969-.

Asian Profile. Hong Kong: Asian Research Service. V. 1–, 1973–.

Asian Review. London. 1886–1966; V. 1–2, no. 4, Nov. 1967–July 1969. Superseded by *Asiatic Review.*

Asian Survey. Berkeley: University of California, Institute of International Studies. V. 1, no. 1–, Mar. 1961. Successor to *Far Eastern Survey.*

Asiatic Quarterly Review, see *Asiatic Review.*

Asiatic Review. Working, Eng.: Oriental University Institute (name changed 1903 to Oriental Institute); London; etc. V. 1, no. 1–10, no. 2, Jan. 1886–Oct. 1890; 2nd series, v. 1, no. 1–v. 10, no. 20, Jan. 1891–Oct. 1895; 3rd series, v. 1, no. 1– v. 34, no. 68, Jan. 1896–Oct. 1912; new (4th) series, v. 1, no. 1–v. 50, no. 184, Jan. 1913–Oct. 1954. Title varies: v. 1–10, 1886–1890, and 4th series, v. 1–2, 1913, issued as *Asiatic Quarterly Review;* 2nd and 3rd series, 1891–1912, issued as *Imperial and Asiatic Quarterly Review.* Succeeded by *Asian Review.*

Atlantic Monthly: A Magazine of Literature, Science, Art, and Politics. Boston: Phillips, Sampson & Co., 1857–. V. 1–, Nov. 1857–.

Atlas. N.Y.: Worley Publishing Co. V. 1–21, no. 3, Mar. 1961–Apr. 1972. Continued by *Atlas World Press Review.*

Atlas World Press Review. N.Y.: Stanley Foundation. V. 21, no. 4–v. 27, no. 2, May 1974– Feb. 1980.

Berkeley J. of Sociology. Berkeley: Dept. of Sociology, University of California. V. 1–, Spring 1955–.

Bridge Magazine. N.Y.. V. 1–, July/Aug. 1971–.

Bulletin of Concerned Asian Scholars. Cambridge, Mass.: Committee of Concerned Asian Scholars. V. 1–, May 1968–.

Bulletin of Department of Archaeology and Anthropology. Taibei: National Taiwan University. 1953–. Chinese title: *Guoli Taiwan daxue kaogu renlei xuekan.*

Bulletin of School of Oriental and African Studies. London: University of London, School of Oriental Studies (name changed 1938 to School of Oriental and African Studies). V. 1–, 1917/20–. Title varies: v. 1–6, 1917/20–1930/32, issued as *Bulletin of the School of Oriental Studies, London Institution;* v. 7–9, 1933/35–1937/39, issued as *Bulletin of the School of Oriental Studies, University of London.*

Bulletin of the Institute of Ethnology, Academia Sinica. Taibei: Zhongyang yanjiuyuan, Minzuxue yanjiusuo. No. 1–, Mar. 1956–. Bilingual: articles in English or Chinese. Chinese title: *Zhongyang yanjiuyuan, Minzuxue yanjiusuo jikan.*

Bulletin on Chinese Education. Peking: Chinese National Association for the Advancement of Education. V. 1–4?, 1922–1926?

Catholic World: A Monthly Magazine of General Literature and Science. N.Y.: L. Kehoe. V. 1–214, Apr. 1865–1971.

Century Magazine. N.Y.: Scribner & Co., 1870–1881; Century Co., 1881–1930. V. 1–120, Nov. 1870–1930.

China Critic. Shanghai. V. 1, no. 1–v. 31, no. 6, May 31, 1928–Nov. 7, 1940.

China Forum. Taibei. 1974–. Bilingual: Chinese and English. Chinese title: *Zhonghua xuebao.*

China J. Shanghai: China Society of Science and Arts; Shanghai Chemical Society. V. 1, no. 1–v. 35, no. 5, Jan. 1923–Nov. 1941. Title varies: v. 1–5, 1923–1927, issued as *China J. of Science and Arts.*

China J. of Science and Arts, see *China J.*

China Law Review. Shanghai: Dong Wu daxue, Falü xueyuan (Suzhou University, Dept. of Law). V. 1, no. 1–v. 11, no. 3?, Apr. 1922–Jan. 1941? Suspended publ. July 1937–May 1940. Bilingual: articles in English or Chinese. Chinese titles: *Faxue jikan; Faxue zazhi.*

The China Magazine. N.Y.: Chinese News Service, 1938–1949. V. 1–19, no. 2, Apr. 1938–Feb. 1949.

China Mainland Review. Hong Kong: Institute of Modern Asian Studies, University of Hong Kong. V. 1–2, Jun. 1965–1967.

China Medical J., see *Chinese Medical J.*

China Monthly Review. Shanghai: Millard Publishing Co. v. 1–124, June 9, 1917–July 1953.

China News Analysis. Hong Kong. No. 1–, Aug. 25 1953.

China Notes. N.Y. V. 1, Sept. 1962–.

China Now. London. No. 1–, May 1970.

China Pictorial. Peking. 1951–.

China Quarterly. London: Congress for Cultural Freedom (Paris); University of London, School of Oriental and African Studies, Contemporary China Institute. No. 1–, Jan.–Mar. 1960.

China Reconstructs. Peking: China Welfare Institute. V. 1, no. 1–, Jan.–Feb. 1952–.

Chinese Report. New Delhi: China Study Center. V. 1, no. 1–, Aug. 1964–.

China Society, Singapore. *Annual of the China Society of Singapore.* 1952–1975.

Chinese Culture. Taibei: Zhongguo wenhua yanjiusuo (Chinese Cultural Research Institute [also called Institute of Chinese Culture and Institute for Advanced Chinese Studies]). V. 1, no. 1–, July 1957–.

Chinese Economic J. and Bulletin. Peiping: Chinese Government Bureau of Economic Information; China [Republic], Shiye bu, Guoji maoyi ju (Ministry of Industry, Bureau of Foreign Trade). V. 1, no. 1–v. 20, no. 6, Jan. 1927–June 1937. Successor to *Chinese Economic Monthly.*

Chinese Economic Monthly. Peking: Chinese Government Bureau of Economic Information. V. 1, no. 1–v. 3, no. 12, Oct. 1923–Dec. 1926. Succeeded by *Chinese Economic J. and Bulletin.*

Chinese Economic Studies. White Plains, N.Y.: International Arts and Sciences Press. V. 1–, Fall 1967–.

Chinese Education. White Plains, N.Y.: International Arts and Sciences Press. V. 1–, Spring 1968–.

Chinese Law and Government. White Plains, N.Y.: International Arts and Sciences Press. V. 1–, Spring 1968–.

Chinese Literature. Peking: Foreign Languages Press. Autumn 1951–.

Chinese Medical J. Peking; Shanghai; Washington D.C.: China Medical Missionary Association (from 1925, Zhongguo yixue hui [Chinese Medical Association]). V. 21, no. 3–v. 85, no. 9, Nov. 1909–Sept. 1966. Supplementary Chengdu ed., v. 61A–v. 63A, no. 5, Oct. 1942–Oct. 1945. Title varies: v. 21, no. 3–v. 45, no. 12, Nov. 1909–Dec. 1931, issued as *China Medical J.*

Chinese Medical J. Taibei: Zhonghua yixue hui (Chinese Medical Association). V. 1, no. 1–, Mar. 1954–. Bilingual: Articles in English or Chinese. Chinese title: *Zhonghua yixue zazhi.*

Chinese Recorder. Foochow; Shanghai: China Christian Educational Association. v. 1, no. 1–v. 72, no. 12?, June 1868–Dec. 1941? Title varies: v. 1, no. 1–v. 45, no. 12, June 1868–Dec. 1914, issued as *Chinese Recorder and Missionary J.;* v. 70, no. 1 to end issued as *Chinese Recorder and Educational Review.*

China Repository. Canton. V. 1, no. 1–v. 20, no. 12, May 1832–1851.

Chinese Social and Political Science Review. Peiping: Chinese Social and Political Science Association. V. 1, no. 1–v. 24 no. 4?, Apr. 1916–Mar. 1941?.

Chinese Sociology and Anthropology. White Plains, N.Y.: International Arts and Sciences Press. V. 1–, Fall 1968–.

Chinese Students' Monthly. Baltimore: Chinese Students'

Alliance of Eastern States, U.S.A. V. 1-v. 26, no. 1, 1905-Dec. 1930.

Chinese Studies in History. White Plains, N.Y. V. 1-, Fall 1967-.

Ch'ing-shih wen-t'i. New Haven, St. Louis: Society for Ch'ing Studies. V. 1, no. 1-, May 1965-.

Christian Century. Chicago: The Christian Century Press. V. 1-, Jan.? 1884-.

Christian Science Monitor. Boston: Christian Science Monitor. 1959-.

Chung Chi J. Hong Kong: Chongji shuyuan (Chung Chi College). V. 1, no. 1-June 1961-. Bilingual: articles in English or Chinese. Chinese title: *Chongji xuebao*.

Chung-kuo yin-hang Bi-monthly Economic Review. Taibei: Bank of China Head Office. 1947-.

Collier's. N.Y.: P.F. Collier. V. 1-139, no. 1, Apr. 28, 1888-Jan. 4, 1857.

Communist Affairs. Los Angeles: University of Southern California, Research Institute on Communist Strategy and Propaganda. V. 1-6, no. 1-2, June 1962-1968.

Contemporary China. Hong Kong: Hong Kong University Press. 1955-.

Contemporary China. N.Y. V. 1-, Oct. 1976.

Contemporary Review. London: A. Strahan. V. 1-Jan. 1866-.

The Cosmopolitan. N.Y. 1886-.

Country Life. London. V. 1-(no. 1), Jan. 18, 1897-.

Current History. N.Y. V. 1, no. 1-, Sept. 1941-.

Current Scene: Developments in Mainland China. Hong Kong. V. 1, no. 1-, May 15, 1961-.

Demography. Chicago: Population Association of America. V. 1-, 1964.

Developing Economies. Tokyo: Institute of Asian Economic Affairs. V. 1-, Jan./June 1963.

East Asian Cultural Studies. Tokyo: The Center for East Asian Cultural Studies.

East Asian Review. Seoul: The Institute for East Asian Studies. V. 1-, Spring 1974-.

East European Quarterly. Boulder, Colo. 1-, 1967-.

East of Asia Magazine. Shanghai. V. 1-5, 1902-1906.

East West Center Review. Honolulu: East West Center Grantees' Association. V. 1-4, no. 3, June 1964-1967/68.

East-West Review. Kyoto: Doshisha University Press. V. 1, Spring 1964-.

Eastern Anthropologists. Lucknow: Ethnographic & Folk Culture Society. 1948-.

Eastern Horizon. Hong Kong. V. 1, no. 1-, July 1960-.

Eastern World (Asian Annual). London. V. 1-25, no. 11/12, May 1947-Nov.-Dec. 1971.

Economic Development and Cultural Change. Chicago: University of Chicago, Research Center in Economic Development and Cultural Change. V. 1, no. 1-, Mar. 1952.

The Economic J.: The J. of the Royal Economic Society. London: MacMillan & Co., Ltd.; N.Y.: The MacMillan Co. V. 1-(no. 1-), Mar. 1891-.

Economic Reporter (Jingji daobao), English supplement. Hong Kong: Economic Information Agency. 1976-.

Ethnology: An International J. of Cultural and Social Anthropology. Pittsburgh: Dept. of Anthropology, University of Pittsburgh. V. 1-, June 1962-.

Eugenics Quarterly. Baltimore: American Eugenics Society. V. 1-15, Mar. 1954-1968.

Eugenics Review. London: The Eugenics Education Society, etc. V. 1-60, Apr. 1909-1968.

Family Planning. London: F. P. Association. V. 1-25, Apr. 1952-Apr. 1976.

Far Eastern Economic Review. Hong Kong. V. 1, no. 1-, Oct. 16, 1946-.

Far Eastern Quarterly. Ann Arbor: Far Eastern Association. V. 1, no. 1-v. 15, no. 4, Nov. 1941- Aug. 1956. Succeeded by *J. of Asian Studies*.

Far Eastern Survey. N.Y.: Institute of Pacific Relations, American Council. V. 1, no. 1-v. 30, no. 2, Mar. 3, 1932-Feb. 1961. Succeeded by *Asian Survey*.

Feminist Studies. N.Y. V. 1-, Summer 1972-.

Folk-Lore: The J. of the Folklore Society. London: Folklore Society. V. 1-, Mar. 1890-.

Folklore Studies. Tokyo, etc. V. 1-21, 1942-62. Continued by *Asian Folklore Studies*, v. 22-, 1963-.

Fortune. Chicago, etc..: Time Inc. V. 1, Feb. 1930-.

Forum. Philadelphia. V. 1-113, Mar. 1886-Mar. 1950.

Free China Review. Taiwan. V. 1-, Apr. 1951-.

The Galaxy: A Magazine of Entertaining Reading. N.Y.: Sheldon. V. 1-25, no. 1, May 1866-Jan. 1878.

Geographical Magazine. London. V. 1, no. 1-, May 1935-.

Good Housekeeping. N.Y. V. 1-, May 1885-.

Harper's Bazaar. N.Y. Hearst Magazines Inc. V. 1-, Nov. 2, 1867-.

Harvard J. of Asiatic Studies. Cambridge, Mass.: Harvard-Yenching Institute. V. 1, no. 1-Apr. 1936-.

Hastings Law J. San Francisco: Hastings College of the Law. V. 1-, Fall 1949-.

History Today. London. V. 1, no. 1-, Jan 1951-.

Hong Kong Law J. Hong Kong. V. 1, no. 1-, Jan 1971-.

Imperial Asiatic Quarterly Review, see *Asiatic Review*.

Independent Woman. Washington, etc.: National Federation of Business and Professional Women's Clubs. V. 1-, 1919-.

Industry of Free China. Taibei: China [Republic], Xingzheng yuan, Jingji anding weiyuanhui, Gongye weiyuanhui (Executive Yuan, Economic Stabilization Board, Industrial Development Commission); Guoji jingji hezuo fazhan weiyuanhui (Council for International Economic Cooperation and Development). V. 1, no. 1, Jan. 1954-. Bilingual: articles in English or Chinese. Chinese title: *Ziyou Zhongguo zhi gongye*.

Information Bulletin. Nanking: Council of International Affairs. V. 1-v. 5, no. 1/2, May 11, 1936-Oct. 27, 1937.

Inprecor: International Press Correspondence. Montrenil, Cedex, France. No. 1-66, 1974?-Jan. 27, 1977; new series: no. 1-18?, Feb.-Dec. 1977.

Institute of Pacific Relations News Bulletin, see *Pacific Affairs*.

International and Comparative Law Quarterly. London: The Society of Comparative Legislation. V. 1-, Jan. 1952-.

International J. of Fertility. Mexico. V. 1-, Oct./Dec. 1955-.

International Labor Review. Geneva. V. 1-, Jan 1921-.

International Review of Missions. Edinburgh: World Council of Churches. V. 1, no. 1-, 1912-.

International Socialist Review:a Monthly J. of International Socialist Thought. Chicago. V. 1-18, no. 8, July 1900-Feb. 1918.

International Studio. N.Y.: John Lane Co., 1817-1921; International Studio Inc., 1922-1931. V. 1-99 (no. 1-411), Mar. 1897-Aug. 1931.

Issues and Studies. Taibei: Zhonghua minguo guoji guanxi yanjiusuo (Institute of International Relations, Republic of China). V. 1, no. 1-Oct. 1964-.

Japan Quarterly. Tokyo. V. 1, no. 1-, Oct.-Dec. 1954.

J. of Applied Sociology. Los Angeles: Southern California Sociological Society and University of Southern California. V. 6, no. 1-v. 11, no. 6, Oct. 1921-July-Aug. 1927. Successor to *Studies in Sociology*. Succeeded by *Sociology and Social Research*.

J. of Asian Affairs. Buffalo: Center for Asian Studies, State University of New York at Buffalo. V. 1–Spring 1976–.

J. of Asian and African Studies. Leiden. V. 1, no. 1–, Jan. 1966–.

J. of Asian Culture. Los Angeles: Graduate Students in Asian Studies at UCLA. V. 1–, Spring 1977–.

J. of Asian History. Wiesbaden. 1–, 1967.

J. of Asian Studies. Ann Arbor: Far Eastern Association (name changed Mar. 1957 to Association for Asian Studies). V. 16, no. 1–, Nov. 1956–. Successor to *Far Eastern Quarterly.*

J. of Comparative Family Studies. Calgary, Alta, s.n. V. 1–, Autumn 1970–.

J. of Family History. Minneapolis: National Council on Family Relations. V. 1–, Autumn 1976–.

J. of Family Issues. Beverly Hills: Sage Publications. V. 1–, Mar. 1980–.

J. of Family Law. Louisville: University of Louisville School of Law. V. 1–, Spring 1961–.

J. of Family Welfare. Bombay. V. 1–, Nov. 1954–.

J. of Home Economics. Baltimore: The American Home Economics Association. V. 1–, Feb. 1909.

J. of Marriage and the Family. Menasha, Wisc.: National Conference on Family Relations (Chicago) (name changed 1948 to National Conference on Family Relations [Chicago; Minneapolis]). V. 1, no. 1–Jan. 1939–. Title varies: v. 1, no. 1–v. 2, no. 4, Jan. 1939–Nov. 1940 issued as *Living;* v. 3, no. 1–v. 25, no. 4, Winter 1941–Nov. 1963, issued as *Marriage and Family Living.*

J. of Oriental Studies. Hong Kong: University of Hong Kong. V. 1, no. 1–, Jan. 1954–. Multilingual: articles in Western languages or Chinese. Chinese title: *Dongfang wenhua.*

J. of Pacific History. Canberra: Australian National University. V. 1–, 1966–.

J. of Peasant Studies. London. V. 1–, 1973/74–.

J. of Projective Techniques and Personality Assessment. Glendale, Ca. V. 1–34, 1936–1970.

J. of Social Forces, see *Social Forces.*

J. of Social Issues. N.Y. V. 1–, Feb. 1945–.

J. of Social Psychology. Worcester. V. 1–, 1930–1981.

J. of Social Science. Limbe, Malawi: University of Malawi. V. 1, 1972–.

J. of Sociology. Taibei: Guoli Taiwan daxue, Faxue yuan, Shehuixue xi (National Taiwan University, College of Law, Dept. of Sociology). No. 1–, Dec. 1963–. Bilingual: articles in English or Chinese. Chinese title: *Shehui xuekan.*

J. of the China Branch of the Royal Asiatic Society. Shanghai. New (2nd) series, v. 19–36, 1884–1906. Successor to and succeeded by *J. of the North-China Branch of the Royal Asiatic Society.*

J. of the China Society. Taibei. V. 1–, 1961–.

J. of the North-China Branch of the Royal Asiatic Society. Shanghai. V. 1–2, 1858–1860. New (2nd) series, v. 1–18, 37–73?, 1864–1883, 1907–1948? Succeeded by and successor to *J. of the China Branch of the Royal Asiatic Society.*

The Labor Monthly: A Magazine of International Labor. London: The Labor Publishing Co., Ltd. V. 1–, July 1921–.

Liberation. N.Y. V. 1–, Mar. 1956–.

Life. Chicago: Time Inc. V. 1–73, Nov. 23, 1936–Dec. 29, 1972; v. 1–, Oct. 1978–.

Literary Digest. N.Y.: Funk & Wagnalls. V. 1–124, v. 125, n. 1–8, Mar. 1, 1890–Feb. 19, 1938.

Literature East and West. College Park, Maryland. V. 1–, 1954–.

Living, see *J. of Marriage and the Family.*

Living Age: The Eclectic Magazine: Foreign Literature. N.Y. & Philadelphia: Leavitt, Trow & Co. V. 1–148, 1844–1907.

Look. Des Moines: Cowles Magazines Inc. V. 1, Jan. 1937–1971.

McCall's. N.Y. 1–, 1870–.

Malayan Economic Review. Singapore: University of Malaya, Economics Society. V. 1, no. 1–, June 1956–.

Man: The J. of the Royal Anthropological Institute. London. V. 1–, Mar. 1966–.

Marriage and Family Living, see *J. of Marriage and the Family.*

Mentor. N.Y.: The Mentor Association Inc. V. 1–23, 1913–1931.

Milbank Memorial Fund Quarterly. N.Y. V. 1, no. 1–, Oct. 1923–. Title varies: v. 1, no. 1–v. 11, no. 4, Oct 1923–Oct 1933, issued as *Milbank Memorial Fund Quarterly Bulletin.*

Missionary Review of the World. Princeton: C.S. Robinson & Co. Printers, 1878–1887, 1888–1939 (new series). N.Y., London: Funk & Wagnalls.

Modern China. Beverly Hills. v. 1–, Jan. 1975–.

Modern Asian Studies. Cambridge, Eng. V. 1, no. 1–, Jan. 1967–.

Monthly Bulletin on Economic China. Tianjin: Nankai daxue, Jingji xueyuan (Nankai University Institute of Economics). V. 7, no. 1–12, Jan.–Dec. 1934. Successor to *Nankai Weekly Statistical Service.* Succeeded by *Nankai Social and Economic Quarterly.*

Monthly Labor Review. Washington, D.C.: U.S. Dept. of Labor, Bureau of Labor Statistics. V. 1, no. 1–, Jul. 1915–. Title varies: v. 1, no. 1–v. 6, no. 6, July 1915–June 1918, issued as *Monthly Review of the U.S. Bureau of Labor Statistics.*

Monthly Review: An Independent Socialist Magazine. N.Y. V. 1–, May 1949–.

Monthly Review of the U.S. Bureau of Labor Statistics, see *Monthly Labor Review.*

Monumenta Serica: J. of Oriental Studies. Peiping: Catholic University of Peking; Tokyo: Society of the Divine Wood Research Institute. V. 1, no. 1–, 1935–.

Nankai Social and Economic Quarterly. Tianjin: Nankai daxue, Jingji xueyuan (Nankai University, Institute of Economics). V. 8, no. 1–v. 11, no. 3/4/v. 12, no. 1/2?, Apr. 1935–Jan. 1941? Suspended publ. July 1937–Jan. 1939. Successor to *Monthly Bulletin on Economic China.*

Nankai Weekly Statistical Service. Tianjin: Nankai daxue, Jingji xueyuan (Nankai University, Institute of Economics). V. 1, no. 1–6, no. 52, Jan. 1928–Dec. 25, 1933. Succeeded by *Monthly Bulletin on Economic China.*

The Nation. N.Y.: Nation Association Inc. V. 1–, June 6, 1865–.

National Taiwan University J. of Sociology. Taibei: Dept. of Sociology, National Taiwan University. 1963–. Bilingual: articles in English or Chinese. Chinese title: *Guoli Taiwan daxue shehui xuekan.*

New China. N.Y.: U.S.-China People's Friendship Association. v. 1–, Sept. 1975–.

New China Review. Shanghai. V. 1, no. 1–v. 4, no. 6, Mar. 1919–Dec. 1922.

New Republic: A J. of Opinion. N.Y.: The Republic Publishing Co., Inc. V. 1–, Nov. 7, 1914–.

New York Academy of Sciences, Transactions. N.Y.: 1881–1897; series 2: 1938–.

New York Times Magazine. N.Y.: The New York Times Co. 1896–.

Newsweek: The Magazine of News Significance. N.Y. V. 1–, Feb. 17, 1933–.

The Nineteenth Century, see *The Twentieth Century.*

The Nineteenth Century and After, see *The Twentieth Century.*

Orient. Hong Kong. V. 1, no. 1–v. 6, no. 8, Aug. 1950–Mar. 1956.

Orientations. Hong Kong. V. 1−, 1970−.
Outlook. Boulder: Mountain View Center for Environmental Education. No. 1−, Winter, 1970.
Overland Monthly. San Francisco: A. Roman & Co. (1868−1875); San Francisco: Overland Publishing Co. (1883−). 1868−1875; 2nd series: 1883−.
Pacific Affairs. Honolulu; N.Y.: Institute of Pacific Relations. v. 1, no. 1, May 26, 1926−. Title varies: May 26, 1926−Apr. 1928 issued as *Institute of Pacific Relations News Bulletin.*
Pacific Historical Review. Glendale, Ca.: American Historical Association, Pacific Coast Branch. V. 1, no. 1−, Mar. 1932−.
The Pacific Sociological Review. Eugene, Oregon: Pacific Sociological Society. V. 1−, 1958−.
The Pacific Spectator. Stanford: Stanford University Press. V. 1−10, Winter 1947−1956.
Papers of the Michigan Academy of Science, Arts, and Letters. N.Y.; Ann Arbor. V. 1−, 1921−. Successor to *Annual Report of the Michigan Academy of Science.*
Peasant Studies Newsletter. Pittsburgh: University of Pittsburgh. V. 1−4, Jan. 1972−1975.
Peking Review. Peking. V. 1, no. 1−v. 9, no. 52, Mar. 4, 1958−Dec. 23, 1966; v. 1967, no. 1 (Jan. 1)−. Successor to *People's China.* Title changed to *Beijing Review* since vol. 22, 1979.
People's China. Peking: Foreign Languages Press. V. 1, no. 1−v. 4, no. 12, Jan. 1, 1950−Dec. 16, 1951; v. 1952, no. 1 (Jan. 1)−v. 1957, no. 24 (Dec. 16). Succeeded by *Peking Review.*
People's Tribune. Peiping. V. 1, no. 1−4, Mar.−June−July 1931; new (2nd) series, v. 1, no. 1−30, no. 8?, Dec. 19, 1931−Apr. 1941?
Philosophy East and West. Honolulu: University of Hawaii Press. V. 1−, 1951−.
Political Quarterly. London. V. 1, no. 1−, Jan. 1930−.
Popular Science Monthly. N.Y.: Popular Science Publishing Co., Inc. V. 1−, May 1872−.
Population Bulletin. Washington: Population Reference Bureau. V. 1−, Sept. 1945−.
Population Index. Princeton University, School of Public and International Affairs; Population Association of America. V. 1, no. 1−, Jan 1935−. Title varies: v. 1, no. 1 issued as *Review of Current Research;* v. 1, no. 2−v. 2, no. 4 issued as *Population Literature.*
Population Literature, see *Population Index.*
Population Review. Madras: Indian Institute for Population Studies. V. 1−, 1957−.
Population Studies: A Quarterly J. of Demography. London: Population Investigation Committee. V. 1, no. 1−. June 1947−.
Problems of Communism. Washington, D.C.: U.S. International Information Administration, Documentary Studies Section; U.S. Information Agency, Special Materials Section. No. 1−4, 1952; v. 2, no. 1−, Jan. 1953−.
Progressive. Madison, Wisc. 1924−1936; n.s., 1936−.
Psychology Today. Del Mar, Ca. V. 1−, May 1967−.
Public Opinion. London: G. Cole. Oct. 5, 1861−June 22, 1951.
Putman's Magazine: Original Papers on Literature, Science, Art, and National Interests. N.Y.: G.P. Putnam & Co. 1853−1870. Title varies: 1853−1857, *Putnam's Monthly Magazine of American Literature, Science and Art.*
Putnam's Monthly Magazine of American Literature, Science and Art, see *Putman's Magazine.*
Quarterly Review of Biology. Baltimore: The Williams & Wilkins Co. V. 1−, Jan. 1926−.

Race and Class. London: Institute of Race Relations. V. 16, no. 2−, Oct. 1974−.
Radical America. Madison, Wisc. V. 1−, 1967?−.
Renditions: A Chinese-English Translation Magazine. Hong Kong: Center for Translation Projects of Chinese University of Hong Kong. No. 1−, Autumn 1973−.
Review of Current Research, see *Population Index.*
The Review of Radical Political Economics. Cambridge, Mass. V. 1−, May 1969−.
Review of Reviews. London: The Review of Reviews. V. 1−87 (No. 1−553), 1890−1936.
The Scholastic: Best High School Writing. N.Y. & Pittsburgh: Scholastic Corporation. 1926−.
School and Society. N.Y., etc. V. 1−100, Jan. 2, 1915−Summer 1972 (No. 1−2342).
Science and Society: A Marxian Quarterly. N.Y.: Science and Society, Inc. V. 1−, Fall 1936−.
Science News. Washington, D.C. V. 1−(no. 1−), Apr. 2, 1921−.
Scientific American. N.Y.: Munn & Co. 1845−1859; new series: 1859−.
Scribner's Magazine. N.Y.: C. Scribner's Sons. V. 1−105, 1887−1939.
Signs: J. of Women in Culture and Society. Chicago: University of Chicago Press. V. 1−, Autumn 1975−.
Sinologica. Basel: Sino-Swiss Society. V. 1, no. 1−, 1947−.
Smithsonian. Washington, D.C. V. 1−, Apr. 1970−.
Social Action. Boston & Chicago: The Pilgrim Press. V. 1−39, Mar. 1935−Dec. 1972.
Social Forces. Chapel Hill, North Carolina. V. 1, no. 1−, Nov. 1922−. Title varies: v. 1, no. 1−v. 3, no. 4, Nov. 1922−May 1925, issued as *J. of Social Forces.*
Social Science and Medicine. Oxford; N.Y.: Pergamon Press. 1967−.
Social Science Quarterly. Austin, Tex. V. 49−, June 1968−.
Socialist Revolution. San Francisco: Agenda Publishing Co. V. 1−7, 1970−1977.
Sociologia Ruralis. Assen, Netherlands. V. 1−, Spring 1960−.
Sociological Abstracts. N.Y. V. 1−, Nov. 1952−.
Sociological Review. Manchester, Eng.: Sherratt & Hughes. Series 2, 1953−.
Sociologus. Berlin. 1925−1933; neue folge, 1951−.
Sociology and Social Research. Los Angeles. V. 12, no. 1−, Sept.−Oct. 1928−. Successor to *J. of Applied Sociology.*
Solidarity. Cairo: Afro-Asian People's Solidarity Organization. No. 1−, Dec. 1974−.
The Southwestern Social Science Quarterly. Austin, Tex.: University of Texas. V. 1−48, June 1920−1968.
Studies in Family Planning. N.Y.: Population Council. No. 1−60 (V. 1), 1963−1970; V. 2−, 1971−.
Survey Graphic. N.Y.: Survey Association, Inc. V. 22−37, 1933−1948.
T'ien Hsia Monthly. Shanghai: Zhongshan wenhua jiaoyuguan (Sun Yat-sen Institute for Advancement of Culture and Education) (Nanking). V. 1, no. 1−v. 12, no. 1, Aug. 1935−Aug.−Sept. 1941.
Time: The Weekly News Magazine. N.Y. V. 1−, Mar. 3, 1923−.
T'oung pao: archives concernant l'histoire, les langues, la géographie et l'ethnographie de l'Asie orientale. Leiden. V. 1, no. 1−v. 10, no. 5, 1890−1899; 2e série, v. 1, no. 1, 1900−.
Tsing Hua J. of Chinese Studies. Peking: Qinghua xuexiao (Tsing Hua College); Peiping; Kunming: Guoli Qinghua xuebaoshe (Tsing Hua Journal Publication Committee). V. 1−v. 4, no. 7, 1916−Jan. 1919; v. 1, no. 1−v. 15, no. 1, June 1924−Oct. 1948. Suspended publ.: July 1937−Apr.

1941, Oct. 1941-Oct. 1947. Taibei: The Tsing Hua Journal Publication Committee. V. 1 (new series), no. 1, June 1956-. Bilingual: articles in English or Chinese. Chinese title: *Qinghua xuebao.*

The Twentieth Century. London: The Nineteenth Century and After. V. 1- 179 (No. 1-1049), Mar. 1877-Apr.-June 1972. Title varies: 1887-Dec. 1900, *The Nineteenth Century: A Monthly Review;* Dec. 1900-Jan. 1901, *The Nineteenth Century and After.*

United Asia: International Magazine of Asian Affairs. Bombay: United Asian Publications. V. 1, no. 1-May-June 1948-.

Urban Anthropology. Brockport, N.Y.: Dept. of Anthropology, SUNY-Brockport. V. 1-, Spring 1972-.

Vogue. N.Y. 1892-.

West and East. Taipei. V. 1-, 1956-. Bilingual: articles in English and Chinese. Chinese title: *Zhong Mei yuekan.*

West China Border Research Society, J. Chengdu. v. 1, 1922/23-1946.

The Woman's J. N.Y.: The Woman Citizen Corporation. V. 1-16, 19117-1931.

Women and Revolution. N.Y. No. 1-, 1972?-.

Women of the Whole World. Berlin: International Women's Democratic Federation. 1946?-.

Women on the March . New Delhi: The Women's Front of the All India Congress Committee. V. 1-, 1957-.

Working Papers for a New Society. Cambridge, Mass.: Cambridge Policy Studies Institute. V. 1-, Spring 1973-.

World Politics: A Quarterly J. of International Relations. New Haven: Yale University, Institute of International Studies. V. 1, no. 1-, Oct. 1948-.

Abbreviations

CB -- Current Background

ECMM -- Extracts from China Mainland Magazine

JPRS -- Joint Publications Research Service

SCMM -- Selections from China Mainland Magazines

SCMP -- Survey of China Mainland Press

SPRCM -- Selections from People's Republic of China Magazines

SPRCP -- Survey of People's Republic of China Press

Bibliographies and Serials

0001 "Annotated Bibliography on Asian Women." In *Asian Women.* Berkeley, 1971, pp. 132-43.

0002 Jacobs, Sue Ellen. *Women in Perspective: A Guide for Cross-Cultural Studies.* Urbana: University of Illinois Press, 1974. [See "China," pp. 34-37.]

0003 Kaplan, Edward H. *Women in Chinese History: An Annotated Bibliography of Some English-Language Works.* Program in East Asian Studies, Publication No. 5. Bellingham, Wash.: Western Washington State College, 1971.

0004 Krichmar, Albert; Smith, Virginia Carlson; and Wiederrecht, Ann E. *The Women's Movement in the Seventies: An International English-Language Bibliography.* Metuchen, N.J.: Scarecrow Press, 1977. [See "China," pp. 76-80.]

0005 Lowe, Chuan-hua. "Twenty Centuries of Chinese Womanhood: Some Highlights, Seen through the Windows of an Introductory Bibliography." *Chinese Librarians Association Newsletter* 2(1976):4:2-8.

0006 Martin, Diana. *Women in Chinese Society.* Commonwealth Bureau of Agricultural Economics Annotated Bibliography No. 28. Oxford, England: Commonwealth Agricultural Bureau, 1974. [Mimeo., 80 titles.]

0007 *Women of China.* Peking, 1952-1966. [Bimonthly magazine published by the All-China Women's Federation. English-language counterpart to *Zhongguo funü.*]

0008 *Women of China (An English Monthly).* 1- (1979-). [Published by Women of China, Beijing.]

Education

EDUCATION: TRADITIONAL CHINA (TO 1911)

0009 Handlin, Joanna F. "Lu K'un's New Audience: The Influence of Women's Literacy on Sixteenth-Century Thought." In *Women in Chinese Society,* ed. Margery Wolf and Roxane Witke, pp. 13-38. Stanford: Stanford University Press, 1975.

0010 Lewis, Ida Belle. *The Education of Girls in China.* New York: Columbia University Teachers College, 1919. [A contemporary's account of changes in female education toward the end of the imperial era. Reprint: 1972.]

0011 Liu, Hsiang. *Typical Women of China.* Trans. Miss A. C. Safford. Shanghai: Kelly & Walsh, 1891. [Abridged from the Chinese work "Records of Virtuous Women of Ancient and Modern Times."]

0012 O'Hara, Albert Richard. *The Position of Women in Early China According to the "Lieh nu chuan," "The Biographies of Eminent Chinese Women."* Catholic University of America Studies in Sociology, Vol. 16. Washington, D.C.: Catholic University, 1945. [2nd ed.: *Lieh nu chuan (The Biographies of Chinese Women).* Hong Kong: Orient, 1955.]

0013 Rawski, Evelyn Sakakida. *Education and Popular Literacy in Ch'ing China.* Ann Arbor: University of Michigan Press, 1979. [See "Female Literacy," pp. 6-8.]

0014 Spade, Beatrice. "The Education of Women in China during the Southern Dynasties." *J. of Asian History* 13(1979):1:15-41.

0015 Swann, Nancy Lee. *Pan Chao: The Foremost Woman Scholar of China, 1st Century A.D.* New York: Century, 1932.

0016 Tsao, Lady [Pan Chao]. *Instructions for Chinese Women and Girls.* Trans. Mrs. S. L. Baldwin. New York: Eaton & Mains, 1900. Cincinnati: Jennings & Pye, 1900.

0017 Williams, Samuel Wells. "Education of Women in China." *Chinese Recorder,* Jan.-Feb. 1880, pp. 40-53.

EDUCATION: THE CHINESE REPUBLIC (1911-1949)

0018 Anderson, Mary Raleigh. *Protestant Mission Schools for Girls in South China (1827 to the Japanese Invasion).* Mobile, Ala.: Heiter-Starke, 1943.

0019 Boyd, C. T., Mrs. *My Chinese Daughter.* N.p.: Wilmette Printing Studio, n.d.

0020 Budd, Josephine E. "Education for Women." In *China,* ed. Orville Anderson Petty, pp. 535-76. Layman's Foreign Missions Inquiry, Factfinders' Reports 5, Supplementary Series, part 2. New York: Harper, 1933.

0021 Burton, Margaret Ernestine. *The Education of Women in China.* New York: Revell, 1911.

0022 Burton, Margaret Ernestine. *Notable Women of Modern China.* New York: Revell, 1912. [On women's education in early 20th-century China, with an emphasis on missionary education. Includes biographies of notable educated Chinese women, among them doctors in missionary hospitals.]

0023 Chang, Hwei-lan. "Chinese Women Leaders in Education." *Chinese Students Monthly* 18(1923):8:36-40.

0024 Foster, Arnold, Mrs. (Amy). *Chinese Schoolgirls in the Valley of the Yangtse.* London: London Missionary Society, 1909.

0025 Hosie, Dorothea, Lady [Soothill]. *The Pool of Ch'ien Lung: A Tale of Modern Peking.* London: Hodder & Stoughton, 1944. [About an English woman's visit to Chinese friends who ran a school for girls in Beijing.]

0026 Hsu, Shou Shang; Ou-yang, Hsiao Lan; and Yoehngoo Tsohsang Wu Lew. "Education of Women in China." In *Education in China: Papers Contributed by Members of Committees of the Society for the Study of International Education,* ed. T. Y. Teng (Ts'ui-ying) and Timothy Tingfang Lew (Liu T'ing-fang), pp. 1-35. Peking: Society for the Study of International Education, 1923. [Trans. from an unpublished Chinese manuscript.]

0027 Jones, M. I. "School of Mothercraft, Huchow, Chekiang." *Chinese Recorder,* Oct. 1924, pp. 665-70.

0028 Kan, Chia-ming. "As a Student at the National Chekiang University during the War of Resistance." *Chinese Studies in History* 14(Fall 1980):59-76. [A personal depiction of the lives and feelings of Chinese students during the Sino-Japanese War. Kan is a woman writer.]

0029 Lewis, I[da] B[elle]. *A Report of the Girls' School in Szechwan Supported by the Women's Foreign Missionary Society of the Methodist Episcopal Church.* Shanghai: Commercial Press, 1921.

0030 Lewis, I[da] B[elle]. *A Report of School in Fukien Supported by the Board of Foreign Missions and the Women's Foreign Missionary Society in the Methodist Episcopal Church.* Shanghai: Commercial Press, 1922.

0031 Lewis, I[da] B[elle]. "China and Christian Education in 1930," *The Christian Advocate* 106(May 28, 1931):682-83.

0032 Lo, Shu Hua. "Chi Chih Yi—A Manchu Woman Philosopher." *Chinese Recorder,* Jan. 1924, pp. 40-42.

0033 Morrison, Elizabeth. "Helping Increase the Literacy of Chinese Women." *Chinese Recorder,* Oct. 1923, pp. 595-600.

0034 Seesholtz, A. G. "In League with Youth." *Chinese Recorder,* Oct. 1923, pp. 608-10.

0035 Tang, Chindon Yiu. "Women's Education in China." *Bulletin on Chinese Education* 2(1923):9:1-36.

0036 Thurston, John Lawrence, Mrs.; and Chester, Ruth M. *Ginling College*. New York: United Board for Christian Colleges in China, 1955.

0037 Turner, H. F. "'Ring out the Old, Ring in the New': New Ideas in Old China. C.E.Z.M.S. Schools in Fuhkien Province...." London: C.E.Z.M.S., 1908.

0038 Wallace, L. Ethel. *Hwa Nan College: The Woman's College of South China*. New York: United Board for Christian Colleges in China, 1956.

0039 Walton, C. M. "Women's Work in Fenchow." *Chinese Recorder*, Sept. 1922, pp. 595-98.

0040 Wei, Wilson Shih-sheng. "The Education of Women in Modern China." M.A. thesis, Stanford University, 1927.

0041 White, F. J. "Coeducation in China." *Chinese Recorder*, Oct. 1919, pp. 666-73.

0042 Women's College, Peking. *Evolution of a Woman's College in China*. Peking, 1914.

EDUCATION: THE PEOPLE'S REPUBLIC OF CHINA (1949–)

0043 Chan, Itty. "Women of China: From the Three Obediences to Half-the-Sky." *J. of Research and Development in Education* 10(Summer 1977):38–52. [The socialization process, human development, and education of women in the context of Chinese society before and after 1949 are examined.]

0044 Eberstade, N. "Women and Education in China: How Much Progress?" *New York Rev. of Books* 26(Apr. 19, 1979):41-45. [Review essay of three books: *China as a Model of Development* by Al Imfeld; *China's Economy and the Maoist Strategy* by John G. Gurley; *China's Economic Revolution* by Alexander Eckstein.]

0045 Epstein, Israel. "Two Girls from Shigatse." *China Reconstructs* 5(Apr. 1956):27.

0046 Han, Tzu. "Teacher of Her People." *China Reconstructs* 5(Oct. 1956):25–27.

0047 Hu, Chih-tao. "A Teacher-Housewife." *China Reconstructs* 2(May–June 1953):10.

0048 "Maidservant Becomes a Teacher." *China Reconstructs* 18(Dec. 1969):36.

0049 Nuckols, Margaret Lynn. "A Comparative Analysis of Selected United Nations Documents Related to Educational Opportunities for Women during the First Development Decade (1960–1970)." Ph.D. dissertation, Florida State University, 1975. [Worldwide coverage, including China.]

0050 Orleans, Leo. *Professional Manpower and Education in Communist China*. Washington, D.C.: National Science Foundation, 1960. [Includes statistics on age and sex structure, female education, and female labor force participation.]

0051 "Schoolteacher, Si Xia." *China Pictorial* 1979:2:7.

0052 *SCMM*, no. 606 (Dec. 18, 1967). "Carry Out the Activity of 'One Helping Another to Form a Red Pair,' Develop and Consolidate the Revolutionary Great Alliance," pp. 1 [From *Hongqi*.]

0053 *SCMP*, no. 100 (Apr. 28, 1951). "Fukien Union Christian University and Hwa Nan Girls College Taken Over and Amalgamated into Foochow University," p. 33

0054 *SCMP*, no. 742 (Jan. 29, 1954). "Educate Rural Women in the Spirit of the General Line of the State," p. 16

0055 *SCMP*, no. 1254 (Mar. 7, 1956). "More Women Intellectuals in China," p. 23

0056 *SCMP*, no. 1476 (Jan. 25, 1957). "Five Good Activities in Cities," p. 14 [On education of women and children.]

0057 *SCMP*, no. 2364 (Oct. 18, 1960). "Lhasa Sets Up First Women's School," p. 24

0058 *SCMP*, no. 2570 (July 29, 1961). "Carry Out Teaching Aimfully and According to the Pupils Taught: A Report on an Investigation in the Problem of Study Among Female Workers (Chekiang)," p. 9

0059 *SCMP*, no. 2579 (Sept. 11, 1961). "Women College Students Graduate in Peking," p. 16

0060 *SCMP*, no. 2694 (March 5, 1962). "5,000 Women Teach in Peking Colleges," p. 21

0061 *SCMP*, no. 3784 (Sept. 10, 1966). "Why Has Ku A-t'ao Changed Completely?" p. 26 [About the education of peasants.]

0062 *SCMP*, no. 4243 (Aug. 15, 1968). "Peasant Women's Study Class," pp. 1 [From New China News Agency.]

0063 *SCMP*, no. 4634 (Mar. 31, 1970). "Sunlight of Mao Tse-tung's Thought Shines on Thousands of Homes." p. 2

0064 *SCMP*, no. 4793 (Nov. 29, 1970). "Girl Student Tells of Re-education by Poor and Lower-middle Peasants," p. 13

0065 *SCMP*, no. 4864 (Mar. 14, 1971). "Women Students from among Workers, Peasants and Soldiers in Peking University," p. 109

0066 *SCMP*, no. 4875 (Mar. 30, 1971). "A School Girl Dedicated to the People," p. 28

0067 *SCMP*, no. 5057 (Jan. 6, 1972). "Let More Young Women and Girls Receive Schooling—the Party Committee of the Kao-t'ou Commune Adopts Various Measures to Give the Overwhelming Majority of Young Women and Girls Schooling," p. 95

0068 *SCMP*, no. 5057 (Jan. 6, 1972). "Liao-nan 'May 7' Middle School Runs an Additional Class for Young Women and Girls," p. 98

0069 *SCMP*, no. 5057 (Jan. 6, 1972). "Seriously Tackle Problem of Girls' Schooling—Chiang Ch'ün, Revolutionary Committee of Chiangtu Hsien, Kiangsu Province," p. 97

0070 *SCMP*, no. 5098 (Mar. 11, 1972). "Woman School Teacher in Northeast China Village," p. 102

0071 *SCMP*, no. 5161 (June 13, 1972). "Unite and Educate Well the Sons and Daughters Who Can Be Educated—CCP Committee of Shanghai State No. 17 Cotton Mill," p. 6

0072 *SCMP*, no. 5206 (Aug. 20, 1972). "Young Woman Teacher Helps Bring Primary School Education to North China Village," p. 116

0073 *SCMP*, no. 5354 (Apr. 2, 1973). "East China Rural Woman Teacher," p. 173

0074 *SCMP*, no. 5370 (Apr. 18, 1973). "A Lively Education in Policy," p. 119

0075 *SCMP*, no. 5375 (May 5, 1973). "Woman Teacher on Central China Lake," p. 116

0076 *SCMP*, no. 5578 (Mar. 12, 1974). "Woman Oil-well Teacher Goes to College," p. 163

0077 Shan, Lingyi; Wang, Chuanfeng; and Zhang, Wenyu. "Difficulties and Worries of Women Teachers in Primary Schools." *Chinese Education* 12(Winter 1979/80):113–15.

0078 *SPRCP*, no. 5888 (June 24, 1975). "More Working Women Attend College in China," p. 17

0079 *SPRCP*, no. 6010 (Dec. 27, 1975). "Daughters and Sons of Emancipated Tibetan Serfs Go to School," p. 198

0080 *SPRCP*, no. 6127 (June 22, 1976). "Young Girl School Graduate: A Fine Example for Chinese Educated Youth," p. 168

0081 "Women Students' Study Group." *Peking Review* 16(Mar. 9, 1973):22-23.

EDUCATION: HONG KONG, TAIWAN, AND OVERSEAS CHINA

0082 Abbott, Elizabeth Lee. "Dr. Hu King Eng, Pioneer." In *The Life, Influence and the Role of the Chinese in the United States, 1776-1960*, pp. 243-49. San Francisco: Chinese Historical Society of America, 1976. [Shows, through the life and career of Dr. Hu King-Eng, the development of organized education for Chinese women by Western women missionaries, and the education of Chinese women in the United States and their impact on the status of women and women's education in China between 1844 and 1929.]

0083 Chen, May Ying. "Teaching a Course on Asian American Women." In *Counterpoint: Perspectives on Asian America*, ed. Emma Gee et al., pp. 234-39. Los Angeles: Asian American Studies Center, University of California, Los Angeles, 1976.

0084 Cheng, Irene [Cheng Ho Ai-ling]. "Women Students and Graduates." In *University of Hong Kong: The First Fifty Years, 1911-1961*, ed. Brian Harrison, pp. 148-58. Hong Kong: Hong Kong University Press, 1962.

0085 Chiang, J. P. "The Home Economics Education in the Philippines and in the Republic of China." M.A. thesis, University of California, Los Angeles, 1969.

0086 Hermalin, Albert I.; Seltzer, Judith A.; and Lin, Chin-hsing. *The Effect of Family Size on Female Educational Attainment in Taiwan.* Taiwan Population Studies, Working Papers, no. 37. Ann Arbor: University of Michigan, Population Studies Center and Taiwan Provincial Institute of Family Planning, 1979.

0087 Huang, Min-chang. "The Effects of the Perception and the Sex of Reading Teachers and the Sex of Students on the Reading Achievement, Attitude, and Reading Class Attendance on Junior High School Students in Taipei, Taiwan." Ed.D. dissertation, Northeast Louisiana University, 1977.

0088 Mitchell, Robert Edward. *Pupil, Parent and School: A Hong Kong Study.* Asian Folklore and Social Life Monographs, 26. Taibei: Orient Cultural Service, 1972.

0089 Rogers, Charles. "Status, Ability, Encouragement, Sex Roles, and Educational Aspirations of Adolescents in Taiwan: A Replicative Study of the Sewell Model." Ph.D. dissertation, University of Illinois, 1976.

0090 Rowe, Elizabeth et al. *Failure in School: Aspects of the Problem in Hong Kong.* London: Oxford University, 1966.

0091 Stoodley, Bartlett H. "Christian Preference and Western Cultural Influence among Chinese College Youth in Hong Kong." *Chung Chi J.* 5(Nov. 1965):21-30.

0092 Wang, Yu Jung. "An Analysis of Male and Female Roles in Chinese Children's Reading Materials Published in Taiwan, China." Ph.D. dissertation, New York University, 1980.

0093 Yan, Kuo-shu; Ko, Yun-ho; and Yang, Pen-hua. "Personality Correlates of Scholastic Achievement among Chinese Junior High School Students." *Bulletin of the Institute of Ethnology, Academia Sinica* 35(Spring 1973):41-86. [Abridged from Chinese original.]

0094 Yen, Han-wen Edwin. "Knowledge, Sources, and Felt Needs of Family Life and Sex Education of Selected College Freshman in Taiwan." Ph.D. dissertation, University of Tennessee, 1977.

Emancipation Movements: History and Ideology

EMANCIPATION MOVEMENTS: GENERAL SURVEYS

0095 Broyelle, Claudie. *Women's Liberation in China.* Atlantic Highlands, N.J.: Humanities Press, 1977. [Translated from the French by Michèle Cohen and Gary Herman.]

0096 Bunch-Weeks, Charlotte. "Asian Women in Revolution—China." *Women: A Journal of Liberation*, Summer 1970, pp. 2-6.

0097 Callis, Maud Eva. "Tradition and Change in the Status of Chinese Women." Ph.D. dissertation, University of Michigan, 1946.

0098 Chen, Kuan-chin. "Emancipation of Women in China." M.A. thesis, Columbia University, 1933.

0099 Cohen, Charlotte Bonny. "Women in China." In *Sisterhood is Powerful*, ed. Robin Morgan, pp. 385-427. N.Y.: Vintage, 1970.

0100 Collins, Leslie Eugene. "The New Women: A Psychohistorical Study of the Chinese Feminist Movement from 1900 to the Present." Ph.D. dissertation, Yale University, 1976.

0101 Cummins, H. W. *The Status of Women in China.* University of Alberta, 1972.

0102 Frenier, Mariam Darce. "Aids and Barriers to Feminism in Modern China: The Effects of War and Economic Change on the Rate of Advance of Chinese Women's Status." *International J. of Women's Studies* 1(May/June 1978):272-80.

0103 Guisso, R. W. L., ed. *Women in China.* Youngstown, N.Y.: Philo, 1981.

0104 Johnson, Kay Ann. "The Politics of Women's Rights and Family Reform in China." Ph.D. dissertation, University of Wisconsin, Madison, 1976.

0105 Kristeva, Julia. *About Chinese Women.* London: M. Boyars, 1977. [Translation of *Des Chinoises* by Anita Barrows. Reprint: N.Y.: Urizen Books, 1981.]

0106 Newcomb, Holly Ellen. "Western Influence and the Transition of Chinese Upper-class Women, 1830s-1930s." M.A. thesis, University of Washington, 1967.

0107 O'Hara, A. R. "The Position of Women in Modern China." In *Research on Changes of Chinese Society* by A. R. O'Hara. Taibei: Orient Cultural Service, 1971.

0108 Rowbotham, Sheila. *Women, Resistance and Revolution.* London: Allen Lane, 1972; N.Y.: Vintage, 1972. [see chapter 7, "When the Sand-Grouse Flies to Heaven," pp. 170-99.]

0109 Shimer, Dorothy Blair, ed. *Rice Bowl Women: Writings by and about Women of China and Japan.* N.Y.: New American Library, 1981. [Collection of stories and memoirs reflecting changing status and ongoing struggle for independence of Chinese and Japanese women over a thousand years.]

0110 Sidel, Ruth. "The Long March of Chinese Women." *Human Behavior* 2(Nov. 1973):15-21.

0111 Snow, Helen Foster [Nym Wales]. *Women in Modern China.* The Hague: Mouton, 1967.

0112 "Three Women—Three Generations." *China Reconstructs* 23(Mar. 1974):14-17.

0113 "The Women's Movement in China." *Chinese Studies in History* 5(Fall 1971):88-108.

0114 "Working Women's Struggle against Confucianism in Chinese History." *Peking Review* 18(Mar. 7, 1975):17–20. [Reprinted in *Chinese Sociology and Anthropology* 7(Summer 1975):4–12.]

0115 Young, Marilyn Blatt. *Women in China: Studies in Social Change and Feminism.* Ann Arbor: Center for Chinese Studies, University of Michigan, 1973.

WOMEN'S TRADITIONAL STATUS

0116 Anderson, Paul. *Pan Chao: A Girl of Old China.* N.Y.: Comet, 1954.

0117 Buck, Samuel [pseud.]. "Ancient Women of China." *Orient* 3(1952-3):1–12.

0118 Chan, Hok-lam. "Li Chih's Family, His Old Home, and His Wife's New Tombstone: An Introduction to the Newly Discovered Cultural Relics Concerning Li Chih." *Papers on Far Eastern History* 17(Mar. 1978):i–xl.

0119 Chan, Hok-lam. "Li Cho-wu's Wife Huang-shih's Grave and Other Memorial Inscriptions." *Papers on Far Eastern History* 17(Mar. 1978):xli–xlix.

0120 Chin, Hsin-ju. "I'm a Sister of China's Last Emperor." *Chinese Studies in History* 13(Summer 1980):89–93. [Author describes changes in her lifestyle as her status changes from high aristocrat to commoner.]

0121 "Chinese Women in Westerners' Eyes." *Chinese Studies in History* 9(Winter 1975–76):37–51.

0122 Chou, Hung-hsiang. "Fu-X Ladies of the Shang Dynasty." *Monumenta Serica* 29(1970–71):346–90.

0123 Chu, Teh. "My Mother." *China Reconstructs* 26(Oct. 1977):14–15.

0124 Ch'ü, T'ung-tsu. *Han Social Structure.* Seattle: University of Washington, 1972. [See "Marriage," ch. 2, pp. 33–48; 'Position of Women," ch. 1 pp. 49–62; "Kinship and Marriage," Documents Section I, pp. 251–321.]

0125 Cooper, Elizabeth. *My Lady of the Chinese Courtyard.* N.Y.: Frederick Stokes, 1914.

0126 Cooper, Elizabeth. *The Harim and the Purdah: Studies of Oriental Women.* London: T. Fisher Unwin, 1915. [See chapters 14–17 on Chinese women, pp. 211–71.]

0127 Creel, H. G. *The Origins of Statecraft in China,* Vol. 1: *Western Chou.* Chicago: University of Chicago, 1970. [References to women's roles, especially within the aristocracy of the Zhou dynasty, are scattered through the text.]

0128 De Mendoza, Juan G. "Chinese Women in Westerners' Eyes." *Chinese Studies in History* 5(Fall 1971):196–202. [Reprint from de Mendoza's *The History of the Great and Mighty Kingdom of China,* originally published in Spanish in 1600.]

0129 Doolittle, Justus. *Social Life of the Chinese.* 2 vols. New York: Harper, 1865. [Subtitled: "With some account of their religious, governmental, educational and business customs and opinions. With special but not exclusive reference to Fuchau." On marriage and family, religion and ritual.]

0130 Eberhard, Wolfram. *Local Cultures of South and East China.* Leiden: Brill, 1968. [Translation by Alide Eberhard of the prewar edition. Research on the possible status of women in neolithic China.]

0131 Faber, Ernst. *The Status of Women in China.* 2nd ed. Shanghai: American Presbyterian Mission, 1897.

0132 Faber, Ernst. *The Famous Women of China.* Shanghai: Society for the Diffusion of Christian & General Knowledge Among the Chinese, 1899.

0133 Fielde, Adele M. *Pagoda Shadows: Studies from Life in China.* W. G. Cothell, 1884. [Exact translations of autobiographical narratives given to the author in the Swatow dialect.]

0134 Gernet, Jacques. *Daily Life in China on the Eve of the Mongol Invasion, 1250–1276.* New York: Macmillan, 1962. [References to women of various classes in thirteenth-century Hangzhou.]

0135 Gray, John H. *China; A History of the Laws, Manners and Customs of the People.* 2 vols. London: Macmillan, 1878. [*Passim.*]

0136 Headland, Isaac Taylor. *Chinese Women from a Chinese Standpoint.* [Pamphlet reprinted from *The Chinese Recorder,* Jan. 1897.]

0137 Hibbert, Eloise Talcott. *Embroidered Gauze; Portraits of Famous Chinese Ladies.* Freeport, N.Y.: Books for Libraries, 1969. [Originally published in 1941.]

0138 Holmgren, Jennifer. "Women's Biographies in the Wei-Shu: A Study of the Moral Attitudes and Social Background Found in Women's Biographies in the Dynastic History of the Northern Wei." Ph.D. dissertation, Australian National University, 1979.

0139 Houghton, Ross C. *Women of the Orient: An Account of the Religious, Intellectual and Social Conditions of Women in Japan, China, India, Egypt, Syria and Turkey.* Cincinnati: Cranston & Stowe, 1877.

0140 Hu, Shih. "A Chinese 'Gulliver' on Women's Rights." *China Review,* Jan.–Mar. 1935, pp. 31–33.

0141 Hu, Shih. *Women's Place in Chinese History.* N.Y.: Trans-Pacific News Service, n.d. [Paper read in 1931.]

0142 Johnston, R. F. *Lion and Dragon in Northern China.* N.Y.: Dutton, 1910. [see chapter 9, "The Women of Weihaiwei," pp. 195–216; chapter 10 "Widows and Children," pp. 217–253.]

0143 K'ang, Yu-wei. *Ta-T'ung Shu: The One World Philosophy of K'ang Yu-wei.* Trans. Lawrence G. Thompson. London: Allen and Unwin, 1958. [1902 original. A Confucian reformer's utopia, proposing abolition of the family.]

0144 Legge, James, trans. The Book of Odes. Volume 5 of The Chinese Classics. London: Henry Frowde, 1871. [Odes 1 21, 158, 22, 95, 93, 99. 81, 58, 102, 76, and 264 give some clues concerning the role of women in Zhou times. There are various later editions.]

0145 Levy, Howard S. *Harem Favorites of an Illustrious Celestial.* Taibei: Chongdai, 1958. [Vignettes concerning Emperor Xuanzong of the Tang and his palace women. Includes a short history of the custom of concubinage in China.]

0146 Li, Dun J. *The Essence of Chinese Civilization.* N.Y.: Van Nostrand, 1967. [See chapter 18, "Women in Chinese Society."]

0147 McNabb, Robert Leroy. *The Women of the Middle Kingdom.* Cincinnati: Jennings & Pye; N.Y.: Eaton & Mains, 1903.

0148 Martin, Bernard. *The Strain of Harmony; Men and Women in the History of China.* London: W. Heinsmann, 1948.

0149 Mels, E. "Women of China." *Harper's Bazaar* 33(Aug. 4, 1900):854–857.

0150 O'Hara, Albert Richard. *The Position of Women in Early China According to the Lieh Nu Chuan, "The Biographies of Eminent Chinese Women."* Catholic University of America Studies in Sociology, Vol. 16. Washington, D.C.: Catholic University, 1945.

0151 O'Hara, Albert Richard. "The Confucian Ideal of Womanhood." *China Society J.* 1963:3:76–83.

0152 O'Hara, Albert Richard. "Woman's Place in Early China." *Free China Review* 13(Mar. 1963):31–35.

0153 Pollard, Edward B. *Women in All Ages and in All Countries: Oriental Women*. Philadelphia: Barrie, 1907. [See chapter 12, "Women of China and Corea," pp. 289-316.]

0154 Ritzman, M. E. "Women's Life in China." *Missionary Review* 34(Fall 1911):93-101.

0155 Shen, Fu. "Six Chapters of a Floating Life by Shen Fu." *T'ien-hsia Monthly* 1(Aug. 1935):72-101, 1(Sept. 1935):208-222, 1(Oct. 1935):316-340, 425-467. [An 18th-century scholar's memoir of his literate wife.]

0156 Sleeman, John H. *White China, an Austral-Asian Sensation*. Sydney: published by the author, 1933. [See pp. 109-135, on the women of China.]

0157 Smith, Arthur. *Village Life in China*. Boston: Little Brown, (1899) 1970. [See chapter 23, "Chinese Country Girls and Women," pp. 258-311.]

0158 Spence, Jonathan. *The Death of Woman Wang*. N.Y.: Viking, 1978. [Chapter 1 "The Woman Who Ran Away," is a case story of a woman's brief escape into an adulterous affair, her return to her husband, and her death at his hands.]

0159 *SPRCM*, no. 813 (Jan. 10, 1975). Sun, Lo-ying and Lu, Li-fen. "On Confucian Persecution of Women in History," p. 52.

0160 Stafford, A. C. *Typical Women of China*. Shanghai: Kelly & Walsh, 1899.

0161 Williams, S. Wells. *The Middle Kingdom: A Survey of the Geography, Government, Literature, Social Life, Arts and History of the Chinese Empire and Its Inhabitants.* 2 vols. N.Y.: C. Scribner's Sons, 1883. [See chapter 14, "Social Life among the Chinese," pp. 782-836.]

0162 Wittfogel, Karl A. "The Society of Prehistoric China." *Zeitschrift für Sozialwissenschaften,* 8(1939):138-86. [Offers a plausible theory of matriarchal society in neolithic China.]

0163 Wolf, Margery. "Chinese Women: Old Skills in a New Context." In *Woman, Culture and Society,* ed. Michelle Zimbalist Rosaldo and Louise Lamphere, pp. 157-72. Stanford, 1975

0164 Wolf, Margery and Witke, Roxanne, eds. *Women in Chinese Society*. Stanford, 1976 [Emphasis on pre-1949 China.]

THE ISSUE OF EMANCIPATION BEFORE 1911

0165 Beahan, Charlotte L. "Feminism and Nationalism in the Chinese Women's Press, 1902-1911." *Modern China* 1(Oct. 1975):379-416.

0166 Beahan, Charlotte. "The Women's Movement and Nationalism in Late Ch'ing China." Ph.D. dissertation, Columbia University, 1976.

0167 Brandauer, Frederick P. "Women in the *Ching-hua yüan*: Emancipation Toward a Confucian Ideal." *J. of Asian Studies* 36(Aug. 1977):647-60.

0168 Burton, Margaret Ernestine. *Notable Women of Modern China*. N.Y.: Fleming W. Revell, 1912.

0169 Chang, Yü-fa. "Women—A New Social Force." *Chinese Studies in History* 11(Winter 1977-78):29-55. [On missionary education, women revolutionaries of 1911, etc.]

0170 Davies, H. "New Women in China." *Review of Reviews* 31(May 1908):374-75.

0171 Drucker, A. R. "Role of the Y.W.C.A. in the Development of the Chinese Women's Movement, 1890-1927." *Social Service Review,* no. 53 (Spring 1979), pp. 421-440.

0172 Eberhard, Wolfram. "Ideas About Social Reforms in the Novel *Ching-hua yüan* [Flowers in the Mirror]." In *Festschrift für Ad. E. Jensen* (Felicitation Volume for Adolf Ellegard Jensen), vol. 1, ed. Eike Haberland, pp. 113-21. Munich: K. Renner, 1964. [Reprinted in W. Eberhard, *Moral and Social Values of the Chinese: Collected Essays.* Chinese Materials and Research Aids Service Center Occasional Series 7 Taibei: Chinese Materials and Research Aids Service Center, 1971, pp. 413-21.]

0173 Evans, Nancy Jane Frances. "Social Criticism in the Ch'ing: The Novel *Ching-hua yüan* [Flowers in the Mirror]." *People's China* 23(July 1970):52-66.

0174 Fan, Wen-lan. "Ch'iu Chin: A Woman Revolutionary." *Women of China,* Oct.-Dec. 1956, pp. 31-33.

0175 "Feminist Movement in China." *Review of Reviews* 39(Jan. 1909):101-102.

0176 Giles, Lionel. "Ch'iu Chin, A Chinese Heroine." *Asiatic Review,* new (4th) series 12, 34(Aug. 1917):125-46.

0177 Lin, Wei-hung. "Activities of Women Revolutionists in the Tung Meng Hui Period (1905-1912)." *China Forum* 2(July 1975):245-300.

0178 Macgowan, Rev. John. *How England Saved China*. London: T.F. Unwin, 1913. [About missionary reforms.]

0179 Michael, Franz. *The Taiping Rebellion,* Vol. 1 *History*. Seattle: University of Washington, 1965. [Contains sections on proposals put forward by the Taiping rebels to "emancipate" women.]

0180 Pao, Chia-lin. "The Feminist Thought in the Hsing-hai [sic] Revolutionary Era, 1898-1911." *China Forum* 1(Jan. 1974):151-80.

0181 Rankin, Mary. *Early Chinese Revolutionaries*. Cambridge: Harvard University, 1971. [Qiu Jin, pp. 40-46; 171-79, and *passim*.]

0182 Rankin, Mary Backus. "The Emergence of Women at the End of the Ch'ing: The Case of Ch'iu Chin." In *Women in Chinese Society,* ed. Margery Wolf and Roxane Witke, pp. 39-66. Stanford, 1976

0183 Ropp, Paul S. "The Seeds of Change: Reflections on the Condition of Women in the Early and Mid-Ch'ing." *Signs* 2(Aug. 1976):5-23.

0184 Sampson, Theos. "Anti-Marriage Associations." *Notes and Queries on China and Japan* 2(Sept. 1868):142-43.

0185 Shih, Vincent Y. C. *The Taiping Ideology, Its Sources, Interpretation and Influences*. Seattle: University of Washington, 1967. [See chapter 3, "Social Ideals and Social Structure," pp. 45-79].

0186 Tsao, Li Yieni. "The Life of a Girl in China." *Annals of the American Academy of Political and Social Sciences* 39(Jan. 1912):62-70.

0187 Wei, Chin-chih. "An Early Woman Revolutionary." *China Reconstructs* 7(June 1962):31-33.

0188 "Women's Rights in China." *Current Literature* 33(July 1902):100.

EMANCIPATION MOVEMENTS: THE CHINESE REPUBLIC (1911-1949)

0189 Andrews, Y. B., Mrs. "The Women of China." In *Camps and Trails in China,* ed. R. C. Andrews and Y. B. Andrews, pp. 67-73. 1918.

0190 Austen, N. "New Women of the Orient." *Current History* 33(Mar. 1931):892-95.

0191 Ayscough, Florence Wheelock. *Chinese Women Yesterday and Today*. Boston: Houghton Mifflin, 1937. [Reprint: N.Y.: Da Capo, 1975. Covers careers of several prominent women.]

0192 Bashford, James Whitford. *China: An Interpretation.* 3rd ed. N.Y.: Abingdon, 1919. [See chapter 5, "Woman's Life in China," pp. 123-45.]

0193 Blake, E. "Position of Women in China." *Living Age,* no. 275 (Dec. 14, 1912), pp. 666-75.

0194 Boggs, L. P. "Position of Women in China." *Popular Science* 82(Jan. 1913):71-75.

0195 Bone, C. "Awakening of the Women of China." *Independent* 77(Sept. 18, 1913):667-70.

0196 Bowden-Smith, A. G. "Manchu Heroine." *Contemporary Review* 103(Apr. 1913):560-64.

0197 Buck, Pearl Sydenstricker. "Chinese Women: Their Predicament in the China of Today." *Pacific Affairs* 4(Oct. 1931):905-909.

0198 Campbell, N. M. "Miss Wu of China; Interview." *Woman's J.* 14(Dec. 1929):18-19.

0199 Carscallen, H. M. "The Status of Women in China." *International Review of Missions,* July 1921, pp. 396-401.

0200 Chang, Shao-wei. "Feminist Movement in China." *China Critic* 5(Dec. 15, 1932):1324-27.

0201 Chao, Buwei Yang. *Autobiography of a Chinese Woman.* Trans. Yuenren Chao. N.Y.: John Day, 1947. [Author was one of the early "emancipated" college-educated women of the 1920s.]

0202 Chiang, Yung-ching. "Hu Han-min's Ideas on Women's Rights and His Achievements." *Chinese Studies in History* 10(Summer 1977):34-72.

0203 "China's Hopes in Her New Women." *Literary Digest* 83(Nov. 15, 1924):38-42.

0204 "China's Modern Women a Curse?" *Literary Digest* 103(Nov. 23, 1929):17.

0205 "China's Modernized Ladies." *Literary Digest* 79(Dec. 8, 1923):18-19.

0206 "Chinese Girl." *Living Age,* no. 273 (May 18, 1912), pp. 442-44.

0207 "Chinese Girl Goes Modern Too." *Asia* 35(Feb. 1935):116-17.

0208 Ching, T. S. and Vaughn, K. E. "What Chinese Women Are Doing." *Missionary Review of the World* 53(Jan. 1930):56-58.

0209 Chou, Tse-tsung. *The May Fourth Movement: Intellectual Revolution in Modern China.* Stanford: Stanford University, 1960. [See "The Emancipation of Woman," pp. 257-59.]

0210 Chow, C. F. "The Awakening of Chinese Women and Celibacy." *Chinese Students Monthly* 19(1923):2:28-29.

0211 Chu, T. C., Mrs. "The Emancipation of Chinese Women." *Chinese Recorder,* Oct. 1919, p. 658.

0212 Close, U. "New Women in a New China." *Ladies Home J.* 50(July 1933):19.

0213 "Defending the Modern Chinese Girl." *Literary Digest* 104(Jan. 11, 1930):20.

0214 Djang, Hsiang-lan. "New Womanhood in Old China." In *Christian Voices in China,* ed. Chester S. Miao, pp. 95-110. N.Y.: Friendship, 1948.

0215 "Feet Unbound; China, Returning to Code of Confucius, Drops Modernisms." *Literary Digest* 122(Sept. 5, 1936):19.

0216 "The Feminist Movement in China." *People's Tribune,* new (2nd) series, 9(June 1935):301-314.

0217 Galbraith, Winifred. *Willow Pattern: A Picture of China Today.* London: Edinburgh House, 1933.

0218 Gamble, Sidney. *Peking, a Social Survey.* N.Y.: George H. Dora, 1921. [Role of women, pp. 36-37; employment of women, p. 327; women in prisons, pp. 309-313.]

0219 Gamewell, M. N., Mrs. *New Life Current in China.* 1919. [See "The New Woman in China," pp. 177-87.]

0220 Green, K. R. "New Horizons for Chinese Women." *Missionary Review of the World* 55(Oct. 1932):537-38.

0221 Hand, Mildred. "China's Awakening Womanhood." *Chinese Recorder,* Dec. 1923, pp. 739-42.

0222 Hannin, Ethel Edith. *Women and the Revolution.* N.Y.: E. P. Dutton, 1939.

0223 Harding, Gardner Ludwig. *Present-day China; a Narrative of a Nation's Advance.* N.Y.: Century, 1916. [See chapter 2, "The Woman's Part," pp. 38-67 and *passim.*]

0224 Hosie, Dorothea Lady [Soothill]. *Portrait of a Chinese Lady and Certain of Her Contemporaries.* London: Hodder & Stoughton, 1929.

0225 Hsieh, Ping-ying. "Letters of a Chinese Amazon." Trans. Lin Yutang. In *Letters of a Chinese Amazon and War-time Essays,* ed. Lin Yutang, pp. 3-37. Shanghai: Commercial Press, 1930.

0226 Hsieh, Ping-ying. *Girl Rebel, the Autobiography of Hsieh Ping-ying.* Trans. Lin Ju-ssu and Lin Wu-shuang. N.p.: Minguang shuju, 1940. [Reprinted as: *The Struggle of a Girl.* Hong Kong: Shijie wenhua chubanshe, n.d. Translation by Tsui Chi: *Autobiography of a Chinese Girl,* London: Allen & Unwin, 1943. American ed.: *Girl Rebel,* N.Y.: John Day.]

0227 Hsu, Meng-hsiung. "The Free Women of Free China." *Asia* 41(Mar. 1941):123-26.

0228 Hu, Hsi-mei. "The Changed Status of Modern Chinese Women." *People's Tribune,* new series, 6(1934):261-64.

0229 Hu, Pingsa [Mrs. T. C. Chu]. *The Changing Chinese Woman.* Peking: Peking Leader, 1926.

0230 Hughee-Hallett, F. *Awakening Womanhood.* London: Church Missionary Society, 1927. [See "Unbinding Women's Minds in China," pp. 55-69.]

0231 Hutchinson, Paul. "China's New Women." In *China's Real Revolution,* pp. 84-105. 1924.

0232 Jen, T'ai. "The Status of Woman in China." *Information Bulletin* (Nanking) 2(1936-37):171-88.

0233 Jenner, Delia. "Women in China: Policy Developments from the 1930s to the 1950s." Ph.D. dissertation, Leeds University, 1974.

0234 Kin, Y. "Women of China." *Asia* 17(Apr. 1917):100-104.

0235 Kinnosuke, A. "New Women in China and Japan." *Review of Reviews* 46(July 1912):71-73.

0236 Koo, W. K. Wellington. "Social and Cultural Changes in China." *China Magazine* 18(Feb. 1948):8-11, 59-62.

0237 Kuo, Helena (Ching-ch'iu). *I've Come a Long Way.* N.Y.: Appleton-Century, 1942.

0238 L. C. C. "The Women's Movement in China During the Last Thirty Years." *China Recorder* 72(Oct. 1941):560-75.

0239 Lu Hsun [Chou, Shu-jen]. "On the Emancipation of Women." In *Selected Works of Lu Hsun,* vol. 3, trans. Yang Hsien-yi and Gladys Yang, pp. 339-41. Peking: Foreign Languages Press, 1959.

0240 Lu Hsun [Chou, Shu-jen]. "On Women's Liberation." *Chinese Literature,* Sept. 1973, pp. 30-32.

0241 Lu Xun [Zhou Shuren]. "What Happens After Nora Leaves Home?" In *Silent China: Selected Writings of Lu Xun,* ed. & trans. Gladys Yang, pp. 148-54. London: Oxford, 1973.

0242 Mei, Anna Kong. "The Modern Chinese Woman: Her Work and Problems." *International Review of Missions* 13(Oct. 1924):565-72.

0243 N., Y. I. "The Awakening Women of China." *Transpacific* 2(1920):3:533-58.

0244 Pajet, J. "China's Women Today." *Eastern World* 1(May 1974):10.

0245 Pan-Pacific Women's Conference. *Women of the Pacific; Being a Record of the Proceedings of the 1st-2nd Pan-Pacific Women's Conference, 1928-30.* 2 vols. Honolulu: Pan-Pacific Union, 1928-1930.

0246 Paterson, I. "Making New Women in China." *Missionary Review of the World* 57(May 1934):225-26.

0247 Pearson, Margaret Jean. "Hsieh Ping-ying: Participant in the Family Revolution in China." M.A. thesis, University of Washington, 1970.

0248 Price, M. "Women Builders of Modern China." *Independent Women* 26(July 1947):186.

0249 Pye, Edith M-. "The Woman's Movement in China." *Asiatic Review,* new (4th) series 25(Apr. 1929):204-219.

0250 Ross, E. A. "Unbinding the Women of China." *Delineator* 79(Apr. 1912):283-84.

0251 Schwarcz, Vera. "Ibsen's Nora: The Promise and the Trap." *Bulletin of Concerned Asian Scholars* 7(Jan./Mar. 1975):3-5.

0252 "Scoring China's Lucy Stoners." *Literary Digest* 100(Feb. 17, 1929):17.

0253 Seesholtz, Ann Groh. "Distinctive Activities and Interests of Chinese Women." In *China,* ed. Orville Anderson Petty, pp. 502-534. N.Y.: Harper, 1933. [Layman's Foreign Missions Inquiry, Factfinders' Reports, 5; supplementary series, part 2.]

0254 Seton, Grace Thompson. "The New Woman." In *Chinese Lanterns,* pp. 185-277. N.Y.: Dodd, Mead & Co., 1924.

0255 Siu, Bobby. *Fifty Years of Struggle: The Development of the Women's Movements in China (1900-1949).* Hong Kong: Revomen, 1975.

0256 Siu, Bobby. *Women of China in Struggle, 1911-1949.* Westport, Conn.: Lawrence Hill, 1981.

0257 Soong, Ching Ling. "The Chinese Woman's Fight for Freedom." *Asia* (N.Y.: American Asiatic Association) 42(July 1942):391-93; 42(Aug. 1942):470-72.

0258 "The Status of Chinese Women." *Chinese Recorder,* June 1925, pp. 348-49. [Editorial.]

0259 Strong, Anna Louise. "New Women of Old Canton." *Asia* (N.Y.: American Asiatic Association) 26(June 1926):493-95, 555-57.

0260 Strong, Anna Louise. "Women of Nationalist China." *Woman Citizen* 12(Nov. 1927):18-19.

0261 "Suffragettes of China." *Literary Digest* 44(Feb. 3, 1912):239.

0262 Tcheng, Soumay. "A Girl from China." *Good Housekeeping* 81(Nov. 1925):14; 82(Dec. 1925):72. [Told by Soumay Tcheng and transcribed by Mrs. John Van Vorst.]

0263 Tseng, P. S. (Pao-sun). "The Chinese Woman, Past and Present." In *Symposium on Chinese Culture,* ed. Sophia H. Chen Zen (Jen Ch'en Hong-che), pp. 281-92. Shanghai: China Institute of Pacific Relations, 1931. [Reprint: N.Y.: Paragon, 1969.]

0264 Twanmoh, Chien-ming. "Hu Shih and Female Emancipation in China." M.A. thesis, Australian National University, 1966.

0265 Van Vorst, Bessie (McGinnis). *A Girl from China (Soumay Tcheng).* N.Y.: Frederick A. Stokes, 1926.

0266 Wei, Cheng Yu-hsia [Mme. Wei Tao-ming]. *My Revolutionary Years.* N.Y.: Charles Scribner, 1943.

0267 Wei, W. L. "Miss Peach Blossom." *Outlook* 154(Jan. 8, 1930):50-51, 78. [Essay on educated women in modern Chinese cities.]

0268 White, J. "Women's Hour in China." *Forum* 57(Apr. 1917):421-28. [On participation of Chinese women in political, economic, and educational endeavors during the early Republic.]

0269 Williams, F. T. "The Status of Women." *Current History* 26(1927):420-25.

0270 Witke, Roxane Heater. "Mao Tse-tung, Women and Suicide in the May Fourth Era." *China Quarterly,* no. 31 (July-Sept. 1967), pp. 128-147.

0271 Witke, Roxane Heater. *Transformation of Attitudes Towards Women During the May Fourth Era of Modern China.* Ann Arbor: University Microfilms, 1971. [Ph.D. dissertation, University of California, Berkeley, 1970.]

0272 "The Women's Movement in China During the Last Thirty Years." *Chinese Recorder,* Oct. 1941, pp. 560-75.

0273 Wong, Dorothy T. "Women as Nationalists." *Current History* 26(1927):425-27.

0274 Woodsmall, Ruth Frances. *Eastern Women Today and Tomorrow.* Boston: Central Committee on the United Study of Foreign Missions, 1933.

0275 Wu, Ting Fang [Wu, Ting-fang]. "Female Changes in China." *Delineator* 99(Oct. 1921):16-17.

0276 Young, Ludvig J-. "The Emancipation of Women in China Before 1920, With Special Reference to Kwangtung." M.A. thesis, Columbia University, 1965.

0277 Young Women's Christian Association. *Present Day China.* Shanghai: Commercial Press, 1927. [Compiled by the student department of the YWCA and YMCA.]

0278 Yule, E. S. "Miss China." *Scribner's Magazine* 71(Jan. 1922):66-79.

0279 Zen, Sophia H. Chen [Mrs. Hong-che]. *The Chinese Woman and Four Other Essays.* 2nd ed. Peiping, 1935.

EMANCIPATION MOVEMENTS IN THE COMMUNIST REVOLUTION, 1921-1949

0280 All China Democratic Women's Federation. *Documents of the Women's Movement in China.* Peking, 1953

0281 All China Democratic Women's Federation. "From Struggle to Victory: Sketches of the Fighting." In *Women of New China.* Peking, 1953

0282 Belden, Jack. *China Shakes the World.* N.Y.: Harper, 1949. [Reprint: N.Y.: Monthly Review, 1970. See chapter 10, "The Revolt of Women," pp. 275-317.]

0283 Buck, P. S. "A Chinese Woman Speaks." *Asia* [Asia and the Americas] 26(Apr. 1926):304-310; 26(May 1926):413-19. [Fictionalized biography.]

0284 Burchett, Wilred, C. *China's Feet Unbound.* London: Lawrence & Wishart, 1952. [See chapter 9, "The Dual Victory of China's Women," pp. 124-43.]

0285 *CB* no. 609 (Oct. 7, 1959). Ts'ai Ch'ang. "Party's Central Line Illuminating Road of Thorough Emancipation of Women in Our Century," p. 36.

0286 Chang, Feng-ju; Li Chih-k'uan; and Liu Chung. "Revolutionary Mother Pao Lien-tzu." In *The People of Taihang,* ed. Sidney L. Greenblatt, pp. 218-45. White Plains, N.Y.: International Arts and Sciences, 1972.

0287 Ch'en, Yü-ying. "Her Revolutionary Spirit Radiates Like a Great Rainbow." *Chinese Studies in History* 12(Summer 1979):61-72. [In praise of Mao Zedong's first wife, Yang Kaihui, a revolutionary martyr.]

0288 The Criticism Group of the People's Literature Publishing House. "Eternal Glory to Martyr Yang K'ai-hui." *Chinese Studies in History* 12(Spring 1979):44-47.

0289 Curtin, Katie. *Women in China*. N.Y.: Pathfinder, 1975. [Topics include women's position in the old society, the Communist Party, and the women's movement before 1949; and women and education.]

0290 Davin, Delia. *The Communist Women's Movement in China, 1945-56*. University of Leeds, 1972.

0291 Davin, Delia. "Women in the Liberated Areas." In *Women in China*, ed. M. Young, pp. 73-92. Ann Arbor: University of Michigan, 1973.

0292 Davin, Delia. *Woman Work: Women and the Party in Revolutionary China*. Oxford: Oxford University, 1976.

0293 De Beauvoir, Simone. *The Long March*. Trans. Austryn Wainhouse. Cleveland: World, 1958 [The role of women is discussed in chapter 3, "The Family."]

0294 Fan, Fang-chün. "Li Lao Ma-ma Has Turned Over." *Chinese Sociology and Anthropology* 9(Winter 1976-77):14-20. [Trans. from *Ten Years of Shanghai Liberation*.]

0295 Frenier, Mariam D. "Women and the Chinese Communist Party, 1921-52: Changes in Party Policy and Mobilization Techniques." Ph.D. dissertation, University of Iowa, 1978.

0296 Ho, Kuo Cheng. "The Status and Role of Women in the Chinese Communist Movement, 1946-1949." Ph.D. dissertation, Indiana University, 1973.

0297 Hsin, Wen-ping. "Martyr Yang K'ai-hui Will Always Live in Our Hearts." *Chinese Studies in History* 12(Summer 1979):54-60.

0298 Hsu, Kuang. "Women's Liberation Through Struggle." *China Reconstructs* 22(Mar. 1973):8-9.

0299 Hsu, Kuang. "Women's Liberation—Part of the Revolutionary Movement." *China Reconstructs* 24(June 1975):2-6.

0300 Hu, Chi-hsi. "The Sexual Revolution in the Kiangsi Soviet." *China Quarterly*, no. 59 (July-Sept. 1974), pp. 477-90. [Emancipation in the Communist rural base area in the 1930s.]

0301 "In Commemoration of the Forty-Sixth Anniversary of the Heroic Martyrdom of Yang K'ai-hui." *Chinese Studies in History* 12(Spring 1979):36-43.

0302 Jackal, Patricia Stranahan. "Changes in Policy for Yanan Women, 1935-1947." *Modern China* 7(Jan. 1981):83-112. [On the development of policy to raise the status of women in the Shaan-Gan-Ning border region.]

0303 K'ang, K'e-ch'ing. "Women Revolutionaries I Have Known (1)." *China Reconstructs* 27(Mar. 1978):2-8.

0304 K'ang K'e-ch'ing. "Women Revolutionaries I Have Known (2)." *China Reconstructs* 27(April 1978):13-16.

0305 K'ang K'e-ch'ing. "Women Revolutionaries I Have Known (3)." *China Reconstructs* 27(May 1978):19-22.

0306 Landy, Laurie. *Women in the Chinese Revolution*. N.Y.: International Social Book Service, 1970.

0307 Liang, Hsing. *Liu Hu-lan*. Peking: Foreign Languages Press, 1953. [Biography of a famous young woman guerrilla and revolutionary martyr, based on interviews carried out in 1951.]

0308 Ling, T. [Ting Ling]. "Thoughts on 8 March (Women's Day)." *New Left Review* 92(July 1975):102-105. [Originally published in 1942.]

0309 Liu, Kuang-p'u and Ch'en Fu-t'ung. "A Woman Farmhand." *Chinese Sociology and Anthropology* 5(Fall/Winter 1972-73):46-66.

0310 Liu, Maoshu. "Xiang Jingyu, Champion of the Chinese Women's Movement." *Women of China* 1980:3:33-35; 1980:4:33-35.

0311 Lu Hsun [Chou, Shu-jen]. "In Memory of Miss Liu Ho-chen." In *Selected Works of Lu Hsun,* vol. 2, trans. Yang Hsien-yi and Gladys Yang, pp. 257-62. Peking: Foreign Languages Press, 1957. [Reprinted in *Chinese Literature*, May, 1959, pp. 34-39.]

0312 Mao, Tse-tung. "Report of an Investigation into the Peasant Movement in Hunan." In *Selected Works,* 2nd ed., vol 1. Peking: Peking Foreign Languages Press, 1965. [Translation from 1960 ed. See part 7, p. 44 (written in 1927).]

0313 "The New Women of a Great Age." *Chinese Education* 6(Sept. 1973):97-104. [About women following Mao Zedong's direction of "resist Japan, save the nation."]

0314 P. R. "Women in Old and New China." *Inprecorr* 11(Feb. 28, 1931):10.

0315 Price, Jane. "Women and Leadership in the Chinese Communist Movement." *Bulletin of Concerned Asian Scholars* 7(Jan.-Mar. 1975):19-24. [Discussion of the relationship between feminism and the revolutionary process, 1921-1945.]

0316 "Revolutionary Grandmothers Still Young in Spirits." *Peking Review* 18(Aug. 22, 1975):22-23.

0317 Ruben, Sanchez. "Communist Heroine Liu Hu-lan." *China Reconstructs* 21(Mar. 1972):3.

0318 Smedley, Agnes. *Portraits of Chinese Women in Revolution*. Ed. J. MacKinnon and S. Mackinnon. Old Westbury, N.Y.: Feminist Press, 1976.

0319 Snow, Helen Foster [Nym Wales]. *The Chinese Communists, Sketches and Autobiographies of the Old Guard*. Conn.: Greenwood Publishing, 1972. [See part 7, "Women."]

0320 *SPRCP*, no. 6241 (Dec. 8, 1976). *"Jen-min jih-pao* Features Commemoration of Martyr Yang K'ai-hui, Close Comrade-in-Arms and Wife of Chairman Mao," p. 155.

0321 *SPRCP*, no. 6242 (Dec. 9, 1976). "Mass Gathering Marks Martyr Yang K'ai-hui's Death," p. 221.

0322 Stein, Guenther. *The Challenge of Red China*. London: Pilot, 1945. [See especially pp. 247-59.]

0323 "The Story of Liu Hu-lan." *China Reconstructs* 19(June 1970):42.

0324 T. H. "Women and Children in the Hupeh-Honan-Anhwei Soviet District." *Inprecorr* 12(Nov. 1932).

0325 Tsin, Ching. "Liu Hu-lan." *Chinese Literature*, Feb. 1972, pp. 15-43. [Reminiscences about a guerrilla heroine.]

0326 Wales, Nym [Helen Foster Snow]. *Red Dust: Autobiographies of Chinese Communists, As Told to Nym Wales*. Stanford: Stanford University, 1952. [See chapter 7: Cai Dingli, woman writer and editor; Kang Keqing, woman peasant partisan.]

0327 Wales, Nym [Helen Foster Snow]. *Notes on the Chinese Student Movement, 1935-36. Guidance Notes Prepared for the Nym Wales Collection on the Far East in the Hoover Institution on War, Revolution and Peace, at Stanford University*. Stanford, 1959 (mimeo).

0328 Walker, Kathy LeMons. "The Party and Peasant Women." In *Chinese Communists and Rural Society, 1927-1934*, ed. Philip C. C. Huang, Lynda Schaefer Bell and Kathy LeMons Walker, pp. 57-82. Berkeley: Center for Chinese Studies, 1978.

0329 Wang, Hsi-t'ang; Lien, Pu-wang; and Yao, I-shan. "The Poor People's Cave." *Chinese Sociology and Anthropology* 5(Fall/Winter 1972-73):85-111. [Includes story of Bao Lianzi, the "revolutionary mother."]

0330 Wang, Yi-chih. "A Great Woman Revolutionary." *China Reconstructs* 14(Mar. 1965):24-27.

0331 Weigelin, Susanne. "The Martyrdom of Yang K'ai-hui." *Eastern Horizon* 16(Mar. 1977):12-14.

0332 "Women's Liberation in the Hunan Peasant Movement." *China Reconstructs* 24(Mar. 1975):40-41.

0333 "Yang K'ai-hui, Wife and Revolutionary Comrade." *China Reconstructs* 26(Dec. 1977):56-58.

0334 Zhang, Hu. "Pioneers in the Chinese Women's Movement." *Women of China* 1980:7:4-5.

EMANCIPATION MOVEMENTS: THE PEOPLE'S REPUBLIC OF CHINA (1949-)

0335 All-China Democratic Women's Federation. "The Women's Movement in China." *Chinese Studies in History* 5(Fall 1971):88-108.

0336 Andors, Phyllis. "Social Revolution and Woman's Emancipation: China During the Great Leap Forward." *Bulletin of Concerned Asian Scholars* 7(Jan.-Mar. 1975):33-42.

0337 Andors, Phyllis. "Politics of Chinese Development: The Case of Women, 1960-1966." *Signs* 2(Autumn 1979):89-119.

0338 Attwood, J. and Garavente, Jean. "Women Inside China." *McCalls,* Nov. 1971, pp. 77+.

0339 Bacon, Margaret. "China: Chinese Women and Their New Status." *Christian Century* 89(Aug. 30, 1972):858.

0340 Bacon, Margaret. "The Egalitarian Concern." *China Notes* 10(1972):2:33-36.

0341 Barrett, Jane. "Women Hold up Half the Sky." In *Women in China,* ed. M. Young, pp. 193-200. Ann Arbor: University of Michigan, 1973.

0342 Bodard, Lucien. "Women of Iron." *Atlantic Monthly* 204(Dec. 1959):95-98.

0343 Brittain, Mary Z. "After Various Twists and Turns." *China Now,* no. 40 (Mar. 1974), pp. 2-4. [On Chinese women's liberation movement.]

0344 Browne, Vivian E. "A Photo Essay on the People's Republic of China." *Heresies: A Feminist Publication on Arts and Politics* 2(1979):4:18-23. [Written by an American black woman on her tour to China in November 1977.]

0345 Buck, Pearl S. "What I Learned from Chinese Women; Interview." Ed. D. McConathy. *Vogue* 159(June 1972):136, 148.

0346 Buxton, Rose and Langton, Patricia. "Women and Socialist Equality." *China Now,* no. 28 (Jan. 1973), pp. 2-4.

0347 Cameron, J. "Women in Red China; Old Condition of the Chinese Woman." *Atlantic Monthly* 196(Oct. 1955):59-64.

0348 "Chairman Mao Writes Inscriptions for the New Journal of Peking University and for 'Women of China.'" *Peking Review* 9(Sept. 2, 1966):5-6.

0349 Chakravarti, Tripurari. "The Position of Women in China." *Bulletin of the Ramakrishna Mission Institute of Culture* 5(1954):257-63.

0350 Chandrasekhar, Sripati. *Red China: An Asian View.* N.Y.: Praeger, 1961. [See "Women in New China," pp. 74-87. Discussion of women's changing legal and economic status.]

0351 Chang, H. M. *The Women in the Capital Are Completely Liberated and Are Leaping Forward, Speeches Given at Second Session of Second National People's Congress, Communist China.* Washington, D.C.: U.S. Joint Publications Research Service, 1960.

0352 Chang, Kuei-mei. "Deepest Love for Chairman Mao's Works and Firmest Belief in Mao Tse-tung's Thought." *Peking Review* 9(Nov. 11, 1966):32-34.

0353 Chen, J. *New Earth.* Peking: New World Press, 1957. [Reprinted in the U.S. by Southern Illinois Press, 1972. Based on first-hand observations in Zhejiang in 1955. Argues that cooperation aided the emancipation of women.]

0354 Chin, Chi-tsu and Hung, Sung. "Men and Women Should Receive Equal Pay for Equal Work: A Critique of an Erroneous Tendency in Allocation in the Villages." *Chinese Sociology and Anthropology* 7(Summer 1975):53-60.

0355 "China's Feminist Movement." *Eastern World* (London) 25(Jan.-Feb. 1971):8-9; and *Current Scene* (Hong Kong) 9(Jan. 7, 1971):18-19.

0356 "China's Women in Socialist Revolution and Socialist Construction." *Peking Review* 13(Mar. 20, 1970):15-20.

0357 "Chinese Women Discuss Life and Work." *Beijing Review* 22(Mar. 9, 1979):19-26.

0358 "Chinese Women Have Equal Political and Social Status with Men." *Economic Reporter* 1(Jan.-Mar. 1973):40-41.

0359 Cohen, Charlotte Bonny. "Experiment in Freedom: Women in China." In *Sisterhood is Powerful,* ed. Robin Morgan, pp. 385-417. N.Y.: Random House, 1970. [A survey of the position of women in traditional and contemporary China, emphasizing the achievements of the communists.]

0360 Croll, Elisabeth Joan. *The Women's Movement in China, a Selection of Readings, 1949-1973.* London: Anglo-Chinese Educational Institute, 1974; and Nottingham, England: Russell Press, 1974.

0361 Croll, Elisabeth Joan. "Half the Sky." *China Now,* no. 48 (Jan. 1975), pp. 9-10.

0362 Croll, Elisabeth Joan. "Social Production and Female Status: Women in China." *Race and Class* 18(Summer 1976):39-52.

0363 Croll, Elisabeth Joan. "The Movement to Criticize Confucius and Lin Piao: A Comment on 'The Women of China' (Vol. 2, No. 1)." *Signs* 2(Spring 1977):721-26.

0364 Croll, Elisabeth Joan. "A Recent Movement to Redefine the Role and Status of Women." *China Quarterly,* no. 71 (Sept. 1977), pp. 591-97.

0365 Croll, Elisabeth Joan. "Female Solidarity as a Power Base in Rural China." *Sociologia Ruralis* 18(1978):2/3:140-157.

0366 Croll, Elisabeth Joan. *Feminism and Socialism in China.* Boston: Routledge and K. Paul, 1978.

0367 Crook, Isabel and David. *The First Years of Yangyi Commune.* London: Routledge and Kegan Paul, International Library of Sociology and Social Reconstruction, 1966. [Chapter 19 deals with women. See in particular: women's work, p. 240; social services, p. 244; women cadres, p. 248; the Yangyi Women's Congress of 1960, p. 251, etc.]

0368 Curtin, Katie. "Women and the Chinese Revolution." *International Socialist Review* 35(Mar. 1974)8-11, 25-40.

0369 Curtin, Katie. *Women in China.* N.Y.: Pathfinder, 1975.

0370 Cusack, Dymphna. *Chinese Women Speak.* London: Angus & Robertson, 1959. [A general account of how modernization and communism changed Chinese women's lives and attitudes during the first decade of the new government.]

0371 Davin, Delia. "The Implications of Some Aspects of C.C.P. Policy Toward Urban Women in the 1950s." *Modern China* 1(Oct. 1975):363-78.

0372 Delmar, Rosalind. "Fighting Traditions." *China Now,* no. 50 (Mar. 1975), pp. 2-4.

0373 Department for International Work, All China Democratic Women's Federation, ed. *Women of China.* Peking: Foreign Languages Press, 1953.

0374 Deza, Alfonso B. "Women of China: They've Come a Long Way." *Impact* 13(June 1978):196-201.

0375 Diamond, Norma. "Collectivization, Kinship and the Status of Women in Rural China." *Bulletin of Concerned Asian Scholars* 7(Jan.-Mar. 1975):25-32.

0376 Dorros, Sybilla Green. "The Status of Women in the People's Republic of China." *Asian Studies* 16(1978):1-50.

0377 *ECMM*, no. 44 (May 1, 1956). "I Accuse Liu Chuan-ching of Maltreating Women," p. 32.

0378 *ECMM*, no. 173 (May 16, 1959). "On the New Stage of the Women's Movement," p. 15. [*Zhongguo funü* editorial.]

0379 *ECMM*, no. 201 (Jan. 1960). Ts'ai Ch'ang. "Party's General Line Illuminates the Path of Emancipation for Our Women." [From *Women of China,* Jan. 1969.]

0380 Fu, Wen. "Doctrine of Confucius and Mencius—the Shackle That Keeps Women in Bondage." *Peking Review* 17(Mar. 8, 1974):16-18.

0381 Goldwater [sic], Janet and Doughty [sic], Stuart [Goldwasser, Janet and Dowty, Stuart]. "Toward Full Emancipation." *China Now,* no. 27 (Dec. 1972), pp. 4-5.

0382 Gordon, Linda. "The Fourth Mountain: Women in China." *Working Paper for a New Society* 1(Fall, 1973):27-39.

0383 "Great Changes in Status of China's Women." *Peking Review* 18(July 4, 1975):16-18.

0384 Greenwood, Sylvia. "Women Hold Up Half the Sky." *China Now,* no. 71 (Apr.-May 1977), pp. 4-5.

0385 Grya, Noel. "Women's Liberation in China." *China Now,* no. 16 (Oct.-Nov. 1971), pp. 4, 10.

0386 Harley, Ann. "Women Hold up Half the Sky." *Convergence* 7(1974):3:18-24. [Discussion of the transformation of women's status in China through political campaigns and small study groups.]

0387 Hinton, Carma. "Women: The Long March Toward Equality." *New China* 1(Spring 1975):26-32.

0388 Hinton, William. *Fanshen: A Documentary of Revolution in a Chinese Village.* N.Y.: Monthly Review, 1966. [For the organization of a women's association, see pp. 157-60; on the struggle for women's rights, pp. 157-60, 396-98, 454-58.]

0389 Hobbs, Lisa. "Has Women's Lib Made it to China?" *Chatelaine* 44(Dec. 1971):25, 60-64.

0390 Hong, Lawrence K. "The Role of Women in the People's Republic of China: Legacy and Change." *Social Problems* 23(June 1976):545-57.

0391 "How to Bring Equal Pay for Equal Work for Men and Women." *Chinese Sociology and Anthropology* 7(Summer 1975):61-73.

0392 Hsin-ning-ts'un Production Brigade, Peking. "Open Fire on the Reactionary Fallacy that 'Males are Exalted and Females are Demeaned.'" (Responsive dialogue.) *Chinese Sociology and Anthropology* 11(Fall 1978):41-44.

0393 Hsu, Kuang. "Women's Liberation through Struggle." *China Reconstructs* 22(March 1973):8-11, 39.

0394 Hsu, Kwang [Hsu, Kuang]. "China's Women: Women's Liberation Is a Component Part of the Proletarian Revolution." *Peking Review* 17(Mar. 8, 1974):12-15.

0395 Huang, L. J. "A Re-evaluation of the Primary Role of the Communist Chinese Women: The Home Maker or the Worker." *Marriage and Family Living,* May 1963.

0396 Hughes, R. "Close-Up of Miss Communist China." *New York Times Magazine,* May 19, 1957, p. 27.

0397 *Hung-ch'i* commentator. "The People's Commune Advances Women's Complete Emancipation." *Peking Review* 3(Mar. 8, 1960):6-9.

0398 "International Working Women's Day: Talking of Women's Liberation." *Peking Review* 16(Mar. 9, 1973):12-15.

0399 Jade [Pseud. (Refugee from Mainland China)]. "Women's Liberation in China." In *Notes on Women's Liberation— We Speak in Many Voices, News and Letters.* Detroit, 1970.

0400 Jancar, Barbara Wolfe. *Women under Communism.* Baltimore: Johns Hopkins, 1978. [See especially appendix 2, "Leading Women in Political and Cultural Life in the People's Republic of China, 1949-1970," pp. 229-97.]

0401 Johnson, Kay Ann. "Women in the People's Republic of China." In *Asian Women in Transition,* ed. Sylvia A. Chipp and Justin J. Green, pp. 62-104. University Park: Pennsylvania State University, 1980. [Discusses reform of marriage and the family, and the economic and political roles of Chinese women.]

0402 Johnson, W. O. "For the Chinese Woman and Child: A New Lifestyle." *Smithsonian* 5(Aug. 1974):38-47.

0403 JPRS 2011 (Apr. 1, 1959). Wang, Ai-chu. "Liberation of Women as Seen from Collective Living." [From *Fudan,* no. 4, pp. 15-18.]

0404 JPRS 2608 (Dec. 1, 1959). "A Further Discussion of the New Stage of the Women's Movement." [From *Zhongguo funü,* no. 23.]

0405 JPRS 5043 (Mar. 1, 1960). Ts'ai, Ch'ang. "Women's Movement in Communist China." [From *Zhongguo funü,* no. 5, pp. 2-7, 8-9.]

0406 JPRS 6483 (Apr. 10, 1960). Chang, Hsiao-mei. "The Women in the Capital are Completely Liberated and are Leaping Forward." [From *Renmin ribao.*]

0407 JPRS 29543 (1960). "Struggle for the Thorough Emancipation of Women." [From *Zhongguo funü,* no. 5, pp. 2-3.]

0408 JPRS 37400 (July 10, 1966). "We Fervently Hope *Chung-kuo fu-nü* Will Become a 'Red' Publication." [From *Zhongguo funü,* no. 7, pp. 30-31.]

0409 JPRS 37400 (July 10, 1966). Liu, Li-wen. "The Poison Flowing from *Chung-kuo fu-nü* Must Be Stopped." [From *Zhongguo funü,* no. 7, p. 31.]

0410 JPRS 40525 (Sept. 10, 1966). "Review of Peking, *Jen-min jih-pao* Editorials for January 1966: Chairman Mao's Inscription for Women's Journal Hailed" [From *Zhongguo funü,* no. 9.]

0411 JPRS 46472 (June 27, 1968). "Revolutionary Women's Movement Praised." [From *Wenhui bao,* p. 4.]

0412 JPRS 61588 (Mar. 12, 1974). "Shanghai Women Workers Group Criticizes Lin, Confucius." [From New China News Agency.]

0413 Kehl, Dorothy. "Women in China: Holding up Half of Heaven." *Bridge* 1(Nov.-Dec. 1971):43-45, 52.

0414 Kingston, M. H. "Reservations about China." *Ms.,* Oct. 1978, pp. 67-68. [Author criticizes the aborting of female fetuses in China, suspecting that sexism still exists in the People's Republic.]

0415 Kraft, Joseph. "The New Maoist Women." *Cosmopolitan,* May 1973, pp. 175-78.

0416 Kristeva, Julia. "On the Women of China." Trans. Ellen C. Kennedy. *Signs* 1(Autumn 1975):57-81.

0417 Kristeva, Julia. *About Chinese Women.* Trans. Anita Barrows. London: Marion Boyars, 1977.

0418 Kwan, Rebecca S. "The Commune, and Family and the Emancipation of Women." *Contemporary China* 3(1958-1959), ed. E. S. Kirby, pp. 146-151. Hong Kong: Hong Kong University, 1960.

0419 Leader, Shelah Gilbert. "Mobilizing 'Half the Sky.'" *Far Eastern Economic Review* 78(Dec. 23, 1972):15-17.

0420 Leader, Shelah Gilbert. "The Emancipation of Chinese Women." *World Politics* 26(Oct. 1973):55-79.

0421 "Liberated Women." *Newsweek* 78(Aug. 16, 1971):32. [On problem of emancipation of women in the People's Republic of China.]

0422 Ling, Chia. "Changed Political Status of Chinese Women." *Women of China* 1957:2:8-10.

0423 Liu, Chao. "Chinese Women: Safeguarding Women's Interests." *Peking Review* 17(Mar. 29, 1974):15-17.

0424 Lu, Y. L. "Liberation of Women." *Peking Review* 15(Mar. 10, 1972):10:10-12.

0425 Lucas, Christopher. *Women of China.* Hong Kong: Dragonfly, 1965. [Anti-communist view arguing Chinese women endure lives of constant turmoil, drabness, and loss of femininity.]

0426 Lund, Caroline. "Women in the Chinese Revolution." *International Socialist Review* 31(June 1970):10-13, 39.

0427 Ma, Hsin-teh. *Chinese Women in the Great Leap Forward.* Peking: Foreign Languages Press, 1960. [Reprint: N.Y.: AMS, 1967.]

0428 Macciocchi, Maria Antonietta. *Daily Life in Revolutionary China.* N.Y.: Monthly Review, 1972. [See "Death of the Housewife," pp. 348-78.]

0429 Macciocchi, Maria Antonietta. "Everyday Life in Revolutionary China." *Monthly Review* 24(1972):2:16-32. [Excerpts from *Everyday Life in Revolutionary China.* N.Y.: Monthly Review, 1972. Includes discussion on women. Author is the Communist Party deputy representing Naples. She and her husband were among the first Western European Communist Party members invited to China after the Cultural Revolution.]

0430 MacFarquhar, E. "Let a Few Flowers Bloom." *Economist,* Dec. 31, 1977, p. 30.

0431 Marvin, Joyce. "Sisterhood is Indeed Powerful." *China Notes* 12(Winter 1973-74):2-4.

0432 Mercer, M. "Liberation, Chinese Style." *McCalls,* Jan. 1976, p. 48.

0433 Milton, Nancy. "Women in China." *Berkeley J. of Sociology* 16(1971-72):106-120.

0434 Moudud, Hasna J. *Women in China.* N.Y.: Advent Books, 1980.

0435 Mututantri, Barbara. "Women in China." *Eastern Horizon* 7(Sept.-Oct. 1968):46-52.

0436 Myrdal, Jan. *Report from a Chinese Village.* Trans. Maurice Michael. London: Heinman, 1965; N.Y.: Pantheon, 1965. [See part 6, "Women," pp. 203-39.]

0437 Myrdal, Jan and Kessle, G. *The Revolution Continued.* N.Y.: Random House, 1972. [Pp. 132-38 deal with Chinese women.]

0438 "New Stage in the Women's Emancipation Movement in China." *Peking Review* 3(Mar. 15, 1960):9-11. [*Renmin ribao* editorial.]

0439 *New Women in New China.* Peking: Foreign Languages Press, 1972.

0440 *New Women in New China.* N.Y.: China Books and Periodicals, 1973.

0441 Nicholson, Susan. "Women's Changing Status in China." *SAIS Review* 19(1975):3:36.

0442 Nishio, Yvonne Wong. "Women in China." In Marchia Jean Chan and Candice Cynda Chan, *Going Back,* pp. 1 1973. [Reports on a vist to China by Chinese American youths.]

0443 O'Hara, Albert Richard. "The Comparative Position of Chinese Women in Communist and Free China." *J. of the China Society* 14-15(1978):1-15.

0444 "The Ongoing Revolution in Women's Liberation in the People's Republic of China." *Far Eastern Reporter,* Sept. 1977, pp. 1-7.

0445 O'Sullivan, Sue. *The Moon for Dinner, Changing Relations—Women in China.* London, 1976 [Backdoor pamphlet no. 1.]

0446 O'Sullivan, Sue. "Transforming Human Relationships." *China Now,* no. 50 (Mar. 1975), pp. 11-12.

0447 *Pen Portraits from New China.* Peking: Foreign Languages Press, 1956. [Includes four portraits of new women, including a doctor and a factory worker.]

0448 "The People's Commune Advances Women's Complete Emancipation." *Peking Review* 3(Mar. 8, 1960):6-9.

0449 "People's Communes and the Emancipation of Women." *Peking Review* 2(Mar. 31, 1959):12-14. [Summary of an article from *Jiefangjun bao.*]

0450 "Questions People Ask—About Chinese Women." *China Reconstructs* 24(June 1975):7-9.

0451 Record, J. C. and Record, W. "Totalist and Pluralist Views of Women's Liberation: Some Reflections on the Chinese and American Settings." *Social Problems* 23(Apr. 1976):402-414.

0452 Ris, H. W. "Chinese Women: New Freedom." *Progressive* 39(Nov. 1975):42-45.

0453 "Role of Women in a Hunan County." *Summary of World Broadcasts,* BBC UK, second series FE/3717 (1971), BII/20.

0454 Rousseau, A. M. "Holding up Half the Heavens: Women in China." *Art in America* 67(Mar. 1979):16+.

0455 Russell, Maud. "Chinese Women: Liberated." *Far Eastern Reporter,* 1970, p. 40.

0456 Salaff, Janet Wietzer and Merkle, Judith. "Women and Revolution: The Lessons of the Soviet Union and China." *Berkeley J. of Sociology* 15(1970):166-91. [Reprint: *Socialist Revolution* 1(July-Aug. 1970):39-72.]

0457 Schuman, J. "Women in China." *Eastern Horizon* 11(1972):3:58-60.

0458 *SCMM,* no. 379 (July 1, 1963). "What Do Women Live For?" [From *Zhongguo funü.*]

0459 *SCMM,* no. 386 (Sept. 16, 1963). "What Do Women Live For?" pp. 12-18.

0460 *SCMM,* no. 390 (Oct. 1, 1963). Liao, Su-hua (Secretary, Supervisory Committee of Chunking CCP Municipal Committee). "What Is Revolutionary Women's True Happiness?" p. 28 [From *Zhongguo funü* 1963, no. 10.]

0461 *SCMM,* no. 401 (Nov. 20, 1963). Feng, Ch'i-yung. "A Thorough Criticism of Feudal Morals," p. 7.

0462 *SCMM,* no. 437 (Oct. 5, 1964). "Raise Your Consciousness and Persist in the Study of Chairman Mao's Works," pp. 11-15. [From *Zhongguo funü* 1964, no. 8.]

0463 *SCMM,* no. 444 (Nov. 23, 1964). Man, Mu-ch'un. "How the Problem of Women Should Be Viewed," pp. 18-22. [From *Hongqi,* 1964, no. 20.]

0464 *SCMM*, no. 448 (Dec. 21, 1964). Mu, Lan-ying. "Be True Daughters of Poor Peasants and Lower Middle Peasants Forever!" p. 30. [From *Zhongguo qingnian* 1964, no. 22.]

0465 *SCMM*, no. 543 (July 10, 1966). *Chung-kuo fu-nü*'s whole body of revolutionary workers. "Expose the Crimes of Black Gang Element Tung Pien," p. 4. [From *Zhongguo funü* 1966, no. 7.]

0466 *SCMM*, no. 543 (July 10, 1966). Liu, Li-wen (Hubei reader). "The Poisonous Influence of *Chung-kuo fu-nü* Must Be Liquidated," p. 11. [From *Zhongguo funü* 1966, no. 7.]

0467 *SCMM*, no. 547 (Oct. 24, 1966). "Class Nature of the Problems of Women Must Not Be Written Off!" pp. 1 [From *Zhongguo funü* 1966, no. 8.]

0468 *SCMM*, no. 547 (Aug. 10, 1966). Kung, Li. "A Refutation of the Anti-Party Absurdity of the Article 'Learn to Act According to Actual Conditions,'" p. 14. [From *Zhongguo funü* 1966, no. 8. About a selected big character poster.]

0469 *SCMM*, no. 548 (Aug. 10, 1966). "The Big Plot of False Discussion and Real Release of Poison—a Critique of Two Big Poisonous Weeds; 'What Do Women Live For?' and 'What Is the Standard for Choosing Spouse?'" p. 22. [From *Zhongguo funü* 1966, no. 8.]

0470 *SCMM*, no. 548 (Oct. 31, 1966). "Expose the Plot, Remove the Poisonous Weed—Excerpts of Articles Criticizing Discussions on 'For What Do Women Live?' and 'What Is the Standard for Choosing Spouse?'" pp. 26-28. [From *Zhongguo funü*, Aug. 10, 1966.]

0471 *SCMM*, no. 552 (Sept. 10, 1966). *Chung-kuo fu-nü* editorial. "Forever Hold High the Great Red Banner of Mao Tse-tung's Thought, Forever Follow Chairman Mao to Make Revolution," p. 6 [From *Zhongguo funü* 1966, no. 9.]

0472 *SCMM*, no. 552 (Sept. 10, 1966). "Warmly Hailing Chairman Mao's Inscription for *Chung-kuo fu-nü*," p. 1. [From *Zhongguo funü* 1966, no. 9.]

0473 *SCMM*, no. 553 (Sept. 10, 1966). *Chung-kuo fu-nü* correspondents. "The Red Guards' Revolutionary Spirit of Rebellion Is Very Good," p. 13 [From *Zhongguo funü* 1966, no. 9.]

0474 *SCMM*, no. 555 (Dec. 2, 1966). "I Shall Always Make Revolution and Always Be Loyal to Chairman Mao Tse-tung's Thought," pp. 6-12. [From *Peking Review*, vol. 9, no. 49 (Dec. 2, 1966)]

0475 *SCMM*, no. 558 (Oct. 17, 1966). *Chung-kuo fu-nü* editorial. "Learn from the Splendid Example of PLA and Study Chairman Mao's Works in a Big Way," p. 22. [From *Zhongguo funü* 1966, no. 11.]

0476 *SCMM*, no. 560 (Nov. 7, 1966). *Chung-kuo fu-nü* editorial. "Long Live the Victory of Chairman Mao's Line," p. 19. [From *Zhongguo funü* 1966, no. 12.]

0477 *SCMM*, no. 564 (Feb. 20, 1967). "Be a Person Useful to the People," p. 30. [From *Zhongguo funü*, Nov. 24, 1966.]

0478 *SCMM*, no. 700 (Feb. 1, 1971). Han, Wen (Revolutionary Committee of Lo-ch'ang *hsien*, Kwangtung). "How We Strengthen Leadership Over the Women's Movement," p. 76

0479 *SCMM*, no. 714 (Sept. 1, 1971). Writing Group, CCP Hunan Provincial Committee. "Bring the Role of Women into Full Play in Revolution and Construction," p. 73. [From *Hongqi*, 1971, no. 10.]

0480 *SCMM*, no. 771 (Mar. 3, 1974). The "Iron Girls" Team of Tachai Brigade. "We Revolutionary Women Bitterly Hate the Doctrines of Confucius and Mencius," p. 36.

0481 *SCMM*, no. 797 (Sept. 20, 1974). Party Branch of Shift B of Weaving Workshop, No. 30 Cotton Textile Mill, Shanghai. "Reveal the Reactionary Features of 'Women's Classics,'" p. 36.

0482 *SCMP*, No. 81 (Mar. 8, 1951). "Women Members of CPV Pledge to Annihilate Enemy," pp. 17-19.

0483 *SCMP*, No. 325 (Apr. 27, 1952). "Chinese Women Enjoying Happy Life After Liberation," p. 18.

0484 *SCMP*, No. 516 (Feb. 11, 1953). "Speech by Shih Liang at PPCC National Committee Session: Women of People's China Today," p. 10.

0485 *SCMP*, No. 527 (Mar. 1953). "China's Emancipated Women," pp. 15-16. [From New China News Agency, Kaifeng, Mar. 1953.]

0486 *SCMP*, No. 558 (Apr. 25, 1953). "Women of New China Today," p. 33. [New China News Agency feature article.]

0487 *SCMP*, No. 760 (Mar. 4, 1954). "Only Socialism Can Fully Free Women, Says Chinese Women's March 9 Appeal," p. 3.

0488 *SCMP*, No. 761 (Mar. 5, 1954). "Chao Chin—Example of Women's Status in New China," p. 29.

0489 *SCMP*, No. 761 (Mar. 7, 1954). "Peking Women Greet Chairman Mao Tse-tung," p. 24.

0490 *SCMP*, No. 761 (Mar. 7, 1954). "Teng Ying-ch'ao Speaks to Peking Women," p. 24.

0491 *SCMP*, no. 1002 (Jan. 9, 1955). "Women's Work in Shanghai during the Past Four Years and the Tasks in the Future," p. 7.

0492 *SCMP*, no. 1003 (Mar. 8, 1955). "*Jen-min jih-pao* Calls on Women to Build Socialism," p. 13.

0493 *SCMP*, no. 1821 (July 13, 1958). "Support Women's Ardor for Socialism," p. 2.

0494 *SCMP*, no. 1973 (Mar. 8, 1959). "Li Teh-chuan on Women's Emancipation in China," p. 3.

0495 *SCMP*, no. 1973 (Mar. 8, 1959). "Women of China, Put Up Skyrocketing Zeal and make Greater Contributions," p. 1.

0496 *SCMP*, no. 2039 (May 8, 1959). "The Breaking Down of the System of Feudal Patriarchy," p. 2

0497 *SCMP*, no. 2065 (July 8, 1959). "Strengthen Political and Ideological Work Among Women Workers," p. 14

0498 *SCMP*, no. 2083 (Aug. 19, 1959). "Review of Women's Work in China," p. 21.

0499 *SCMP*, no. 2206 (Feb. 24, 1960). Ts'ai Ch'ang. "Women's Movement in China Enters on New Stage," p. 8.

0500 *SCMP*, no. 2210 (Feb. 29, 1960). *Red Flag* commentator. "The P.C. [people's commune]—a Good Set-up for the Thorough Liberation of Women," p. 2.

0501 *SCMP*, no. 2210 (Feb. 29, 1960). "20,000,000 Emancipated Women in Central China Province," p. 22.

0502 *SCMP*, no. 2210 (Mar. 1, 1960). "Women of Rural China on the Road to Complete Liberation," p. 8

0503 *SCMP*, no. 2211 (Feb. 24, 1960). Ts'ai Ch'ang. "Mobilize Women Further to Take a Continuing Leap Forward in 1960, Holding Aloft the Banner of Mao Tse-tung's Thought," p. 1.

0504 *SCMP*, no. 2211 (Mar. 2, 1960). Jui, Wan. "Women's Role in Building Socialism in China," p. 13.

0505 *SCMP*, no. 2211 (Mar. 2, 1960). "Women's Status in China," p. 12.

0506 *SCMP*, no. 2215 (Mar. 8, 1960). *Jen-min jih-pao* editorial. "New Stage in the Women's Emancipation Movement in Our Country," p. 6

0507 *SCMP*, no. 2350 (Sept. 27, 1960). "Urban Communes Set Chinese Women Free," p. 10.

0508 *SCMP*, no. 2454 (Mar. 7, 1961). "Women in Dragon Beard Ditch—Former Peking Slum Area," p. 16

0509 *SCMP*, no. 2702 (Mar. 8, 1962). *Jen-min jih-pao* editorial. "Conduct Work on Women in a More Practical, Thoroughgoing and Attentive Way," p. 5.

0510 *SCMP*, no. 3784 (Sept. 10, 1966). "Chairman Mao's Works Bring Light to My Mind—Outline of a Speech by Ku A-t'ao, an Activist in the Study of Chairman Mao's Works," p. 20.

0511 *SCMP*, no. 4233 (June 14, 1968). "Attach Full Importance to the Role Played by Women," pp. 12–13. [From *Wenhui bao*, Shanghai.]

0512 *SCMP*, no. 4991 (Sept. 24, 1971). "Fokang *Hsien*, Kuangtung Province Strengthens Leadership Over Women's Work," p. 150.

0513 *SCMP*, no. 5086 (Feb. 23, 1972). "Women of Our Country Play a Major Role in the Three Major Revolutionary Movements," p. 19

0514 *SCMP*, no. 5905 (Mar. 6, 1972). "Conduct Penetrating Line Education and Raise Women's Consciousness of Line Struggle—in Compliance with Chairman Mao's Teachings, the CCP Committee of Hsingt'ai *Hsien* Strengthens Leadership over Women-Related Work," p. 173

0515 *SCMP*, no. 5096 (Mar. 6, 1972). "Men and Women Must Receive Equal Pay for Equal Work," p. 8.

0516 *SCMP*, no. 5103 (Mar. 19, 1972). "Give Full Play to Women's Role in the Three Major Revolutionary Movements—Party Committee of Hsingt'ai *Hsien* Puts Line Education First in Guiding Woman Work," p. 90.

0517 *SCMP*, no. 5103 (Mar. 19, 1972). "Make a Good Job of the Work on Women—a *Jen-min jih-pao* Short Comment," p. 87.

0518 *SCMP*, no. 5334 (Mar. 4, 1973). "Chinese Women Have Equal Political and Social Status with Men," p. 138

0519 *SCMP*, no. 5337 (Mar. 8, 1973). *Jen-min jih-pao* editorial. "Working Women are Great Revolutionary Force," p. 59.

0520 *SCMP*, no. 5338 (Mar. 8, 1973). "Use Marxism-Leninism and Mao Tse-tung's Thought to Educate the Broad Masses of Women," p. 89.

0521 *SCMP*, no. 5383 (May 13, 1973). "A *Hsien* Party Committee in Fukien Conscientiously Carries out Policy of Equal Pay for Equal Work Done by Men and Women," p. 17.

0522 *SCMP*, no. 5407 (June 22, 1973). "Shanghai Girl Shows Fine Communist Spirit," p. 76.

0523 *SCMP*, no. 5460 (Sept. 9, 1973). "Women Prop up Half the Heavens," p. 310. [From Jianming Commune Series (Four).]

0524 *SCMP*, no. 5515 (Dec. 10, 1973). "Big Changes in Status of Women in the Chinese Countryside," p. 109

0525 *SCMP*, no. 5554 (Feb. 6, 1974). "Why a Peking Woman Worker Criticizes Confucius," p. 174.

0526 *SCMP*, no. 5559 (June 27, 1974). Ch'ing, Fu-wen. "The Ways of Confucius and Mencius are Ropes that Bind and Enslave Women," p. 1.

0527 *SCMP*, no. 5572 (Mar. 4, 1974). "Well-Known Educated Young Women in Chinese Countryside Criticize Lin Piao and Confucius," p. 141.

0528 *SCMP*, no. 5573 (Mar. 5, 1974). "Women in Lu Hsun's Home *Hsien* Denounce Feudal Ethics, Criticize Lin Piao and Confucius," p. 179.

0529 *SCMP*, no. 5573 (Mar. 6, 1974). "Women in East China *Hsien* Criticize Confucius, Lin Piao Slanders of Women," p. 181.

0530 *SCMP*, no. 5574 (Mar. 7, 1974). "Chinese Women Criticize Lin Piao and Confucius," p. 19.

0531 *SCMP*, no. 5574 (Mar. 8, 1974). "Tachai Women Criticize Lin Piao and Confucius," p. 60.

0532 *SCMP*, no. 5575 (Mar. 8, 1974). "Chinese Women Advance Along Socialist Road," p. 56.

0533 *SCMP*, no. 5575 (Mar. 8, 1974). *Jen-min jih-pao* editorial. "Let All Women Rise Up," p. 51.

0534 *SCMP*, no. 5576 (Mar. 9, 1974). "Peking Press Carries Articles by Chinese Women Criticizing Lin Piao and Confucius," p. 88.

0535 *SCMP*, no. 5577 (Mar. 11, 1974). "Chinese Fisherwomen Criticize Lin Piao's Contempt for Women's Notions as Reactionary," p. 129.

0536 *SCMP*, no. 5578 (Mar. 12, 1974). "Women Workers' Marxism-Leninism Study Group," p. 161

0537 *SCMP*, no. 5607 (Apr. 24, 1974). "North China Peasant Women's Sports Team Criticizes Lin Piao, Confucius," p. 25.

0538 *SCMP*, no. 5717 (Sept. 30, 1974). "Emancipation of Chinese Women Acclaimed amid National Day Celebrations," p. 179.

0539 Selden, M. "What Men Can Do Women Can Do Also." *China Policy Study Group Broadsheet* 10:2(1973).

0540 The Seven Sisters After-Work Study Group, the Subsidiary Tools Factory of the Peking Motorcar Manufacturing Plant. "Study for the Thorough Liberation of Women." *Chinese Sociology and Anthropology* 7(Summer 1975):13–26.

0541 Sladetien, Joseleyne. "Women's Place in the People's Republic of China: Ideology and Practice." *Asian Profile* 5(Oct. 1977):409–18.

0542 Smedley, Agnes. *Portraits of Chinese Women in Revolution*. N.Y.: Feminist Press, 1976.

0543 Snow, Helen. *Women in Modern China*. N.Y.: Humanities Press, 1968.

0544 "Socialism Brings Women Genuine Emancipation." *Women of China* 1966:2:1.

0545 "Solving Women's Problems." *China Reconstructs* 10(Nov. 1961):39.

0546 "Some Facts about Women in China." *China Reconstructs* 22(Mar. 1972):7.

0547 "Some More Facts on Women." *People's China* 5(Mar. 1, 1952):22.

0548 Soong, Ching Ling. "Women's Liberation in China." *Peking Review* 15(Feb. 11, 1972):6–7.

0549 Soong, Ching-ling. "China's Women in Our New Long March." *China Reconstructs* 28(Mar. 1979):6–7.

0550 "Spare Rib, Sweet and Sour." *Economist* 245(Dec. 2, 1972):51. [Account of women's continuing struggle for equal status and equal pay in China.]

0551 *SPRCP*, no. 5813 (Mar. 5, 1975). "Women of China Today," p. 55

0552 *SPRCP*, no. 5814 (Mar. 7, 1975). "Chinese Women Criticize Confucian-Mencian Concept of Male Supremacy," p. 92.

0553 *SPRCP*, no. 5815 (Mar. 9, 1975). "Chinese Working Women Are Masters of Socialist New Culture," p. 133.

0554 *SPRCP*, no. 5816 (Mar. 9, 1975). "Women of New China," p. 190.

0555 *SPRCP*, no. 5820 (Mar. 17, 1975). "Women in North China County Demolish Confucian Concept," p. 179.

0556 *SPRCP*, no. 5831 (Mar. 8, 1975). The Theory Group of the Message Station of a certain PLA unit. "Women Are a Great Force in the Revolution," p. 11.

0557 *SPRCP*, no. 5881 (June 13, 1975). "Tremendous Changes in Status of Women in China," p. 113.

0558 *SPRCP*, no. 5882 (June 15, 1975). "Women of New China 'Hold up Half of Sky' in Socialist Revolution and Construction," p. 170.

0559 *SPRCP*, no. 5883 (June 15, 1975). "'Women in China,' Exhibition Closes in Berne," p. 235.

0560 *SPRCP*, no. 5886 (June 20, 1975). "Elderly Women in Old Revolutionary Base Areas Make Continuous Progress," p. 103.

0561 *SPRCP*, no. 5889 (June 25, 1975). "How Women of China Achieve Emancipation through Revolutionary Struggle," p. 70.

0562 *SPRCP*, no. 5897 (July 6, 1975). "Yenan Cadres Discuss Women's Emancipation," p. 231.

0563 *SPRCP*, no. 5948 (Sept. 20, 1975). "'Women of China Today,' Photo Exhibition Opens in Brussels," p. 210.

0564 *SPRCP*, no. 6054 (Mar. 6, 1976). "Shanghai Women Workers Study Marxism-Leninism," p. 15.

0565 *SPRCP*, no. 6055 (Mar. 7, 1976). "Women Prop up Half of Sky," p. 56.

0566 *SPRCP*, no. 6063 (Feb. 1, 1976). The Women Commentators Group of Chinese Brigade, Ch'iangkang Fishery Commune, Tungt'ai County, Kiangsu Province. "Discredit by Criticism the Old Idea of 'Valuing Boys above Girls,'" p. 255.

0567 *SPRCP*, no. 6150 (July 24, 1976). "Young Woman in Northwest China Breaks with Old Traditional Ideas," p. 136.

0568 *SPRCP*, no. 6167 (Aug. 20, 1976). "Women of Central China County Hold up Half of Heaven," p. 213.

0569 *SPRCP*, no. 6168 (Aug. 21, 1976). "*Jen-min jih-pao* Features Heroic Exploits of Seven Young Women," p. 21.

0570 *SPRCP*, no. 6178 (Sept. 4, 1976). "*Jen-min jih-pao* Article: Chinese Women Advance Boldly in Struggle," p. 78.

0571 Stacey, Judith. "When Patriarchy Kowtows: The Significance of the Chinese Family Revolution for Feminist Theory." *Feminist Studies* 2(1975):2/3:64–112.

0572 Stacey, Judith. "A Feminist View of Research on Chinese Women." *Signs* 2(Winter 1976):485–497.

0573 Su, Huei. "Three Major Problems Confronting Chinese Communist Women's Movement." *Asian Outlook* 13(Oct. 1978):34–40.

0574 Sung, Hsin-ju. "Women Win Liberation Through Revolutionary Struggle." *China Reconstructs* 24(June 1975):13–16.

0575 Tavris, Carol. "Women in China: The Speak-Bitterness Revolution." *Psychology Today* 7(1974):12:43.

0576 Teng, Ying-ch'ao. "Chinese Women Help Build New China." *People's China*, Mar. 16, 1950, pp. 3–5.

0577 Teng, Ying-ch'ao. "China Women Advance." *People's China*, Dec. 1, 1952, pp. 9–12.

0578 Teng, Ying-ch'ao. *The Women's Movement in New China*. Peking: Foreign Languages Press, 1952. [By the president of the women's federation.]

0579 Teng, Ying-ch'ao. "Towards the Thorough Emancipation of Women." *Peking Review*, 3(Mar. 15, 1960):6–9.

0580 Teng, Ying-ch'ao. "Report on the Present Course and Tasks of the Chinese Women's Movement." *Chinese Studies in History* 5(Fall 1971):76–87.

0581 Tien, H. Y. *The Changing Status of Women in China*. Ohio State University, 1973.

0582 Tien, J. S. "Unbound: The Women of New China." *Intellect* 106(Aug. 1977):37–41.

0583 "To Our Readers: Socialism Brings Women Genuine Emancipation." *Women of China* 1966:2:1.

0584 Tretiak, L. D. "Women in China: The Distance Travelled." *Canadian Forum* 54(Spring 1974):20–22.

0585 Tsao, M. Ch. "The Status of Women in the World Today: China." *Review of Contemporary Law* 7(1960):1:54–60.

0586 Tsui, Yu-lan. "How We Women Won Equality." *China Reconstructs* 23(Mar. 1974):2–5.

0587 "Ugly and the Beautiful." *Time* 75(Mar. 21, 1960):32. [On the change in women's status in the People's Republic of China.]

0588 Weinbaum, Batya. "Women in Transition to Socialism: Perspectives on the Chinese Case." *The Review of Radical Political Economics* 8(Spring 1976):34–58.

0589 Weiss, Ruth. "From Confucian Obedience to Propping up Half the Sky." *Eastern Horizon* 14(1975):2:25–34.

0590 Weiss, Ruth. "The Women One Meets." *Eastern Horizon* 14(1975):3:16–20.

0591 Whitehead, Raymond L. "Democracy and Emancipation of Women." *Eastern Horizon* 12(1973):2:62–64. [Review of Jack Chen's *New Earth*.]

0592 Whitehead, Rhea M. "Women in China Today." *China Notes* 9(Spring 1971):13–16.

0593 Whitehead, Rhea. "Women in China." *IDOC/International Documentation*, no. 67 (Nov. 1974), pp. 27–32. [Role of women and their relationships with men in the People's Republic of China.]

0594 "Women Active on Various Fronts." *Peking Review* 15(Mar. 10, 1972):11.

0595 "Women as a Revolutionary Force." *Philippine Historical Association Historical Bulletin* 19(Jan.–Dec. 1975):92–99. [Interview with Han Suyin.]

0596 "Women Builders of Socialism." *Peking Review* 1(Dec. 9, 1958):12.

0597 *Women in China Today*. Peking: All-China Democratic Women's Federation, 1952.

0598 *Women in New China*. Peking: Foreign Languages Press, 1950.

0599 "Women in People's China." *China Now*, no. 5 (Sept.–Oct. 1970).

0600 "Women in the Villages Are a Great Revolutionary Force." *Chinese Sociology and Anthropology* 7(Summer 1975):45–52.

0601 *Women of China*. Peking: Foreign Languages Press, 1953.

0602 "Women of China." *Peking Review* 15(Feb. 11, 1972):8–9.

0603 "Women to the Fore." *Peking Review* 3(Feb. 23, 1960):4–5.

0604 "Women to the Fore." *Peking Review* 9(Mar. 11, 1966):3.

0605 "The Women's Movement in China—an Interview with Luo Qiong." *China Reconstructs* 28(Mar. 1979):33–36.

0606 Wood, S. "Women's Liberation." *China Policy Study Group Broadsheet* 8(1971):9.

0607 "Working Women Are a Great Revolutionary Force." *Peking Review* 16(Mar. 16, 1973):5–6. [From *Renmin ribao* editorial.]

0608 "Working Women on Various Fronts." *Peking Review* 18(Mar. 28, 1975):22–23.

0609 Ying, Kuei-fang. "The Current Women's Movement on the Chinese Mainland." *Issues and Studies* 10(July 1974):50–63.

0610 Yu, H. "China: Women's Liberation Movement." *Christian Century* 88(Feb. 24, 1971):270.

EMANCIPATION MOVEMENTS: MINORITIES

0611 Brown, M. "Emancipation by Decree; Mohammedan Women of Chinghai in North China." *Independent Woman* 28(Mar. 1949):69.

0612 "Heroic Mother and Daughter of the Grassland." (Reportage.) *Chinese Literature,* Oct. 1968, pp. 33-40.

0613 "A Heroine on the Grasslands." (Reportage.) *Chinese Literature,* July 1971, pp. 89-95.

0614 Russell, Flo. "Women of Tibet Have Become Masters of their Own Affairs." *Women of China,* 1965:6:12-14.

0615 *SCMM,* no. 261 (Aprl 1, 1961). "Paean of the Emancipated Women of Tibet," p. 35.

0616 *SCMM,* no. 682 (May 1, 1970). Yang, Kuei-fang (Hui nationality). "Mao Tse-tung Thought Guides Us Women Forward Forever," p. 86. [From *Hongqi,* May 1, 1970.]

0617 *SCMP,* no. 1854 (Aug. 21, 1958). "Women of the National Minorities in Yunan Make Great Leap Forward," p. 15.

0618 *SCMP,* no. 3408 (Feb. 27, 1965). "Emancipated Women Serfs and Slaves of Tibet," p. 24.

0619 *SCMP,* no. 4351 (Jan. 28, 1969). "Young Heroines on Inner Mongolian Grasslands Repudiate 'Philosophy of Survival,'" p. 11. [From New China News Agency, Huhehot.]

0620 *SCMP,* no. 4523 (Oct. 17, 1969). "Five Old Women of Mongolian Nationality Who Study Chairman Mao's Works in a Living Way," p. 15. [From New China News Agency, Shenyang.]

0621 *SCMP,* no. 4865 (Mar. 15, 1971). "Women on Inner Mongolian Grassland," p. 163.

0622 *SCMP,* no. 5094 (Mar. 5, 1972). "Women of Minority Nationalities Play Important Role on Mongolian Grasslands," p. 145.

0623 *SCMP,* no. 5578 (Mar. 12, 1974). "Inner Mongolian Woman Cadre Criticizes Theory of 'Mandate of Heaven,'" p. 156.

0624 Smedley, Agnes. "Five Women of Mukden." *New Republic* 63(June 11, 1930):99-101.

0625 *SPRCP,* no. 5812 (Mar. 5, 1975). "Former Slave on Emancipation of Working Women in Tibet," p. 22.

0626 *SPRCP,* no. 6052 (Mar. 3, 1976). "Social Status of Hui Women in Northwest China," p. 135.

0627 *SPRCP,* no. 6055 (Mar. 8, 1976). "Tibetan Women make Revolution," p. 59.

0628 Teng, Yuan-ying. "A Miao Woman's Story." *China Reconstructs* 22(Aug. 1973):42-45.

0629 "Tibetan Slave Girl, Chhodnam Drolma." *Chinese Literature,* May 1966, pp. 46-56.

0630 Winnington, Alan. *The Slaves of the Cool Mountains; the Ancient Social Conditions and Changes Now in Progress on the Remote Southwestern Borders of China.* London: Lawrence and Wishart, 1959.

0631 Yang, Kuei-fang. "Mao Tse-tung Thought Guides Us Women to March Forward Forever." *Chinese Sociology and Anthropology* 7(Summer 1975):27-36. [Yang is of Hui nationality.]

0632 Yi, Chun. "A New Life for Tibetan Women." *Women of China* 1964:6:20-21.

EMANCIPATION MOVEMENTS: HONG KONG, TAIWAN, AND OVERSEAS CHINA

0633 Armbruster, W. "Women's Equality: Fighting for More." *Far Eastern Review,* May 14, 1976, p. 30. [On women of Taiwan.]

0634 Barnett, William K. "An Ethnographic Description of San-lei Ts'un, Taiwan, with Emphasis on Women's Roles, Overcoming Research Problems Caused by the Presence of a Great Tradition." Ph.D. dissertation, Michigan State University, 1970.

0635 Diamond, Norma. "The Status of Women in Taiwan: One Step Forward, Two Steps Back." In *Women in China,* ed. M. Young, pp. 211-42. Ann Arbor: University of Michigan, 1973.

0636 Diamond, Norma. "Women under Kuomintang Rule: Variations on the Feminine Mystique." *Modern China* 1(Jan. 1975):3-45.

0637 Fessler, Loren. *Women in Hong Kong.* American Universities Field Staff Reports East Asia Series 23:1 (1976).

0638 O'Hara, Albert R. "The Position of Women in Modern China." *J. of the China Society* 9(1972):77-85. [Emphasizes the situation in Taiwan.]

0639 Sankar, Andrea Patrice. "The Evaluation of the Sisterhood in Traditional Chinese Society: From Village Girls' Houses to Chai T'angs in Hong Kong." Ph. D. dissertation, University of Michigan, 1978.

0640 Sinanian, Natalie J.R. "A Comparative Study of Women and the Modernization Process in Taiwan and Japan." SP.A., Western Michigan University, 1975.

0641 *SPRCP,* no. 6055 (Mar. 8, 1976). "Taiwan Women in Abyss of Misery," p. 61.

0642 Ts'ai, Ch'ing-yuan. "Women of Free China." *Free China Review* 26(Aug. 1976):13-18.

0643 Tsai, Yung-mei. "Urbanism and Restrictions on Women's Socioeconomic Roles: An Analysis of Communities in Taiwan." *J. of Asian and African Studies* (Leiden) 13(July-Oct.1978):256-264. [Discusses problems of labor force, fertility, and marriage. Author argues that woman's role is less restricted in urban areas than in rural areas, and that a feminist subculture is being formed in the cities.]

0644 Wong, Aline K. "Women in Singapore: A Report." *Signs* 2(Autumn 1976):213-218.

Health and Population

MATERNITY AND CHILD CARE: TRADITIONAL AND REPUBLICAN CHINA (TO 1949)

0645 Best, A. E. "Chinese Folklore, Relating to Conception and Maternity." *Chinese Medical J.* 40(June 1926):564-74.

0646 Chow, Tse-tsung. "The Childbirth Myth and Ancient China Medicine: A Study of Aspects of the *Wu* Tradition." In *Ancient China: Studies in Early Civilization,* ed. David T. Roy and Tsuen-hsuin, pp. 43-90. Hong Kong: Chinese University Press, 1978.

0647 Guy, R. A. "The Diet of Nursing Mothers and Young Children in Peiping." *Chinese Medical J.* 50(Apr. 1936):434-42.

0648 Huang, H. H. and Wang, T.H. "A Survey of the Maternity and Child Health Work in Nanking Municipality." *Chinese Medical J.* 50(Apr. 1936):554-61.

0649 Imahari, Seiji. "A Study of the Protective Institutions for Babies in the Sung Period." *Hiroshima Daigaku, Bungaku-bu kiyo* 8(Oct. 1955):127-51. [In Japanese with an English summary at the end.]

0650 Johnston, Reginald Fleming. "A Note on Multiple Births in China." *New China Review* 2(Aug. 1920):415-18.

0651 Laufer, Berthold. "Multiple Births among the Chinese." *New China Review* 2(Apr. 1920):109–136.

0652 Pillsbury, Barbara L. K. "Doing the Month: Confinement and Convalescence of Chinese Women after Childbirth." *Social Science and Medicine* 12(Jan. 1978):11–22. [The traditional Chinese custom requiring women to be confined to the home for a full month after giving birth and to observe certain rules during that month is analyzed from the perspectives of ethnomedicine, classical Chinese medical theory, and Western medicine.]

0653 Poulter, Mabel C. "Obstetrical Experiences in Futsing City [i.e., Fuqing *xian*], Fukien, China." *Chinese Medical J.* 35(July 1921):331–47.

0654 Topley, Marjorie. "Cosmic Antagonisms: A Mother-Child Syndrome." In *Religion and Ritual in Chinese Society,* ed. Arthur P. Wolf, pp. 233–249. Stanford: Stanford University, 1974.

0655 Tsay, Queenie. "Chinese Superstitions Relating to Child Birth." *Chinese Medical J.* 32(Nov. 1918):533–536.

0656 Wong, K. and Wu, L. *History of Chinese Medicine.* 2nd ed. Shanghai: National Quarantine Service, 1936. [Has sections on obstetrics.]

MATERNITY AND CHILD CARE: THE PEOPLE'S REPUBLIC OF CHINA (1949–)

0657 Chen, K. Y. "Two Mothers Everywhere." *People's China* 2(1955):16:28.

0658 Ch'en, Wen-chen. "A Clinical Analysis of 8063 Cases of Painless Labor by the Psychoprophylactic Method." *Chinese Medical J.* 75(May 1957):337–43.

0659 Chu, Fu-t'ang. "Progress of Pediatric Work in China in the Past Eight years." *Chinese Medical J.* 83(Dec. 1964):795–802.

0660 Chung-hua fu-ch'an-k'o tsa-chih. "Investigation of and Analysis of the Childbirth and Menstrual Conditions of 22,251 Rural and Urban Hupei Women." *Chinese J. of Obstetrics and Gynecology* 8(1960):5–11.

0661 *Culture, Education and Health in New China.* Peking: Foreign Languages Press, 1952. [Includes statistics on midwives and infant mortality.]

0662 *ECMM*, no. 1154 (Oct. 8, 1955). "Inner Mongolia Holds First Session of Women and Children Health Work Conference," p. 13.

0663 Flax, Michael Howard. "Day Care Services in the People's Republic of China and the United States with a Focus upon Children's Interpersonal Aggression." Ph.D. dissertation, Boston University, 1978. [Relation between child care system and women's societal roles is discussed.]

0664 "For Safe and Happy Motherhood." *China Reconstructs* 3(Mar. 1954):33.

0665 "For the Better Health of Women—International Peace Maternity and Chinese Health Hospitals." *China Reconstructs* 27(June 1978):11–16.

0666 "Health Care for Women and Children." *China Reconstructs* 25(Sept. 1976):43–46.

0667 L. V. "Mother and Child Care in New China." *People's China* 1952:6:22.

0668 Li, Shen. "Maternity and Child Welfare in People's Communes." *Chinese Medical J.* 78(June 1959):576–79.

0669 Minkowski, Alexandre. "Health of Mother and Child: The Experience in the People's Republic of China, the Democratic Republic of Viet-nam and Cuba." *Impact of Science on Society* 23(1973):1:29–40.

0670 Mu, Cheng. "Women's and Children's Health Work." *China Reconstructs* 27(July 1978):29–31.

0671 *SCMM*, no. 364 (Apr. 1, 1963). "Can Late Marriage Cause Difficult Labor?" p. 36.

0672 *SCMP*, no. 1002 (Mar. 7, 1955). "Mother, Children Care Work in China Reviewed," p. 7.

0673 *SCMP*, no. 1059 (May. 31, 1955). "Health Service for Women and Children Continuously Developed in Recent Years," p. 22

0674 *SCMP*, no. 1183 (Dec. 2, 1955). "Maternity and Child Welfare Meeting Ends," p. 15.

0675 *SCMP*, no. 1419 (Nov. 25, 1956). "Infant and Mother Mortality Drops," p. 6.

0676 *SCMP*, no. 1432 (Nov. 7, 1956). "Pregnant and Breast Feeding Women Workers Given Break in Kiangsu Factories," p. 24.

0677 *SCMP*, no. 1432 (Nov. 22, 1956). "Textile Worker Union Resolution on Correction of the Practice of Granting Miscarriage Leave on Production of Womb," p. 18.

0678 *SCMP*, no. 1432 (Nov. 24, 1956). "Peking Women Cadres to Get Allowances When Giving Birth at Home," p. 18.

0679 *SCMP*, no. 1487 (Mar. 3, 1957). "Maternity and Child Health Service Improve in Rural Areas," p. 14.

0680 *SCMP*, no. 2212 (Mar. 3, 1960). "Women and Child Care in China."

0681 *SCMP*, no. 2695 (Mar. 6, 1962). "Health of Women and Children of Small Minority in China Protected," p. 32.

0682 *SCMP*, no. 3175 (Mar. 6, 1964). "Mother and Child Care in China," p. 17.

0683 *SCMP*, no. 5448 (Aug. 23, 1973). "South China *Hsien* Improves Maternity and Child Care Work," p. 22.

0684 *SCMP*, no. 5633 (May 31, 1974). "Veteran Pediatrician on Child Care in New China," p. 110.

0685 *SCMP*, no. 5638 (June 18 1974). "China's Multi-National Autonomous Regions Improve Maternity and Child Care," p. 117.

0686 Sidel, Ruth. *Women and Child Care in China: A Firsthand Report.* N.Y.: Hill and Wang, 1972.

0687 *SPRCP*, no. 5885 (Jan. 19, 1975). "Maternity and Child Care in China," p. 60.

0688 *SPRCP*, no. 5907 (July 23, 1975). "Shanghai Babies Get Tender Care," p. 163.

0689 *SPRCP*, no. 6128 (June 23, 1976). "Maternity and Child Care in East China County," p. 216.

0690 *SPRCP*, no. 6162 (Aug. 12, 1976). "Maternity and Child Care in Multinational County," p. 205.

0691 "Treating Ectopic Pregnancy without Operation." *Peking Review* 15(Apr. 7, 1972):22–23.

0692 Tsui, Ching-tai. "New Birth." *China Reconstructs* 3(May 1954):32.

0693 Wei, Wen. "Child Care in New China." *Comparative Medicine: East and West* 5(Fall-Winter 1977):297–99.

0694 Yi, Ke. "Maternity and Childcare." *Peking Review,* 15(June 9, 1972):14.

MATERNITY AND CHILD CARE: HONG KONG, TAIWAN, AND OVERSEAS CHINA

0695 Chi, I. C. [Ch'i I-cheng]; Chow, L. P. [Chou Lien-pin]; and Rider, Rowland V. "The Randomized Response Technique as Used in the Taiwan Outcome of Pregnancy Study." *Studies in Family Planning* 3(Nov. 1972):265–69.

0696 Chu, Cheng-ping. "A Study of the Effects of Maternal Employment for the Preschool Children in Taiwan." *Acta Psychologica Taiwanica* 12(Mar. 1970):80–85.

0697 Gould-Martin, Katherine. "Women Asking Women: An Ethnography of Health Care in Rural Taiwan." Ph.D. dissertation, Rutgers, 1976.

0698 Ikeda, Toshio. "Custom Concerning Birth among the Formosan Chinese." *Minzoku gokka kenkyū* 19(Sept. 1955):153-63. [In Japanese. English summary on pp. 152-53.]

0699 Johnson, Elizabeth. "Women and Childbearing in Kwan Mun Hau Village: A Study of Social Change." In *Women in Chinese Society*, ed. Margery Wolf and Roxane Witke, pp. 215-42. Stanford: Stanford University, 1975.

0700 Kang-Wang, J. F. "Midwife in Taiwan: An Alternative Model for Maternity Care." *Human Organization*, no. 39 (Spring 1980), pp. 70-79.

0701 Kriger, Sara F. "Attitudes toward Child-rearing as Avowed by Middle-class White Anglo-Saxon Protestant (WASP), Jewish and Chinese Mothers." M.A. thesis, Sacramento State College, 1969. ["Chinese" refers to American Chinese.]

0702 "Our Chinese Nursing Project." *Independent Woman* 34(Aug. 1955):17-18. [As observed by Mrs. Oswald B. Lord in Taibei.]

0703 Seligmann, J. "Tanka Syndrome: Effects of Nursing Babies on One Side Only; Chinese Boat Women Study." *Newsweek* 90(Sept. 12, 1977):52.

0704 Takeshita, John Yuzuru; Reng, J. Y.; and Liu, Paul K. C. [Liu K'o-chih]. "A Study of the Effectiveness of the Prepregnancy Health Program in Taiwan." *Eugenics Quarterly* 11(Dec. 1964):222-33.

0705 Wang, Jen-ying. "Cultural Ecology and Child-bearing Patterns: A Comparative Study of Two Chinese Villages." Ph.D. dissertation, University of North Carolina at Chapel Hill, 1976. [Emphasizes cultural-ecological factors affecting the natality differentials between two villages in Taiwan.]

HEALTH AND HEALTH WORKERS: TRADITIONAL AND REPUBLICAN CHINA (TO 1949)

0706 Burton, E. D. et al. "Report on Medical Schools in China Connected with Christian Missions." *China Medical J.*, Nov. 1922, pp. 509-525.

0707 Burton, Margaret. "A Woman Pioneer of the East." *World Outlook* 2(Apr. 1916):11.

0708 Faust, Ernest Caroll. "Social Diseases in China." *Social Pathology* 1(1925):6:274-77.

0709 Greene, R. S. "Public Health and the Training of Doctors and Nurses in China." *International Review of Missions*, Oct. 1925, 481-98.

0710 Lamson, Herbert Day. *Social Pathology in China: A Source Book for the Study of Problems of Livelihood, Health, and the Family.* Shanghai: Commercial Press, 1934.

0711 Oldt, Frank. "Tuberculosis in Kwangtung, According to Age, Sex, Occupation, and Economic Condition." *Chinese Medical J.* (Peking) 47(Feb. 1933):111-127.

0712 Powell, Charles A. *Bound Feet.* Boston: Warren Press, 1938. [Diary of a Western M.D. in inland China.]

0713 Purwin, L. and Block, R. H. "Nurses for China." *Independent Woman* 23(Mar. 1944):66-67+.

0714 Tao, S. M. "Medical Education of Chinese Women." *Chinese Medical J.* (Peking) 47(Oct. 1933):1010-1028.

0715 Tseng, Lily. "Midwifery." *Chinese Medical J.* 44(May 1930):431-45.

0716 Wang, Kai-hsi. "Three Women Pioneers of Modern Medicine in China." *Chinese Medical J.* 65(Jan./Feb. 1947):5-10.

0717 Wong, K. Chimin [Wang Chi-min]. "The Social Evil in China." *Chinese Medical J.* 34(Nov. 1920):630-34.

HEALTH AND HEALTH WORKERS: THE PEOPLE'S REPUBLIC OF CHINA (1949-)

0718 "Big Ovarian Tumour Removed in Commune Clinic." *Peking Review* 15(Dec. 15, 1972):23.

0719 "Chairman Mao Gave Her a New Life." (Reportage.) *Chinese Literature* 1969:4:3-30.

0720 Chen, Chung-hsien. "A Nurse's Story." *China Reconstructs* 12(Dec. 1963):27-29.

0721 Chen, Pi. "Women Doctor in the Mountains." *Chinese Literature* 1970:12:76.

0722 Chiang, An-hui. "A Woman Doctor Writes: Life at Our House." *China Reconstructs* 10(Nov. 1961):10.

0723 Chien, Tze. "The Story of Two Women Doctors." *Peking Review* 2(Feb. 17, 1959):15-16.

0724 Chin, Yueh-ying. "Country Midwife." *China Reconstructs* 8(May 1959):22-24.

0725 Eloesser, Leo. "Assembly Line for County Midwives." *Pacific Spectator* 7(Spring 1953):232-42.

0726 "For the Better Health of Women: International Peace Maternity and Child Health Hospital." *China Reconstructs* 27(June 1978):11-16.

0727 "Health Care for Rural Women." *China Reconstructs* 8(Apr. 1959):38.

0728 Hicks, Cherrill. "Veteran Gynaecologist." *China Now*, no. 82 (Jan./Feb. 1979), pp. 27-28.

0729 Horn, Joshua S. *Away With All Pests.* N.Y.: Monthly Review, 1969.

0730 JPRS, no. 37161 (May 24, 1966). "Chinese Forum on Gynecological Cancer," p. 125. [From New China News Agency.]

0731 JPRS, no. 52693 (Mar. 23, 1971). "Book on Female Health Care Revised," pp. 3-4. [From *Funü baojian zhishi.*]

0732 JPRS, no. 64393-0024 (Dec. 1, 1974). "Medical Team Treats Women's Diseases." [From *Wenhui bao.*]

0733 JPRS, no. 64393-0025 (Dec. 7, 1974). "Giant Tumor Removed from Pregnant Woman." [From *Zhongguo xinwen.*]

0734 Liu, Bingqi and Zhang, Tianlai. "A Plastic Surgeon's Career." *China Reconstructs* 30(July 1981):32-33. [A story of a woman plastic surgeon in the PRC.]

0735 "A Model Woman Doctor." *Peking Review* 16(May 25, 1973):22-23.

0736 Mu, Cheng. "Women's and Children's Health Work." *China Reconstructs* 27(July 1978):29-31.

0737 "Nurse Becomes Doctor." *Women of China* 1966:1:17-19.

0738 Salaff, Janet Weitzner. "The Role of the Family in Health Care." In *Medicine and Public Health in the People's Republic of China*, ed. Joseph R. Quinn, pp. 23-53. Washington, D.C.: U.S. Department of Health, Education and Welfare, Public Health Service, National Institute of Health, 1972.

0739 Sidel, Ruth. "Women in Medicine in China." *Eastern Horizon* 12(1973):4:57-60.

0740 *SCMM*, no. 364 (Apr. 1, 1963). "Give the Revolutionary Task Top Priority," p. 40.

0741 *SCMM*, no. 595 (Oct. 2, 1967). "How She Devotedly Serves the Commune Members for the Last Five Years—a Story of Tung Hai-chen, Health Worker of Hsutotzu Production Brigade, Wanhsiang Commune," pp. 24-28.

0742 *SCMP*, no. 1299 (May 16, 1956). "Safeguard the Health of Women and Children in Rural Areas," p. 5.

0743 *SCMP*, no. 1628 (Sept. 28, 1957). "Group of Voluntary Women Health Workers Trained in Yatung, Tibet," p. 37.

0744 *SCMP*, no. 1935 (Dec. 19, 1958). "Chairman Mao and the Nurse," p. 3.

0745 *SCMP*, no. 2463 (Mar. 19, 1961). "Minister of Health on Labor Protection for Women."

0746 *SCMP*, no. 2708 (Mar. 8, 1962). "Properly Carry Out '4 Period' Protection for Women Workers," p. 5.

0747 *SCMP*, no. 4323 (1968). "Young Woman Doctor in North China Mountainous Area," pp. 14–16. [From New China News Agency, Beijing.]

0748 *SCMP*, no. 4369 (Feb. 27, 1969). "Woman Medical Worker in Northwest China Praised by Poor Herdsmen for Devoted Service," p. 16. [From New China News Agency, Lanzhou.]

0749 *SCMP*, no. 4385 (Mar. 21, 1969). "She Serves the People Wholeheartedly," p. 12. [From New China News Agency, Shengyang. In praise of an exemplary PLA nurse.]

0750 *SCMP*, no. 4551 (Nov. 1969). "PLA Nurse Chen Shu-ching Serves People Wholeheartedly," p. 12. [From New China News Agency, Nanning.]

0751 *SCMP*, no. 4826 (Dec. 16, 1970). "A Woman Veterinary of a Commune—Chun Yen," p. 27. [From China News Service.]

0752 *SCMP*, no. 4859 (Mar. 3, 1971). "Fight for Women's Better Health—an Investigative Report on General Treatment of Gynecological Diseases in Jutung *Hsien*," p. 86.

0753 *SCMP*, no. 4870 (Mar. 22, 1971). "Barefoot Women Doctors on Tibetan Plateau," p. 183.

0754 *SCMP*, no. 4883 (Apr. 13, 1971). "Woman Army Surgeon Firmly Carries Out Chairman Mao's Proletarian Revolutionary Line in Medical and Health Work," p. 140.

0755 *SCMP*, no. 4938 (July 7, 1971). "Woman Doctor on Inner Mongolian Grassland Serves People Wholeheartedly," p. 259.

0756 *SCMP*, no. 5027 (Nov. 2, 1971). "Omanchu—Tibetan Woman Barefoot Doctor," p. 240.

0757 *SCMP*, no. 5336 (Mar. 6, 1973). "Barefoot Tibetan Woman Doctor," p. 19.

0758 *SCMP*, no. 5340 (Mar. 13, 1973). "Actively Prevent and Cure Women's Diseases, Protect the Women Labor Force—CCP Committee of Changsha *Hsien*, Hunan Province," p. 173.

0759 *SCMP*, no. 5350 (Mar. 27, 1973). "A Model Chinese Woman Doctor," p. 16.

0760 *SCMP*, no. 5582 (Mar. 19, 1974). "Jentso—a Young Tibetan Woman Barefoot Doctor," p. 123.

0761 *SCMP*, no. 5661 (July 13, 1974). "Liu Hsiang-ping Meets American Medical Association Delegation," p. 183.

0762 *SPRCP*, no. 5824 (Mar. 15, 1975). "A Woman Barefoot Doctor Eager to Make a Success of Family Planning," p. 128.

0763 *SPRCP*, no. 5843 (Apr. 19, 1975). "Women Barefoot Doctors Play a Major Role in Maternity and Child Care," p. 164.

0764 *SPRCP*, no. 5887 (June 22, 1975). "New China Insures Health and Safety of Women Workers," p. 150.

0765 *SPRCP*, no. 5894 (July 1, 1975). "Peking Women Get Early Check-up for Tumors and Cancer," p. 81.

0766 *SPRCP*, no. 5909 (July 26, 1975). "More Women Doctors Trained," p. 54.

0767 *SPRCP*, no. 5921 (Aug. 13, 1975). "Woman Doctor on Chinghai Grasslands," p. 185.

0768 *SPRCP*, no. 6041 (Feb. 16, 1976). "Mongolian Woman Doctor," p. 92.

0769 *SPRCP*, no. 6065 (Mar. 21, 1976). "Woman Barefoot Doctor of Kazakh Nationality in Sinkiang," p. 70.

0770 *SPRCP*, no. 6125 (June 18, 1976). "Shanghai Girl Doctor Settles Down in Tibet," p. 73.

0771 *SPRCP*, no. 6129 (June 25, 1976). "Women Barefoot Doctors in Mountainous County Promote Maternity and Child Hygiene," p. 26.

0772 *SPRCP*, no. 6226 (Nov. 14, 1974). "Health Facility for Women and Children in South China Region," p. 154.

0773 "The Story of Two Women Doctors." *Peking Review* 2(Feb. 17, 1959):15–17.

0774 Su, Yu-fu. "Pioneering in Women's Health Work." *China Reconstructs* 11(Jan. 1962):28.

0775 Tuan, Ti-wei. "A Girl Veterinarian." *China Reconstructs* 11(Sept. 1962):35–36.

0776 Wood, Shirley. "Lili Becomes a 'Barefoot Doctor.'" *China Now* 4(Aug. 1970):1–4.

FOOTBINDING AND INFANTICIDE

0777 A. C. D. "Female Infanticide, From an Unpublished History of Amoy." *China Review* 2(July–Aug. 1873):55–58.

0778 Anon. "Letter about Footbinding." *Spectator*, Mar. 19, 1898, pp. 406–407.

0779 Anon. "Small Feet of the Chinese Females; Remarks in the Origin of the Custom of Compressing the Feet; the Extent and Effects of the Practice; with an Anatomical Description of a Small Foot." *The Chinese Repository* 3(Apr. 1835):537–42.

0780 Arlington, Lewis C. "Footbinding." *The New China Review* 1(Mar. 1919):92–94.

0781 Arlington, Lewis C. "Further Notes on Footbinding." *New China Review* 2(1920):211–14.

0782 Chan, Lily M. "Footbinding in Chinese Women and Its Psycho-social Implications." *Canadian Psychiatric Association J.* 15(1970):2:229–31.

0783 Chau, Virginia Chi-tin. "The Anti-footbinding Movement in China (1850–1912)." M.A. thesis, Columbia, 1966.

0784 "China's Unwanted Babies." *Literary Digest* 117(Mar. 24, 1934):17.

0785 Dudgeon, John Hepburn. "The Small Feet of Chinese Women." *Chinese Recorder* 2(Sept. 1869):93–96; 2(Oct. 1869):130–33.

0786 Gamble, Sidney David. "The Disappearance of Footbinding in Tinghsien [Hebei]." *Amer. J. of Sociology* 49(Sept. 1943):181–83.

0787 Greenhalgh, Susan. "Bound Feet, Hobbled Lives: Women in Old China." *Frontiers* 2(Spring 1977):7–21.

0788 Levy, Howard Seymour. *Chinese Footbinding: The History of a Curious Erotic Custom.* New York: W. Rawls, 1966. [The major monograph on this custom.]

0789 McDougall, Colin. "Chinese Footbinding." Ph.D. dissertation, University of Edinburgh, 1958.

0790 Pang, Yong-pil. "Footbinding in China." *J. of Asian Culture* 3(Spring 1979):96–108.

0791 "The Prevalence of Infanticide in China." *J. of the Royal Asiatic Society—China Branch*, new (2nd) series, 20(1885):1:25–68.

0792 Suh-ho. "In Praise of Footbinding." *New Republic,* Dec. 18, 1915, pp. 170–72.

DEMOGRAPHIC PATTERNS AND POPULATION POLICY

0793 Aird, John Shields. "Population Policy in Mainland China." *Population Studies* 16(July 1962):38–59.

0794 Aird, John Shields. "Population, Planning and Economic Development in Mainland China in a Decade of Crisis." *Population Bulletin* 19(Aug. 1963):114–35.

0795 Aird, John Shields. "Population Policy and Demographic Prospects in the People's Republic of China." In *People's Republic of China: An Economic Assessment,* comp. Joint Economic Committee, U.S. Congress, pp. 220–331. Washington, D.C.: U.S. Government Printing Office, 1972.

0796 Aird, John Shields. "Recent Provincial Population Figures." *China Quarterly,* no. 73 (Mar. 1978), pp. 1–44.

0797 Avery, Roger Christopher. "The Age Pattern of Fertility and the Demographic Transition." Ph.D. dissertation, University of California, Berkeley, 1974.

0798 Bendel, Jean-Pierre and Hua, Chang-i. "An Estimate of the Natural Fecundability Ratio Curve." *Social Biology* 25(Fall, 1978):210–27. [Based on data from Taiwan.]

0799 Chang, Ming-cheng. "Migration and Fertility in Taiwan." Ph.D. dissertation, University of Pennsylvania, 1978.

0800 Ch'en, Ta. *Population in Modern China.* Chicago: Chicago University, 1946.

0801 Chiao, Chi-ming. "A Study of the Chinese Population." *Milbank Memorial Fund Quarterly Bulletin* 11(Oct. 1933) and 12(Jan., Apr., July 1934).

0802 "China Achieves Initial Success in Planned Population Growth." *Economic Reporter* [Hong Kong] 3(July–Sept. 1974):2–3.

0803 "China Cracks Down." *World Press Review* 28(Feb. 1981):58. [A report on Beijing's population control program.]

0804 Cho, Lee-jay and Kobayashi, Kazumasa, eds. *Fertility and Transition of the East Asian Population.* Monographs of the Center for Southeast Asian Studies, Kyoto University, English-language Series, No. 13. Honolulu: University of Hawaii, 1979. [Focusing on the relationship between the general Chinese background and the demographic transition.]

0805 Conger, Darius J. and Luan, David C. "Dynamic Properties of Taiwanese Fertility, 1950–1972." *Studies in Comparative International Development* 14(Summer 1979):54–74.

0806 Coughlin, Richard James. "Population Controls in China." In *Symposium on Economic and Social Problems of the Far East,* ed. Edward Franciszek Szczepanik, pp. 389–99. Hong Kong: Hong Kong University, 1962.

0807 *ECMM,* no. 142 (Sept. 15, 1958). Min Tzu. "It Is Good to Have a Large Population," pp. 25–32. [From *Jihua jingji,* June 9, 1958.]

0808 Ehrlich, P. R. and Holdren, J. P. "Neither Marx Nor Malthus." *Saturday Review* 54(Nov. 6, 1971):88.

0809 Falkenheim, Victor Carl. "Communist China's Population Policy." M.A. thesis, Columbia, 1964.

0810 Freedman, Ronald; Moots, Baron; and Wei, Sou-pen. *Differential Fertility in Taiwan: 1972–1974.* Taiwan Population Studies Working Papers, no. 41. Ann Arbor: University of Michigan, Population Studies Center and Taiwan Provincial Institute of Family Planning, 1979.

0811 Goodstadt, Leo F. "Official Targets, Data, and Policies for China's Population Growth: An Assessment." *Population and Development Review* 4(June 1978):255–75.

0812 Lam, Peggy and Smith, Doreen. "Hong Kong." *Studies in Family Planning* 11(Nov. 1980):316–20. [Special issue: "East Asia Review, 1978–1979." The article reviews population policy in Hong Kong.]

0813 Lamson Herbert Day. "Population Studies: Size of the Chinese Family in Relation to Occupation, Age, and Education." *Chinese Economic J.* 11(Dec. 1932):478–96.

0814 Lamson, Herbert Day. "Differential Reproduction in China." *Quarterly Review of Biology* 10(Sept. 1935):308–21.

0815 Lin, Rui-sui. "Correlates of Sub-areal Differential Fertility in Taiwan." *National Taiwan University J. of Sociology* 12(July 1977):101–16.

0816 Liu, K. C. and Sun, T. H. "The Determinants of Fertility Transition and Their Implications in Taiwan, R.O.C." *Industry of Free China* 52(Aug./Sept. 1979):9–25.

0817 Morrison, R. L., Jr. and Salmon, J. D. "Population Control in China: A Reinterpretation." *Asian Survey* 13(Sept. 1973):873–90.

0818 Mosher, Steven W. "Birth Seasonality among Peasant Cultivators: The Interrelationship of Workload, Diet, and Fertility." *Human Ecology* 7(June 1979):151–81. [An analysis of the situation in a rural fishing community on Taiwan.]

0819 Ni, Ernest [Ni, In-hsin]. "Marital Status and Family Size in China." M.A. thesis, University of Chicago, 1945.

0820 Ni, Ernest In-hsin. *Social Characteristics of the Chinese Population Structure and Urbanism of a Metropolitan Community.* Chicago: University of Chicago, 1948. [A study of the social characteristics, including age and sex structure, marital status, fertility rate, educational status, etc., of the Chinese men and women of the Kunming area in 1942–1944.]

0821 Orleans, Leo A. "Dealing with Population Problems." *Bulletin of Atomic Scientists* 22(June 1966):22–26.

0822 Orleans, Leo A. "Evidence from Chinese Medical Journals on Current Population Policy." *China Quarterly,* no. 40 (1969), pp. 137–46.

0823 Orleans, Leo A. "Propheteering: The Population of Communist China." *Current Scene* 7(Dec. 15, 1969):13–19.

0824 Orleans, Leo A. "China: Population in the People's Republic." *Population Bulletin* 27(Dec. 1971):5–37.

0825 Orleans, Leo A. *Every Fifth Child: The Population of China.* London: Eyre Methuen, 1972.

0826 Pan, Chia-lin. "An Estimate of the Long-term Birth Rate of the Agricultural Populations of China." *Demography* 3(1966):204–208.

0827 Sarker, Subhash Chandra. "Population Planning in China." *Population Review* 2(July 1958):49–58.

0828 *SCMP,* no. 5689 (Aug. 23, 1974). "China Achieves Initial Success in Planned Population Growth," p. 103.

0829 Snow, Edgar. "Population Care and Control." *New Republic* 164(May 1, 1971):20–22.

0830 Taeuber, Irene Barnes. "Population Policy in Communist China." *Population Index* 22(Oct. 1956):261–74.

0831 Tien, H. Yuan [T'ien, Hsin-yüan], ed. *Population Theory in China.* White Plains, N.Y.: M. E. Sharpe, 1980.

0832 United States, Library of Congress, Congressional Research Service. *China's Experience in Population Control: The Elusive Model: Prepared for the Committee on Foreign Affairs, U.S. House of Representatives.* Washington, D.C.: U.S. Government Printing Office, 1974.

0833 Wang, C. M. and Sun, T. H. "Taiwan, Republic of China." *Studies in Family Planning* 11(Nov. 1980):343-47. [Special issue: "East Asia Review, 1978-1979." The article reviews population policy in Taiwan.]

0834 Wertheim, W. F. "Recent Trends in China's Population Policy." *Science and Society* 30(Spring 1966):129-35.

0835 Wolf, Arthur Paul. "The Women of Hai-shan: A Demographic Portrait." In *Women in Chinese Society,* ed. Margery Wolf and Roxane Witke, pp. 89-110. Stanford: Stanford University, 1975.

0836 Yu, Y. C. "The Demographic Situation in China." *Population Studies* (London) 32(Nov. 1978):427-47. [Covers the period 1953-1978.]

0837 Yu, Y. C. "The Population Policy of China." *Population Studies* 33(Mar. 1979):125-42.

BIRTH CONTROL: GENERAL; TRADITIONAL AND REPUBLICAN CHINA (TO 1949)

0838 Himes, Norman E. *Medical History of Contraception.* N.Y.: Gamut Press, 1963. [See pp. 108-113 on Chinese contraceptives and abortifacients.]

0839 Lamson, Herbert Day. "Educated Women and Birth Control in China." *Chinese Medical J.* 44(Nov. 1930):1100-1109.

0840 Lamson, Herbert Day. "Family Limitation among Educated Chinese Married Women: A Study of the Practice and Attitudes of 120 Women." *Chinese Medical J.* 47(May 1933):493-503.

0841 Su, Ru-chiang. "Birth Control in China." M.A. thesis, University of Chicago, 1946.

BIRTH CONTROL: THE PEOPLE'S REPUBLIC OF CHINA (1949-)

0842 Aird, John Shields. "Fertility Decline and Birth Control in the People's Republic of China." *Population and Development Review* 4(June 1978):225-54.

0843 "Baby Budgeting." *Economist,* no. 274 (Mar. 1, 1980), p. 38. [About a birth control plan in Guangdong.]

0844 Beedham, B. "One Is Best, Two Is Most." *Economist,* no. 273 (Dec. 29, 1979), pp. 24-25. [About birth control in the PRC.]

0845 Bianco, Lucien. "Birth Control in China: Local Data and Their Reliability." *China Quarterly,* no. 85 (Mar. 1981), pp.119-37.

0846 "Birth Control in China." *People's China* 11(June 11, 1957):25-29.

0847 "Birth Control Receives Renewed Attention." *Current Scene* 11(May 1973):11-13.

0848 "Birth Pains." *Economist,* no. 270 (Feb. 10, 1979), pp. 76, 79. [About birth control in the PRC.]

0849 Camp, Sharon L., ed. *Birth Planning in China.* Draper Fund Report, no. 8. Washington: Population Crisis Committee, 1980.

0850 *CB,* no. 405 (July 26, 1956). Shao, Li-tzu. "The Problem of Birth Control," pp. 16-18.

0851 *CB,* no. 445 (Apr. 5, 1957). Chung, Hui-lan. "Population and Birth Control," p. 14-21.

0852 *CB,* no. 445 (Apr. 5, 1957). Li, Chien-sheng. "Do Not Perform Artificial Abortion Unless Absolutely Necessary," pp. 6-8.

0853 *CB,* no. 445 (Apr. 5, 1957). Li Teh-chuan. "Birth Control and Planned Families," pp. 1-5.

0854 *CB,* no. 445 (Apr. 5, 1957). Shao, Li-tzu. "Planned Parenthood," pp. 9-13.

0855 "Changing Customs and Habits (Comic Dialogue)." *Chinese Sociology and Anthropology* 11(Fall 1978):25-33.

0856 Chen, Muhua. "Birth Planning in China." Trans. Pi-chao Chen. *International Family Planning Perspectives* 5(Sept. 1979):92-101.

0857 Chen, Pi-chao. "The Politics of Population in Communist China: A Case Study of Birth Control Policy, 1949-1965. Ph.D. dissertation, Princeton University, 1966.

0858 Chen, Pi-chao. "China's Birth Control National Programme, 1954-64." *Population Studies* 24(July 1970):141-58.

0859 Chen, Pi-chao, and Miller, Ann. *The 'Planned Birth' Program of the People's Republic of China, with a Brief Analysis of Its Transferability.* N.Y.: Southeast Asia Development Advisory Group of the Asia Society, 1974. [SEADAG Papers on Problems of Development in Southeast Asia.]

0860 "Chinese View: Birth Control Is a Must." *Look* 20(Nov. 13, 1956):48.

0861 Chou, Ngo-fen. "Birth Control in China." *J. of Family Welfare* (Bombay) 4(Nov. 1957):17-22.

0862 Chu, Leonard L. *Planned Birth Campaigns in China, 1949-1976.* Honolulu: East-West Center, 1977.

0863 Cousins, Norman. "Solutions Are Possible." *Saturday Review,* Feb. 16, 1980, p. 6. [A discussion of birth control in the PRC.]

0864 Culliton, Barbara J. "China's New Birth Policy: One Baby is Enough." *Science,* Oct. 26, 1979, p. 429.

0865 Djerassi, Carl. *The Politics of Contraception.* 2 vols. Stanford: Stanford Alumni Association, 1979. [In Volume 2 the author discusses future prospects for male and female contraceptives and population programs, etc. in China.]

0866 Dreijmanis, John. "The Politics of Birth Prevention: A Comparison of the Chinese and Japanese Approaches." *Population Review* 12(Jan.-Dec. 1968):23-68

0867 *ECCM,* no. 2 (Nov. 4 & 5, 1955). "How to Approach the Problem of Birth Control," p. 8.

0868 Ellithorpe, H. "China's All-out Push to Slash Its Birth Rate." *Business Week,* Nov. 19, 1979, p. 67.

0869 "Family Planning in China." *Scientific American,* Nov. 1972, pp. 50-51.

0870 Faundes, Anibal and Luukkainen, Tapani. "Health and Family Planning Services in the Chinese People's Republic." *Studies in Family Planning* 3(July 1972):165-76.

0871 Fessler, Loren. *Delayed Marriage and Planned Birth: Translation of a Chinese Birth Control Manual.* American University Field Staff, Reports Service, East Asia Series 20(Jan. 1973):1-14.

0872 Fraser, S. E. "One Is Fine, Two Is More than Adequate." *Far Eastern Economic Review,* Oct. 5, 1979, pp. 61-62. [On the family planning situation in China.]

0873 Freeberne, John Derek Michael. "The Spectre of Malthus: Birth Control in Communist China." *Current Scene* 2(Aug. 15, 1963):1-14. [Reprinted as "Birth Control in China," in *Population Studies* 18(July 1964):5-16; and *This is China: Analyses of Mainland Trends and Events,* ed. Francis Harper, pp. 1-18 (Hong Kong: Dragonfly Books, 1965).]

0874 Guan, Zaihan. "Birth Control: A Pressing Matter for the Moment." *Eastern Horizon* 18(Sept. 1979):5-7.

0875 Han, Suyin [Chow, Elizabeth K.]. "Birth Control in China—Recent Aspects." *Eugenics Review* 52(Jan. 1960):19-22.

0876 Han, Suyin. [Chow, Elizabeth K.]. "Family Planning in China Today." *Eastern Horizon* 4(Nov. 1965):5-8.

0877 Han, Suyin [Chow, Elizabeth K.]. "Family Planning in China." *Japan Quarterly* 17(Oct.-Dec. 1970):433-42.

0878 Han, Suyin [Chow, Elizabeth K.]. "Population Growth and Birth Planning." *China Now* 43(July/Aug. 1974):8-11.

0879 Heenan, Brian. "Curbing Birth Rates." *Far Eastern Economic Review,* Dec. 16, 1965, p. 514-17.

0880 Hsü, Lin. "Yu-hua and Her Family (Shantung Monologue in Quick Time)." *Chinese Sociology and Anthropology* 11(Fall 1978):34-37. [Propaganda on family planning in the PRC.]

0881 Hsü, Pao-ch'eng. "Family Planning Is Good (Quick Patter Choral Dialogue)." *Chinese Sociology and Anthropology* 11(Fall 1978):6-11. [Propaganda on family planning in the PRC.]

0882 Hsu, S. C. [Hsü, Shih-chü]. "Summary Report of Present Status of Family Planning Programs in East Asia." *Chinese Medical J.* (Taiwan) 15(June 1968):89-118.

0883 Hughes, R. "China Makes a Bitter Retreat." *New York Times Magazine,* July 15, 1962, p. 5+.

0884 "In China, Three's a Crowd." *Newsweek* 94(Nov. 26, 1979):97. [A discussion of China's birth control drive.]

0885 JPRS, no. 796D (June 30, 1959). "Women." "Birth Control."

0886 JPRS, no. 52013 (Dec. 17, 1970). "Pamphlet Promoting Planned Parenthood and Late Marriage," pp. 7-8.

0887 Kane, Penny. "Birth Planning." *China Now,* no. 86 (Sept./Oct. 1979), pp. 21-23.

0888 Kane, Penny. "Family Planning in Sichuan." *China Now,* no. 95 (Mar./Apr. 1981), pp. 20-21.

0889 Katagiri, T. and Terao, Takuma. "Wide Range of Family Planning." *China Now,* no. 23 (July 1972), pp. 5-6.

0890 [La Dany Ladislao]. "Limitations of Births and Ma Yin-ch'u." *China News Analysis,* Feb. 26, 1960, pp. 1-7.

0891 Laidlaw, Karen A. and Stockwell, Edward G. "Fertility Control Programs in Asia: Another Look at the Data." *Asian Survey* 20(Aug. 1980):803-11. [Includes discussion on the PRC.]

0892 Lal, Amrit. "Fertility Management and Concern with Overpopulation in Mainland China." *Eugenics Quarterly* 11(Sept. 1964):170-74.

0893 "Let Only Two Children Bloom." *Scientific American,* Apr. 1980, p. 64. [On China's birth control problems.]

0894 Liu, Liang-ch'ung. "Family Planning is Good (Comic Dialogue)." *Chinese Sociology and Anthropology* 11(Fall 1978):12-24.

0895 Loraine, J. A. "Population and Birth Control in China." *Contemporary Review* 239(Sept. 1981):126-30.

0896 Lu, Zilan. "Flower Intrauterine Contraceptive Device." *Chinese Medical J.* 93(1980):8:528-30. [Observations of 4,321 fertile women using the flower intrauterine device from 1965 to 1977. Material was collected from hospitals in Guangdong province.]

0897 Lyle, Katherine Ch'iu. "Birth Control in China: A Research Bibliography." *International Review of Modern Sociology* 4(1974):1:94-99.

0898 Lyle, Katherine Ch'iu. "China's Birth Planning: Organization Since the Cultural Revolution." *Human Organization* 39(Summer 1980):197-201.

0899 Lyle, Katherine Ch'iu. "Planned Birth in Tianjin." *China Quarterly,* no. 83 (Sept. 1980), pp. 551-67.

0900 Mauldin, Wayman Parker. "Fertility Control in Communist Countries: Policy and Practice." In *Population Trends in Eastern Europe, the USSR, and Mainland China,* comp. Milbank Memorial Fund, pp. 179-223. N.Y.: Milbank Memorial Fund, 1960.

0901 Morrison, Raymond L. and Salmon, Jack D. "Population Conrol in China: A Reinterpretation." *Asian Survey* 13(Sept. 1973):873-90.

0902 Ng, Pedro Pak-tao. "Planned Fertility and Fertility Socialization in Kwangtung Province." *China Quarterly,* no. 78 (June 1979), pp. 351-59.

0903 Nossal, Frederick. "Birth Control: China's Second Experiment." *Nation,* June 15, 1963, pp. 503-505.

0904 Orleans, Leo A. "Birth Control: Reversal or Postponement?" *China Quarterly,* no. 3 (July-Sept. 1960), pp. 59-73.

0905 Orleans, Leo A. "A New Birth Control Campaign?" *China Quarterly,* no. 12 (Oct.-Dec. 1962), pp. 207-210.

0906 Orleans, Leo A. "Comment: Birth Control in Communist China." *China Quarterly,* no. 14 (Apr.-June 1963), pp. 226-29. [Rejoinder to H. Yuan Tien's comment (see #0936).]

0907 Orleans, Leo A., ed. *Chinese Approaches to Family Planning.* London: MacMillan, 1979. [The book has three sections: a brief history of family planning in China since 1949, a translation of a booklet of source materials on family planning, and a translation of *Questions and Answers on Information about Family Planning.*]

0908 People's Health Press. "Literature and Art Propaganda: Source Materials on Family Planning." *Chinese Sociology and Anthropology* 11(Fall 1978):3-103. [Consists of choral dialogue, monologue, drama, short skits and singing performances published for propagandizing family planning in the PRC.]

0909 Salaff, Janet Weitzner. "Institutionalized Motivation for Fertility Limitation in China." *Population Studies* 26(July 1972):233-62.

0910 SCMM, no. 364 (Apr. 1, 1963). "The Positive Significance of Planned Family." p. 38

0911 SCMM, no. 383 (July 28, 1963). "Contraception Will Not Impair One's Health," pp. 42-43. [From *Zhongguo qingnian.*]

0912 SCMP, no. 5268 (Nov. 20, 1972). "Educate the Young People to Practice Late Marriage and Family Planning," pp. 14-15.

0913 SCMP, no. 5335 (Mar. 5, 1973). "Family Planning in China," p. 173.

0914 SCMP, no. 5435 (July 30, 1973). "Effectively Strengthen the Party's Leadership Over the Family Planning Work—the Party Committee of T'aihu Fishery Commune on the Outskirts of Wuhsi Municipality, Kiangsu," p. 59.

0915 SCMP, no. 5534 (Dec. 25, 1973). "Family Planning Is Good," p. 47.

0916 SCMP, no. 5694 (Aug. 31, 1974). "Family Planning Gains Popularity in China," p. 149.

0917 SPRCP, no. 5801 (Feb. 5, 1975). "Cadres and Masses at the Hsiaochinchuang Production Brigade Take the Political Evening School as the Battlefield to Criticize the Old Ideas of the Exploiting Classes and Promote Family Planning Work," p. 179.

0918 SPRCP, no. 5801 (Feb. 5, 1975). "Criticize the Doctrines of Confucius and Mencius and Do a Good Job in Family Planning—the Party Branch of the Huahsi Production Brigade of the Huashih Commune in Chiangying Hsien, Kiangsu Province," p. 176.

0919 SPRCP, no. 5801 (Feb. 5, 1975). "Family Planning Has Liberated Women for Manual Work," p. 181.

0920 *SPRCP,* no. 5824 (Mar. 15, 1975). "Party Committee of the Tangchung Freshwater Fisheries Commune Develops Work in Family Planning, Thoroughly Criticizes Lin Piao and Confucius and Vigorously Fosters Socialist New Practice," p. 126.

0921 *SPRCP,* no. 5824 (Mar. 15, 1975). "Properly Grasp the Revolution in the Ideological Sphere and Do a Good Job in Family Planning—the Revolutionary Committee of Wuhsing County, Chekiang Province," p. 123.

0922 *SPRCP,* no. 5841 (Apr. 14, 1975). "Criticism of Old Ideas Is Good for Family Planning—Chiang Yü-chen, Poor Peasant Commune Member of the Chenliao Production Brigade, Chiehyang County, Kwangtung," p. 42.

0923 *SPRCP,* no. 5841 (Apr. 14, 1975). "Do a Good Job in Family Planning and Liberate the Labor Force of Women," p. 39.

0924 *SPRCP,* no. 5841 (Apr. 14, 1975). "Family Planning Has Brought Advantages to the Revolution and Production—the Party Branch of Production Brigade No. 6 of the Fenghsi Commune, Jutang County, Kiangsu Province," p. 44.

0925 *SPRCP,* no. 5890 (June 27, 1975). "Family Planning and Emancipation of Women in China," p. 116.

0926 *SPRCP,* no. 6063 (Feb. 1, 1976). "Carry out Family Planning Properly in Order to Consolidate the Dictatorship of the Proletariat—CCP Committee of Nanwangchuang Commune, Anp'ing County, Hopei Province," p. 233.

0927 *SPRCP,* no. 6063 (Feb. 1, 1976). "Family Planning is Good," p. 230.

0928 *SPRCP,* no. 6063 (Feb. 1, 1976). "A New Look Appears in Family Planning Work in Shihfang County," p. 228.

0929 *SPRCP,* no. 6101 (May 4, 1976). "Late Marriage and Family Planning Are Good," p. 6.

0930 *SPRCP,* no. 6105 (May 11, 1976). "Ch'in County in Shensi Has Done a Good Job in the Practice of Family Planning," p. 223.

0931 *SPRCP,* no. 6105 (May 11, 1976). "Late Marriage and Family Planning Become a Common Practice in Shanghai Iron and Steel Plant No. 5—All Youngsters of the Factory Concentrate Their Energy on Actively Criticizing Teng Hsiao-p'ing, Thus Becoming an Exuberant Force in the Three Great Revolutionary Movements," p. 221.

0932 Sun, Tsai-hua. "Going to Meet Maternal Grandmother (Local Duodrama)." *Chinese Sociology and Anthropology,* 11(Fall 1978):45–58. [Family planning propaganda from the PRC.]

0933 Taeuber, Irene Barnes and Orleans, Leo A. "National Programs: Achievements and Problems, Mainland China." In *Family Planning and Population Programs: A Review of World Developments,* ed. Bernard Berelson et al, pp. 31–54. Chicago: University of Chicago, 1966. [Proceedings of International Conference on Family Planning Programs, Geneva, 1965.]

0934 Terrill, R. "China, Birth Control and Babies." *New Republic* 152(Feb. 6, 1965):13–14.

0935 Tien, H. Yuan [T'ien, Hsin-yüan]. "Induced Abortion and Population Control in Mainland China." *Marriage and Family Living* 25(Feb. 1963):35–43.

0936 Tien, H. Yuan [T'ien, Hsin-yüan]. "'Birth Control in Communist China' (With a Reply by Leo A. Orleans)." *China Quarterly,* no. 14 (Apr.–June 1963), pp. 218–29. [See #0906.]

0937 Tien, H. Yuan [T'ien, Hsin-yüan]. "Birth Control in Mainland China: Ideology and Politics." *The Milbank Memorial Fund Quarterly* 41(July 1963):269–90.

0938 Tien, H. Yuan [T'ien Hsin-yüan]. "Birth Control in Mainland China: Ideology and Politics." *Eugenics Review* 55(Jan. 1964):213–21.

0939 Tien, H. Yuan [T'ien Hsin-yüan]. "Sterilization, Oral Contraception, and Population Control in China." *Population Studies* 18(Mar. 1965):215–35.

0940 Tien, H. Yuan [T'ien Hsin-yüan]. "Marital Moratorium and Fertility Control in China." *Population Studies* 24(Nov. 1970):311–23.

0941 Tien, H. Yuan [T'ien Hsin-yüan]. "Fertility Decline via Marital Postponement in China." *Modern China* 1(Oct. 1975):447–62.

0942 Tien, H. Yüan [T'ien, Hsin-yüan]. "Wan, Xi, Shao: How China Meets Its Population Problems." *International Family Planning Perspectives* 6(June 1980):65–73. [The author uses data from the administrative records of population programs in four communes to examine the current extent of use of the pill, IUD, sterilization, and abortion in China.]

0943 Triviere, Leon. "Family Planning in China." *Mission Bulletin* (Hong Kong) 9(Nov. 1957):580–85.

0944 Tso, An-hua. "Family Planning in Jutung County." *Peking Review* 21(Apr. 7, 1978):18–22.

0945 United States, Library of Congress, Congressional Research Service. *China's Experience in Population Control: The Elusive Model: Prepared for the Committee on Foreign Affairs, U.S. House of Representatives.* Washington, D.C.: U.S. Government Printing Office, 1974.

0946 Varma, Asha. "Birth Control and Planned Parenthood in China." *China Report* (New Delhi) 7(Mar.-Apr. 1971):41–48.

0947 White, Lynn T. III. *Careers in Shanghai: The Social Guidance of Personal Energies in a Developing Chinese City, 1949–1966.* Berkeley: University of California, 1978. [Birth control and family patterns in the city during the 1950s and 1960s are discussed in chapter 4, pp. 106–206.]

0948 Ying, Kuei-fang. "The Birth Control Movement on the Chinese Mainland." *Issues and Studies* 10(Feb. 1974):80–89.

0949 Yu, H. "China: Politics in Command Slogan." *Christian Century* 88(Jan. 27, 1971):142. [Includes discussion of contraceptive use.]

0950 "Yü-hua and Her Family (Shantung Monologue in Quick Time)." *Chinese Sociology and Anthropology* 11(Fall 1978):34–37. [Propaganda material on family planning.]

0951 Zhang, Pei-Zhu. "Five Years Experience with the Copper T 200 in Shanghai: 856 Cases." *Contraception* 22(Dec. 1980):561–71.

BIRTH CONTROL: HONG KONG, TAIWAN, AND OVERSEAS CHINA."

0952 Anderson, John Ellis. "Area Variation in Fertility Trends in Taiwan, 1952–1970: Diffusion or Development Process." Ph.D. thesis, University of Michigan, 1974.

0953 Arnold, Fred Sidney. "A Model Relating Education to Fertility in Taiwan." Ph.D. dissertation, University of Michigan, 1972.

0954 Bedwany, Theresa Labib. "The Status of Women and Population Control: The Relationship of Gross Reproduction Rate and Selected Indicators of the Status of Women in Developed and Developing Countries." Ph.D. dissertation, Michigan State, 1974. [Includes women in Taiwan.]

0955 Berelson, Fernand and Freedman, Ronald. "A Study in Fertility Control." *Scientific American,* May 1964, pp. 29–37. [Includes discussion on Taiwan.]

0956 Cernada, George Peter. "Basic Beliefs about Human Life Relating to Ethical Judgments Family Planning Field Workers make about Induced Abortion: Taiwan, 1973." Ph.D. dissertation, University of California, Berkeley, 1975.

0957 Cerneda, George Peter and Chow, L.P. [Chou Lien-pin]. "The Coupon System in an Ongoing Family Planning Program." *American J. of Public Health* 59(Dec. 1969):2199–2208.

0958 Cerneda, George Peter and Lu, Laura P. "The Kaoshiung Study." *Studies in Family Planning* 3(Aug. 1972):198–203.

0959 Chan, K. C. "Hong Kong: Oral Contraceptive Follow-up Study." *Studies in Family Planning* 2(Mar. 1971):70–74.

0960 Chan, K. C. "Hong Kong: Report of the IUD Reassurance Project." *Studies in Family Planning* 2(Nov. 1971):225–33.

0961 Chang, Kung-kong. "A Decision Making System for a Family Planning Program: A Case Study of Taiwan." Ph.D. dissertation, North Carolina, 1971.

0962 Chang, M. C.; Cernada, George Peter; and Sun, T. H. [Sun Te-hsiung]. "A Field-Worker Incentive Experimental Study." *Studies in Family Planning* 3(Nov. 1972):270–72.

0963 Chen, F. L. et al. "Taiwan: First Island-wide Pill Acceptor Follow-up Survey." *Studies in Family Planning,* no. 60 (Dec. 1970), pp. 18–23.

0964 Chen, Shao-hsing [Ch'en Shao-hsing]; Wang Yao-tung; and Foley, Frederick Joseph. "Pattern of Fertility in Taiwan: Report of a Survey Made in 1957." *J. of Social Science* (Taibei) 13(1963):209–94.

0965 Chi, I. C. [Ch'i I-cheng] and Mao, W. P. [Mao Wen-ping]. "Male Attitude toward Birth Control in Musa, Taipei County [Mu-shan hsiang, T'ai-pei hsien], Taiwan." *Chinese Medical J.* (Taibei) 14(Mar. 1967):71–86.

0966 Chi, I. C. [Ch'i I-cheng]; Chow, L. P. [Chou Lien-pin]; and Rider, Rowland Von. "The Randomized Response Technique as Used in the Taiwan Outcome of Pregnancy Study." *Studies in Family Planning* 3(Nov. 1972):265–69.

0967 Chow, L. P. [Chou, Lien-pin], et al. "A Fertility Survey of Taiwan." *Chinese Medical J.* (Taibei) 12(Sept. 1965):177–94.

0968 Chow, L. P. [Chou, Lien-pin]. "A Programme to Control Fertility in Taiwan." *Population Studies* 19(Nov. 1965):155–66.

0969 Chow, L. P. [Chou, Lien-pin]. "Evaluation of a Family Planning Programme in China (Taiwan)." In *World Population Conference, 2nd, Belgrade, 1965, Proceedings,* vol. 2, pp. 265–69. N.Y.: United Nations, 1967.

0970 Chow, L. P. [Chou, Lien-pin]. "Evaluation Procedures for a Family Planning Program." In *Family Planning and Population Programs: A Review of World Developments,* ed. Bernard Berelson, et al., pp. 675–89. Chicago: University of Chicago, 1966. [Proceedings of the International Conference on Family Planning Programs, Geneva, 1965.]

0971 Chow, L. P. [Chou, Lien-pin]. "A Study on the Demographic Impact of an IUD Planning Programme." *Population Studies* 22(Nov. 1968):347–60.

0972 Chow, L. P. [Chou, Lien-pin]. "Current Fertility in Taiwan." *Industry of Free China* 32(Dec. 1969):12–26.

0973 Chow, L. P. [Chou, Lien-pin]. "Family Planning in Taiwan, Republic of China: Progress and Prospects." *Population Studies* 24(Nov. 1970):339–52.

0974 Chow, L. P. [Chou, Lien-pin]. "The Island-wide Family Planning Programme in Taiwan: Analysis of the Accomplishments of the Past Eight Years." *Population Studies* 28(Mar. 1974):107–126.

0975 Chow, L. P. [Chou, Lien-pin]., et al. "Correlates of IUD Termination in a Mass Family Planning Program: The First Taiwan IUD Follow-up Survey." *Milbank Memorial Fund Quarterly Bulletin,* vol. 46, no. 2, part 1 (Apr. 1968), pp. 215–35.

0976 Chow, L. P. [Chou, Lien-pin] and Hsu, S. C. [Hsü, Shih-chü]. "A Chinese View of Family Planning in the Developing World." In *Fertility and Family Planning: A World View,* ed. S. J. Behrman, Leslie Corsa, and Ronald Freeman, pp. 451–66. Ann Arbor: University of Michigan, 1969. [Data from Taiwan.]

0977 Chun, Daphne [Ch'in, Hui-chen]. "National Programs: Achievements and Problems, Hong Kong." In *Family Planning and Population Programs: A Review of World Developments,* ed. Bernard Berelson, et al., pp. 71–84. Chicago: University of Chicago, 1966. [Proceedings of International Conference on Family Planning Programs, Geneva, 1965.]

0978 Chun, Daphne [Ch'in Hui-chen]. "Family Planning and the Population Problems of Hong Kong." *World Population Conference, 2nd, Belgrade, 1965, Proceedings,* vol. 2, pp. 270–73. N.Y.: United Nations, 1967.

0979 Clinton, J. Jarrett and Baker, Jean, eds. "East Asia Review, 1978–1979." *Studies in Family Planning* 11(Nov. 1980):311–50. [Includes reviews written by officials of national family planning programs in Taiwan, Hong Kong, and other Asian countries.]

0980 Collver, Alden Speare, Jr. and Liu, Paul K. C. [Liu K'o-chih]. "Local Variations of Fertility in Taiwan." *Population Studies* 20(Mar. 1967):329–42.

0981 Coombs, Lolagene C. "Prospective Fertility and Underlying Preferences: A Longitudinal Study in Taiwan." *Population Studies* 33(Nov. 1979):447–55.

0982 Coombs, Lolagene C. *Economic Factors in Fertility Decisions: The Role of Cost and Benefits.* Taiwan Population Studies Working Papers, no. 45. Ann Arbor: University of Michigan Population Studies Center and Taiwan Provincial Institute of Family Planning, 1980. [Investigates how family economic conditions and the perceptions of costs and benefits affect preferences for number of children in Taiwan families.]

0983 Coombs, Lolagene C. and Chang, Ming Cheng. *Consistency of Fertility Attitudes Between Marital Partners and Its Role in Subsequent Fertility.* Taiwan Population Studies Working Papers, No. 43. Ann Arbor: University of Michigan Population Studies Center and Taiwan Provincial Institute of Family Planning, 1979. [A study on marital attitudes and fertility in Taiwan, using 1969 and 1970 surveys and 1970–74 follow-up data.]

0984 Coughlin, Richard James and Coughlin, Margaret Morgan. "Fertility and Birth Control among Low Income Chinese Families in Hong Kong." *Marriage and Family Living* 25(May 1963):171–77.

0985 Eberhard, Wolfram. "Family Planning in a Taiwanese Town." In *Settlement and Social Change in Asia, Collected Papers of Wolfram Eberhard,* vol. 1, pp. 204–254. Hong Kong: Hong Kong University, 1967.

0986 Fessler, Loren. "Taiwan as a Model for Family Planning." *American Universities Field Staff, Report Service, East Asia Series* 17(1970):7:1–9.

0987 Finnigan, O· D· and Keeny, Spurgeon Milton. "Taiwan, 1970: Report on the National Family Planning Programs." *Studies in Family Planning* 2(Mar. 1971):63–69.

0988 Freedman, Deborah Selin. "The Relationship of Family Planning to Savings and Consumption in Taiwan." *Demography* 9(Aug. 1972):499–505.

0989 Freedman, Ronald. "Changing Fertility in Taiwan." In *Human Fertility and Population Problems,* ed. Roy O. Grup, pp. 106–131. Schenkman Publication Co., 1963.

0990 Freedman, Ronald. "Sample Surveys for Family Planning Research in Taiwan." *Public Opinion Quarterly* 28(Fall 1964):373–82.

0991 Freedman, Ronald. "The Accelerating Fertility Decline in Taiwan." *Population Index* 31(Oct. 1965):430–35.

0992 Freedman, Ronald, et al. "Hong Kong's Fertility Decline, 1961-1968." *Population Bulletin* 36(Jan.-Mar. 1970):3–18.

0993 Freedman, Ronald and Adlakha, A. L. "Recent Fertility Declines in Hong Kong; The Role of the Changing Age Structure." *Population Studies* 22(July 1968):181–98.

0994 Freedman, Ronald; Hermalin, Albert and Chang, Ming-cheng. "Do Statements about Desired Family Size Predict Fertility? The Case of Taiwan, 1967–1970." *Demography* 12(Aug. 1975):407–416.

0995 Freedman, Ronald and Sun, T. H. [Sun Te-hsiung]. "Fertility Trends in Taiwan, 1951–1970." *Population Index* 38(Apr.-June, 1972):141–66.

0996 Freedman, Ronald and Takeshita Y. John. "Studies of Fertility and Family Limitation in Taiwan." *Eugenics Quarterly* 12(Dec. 1965):233–50.

0997 Freedman, Ronald and Takeshita, Yuzuru John. *Family Planning in Taiwan: An Experiment in Social Change.* Princeton: Princeton University, 1969.

0998 Freedman, Ronald; Takeshita, Y. John; and Sun, T. H. "Fertility and Family Planning in Taiwan: A Case Study of the Demographic Transition." *American J. of Sociology* 70(July 1964):16–27.

0999 Gillespie, Robert W. *Family Planning on Taiwan, 1964–1965.* Taizhong, 1965.

1000 Heidt, Sarajane. "Knowledge and Its Consequences: the Impact of Information on a Family Planning Program." *American Behavioral Scientist.* 12(Nov.-Dec. 1968):43–48.

1001 Hermalin, Albert I. *Spatial Analysis of Family Planning Program Effects in Taiwan 1966–1972.* East-West Population Institute, Papers 48. Honolulu: East-West Population Institute, 1978.

1002 Hermalin, Albert I.; Freedman, Ronald; Sun Te-hsiung and Chang Ming-cheng. "Do Intentions Predict Fertility? The Experience in Taiwan, 1967–1974." *Studies in Family Planning* 10(Mar. 1979):75–95.

1003 Hermalin, Albert I; Seltzer, Judith A.; and Lin, Chin-hsing. *The Effect of Family Size on Female Educational Attainment in Taiwan.* Taiwan Population Studies Working Papers, no. 37. Ann Arbor: University of Michigan Population Studies Center and Taiwan Provincial Institute of Family Planning, 1979.

1004 Hsu, S. C. [Hsü, Shih-chü]. "Report on the Development of the Family Planning Program in Taiwan." *Eugenics Quarterly* 10(Sept. 1963):135–38.

1005 Hsu, S. C. [Hsü, Shih-chü]. "Personnel Problems in Family Planning Programs." In *Family Planning and Population Programs: A Review of World Developments,* ed. Bernard Berelson, et al., pp. 335–43. Chicago: University of Chicago, 1966. [Proceedings of International Conference on Family Planning Programs, Geneva, 1965.]

1006 Hsu, S. C. [Hsü, Shih-chü]. "Promotion and Progress of Family Planning Action Program in Taiwan." *Industry of Free China* 26(Oct. 1966):37–42.

1007 Hsu, S. C. [Hsü, Shih-chü]. "Teaching of Fertility Regulation in Medical Schools in Taiwan." *Chinese Medical J.* (Taibei) 13(Dec. 1966):319–25.

1008 Hsü, Shih-chü. "Family Planning in Taiwan, 1949–1970." *Industry of Free China* 34(Dec. 1970):2–20.

1009 Hsu, T. C. [Hsü, Shih-chü] and Chow, L. P. [Chou, Lien-pin]. "National Programs: Achievements and Problems, Taiwan, Republic of China." In *Family Planning and Population Programs: A Review of World Developments,* ed. Bernard Berelson, et al., pp. 55–70. Chicago: University Press, 1966. [Proceedings of International Conference on Family Planning Programs, Geneva, 1965.]

1010 Hsu, T. C. [Hsü, Shih-chü] and Chow, L. P. [Chou, Lien-pin]. "The Program for Intrauterine Contraceptive Devices in Taiwan." *Industry of Free China* 23(Jan. 1965):43–48.

1011 Hsu, S. C. [Hsü, Shih-chü]; Wei H. Y. and Niu L. C. "Country Report: Taiwan: Family Planning Programme in Taiwan." In *Proceedings of Combined Conference on Evaluation of Malaysia National Family Planning and East Asia Population Programmes,* pp. 256–60. Kuala Lumpur: National Family Planing Board, Malaysia, 1970.

1012 Jain, Anrudh Kumar. "Fecundity Components in Taiwan: Application of a Stochastic Model of Human Reproduction." Ph.D. dissertation, University of Michigan, 1968.

1013 Jain, Anrudh Kumar. "Socio-economic Correlates of Fecundability in a Sample of Taiwanese Women," *Demography* 6(Feb. 1969):75–90.

1014 Jain, Anrudh Kumar. "Fecundability and Its Relation to Age in a Sample of Taiwanese Women," *Population Studies* 23(Mar. 1969):69–85.

1015 Jain, Anrudh Kumar. "Fetal Wastage in a Sample of Taiwanese Women." *Milbank Memorial Fund Quarterly,* vol. 47, no. 3, part 1 (July 1969), pp. 297–306.

1016 Jain, Anrudh Kumar. "Pregnancy Outcome and the Time Required for the Next Conception." *Population Studies* 23(Nov. 1969):421-33.

1017 Keeny, Spurgeon Milton. "Country Profiles: Taiwan." *Studies in Family Planning* 50(Feb. 1970):1–15. [Supplement.]

1018 Keeny, Spurgeon Milton and Cernada, George Peter. "Taiwan, 1969: Report on the National Family Planning Programs." *Studies in National Family Planning* 54(June 1970):8–16.

1019 Kindermann, Charles Robert. "Perception and Source of Information: Their Effect on Contraception Use in Taiwan." Ph.D. dissertation, University of Michigan, 1969.

1020 Koo, Helen Ping-ching [Mrs. Richard Billsborrow]. "Use of Induced Abortion and Contraception in Taiwan: A Multivariate Analysis." Ph.D. dissertation, University of Michigan, 1973.

1021 Laidlaw, Karen A. and Stockwell, Edward G. "Fertility Control Programs in Asia: Another Look at the Data." *Asian Survey* 20(Aug. 1980):803–811. [Includes discussion on Taiwan and Hong Kong.]

1022 Lam, Peggy. "East Asia Review, 1971: Hong Kong." *Studies in Family Planning* 3(July 1972):125–27.

1023 Lam, Peggy. "The Hong Kong Experience in Promoting Sterilization." In *Voluntary Sterilization: A Decade of Achievement,* ed. Marilyn E. Schima and Ira Lubell. Proceedings of the 4th International Conference on Voluntary Sterilization, May 7-10, 1979, Seoul, Korea. N.Y.: Association for Voluntary Sterilization, 1980.

1024 Lee, T. M. [Li, Tung-ming] and Chow L. P. [Chou, Lien-pin]. "Mailing to the Recent Postpartum Women to Encourage Loop Acceptance." *Chinese Medical J.* (Taibei) 16(Sept. 1969):206-214.

1025 Lee, T. Y. "East Asia Review, 1971: Taiwan." *Studies in Family Planning* 3(July 1972):145-50.

1026 Lieh-Mak, F.; Tam, Y. K.; and Ng, S. "Hong Kong Married Abortion Applicants: A Comparison with Married Women Who Elect to Complete Their Pregnancies." *J. of Bio-Social Science* 13(Jan. 1981):71-80.

1027 Liu, P. T. and Chow, L. P. [Chou, Lien-pin]. "A Stochastic Approach to the Estimation of the Prevalence of the IUD: Example of Taiwan, Republic of China." *Demography* 8(Aug. 1971):341-52.

1028 Lu, Laura P.; Chen, H. C.; and Chow, L. P. [Chou, Lien-pin]. "An Experimental Study of the Effect of Group Meetings on the Acceptance of Family Planning in Taiwan," *J. of Social Issues* 23(Oct. 1967):171-77.

1029 Mauldin, Wayman Parker; Nortman, Dorothy; and Stephen, Frederick F. "Retention of IUD's: An International Comparison." *Studies in Family Planning* 18(Apr. 1967):1-12. [Includes discussion on Hong Kong.]

1030 Mitchell, Robert Edward. "Hong Kong: An Evaluation of Field Workers and Decision Making in Family Planning Programs." *Studies in Family Planning* 30(May 1968):7-12.

1031 Mitchell, Robert Edward. "Changes in Fertility Rates and Family Size [in Hong Kong] in Response to Changes in Age at Marriage, the Trend away from Arranged Marriages, and Increasing Urbanization." *Population Studies* 25(Nov. 1971):481-89.

1032 Mitchell, Robert Edward. "Husband-Wife Relations and Family-Planning Practice in Urban Hong Kong." *J. of Marriage and the Family* 34(Feb. 1972):139-46.

1033 Mode, Charles J. and Soyka, Michael G. "Linking Semi-Markov Processes in Times Series: An Approach to Longitudinal Data Analysis." *Mathematical Biosciences,* 51(1980):141-64. [Data on approximately 6,000 Taiwanese women who were given IUDs between 1962 and 1965.]

1034 Mohapatra, Partha Sarathi. "The Effect of Age at Marriage and Birth Control Practices on Fertility Differentials in Taiwan." Ph.D. dissertation, University of Michigan, 1966.

1035 Mueller, E. "Economic Motives for Family Limitation: A Study Conducted in Taiwan." *Population Studies* 26(Nov. 1972):383-403.

1036 Nair, N. K. and Chow, L. P. [Chou, Lien-pin]. "Fertility Intentions and Behavior: Some Findings from Taiwan." *Studies in Family Planning* 11(July/Aug. 1980):255-63.

1037 Peng, J. Y.; Chow, L. P. [Chou, Lien-pin]; and Corsa, Leslie. "Medical Correlates of Termination of Use of Intrauterine Contraceptive Devices in Taichung." *International J. of Fertility* 15(June 1970):120-26. [Reprinted as "Taiwan Medical Correlates of Termination of Use of Intrauterine Devices." *Studies in Family Planning* 60(Dec. 1970):24-27.]

1038 Pickens, Gary; and Soyka, Michael. "Effects of Changed Contraception Patterns of Fertility in Taiwan: Applications of a Non-Markovian Stochastic Model." *International J. of Bio-Medical Computing* 11(Jan. 1980):1-19.

1039 Potter, R. G. "Taiwan's Family Planning Program." *Science* 160(May 1968):848-53.

1040 Potter, R. G., et al. "Measuring Potential Fertility through Null Segments: An Exploratory Analysis." *Social Biology,* no. 26 (Winter 1979), pp. 314-29. [On Taiwan.]

1041 Ross, John. A. and Koh, Kap-suk. "Transition to the Small Family: A Comparison of 1964-1973 Time Trends in Korea and Taiwan." *J. of the Population Association of Korea,* no. 1 (1977), pp. 14-31.

1042 Rutstein, Shea Oscar. "The Influence of Child Mortality on Fertility in Taiwan: A Study Based on Sample Surveys Conducted in 1967 and 1969." Ph.D. dissertation, University of Michigan, 1971.

1043 Schultz, T. Paul. *Evaluation of Population Policies: A Framework for Analysis and Its Application to Taiwan's Family Planning Program.* Santa Monica, Calif.: Rand Corp., 1971.

1044 Siddiqui, Mohammed K. "The Initiation of Contraception in Taiwan." Ph.D. dissertation, University of Michigan, 1979.

1045 Speare, A.; Speare Mary; and Lin, Hui-sheng. "Urbanization, Non-familial Work, Education and Fertility in Taiwan." *Population Studies* 27(July 1973):323-34.

1046 Srikantan, Kodaganallur Sivaswamy. "Effects of Neighborhood and Individual Factors on Family Planning in Taichung." Ph.D. dissertation, University of Michigan, 1967.

1047 Sun, T.H. [Sun, Te-hsiung]. "Socio-Structural Analysis of Fertility Differentials in Taiwan." Ph.D. dissertation, University of Michigan, 1968.

1048 Sun, T.H. [Sun, Te-hsiung]. "Demographic Evaluation of Taiwan's Family Planning Program." *Industry of Free China* 49(May 25, 1978):11-27.

1049 Taiwan Population Studies Center. *Taiwan's Family Planning in Charts.* 2nd ed. Taibei: Taiwan Provincial Department of Health, 1967.

1050 Takeshita, John Yuzuru. "Lessons Learned from Family Planning Studies in Taiwan and Korea." In *Family Planning and Population Programs: A Review of World Developments,* ed. Bernard Berelson, et al., pp. 691-710. Chicago: Chicago University, 1966.

1051 Tu, G. L. T. "Recent Fertility Trends in Taiwan." *Industry of Free China* 28(Dec. 1967):2-22.

1052 Tuan, Chi-hsien. "Reproductive Histories of Chinese Women in Rural Taiwan." *Population Studies* 12(July 1958):40-50.

1053 Wang, Janet F. "Education and Fertility Behavior: A Case Study in Taipei, Taiwan." Ph.D. dissertation, University of Pittsburgh, 1980.

1054 Wang, Yi-chang. "The Medical Practitioners' Points of View on Birth Control: A Survey of Selected Practitioners on OBG, Non-OBG and Midwives in Taipei City." *Chinese Medical J.* (Taibei) 16(Mar. 1969):43-54.

1055 Women in the Birth Control Movement and in Maternal and Child Health. Oral History, 1973-1975. 11 vols. and 66 tapes, unpublished guide. [Includes an interview with physician Julia Tsuei, fellow of the Sanger Research Bureau, family planning worker in Taibei, Taiwan, and founder with Elizabeth Arnold of the Demonstration Project in Taibei.]

Labor and Production

ECONOMIC DEVELOPMENT, GENERAL

1056 Andors, Phyllis. "Social Revolution and Woman's Emancipation: China during the Great Leap Forward." *Bulletin of Concerned Asian Scholars* 7(Jan./Mar. 1975):33–42.

1057 Andors, Phyllis. "Politics of Chinese Development: The Case of Women, 1960–1966." *Signs* 2(Autumn 1976):89–119.

1058 Boserup, Ester. *Women's Role in Economic Development.* London: Allen and Unwin, 1970. [For Chinese women in trade and commerce, see pp. 89–98; for hostility toward education for Chinese girls, pp. 121–22; for Chinese patterns of employment of women, pp. 180–82.]

1059 Solidum, Estella D. "The Perceptions of Women of Their Role in National Development and of How Culture Limits Such a Role." *Asian and Pacific Quarterly of Cultural and Social Affairs* 8(Summer 1976):22–30. [Taibei, Seoul, and Tokyo women interviewed.]

URBAN AND INDUSTRIAL LABOR: THE CHINESE REPUBLIC (1911–1949)

1060 Burr, John S. "Shanghai Factory Conditions." *China Quarterly* (Shanghai) 1(Summer 1936):31–39.

1061 Burton, Margaret Ernestine. *Women Workers of the Orient.* West Medford, Mass.: The Central Committee of the United Study of Foreign Missions, 1918. [Includes Chinese women working in factories, at home, in hospitals, etc; also includes Chinese businesswomen, women physicians, social workers, etc.]

1062 Chang, E. "Chinese Women's Place in Journalism." *Chinese Students Monthly* 18(1923):5:50–55.

1063 Chen, Ta [Ch'en, Ta]. "Wages and Hours of Labor in Five Chinese Cities [Shanghai, Nanking, Peking, Taiyuan, and Amoy], 1917–1920." *Monthly Labor Review* 13(Aug. 1921):3–15. [Includes statistics on women's wages and working hours.]

1064 Chen, Ta [Ch'en, Ta]. "Working Women in China." *Monthly Labor Review* 15(Dec. 1922):142–49.

1065 "Child and Woman Labor in China, 1930." *Nankai Weekly Statistical Service* 4(Mar. 2, 1931):49, 51–54.

1066 Ching, Chung Shou and Bagwell, May. *Women in Industry in the Chapei, Hongkew and Pootung Districts of Shanghai.* Shanghai: Y.W.C.A. of China, National Committee, 1931.

1067 "Conference on Women's Work: a New Era for Women's Work." *Chinese Recorder*, Feb. 1920, pp. 118–23.

1068 E. E. [Entwistle]. *Working Girls of China: For Senior Girls.* London: United Council for Missionary Preparation, 1920.

1069 Epstein, Israel. *Notes on Labor Problems in Nationalist China.* N.Y.: International Secretariat, Institute of Pacific Relations, 1949. [Chapter 5, "Women and Children in Industry," describes woman workers in wartime industry.]

1070 "Factory Labor in Shanghai, 1929." *Nankai Weekly Statistical Service* 6(Sept. 25, 1933):179, 181–82.

1071 Fang, Fu-an. *Chinese Labor: An Economic and Statistical Survey of Labor Conditions and Labor Movements in China.* Shanghai: Kelly and Walsh; London: King, 1931. [Women's working conditions of are described in chapter 5.]

1072 Federation of Woman's Boards of Foreign Missions. *Report of the Deputation,* 1920. [See "Women in Industry," pp. 39–47.]

1073 Feng, Cheng-hai. "Labor Conditions in China during 1934." *Chinese Economic Journal and Bulletin* 16(1935):2:185–99.

1074 Fong, H. D. [Fang Hsien-t'ing]. "Industrialization and Labor in Hopei, with Special Reference to Tientsin." *Chinese Social and Political Science Review* 15(Apr. 1931):1–28. [See "Child and Woman Labor," pp. 20–22.]

1075 Hinder, Eleanor M. "China's New Factory Law as Affecting Women and Children." *Chinese Recorder* 62(Mar. 1931):149–55.

1076 Koo, D. Y. "Women's Place in Business." *Chinese Students Monthly* 18(1922):1:34–36.

1077 Koo, Ping Yuan. *China's Labor Laws, 1929–1935.* Shanghai: Commercial Press, 1935.

1078 Kuo, Ping-wen. "Labor Conditions and Labor Regulation in China." *International Labor Review* 10(Dec. 1924):1005–1028.

1079 Kyong, Bae-tsung. *Industrial Women in Wusih, a Study of Industrial Conditions.* National Committee of the Y.W.C.A. in China, 1929.

1080 Ma, K. C., trans. "History of a Shanghai Tobacco Company." *Chinese Sociology and Anthropology* 6:1 (Fall 1973); 6:2 (Winter 1973); 6:3–4 (Spring–Summer 1974); 7:1 (Fall 1974). [Book length translation of a work published by the Shanghai Academy of Sciences in 1960 on an industry that used a largely female labor force.]

1081 Nee, P. "The Strike of the Working Women in the Shanghai Filatures." *Chinese Students Monthly* 19(1924):3:21–23.

1082 Ostrofsky, Diane Betty. "The Role of Women in the Chinese Labor Movement, 1919–1927." M.A. thesis, Columbia University, 1967.

1083 Paddock, A. E. "Hair Nets." *Survey* 48(Sept. 1, 1922):663–65.

1084 Rietveld, Harriet. "Women and Children in Industry in Chefoo." *Chinese Economic Monthly* 3(Dec. 1926):559–62.

1085 Roman, A. "Factory Workers of China." *Asia* [Asia and the Americas] 36(Oct. 1936):636–40.

1086 "Statistics on Factory Workers in Tientsin, 1928." *Nankai Weekly Statistical Service* 2(Oct. 7, 1929):1, 4.

1087 Strong, A. L. "Some Hankow Memories of a Women's Union." *Asia* [Asia and the Americas] 28(Oct. 1928):794–97.

1088 T'ao, Ling and Johnson, Lydia. *Women in Tientsin Industries: a Study of the Working Conditions of Women and Girls.* Beijing: Peking Leader Press, 1928.

1089 Tayler, John Bernard and Zung, W. T. "Labour and Industry in China." *International Labor Review* 8(July 1923):1–20.

1090 T'ien, Ju-k'ang. "Female Labor in a Cotton Mill [in Kunming]." Trans. Francis L. K. Hsu. In *China Enters the Machine Age: A Study of Labor in Chinese War Industry,* by Kuo-heng Shih, ed. Fei Hsiao-tung [Fei Hsiao-t'ung], pp. 178–95. Cambridge, Mass.: Harvard University, 1944.

1091 Tsha, T. Y. [Ts'ai Cheng-ya]. "Labor Legislation, Wages and Hours in Shanghai." *China Critic* 4(July 23, 1931):705–709.

1092 Tsha, T. Y. [Ts'ai Cheng-ya]. "A Study of the Wage Rates in Shanghai, 1930–34." *Nankai Social and Economic Quarterly* 8(Oct. 1935):459–510.

1093 Tso, S. K. Sheldon [Chu, Shih-k'ang]. "Present Labor Conditions in China." *Monthly Labor Review* 26(Apr. 1928):44-55.

1094 "Wages, Hours and Family Budget of the Chinese Laborers, 1930." *Nankai Weekly Statistical Service* 4(Sept. 21, 1931):177, 179-80.

1095 "Wages in Tientsin Industries." *Chinese Economic Monthly* 3(Oct. 1926):418-22.

1096 "Wages of Handicraft Workers in Peiping, 1862-1927." *Nankai Weekly Statistical Service* 3(Feb. 24, 1930):35, 38-40.

1097 Wagner, Augusta Bertha. "Some Aspects of Chinese Labor Conditions." M.A. thesis, Columbia University, 1930.

1098 Wales, Nym, pseud. [Snow, Helen Foster]. *The Chinese Labor Movement.* N.Y.: John Day, 1945. [Includes discussion on women in industry.]

1099 Walton, Cara May. "Women's Work in Fenchow [i.e. Fengzhou, Fengyang *xian*, Shanxi]." *Chinese Recorder* 53(Sept. 1922):595-98.

1100 Wikander, Ingeborg. "The Preservation of the Old Chinese Art of Textile Work." *Chinese Recorder*, Oct. 1922, pp. 639-42.

1101 "Women's Work in Kwangtung Province." *Chinese Economic J. and Bulletin* (Peking) 1(June 1927):564-78.

1102 Woo, Sun-pei. "China's Silk Industry in 1946." *China Trade Monthly* 1(Jan. 1947):25-27+.

1103 "Working Conditions in Shanghai Cotton Mills." *International Labour Review* 20(1929):251-54.

1104 Y.W.C.A. United States National Board, Education and Research Division with Y.W.C.A. Industrial Dept. "China." In *Women in Industry in the Orient: A Sourcebook,* comp. by the organization cited, pp. 75-65. N.Y.: Women's Press, 1926.

1105 Zung, Wei-tsung. "The Chinese Church and the New Industrial System." *Chinese Recorder*, Mar. 1922, pp. 186-90. [The author calls for the equality of Chinese woman workers.]

RURAL AND AGRICULTURAL LABOR: THE CHINESE REPUBLIC (1911-1949)

1106 Fei, Hsiao-tung [Fei, Hsiao-t'ung]. "Agricultural Labor in a Yunnan Village [Lu village, Lufeng *xian*]." *Nankai Social and Economic Quarterly* 12(Jan. 1941):146-68.

1107 Gamble, Sidney D. *Ting Hsien: A North China Rural Community.* Stanford: Stanford University, 1954. [Includes women's activities in home industry during the 1920s and 1930s.]

1108 Hommel, Rudolf P. *China at Work: An Illustrated Record of the Primitive Industries of China's Masses.* N.Y.: John Day, 1937. [Reprint: M.I.T. Press, 1969. See especially chapter 3, "Tools for Making Clothing," pp. 161-218.]

1109 Spencer, C. "Chinese Boat Woman." *Asia* [Asia and the Americas] 37(Dec. 1937):879-81.

1110 Tsin, Yu. "The Working Women of Soviet China." *Inprecorr* 12(Jan. 14, 1932).

1111 Yang, Martin C. *A Chinese Village: Taitou, Shantung Province.* N.Y.: Columbia University, 1945. [Sociological description of a Shandong village and, in passing, of the life of women during the early 20th century.]

Note: See also "Family in Republican China."

WOMEN IN PRODUCTION, GENERAL: THE PEOPLE'S REPUBLIC OF CHINA (1949-)

1112 *CB*, no. 579 (May 25, 1959). Ts'ai Ch'ang. "The Role of Women in Socialist Construction," pp. 9-12.

1113 *CB*, no. 579 (May 25, 1959). Li, Tung-ch'ing. "Women Accomplish Miraculous Feats in the Leap Forward," pp. 13-16.

1114 Chang, Hsiang-yu [Chang, Hsiang-yü]. "My Rebirth." In *Chinese Women in the Great Leap Forward,* pp. 50-56. Peking: Foreign Languages Press, 1960.

1115 "Chekiang Article on Women's Work." *Summary of World Broadcasts,* BBC, UK.FE/3665 (1971), B11/14.

1116 "Chekiang Conference on Deployment of Women Workers and Cadres." *Summary of World Broadcasts,* BBC, UK.FE/3660 (1971), B/19.

1117 *Chinese Women in the Great Leap Forward.* Peking: Foreign Languages Press, 1960.

1118 Chou, M. J. "Women Workers and Their Children." *China Reconstructs* 2(May-June, 1953):28.

1119 Chow, Fan. "Weather Girls." *Orientations* 10(Oct. 1979):6-7. [A report on two Chinese women who set up a weather station in Xin'gan county, Jiangxi.]

1120 *ECMM*, no. 168 (Mar. 6, 1959). "Women: An Important Force in Socialist Construction," p. 24.

1121 *ECMM*, no. 1152 (Oct. 8, 1955). "All China Democratic Women's Federation Organizations Instructed to Mobilize Women to Increase Production and Practice Economy," p. 6.

1122 "Five Women." *China Reconstructs* 2(July-Aug. 1953):43. [Model women workers in various fields.]

1123 Hickey, Margaret. "China Dateline." *National Business Woman* 61(Jan./Feb. 1980):9-11. [A report based on observation, including work conditions of women in China.]

1124 Hung, Ying. "Chinese Women Achieve Economic Independence." *Economic Reporter,* July/Sept. 1973, pp. 32-33.

1125 JPRS, no. 35082 (Mar. 7, 1966). "New China's Women Workers." [From *Zhongguo xinwen*, pp. 9-10.]

1126 Li, Chen. "Chinese Women: Women Take Part in Productive Labour." *Peking Review* 17(Mar. 22, 1974):17-19.

1127 "New Jobs for Women." *China Reconstructs* 9(Apr. 1960):38.

1128 "Ordinary but Outstanding Women: A Fishing Team, a Drilling Group, Hoche Girl Joins Army, Lung Mei Goes to College, Saving a Train." *Peking Review* 16(Mar. 30, 1973):22.

1129 *SCMM*, no. 562 (Feb. 6, 1967). "Take Part in Labor, Promote Revolutionization of Family Dependents," pp. 13-18. [From *Shuili yu dianli*, no. 5 (Mar. 5, 1966).]

1130 *SCMM*, no. 714 (Sept. 1, 1971). Writing Group, CCP Hunan Provincial Committee. "Bring the Role of Women into Full Play in Revolution and Construction," p. 73. [From *Hongqi*, 1971, no. 10.]

1131 *SCMP*, no. 291 (Mar. 7, 1952). "Achievements in Constructive Work by Women of New China," p. 21.

1132 *SCMP*, no. 609 (July 11, 1953). "Chinese Women in Construction Work," p. 9.

1133 *SCMP*, no. 1002 (Mar. 7, 1955). "Women Worker Ranks Continue to Swell in China," p. 5.

1134 *SCMP,* no. 1245 (Mar. 7, 1956). "Liberation Brings Women Jobs," p. 20.

1135 *SCMP,* no. 1258 (Mar. 8, 1956). "Fully Promote the Positive Role of Women in Socialist Construction," p. 17. [*Renmin ribao* editorial.]

1136 *SCMP,* no. 1378 (Sept. 26, 1956). "Yang Chih-hua Speaks on Women Workers at September 26th Meeting of Communist Party Congress," p. 7.

1137 *SCMP,* no. 1487 (Mar. 7, 1957). "More Women Workers in China Today," p. 18.

1138 *SCMP,* no. 1491 (Mar. 3, 1957). "Higher Women Intellectuals of Peking in Socialist Construction," p. 20.

1139 *SCMP,* no. 1783 (May 24, 1958). "Szechuan Women Contribute to Production," p. 41.

1140 *SCMP,* no. 1791 (June 2, 1958). Tsao, Kuan-chun. "Further Liberate Women's Labor Capacity and Channel this Force to Building up Socialism in a Better Way," p. 4.

1141 *SCMP,* no. 1843 (Aug. 25, 1958). "Exhibition on Women's Part in National Construction," p. 3.

1142 *SCMP,* no. 1922 (Jan. 4, 1959). "Chinese Women's Achievements in 1958," p. 2.

1143 *SCMP,* no. 1971 (Mar. 6, 1959). "Chinese Women's Great Contribution to Production," p. 14.

1144 *SCMP,* no. 2083 (Aug. 19, 1959). "Review of Women's Work in China," p. 21.

1145 *SCMP,* no. 2708 (Mar. 7, 1962). "Women throughout Kwangtung Province Made Great Contributions to Production and Construction Front Last Year," p. 10.

1146 *SCMP,* no. 4861 (Mar. 10, 1971). "East China Women Workers Play Important Role in Socialist Construction," p. 184.

1147 *SCMP,* no. 5098 (Mar. 11, 1972). "Peking Women Play Important Role in Revolution and Production," p. 103.

1148 *SCMP,* no. 5337 (Mar. 8, 1973). "Working Women Are Great Revolutionary Force," p. 59. [*Renmin ribao* editorial.]

1149 *SCMP,* no. 5423 (July 16, 1973). "Peking Women Play Important Role in Revolution and Construction," p. 176.

1150 *SCMP,* no. 5577 (Mar. 10, 1974). "Women in Hsiyang *Hsien* Play Important Role in Socialist Revolution and Construction," p. 131.

1151 Sheth, Ketaki. "Is Asian Life Improving?" *World Press Review* 27(June 1980):41-42. [Author argues that women are doing more work for less money in China.]

1152 "Women Builders of Socialism." *Peking Review* 1(Dec. 9, 1958):12.

1153 "Women on the Production Front." *Peking Review* 8(Mar. 12, 1965):30.

1154 "Women to the Fore." *Peking Review* 9(Mar. 11, 1966):3. [Summarizes achievements of women in labor, especially in Daqing and Dazhai.]

1155 "Women Workers in Emulation Drive." *People's China* 3(1951):4:20.

1156 "Working Women Are a Great Revolutionary Force." *Peking Review* 16(Mar. 11, 1973):5-6. [*People's Daily* editorial.]

1157 Yang, C. H. "Concretely Applying Party Policies to the Work of Women Workers." *Women of China* 1961:12:1, 4.

URBAN AND INDUSTRIAL LABOR: THE PEOPLE'S REPUBLIC OF CHINA (1949-)

1158 Chen, Fang. "Policewomen in Shanghai." *Economic Reporter,* July-Sept. 1973, pp. 32-33.

1159 Chen, Han-seng. "Porcelain-making Modernized." *China Reconstructs* 13(Aug. 1964):15-16.

1160 Chen, Han-seng. "Textile Workers' Standard of Living Rises." *China Reconstructs* 21(Dec. 1972):35-37.

1161 Chen, Han-seng. "Peasant Girl Now a Trade-Union Leader." *China Reconstructs* 22(Oct. 1973):26-27.

1162 Chin, Chin-chih. "Businessman's Wife." *China Reconstructs* 5(July 1956):27-29.

1163 Ching, Hung. "Report from Tach'ing Oilfield: A Women's Oil Team." *Peking Review* 15(July 14, 1972):19-20.

1164 "A Cotton Mill Reborn." *China Pictorial* 1967:6:24-29.

1165 Croll, Elisabeth Joan. "Trade Union Women." *China Now,* no. 50 (Mar. 1975), pp. 7-9.

1166 Davin, Delia. "The Implications of Some Aspects of C.C.P. Policy Toward Urban Women in the 1950s." *Modern China* 1(Oct. 1975):363-78.

1167 *ECMM,* no. 55 (Oct. 1, 1956). "She Holds 13 Different Jobs," p. 16.

1168 *ECMM,* no. 153 (Jan. 12, 1959). "A Discussion of the Problem of Piece Wages," pp. 18-23. [From *Caijing yanjiu,* 1958, no. 6.]

1169 Emerson, John Philip. *Sex, Age and Level of Skill of the Non-Agricultural Labour Force of Mainland China.* Washington, D.C.: U.S. Bureau of the Census, Foreign Demographic Analysis Division, 1965.

1170 Fang, Chi. "Notable Advance in Woolen Textiles." *China Reconstructs* 13(June 1964):2-4.

1171 Fang, Kuei-mei. "Two Societies, Two Different Lives." *China Pictorial* 1973:3:8-11. [About equal work and equal pay in China.]

1172 Goldwasser, Janet and Dowty, Stuart. "Chinese Factories Are Exciting Places." *Eastern Horizon* 11(1972):5:39-51; 11(1972):6:49-60. [See "Holding up Half the Sky" and "Woman's Work is Never Done" in part 2, pp. 49-52.]

1173 "A Good Ticket Seller." *China Reconstructs* 19(Nov. 1970):34-35.

1174 Hsu, C. "A Woman General Foreman." *People's China* 1(1955):6:19.

1175 Hu, Chin. "Breaking Down Male Supremacy: Mobile Chairs for Spinners." *China Reconstructs* 24(Mar. 1975):5.

1176 *Important Labour Laws and Regulations of the People's Republic of China.* Peking: Foreign Languages Press, 1961.

1177 "The Iron-Girl Well-Sinking Team." *China Reconstructs* 19(Nov. 1970):33.

1178 JPRS, no. 37246 (July 5, 1966). "China's Textile Workers Developed Textile Technology." [From *Da gong bao,* p. 2.]

1179 JPRS, no. 47818 (Dec. 22, 1968). "Daughter Following Mao's Road Supported," pp. 59-60. [From *Gongren zaodanbao,* p. 2.]

1180 JPRS, no. 51280 (Aug 11, 1970). "Mass Criticism at Shenyang Woolen Textile Mill," p. 1. [From *Renmin ribao.*]

1181 Opper, Michael. "Factory Born of Women." *Eastern Horizon* 14(1975):3:21-23.

1182 Opper, Michael. "Women Power." *China Now,* no. 57 (Dec. 1975), pp. 7-8. [About a metallurgical factory.]

1183 Penn, Colin. "At Taching." *China Now,* no. 50 (Mar. 1975), pp. 9-10. [About women working in oilfields.]

1184 "Policewomen." *Peking Review* 16(Jan. 5, 1973):31.

1185 *SCMM*, No. 304 (Dec. 1, 1962). "Why Their Work on Women Workers is Successful—an Account of Experience in Work on Women Workers of the 1st Maintenance Center of Peking Municipal Omnibus Corporation," p. 12.

1186 *SCMM*, No. 304 (Dec. 1, 1962). Yang, Chih-hua. "Concretely Implement the Party's Policies on Women Workers," p. 10.

1187 *SCMM*, no. 548 (Oct. 1, 1966). Hu, Fa-lien (a woman worker of Tach'ing Oilfield). "Manage Well Oil-Wells for the People," p. 11. [From *Hongqi*, 1966, no. 13.]

1188 *SCMM*, no. 552 (Aug. 24, 1966). Liang, Yen (telephone operator, Canton, College of Physical Culture). "Listen to Chairman Mao's Instructions and Serve the People Wholeheartedly," p. 3.

1189 *SCMP*, no. 78 (Mar. 5, 1951). "31 Girls Trained as Tractor Operators in Peking Suburbs."

1190 *SCMP*, no. 79 (Mar. 6, 1951). "Women Workers Play Important Role in China's Industry."

1191 *SCMP*, no. 132 (June 8, 1951). "Women Tram and Bus Drivers Appear in Peking," p. 11.

1192 *SCMP*, no. 139 (July 20, 1951). "Women Crew of 'March 8th' Locomotive Take up Challenge of Soviet Sisters," p. 11.

1193 *SCMP*, no. 761 (Mar. 6, 1954). "Chinese Women Join Ranks of Industrial Workers," p. 28.

1194 *SCMP*, no. 778 (Mar. 8, 1954). "Women's Enormous Contribution to Industrial Production," p. 13.

1195 *SCMP*, no. 1002 (Mar. 7, 1955). "Peking Has Women Factory Directors," p. 6.

1196 *SCMP*, no. 1109 (Aug. 10, 1955). "Peking Women Take to Industry in Peking," p. 23.

1197 *SCMP*, no. 1240 (Feb. 18, 1956). "Preparatory Committee Formed for Conference of Women in Industry and Commerce," p. 5.

1198 *SCMP*, no. 1240 (Feb. 19, 1956). "National Conference of Women in Industry and Commerce to Be Convened," p. 3.

1199 *SCMP*, no. 1261 (Mar. 29, 1956). "Conference of Representative Conference of Wives of Industrialists, Merchants," p. 15.

1200 *SCMP*, no. 1270 (Apr. 8, 1956). "National Conference of Wives of Businessmen and Business Women Addresses Open Letter to Women of Business Circles in China," p 7.

1201 *SCMP*, no. 1276 (Apr. 8, 1956). "Fully Promote the Positive Role of Business Women in Socialist Transformation," p. 2 [*Renmin ribao* editorial.]

1202 *SCMP*, no. 1344 (July 20, 1956). "Care or Discrimination—Peking Bus Company's Ban on Women Workers," p. 17.

1203 *SCMP*, no. 1547 (June 4, 1957). "Workers Families Hold National Conference," p. 9.

1204 *SCMP*, no. 1848 (Aug. 14, 1958). "On the Transformation of Wives of Capitalist Industrialists and Businessmen," p. 4.

1205 *SCMP*, no. 1967 (Mar. 2, 1959). "Women Mechanize Chinese Restaurant in Harbin," p. 22.

1206 *SCMP*, no. 1971 (Mar. 8, 1959). "Chinese Women Operate a Tin Mine," p. 16.

1207 *SCMP*, no. 1973 (Mar. 6, 1959). "Peking Women's Part in the Leap Forward," p. 10.

1208 *SCMP*, no. 1999 (Apr. 20, 1959). "Women Police Direct Peking Traffic," p. 32.

1209 *SCMP*, no. 2007 (May 30, 1959). "Number of Women Workers Doubled," p. 15.

1210 *SCMP*, no. 2021 (May 15, 1959). "Women Taxi Drivers in Peking," p. 10.

1211 *SCMP*, no. 2136 (Nov. 7, 1959). "Wide Representation of Women Workers at Conference," p. 5.

1212 *SCMP*, no. 2206 (Feb. 24, 1960). "One Million Working Women in Chinese Capital," p. 16.

1213 *SCMP*, no. 2212 (Mar. 3, 1960). "Chinese Women Workers Set Good Production Records," p. 2.

1214 *SCMP*, no. 2212 (Mar. 3, 1960). "Outstanding Chinese Working Women Elected," p. 1.

1215 *SCMP*, no. 2454 (Mar. 5, 1961). "Peking Working Women's Contribution in Past Year," p. 14.

1216 *SCMP*, no. 2454 (Mar. 6, 1961). "Chungking Women Active in Production Work," p. 17.

1217 *SCMP*, no. 2454 (Mar. 7, 1961). "More Women Workers in Peking," p. 16.

1218 *SCMP*, no. 2454 (Mar. 7, 1961). "Shanghai Women Help in City Advance," pp. 16–17.

1219 *SCMP*, no. 2455 (Mar. 8, 1961). "Woman Director of Shanghai Factory Interviewed," p. 9.

1220 *SCMP*, no. 2692 (Mar. 1, 1962). "China's Leading Steel Center Has More Women Technicians," p. 20.

1221 *SCMP*, no. 2692 (Mar. 1, 1962). "Women Tractor Drivers and Technicians in China's Rural Communes," p. 20.

1222 *SCMP*, no. 2694 (Mar. 5, 1962). "Peking Women Textile Workers," p. 20.

1223 *SCMP*, no. 3175 (Mar. 5, 1964). "China's Noted Woman Lathe Turner," p. 24.

1224 *SCMP*, no. 3175 (Mar. 6, 1964). "Outstanding Shanghai Woman Spinner," p. 19.

1225 *SCMP*, no. 3176 (Mar. 7, 1964). "Advanced Shanghai Woman Worker Honored," p. 17.

1226 *SCMP*, no. 3652 (Mar. 3, 1966). "Young Postwoman Honored as Model Worker," p. 17.

1227 *SCMP*, no. 3653 (Mar. 3, 1966). "The Women of Tach'ing Oilfied Play a Revolutionary Role," pp. 23–24.

1228 *SCMP*, no. 3655 (Mar. 8, 1966). "Outstanding Woman Worker in China's Motor Vehicle Industry," p. 23.

1229 *SCMP*, no. 3808 (Oct. 22, 1966). "Chinese Newspapers Praise Yü Feng-ying, Chairman Mao's Good Worker," p. 20.

1230 *SCMP*, no. 3810 (Oct. 22, 1966). "Make Revolution at the Very Center of One's Being—Learn from Yü Feng-ying, Good Worker of Chairman Mao," p. 25.

1231 *SCMP*, no. 3811 (Oct. 26, 1966). "Excerpts of Diary of Chinese Woman Worker Yü Feng-ying," p. 23.

1232 *SCMP*, no. 4376 (Mar. 9, 1969). "Women of Taching Oilfield Active in the Three Great Revolutionary Movements," p. 12. [From New China News Agency, Beijing.]

1233 *SCMP*, no. 4618 (Mar. 12, 1970). "Woman Turbine Generator Operator in Shanghai," p. 100.

1234 *SCMP*, no. 4739 (Sept. 1, 1970). Chi, Wei-wen. "Rousing Workers' Dependents to Take Part in Collective Productive Labor," p. 55.

1235 *SCMP*, no. 4862 (Mar. 11, 1971). "Chinese Women Electricians Conduct Free Live-Line Operation," p. 25.

1236 *SCMP*, no. 4862 (Mar. 11, 1971). "Outstanding Peking Woman Shop Assistant," p. 26.

1237 *SCMP*, no. 4876 (Apr. 1, 1971). "'Iron Girls' Oil Extracting Team in Tach'ing," p. 77.

1238 *SCMP*, no. 5094 (Mar. 5, 1972). "Women in Tach'ing Oilfield Take Part in Production," p. 142.

1239 *SCMP*, no. 5095 (Mar. 6, 1972). "Hundreds of Thousands of Women Workers on Shanghai's Industrial and Communications Fronts Forge Ahead Brimming Over with Vim and Vigor, Under Guidance of Chairman Mao's Proletarian Revolutionary Line," p. 177.
1240 *SCMP*, no. 5095 (Mar. 6, 1972). "Chinese Women Start an Oil Refinery," p. 180.
1241 *SCMP*, no. 5095 (Mar. 7, 1972). "Woman Train Crew in Northeast China," p. 183.
1242 *SCMP*, no. 5096 (Mar. 8, 1972). "Outstanding Woman Bus Conductor in Peking," p. 22.
1243 *SCMP*, no. 5109 (Mar. 26, 1972). "Women in North China City Take Part in Production," p. 32.
1244 *SCMP*, no. 5135 (May 6, 1972). "Young Woman Worker of Tach'ing Oilfield Practices Economy," p. 123.
1245 *SCMP*, no. 5267 (Nov. 21, 1972). "Policewomen in Shanghai," p. 212.
1246 *SCMP*, no. 5337 (Mar. 8, 1973). "Chinese Women Textile Workers Manage Cotton Mills," p. 65.
1247 *SCMP*, no. 5339 (Mar. 11, 1973). "Young Women Workers in Northeast China Port City," p. 142.
1248 *SCMP*, no. 5341 (Mar. 14, 1973). "More Women in Shanghai Engaged in Productive Work," p. 17.
1249 *SCMP*, no. 5342 (Mar. 15, 1973). "Shanghai Women Operate on 220,000-volt Transmission Lines," p. 59.
1250 *SCMP*, no. 5405 (June 19, 1973). "Women Electricians on Southwest China Plateau," p. 213.
1251 *SCMP*, no. 5487 (Oct. 21, 1973). "Noted Chinese Silk Tapestry Factory Trains Worker-cadres," p. 190.
1252 *SCMP*, no. 5578 (Mar. 12, 1974). "Woman Oil-Well Tender Goes to College," p. 162.
1253 *SCMP*, no. 5579 (Mar. 13, 1974). "Women Truck Drivers in Southwest China," p. 22.
1254 *SCMP*, no. 5580 (Mar. 15, 1974). "Brave Women Navigators in East China," p. 55.
1255 *SCMP*, no. 5584 (Mar. 21, 1974). "Woman Worker-Technicians in Shanghai," p. 28.
1256 *SCMP*, no. 5588 (Mar. 6, 1974). The Women Oil Extracting Team of the Tach'ing Oilfield. "Smashing the Iron Chains of 1,000 Years Standing; Women Prop up 'Half the Sky,'" p. 19.
1257 *SCMP*, no. 5592 (Mar. 31, 1974). "Women's Motorboat Team on Central China River," p. 183.
1258 "Silk Weaving in China." *China Reconstructs* 4(Nov. 1955):15.
1259 *SPRCP*, no. 5811 (Mar. 3, 1975). "Women Workers Play Significant Role in Rolling Stock Plant," p. 205.
1260 *SPRCP*, no. 5813 (Mar. 6, 1975). "All Women Well Drilling Team in North China Village," p. 58.
1261 *SPRCP*, no. 5816 (Mar. 10, 1975). "China Trains Women Diesel Locomotive Drivers," p. 178.
1262 *SPRCP*, no. 5818 (Mar. 14, 1975). "Women Workers at China's Big Oilfield," p. 83.
1263 *SPRCP*, no. 5829 (Mar. 30, 1975). "Women Play Big Role at Port of Shanghai," p. 151.
1264 *SPRCP*, no. 5833 (Apr. 6, 1975). "Steerswomen on Yangtze River Liner," p. 126.
1265 *SPRCP*, no. 5871 (May 29, 1975). "Women Workers in Silk Industry of East China Coastal Province," p. 85.
1266 *SPRCP*, no. 5883 (June 17, 1975). "Chinese Women Active in Tach'ing Oilfield," p. 211.
1267 *SPRCP*, no. 5892 (June 29, 1975). "Women Administrators in East China Filature," p. 204.
1268 *SPRCP*, no. 5893 (July 1, 1975). "Women Workers in Peking Rise as Activists in Marxist Study," p. 21.
1269 *SPRCP*, no. 6053 (Mar. 5, 1976). "Women at Tach'ing Oilfield, " p. 169.
1270 *SPRCP*, no. 6057 (Mar. 10, 176). "More Women's Livewire Operation Groups in China," p. 134.
1271 *SPRCP*, no. 6197 (Sept. 30, 1976). "Women Textile Workers Honor Memory of Chairman Mao," p. 30.
1272 *SPRCP*, no. 6215 (Oct. 29, 1976). "Women Drillers at Tach'ing Oilfield," p. 103.
1273 Su, M. "A Woman Train Crew." *People's China* 3(1951):9:40.
1274 Sun, Hsiao-chu. "Girl Dispatcher." *China Reconstructs* 3(Mar.–Apr. 1954):31.
1275 "Textile Worker—Central Committee Member." *China Reconstructs* 21(July 1972):8–11.
1276 "Textile Workers Repudiate China's Khrushchev." *China Reconstructs* 17(Feb. 1968):40–43.
1277 Thorborg, Marina. "Women in Non-Agricultural Production in Post-Revolutionary China." Ph.D. dissertation, Uppsala University, Sweden, 1980.
1278 Tie, Yun. "From Textile Worker to Minister." *China Reconstructs* 30(July 1981):6–9.
1279 Tien, Kuei-ying. "My School Life." *People's China*, Apr. 16, 1954, pp. 25–27. [The story of China's first woman locomotive driver.]
1280 Tung, Mei. "She's Walked Across China." *China Reconstructs* 23(July 1974):44–45. [About a model woman metallurgical field surveyor.]
1281 Wan, Shan-hung and Hung Tieh-shan. "The Iron Girl" (Reportage). *Chinese Literature* 1971:5:59–66.
1282 Wang, Hsin-chen. "Proletarian Revolutionary Woman Fighter." *Peking Review* 11(May 3, 1968):23–25, 33. [In praise of a woman textile worker in Shanghai.]
1283 Wang, Tung-ching. "Women Workers in Our Mill." *Women of China* 1964:5:12–13.
1284 Wen, Chun-chuan and Shan, Fu. "The Girl at the Control Board." *People's China*, May 1, 1955, p. 23. [Woman leader in an iron and steel factory.]
1285 "Women Drill Team." *China Pictorial* 1977:2–3:52–53.
1286 "Women Drive Trams in Peking." *China Reconstructs* 1(Jan.–Feb. 1952):34.
1287 "Women's Oil Extracting Team." *China Reconstructs* 24(June 1975):22–27.
1288 Yang, Ai-wen. "Every Conductress a Walking Map." *China Reconstructs* 9(June 1960):13.
1289 Yang, H. C. "The Life of Our Women Textile Workers." *Women of China*, June 1953, pp. 17–26.

HOUSEWIVES AND PRODUCTION: THE PEOPLE'S REPUBLIC OF CHINA (1949–)

1290 Alley, Rewi. "Oilfield Wives Farm the Gobi." *China Reconstructs* 22(Dec. 1973):32–34.
1291 *CB*, no. 579 (May 25, 1959). Chang, Hsiao-mei. "The Broad Masses of the Housewives Take up the Posts of Social Labor," pp. 17–19.
1292 *ECCM*, no. 163 (Apr. 6, 1959). Wang, Hai-p'o. "Questions Concerning the Establishment of People's Communes in Urban Streets," pp. 19–30. [From *Jiaoxue yu yanjiu* 1958, no. 11.]
1293 Han, Suyin. "A Housewife." *Eastern Horizon* 9(1970):1:7–11. [Discusses family life in Bengbu New Village, Shanghai, and the effects of industrialization on women workers as well as housewives.]
1294 "Housewives Take Part in Productive Labor." *China Reconstructs* 18(Dec. 1969):37.

1295 "Housewives' Workshops." *Peking Review* 16(Mar. 23, 1973):22.

1296 JPRS, no. 36983 (June 9, 1966). "Housewives Make up Labor Force for Lau-chan Neighborhood Industries," p. 95.

1297 JPRS, no. 40614 (Mar. 5, 1966). "Family Dependents Mobilized to Perform Fruitful Work," pp. 64–67. [From *Shuili yu dianli*.]

1298 Moos, Elizabeth. "Women's Place is in the Factory." *New China* 1(Spring 1975):28. [On housewife factory workers.]

1299 Nien, Chi. "Housewives Set up a Factory." *Women of China* 1964:5:8–11.

1300 "Peking's Community Factories." *Peking Review* 3(Mar. 29, 1960):3–4.

1301 SCMP, no. 1830 (July 31, 1958). "Housewives Taking Part in Industrial Production," p. 5.

1302 SCMP, no. 1913 (Dec. 9, 1953). "City Housewives Join Production Work," p. 9.

1303 SCMP, no. 1970 (Mar. 7, 1959). "Growing Membership of Tientsin's First Housewives Cooperatives," p. 28.

1304 SCMP, no. 2149 (Nov. 20, 1959). "Housewives in Peking in Social Labor," p. 20.

1305 SCMP, no. 2149 (Nov. 24, 1959). "Dependents of Workers and Housewives Serve Workers to Aid Big Leap Forward of Production in Shanghai," p. 16.

1306 SCMP, no. 2210 (Feb. 29, 1960). "China's Housewives Serve Production," p. 6.

1307 SCMP, no. 2249 (Apr. 27, 1960). "Former Housewives Head Central China Community Factory," p. 15.

1308 SCMP, no. 2251 (Apr. 28, 1960). "Shanghai Housewives Enjoy New Life," p. 6.

1309 SCMP, no. 2253 (Apr. 29, 1960). "More Chinese Housewives Become Workers," p. 24.

1310 SCMP, no. 2336 (Sept. 6, 1960). "Housewife Workers Are Rising Force on China's Industrial Front," p. 2.

1311 SCMP, no. 2350 (Sept. 27, 1960). "Urban Communes Set Chinese Women Free," p. 10.

1312 SCMP, no. 2454 (Mar. 7, 1961). "Women in Dragon Beard Ditch—Former Peking Slum Area," p. 15.

1313 SCMP, no. 2502 (May 16, 1961). "Chinese Women Active in Urban People's Communes," p. 8.

1314 SCMP, no. 3409 (Feb. 28, 1965). "Northeast China Housewives Tell Revolutionary Stories," p. 22.

1315 SCMP, no. 4870 (Mar. 23, 1971). "Oil Workers' Wives Run Farm," p. 181.

1316 SCMP, no. 4905 (May 15, 1971). "Housewives in Sinkiang PLA Production and Construction Corps Carry out Chairman Mao's May 7 Directive," p. 77.

1317 SCMP, no. 5088 (Feb. 25, 1972). "Workers' Wives in Northeast China City Take Part in Socialist Construction," p. 125.

1318 SCMP, no. 5096 (Mar. 7, 1972). "Housewives Start Factory from Scratch in Central China Province," p. 21.

1319 SCMP, no. 5097 (Mar. 9, 1972). "Housewives' Co-op in Shanghai Makes Tele-Communication Equipment," p. 61.

1320 SCMP, no. 5264 (Nov. 17, 1972). "Housewives Expand Factory in Northeast China," p. 70.

1321 SCMP, no. 5547 (Jan. 25, 1974). "How 27 Housewives Re-open a Fire-Clay Mine in Northeast China," p. 107.

1322 SCMP, no. 5615 (May 5, 1975). "Wives of Workers Run Farms at Northwest China Oilfield," p. 97.

1323 SPRCP, no. 5814 (Mar. 7, 1975). "Wives of Workers Run Farms at Northwest China Oilfield," p. 97.

1324 SPRCP, no. 5873 (June 1, 1975). "Housewives Run Factory Well in Northeast China City," p. 176.

1325 SPRCP, no. 6085 (Apr. 19, 1976). "More Peking Housewives Join Productive Labor," p. 250.

1326 "Street Factories." *China Reconstructs* 22(Aug. 1973):9–11.

RURAL AND AGRICULTURAL LABOR: THE PEOPLE'S REPUBLIC OF CHINA (1949–)

1327 "At the Foot of Hawk's Nest Mountain" [PLA Wives Building a Farm in Kirin Province] (Reportage). *Chinese Literature* 1968:10:14–23.

1328 Chan, Anita. "Rural Chinese Women and the Socialist Revolution: An Inquiry into the Economics of Sexism." *J. of Contemporary Asia* 4(1974):2:197–208.

1329 Chia, La-hsiang. "Women Cotton Growers." *China Reconstructs* 23(June 1974):36–38.

1330 "China: Girls Get Bored on the Farm." *Economist*, Apr. 7, 1973, pp. 35–36.

1331 Chou, Keh-chou. "Breaking Down Male Supremacy: How Our Village Got Equal Pay for Equal Work." *China Reconstructs* 24(Mar. 1975):6–9.

1332 Chou, Pien. "The Women of Wukung Village." *Women of China* 1964:1:7–9.

1333 "The Commune: A New Way of Life in the Village." *Peking Review* 1(Sept. 30, 1958):21–24.

1334 Croll, Elisabeth Joan. *Socialist Development Experience: Women in Rural Production and Reproduction in the Soviet Union, China, Cuba and Tanzania.* Brighton, England: Institute of Development Studies at the University of Sussex, 1979.

1335 Croll, Elisabeth Joan. *Women in Rural Development in the People's Republic of China.* Geneva: International Labor Office, 1979.

1336 Crook, David and Isabel. *The First Years of the Yangyi Commune.* London: Routledge and Kegan Paul, 1966.

1337 Davin, Delia. "Women in the Countryside of China." *Current History* 69(Sept. 1975):94–96+.

1338 Diamond, Norma. "Collectivization, Kinship, and the Status of Women in Rural China." *Bulletin of Concerned Asian Scholars* 7(Jan./Mar. 1975):25–32.

1339 Donnelly, Jannete C. "Women in the Northern Wilderness." *Eastern Horizon* 16(Apr. 1977):7–10.

1340 ECCM, no. 117 (Nov. 5, 1955). "Mobilize Women to Join the Cooperativization Movement," p. 14. [*Renmin ribao* editorial.]

1341 ECCM, no.155 (Oct. 16, 1958). Chang, Yu-san. "An Investigation of Supply-Wage System in a People's Commune in Shansi," pp. 21–26. [From *Hongqi*, 1958, no. 10.]

1342 Fairfax-Cholmeley, Elsie. "A Look at the People's Communes." *New World Review* 27(Feb. 1959):20–27.

1343 Fairfax-Cholmeley, Elsie. "Peasant Woman Leader." *Eastern Horizon* 4(Nov. 1965):44–48.

1344 "For Good Living in the Communes." *Peking Review* 2(Jan. 6, 1959):20.

1345 Hinton, William. "Two Ordinary Girls." *China Reconstructs* 2(Sept.–Oct. 1953):21. [About two model women, a farm worker and a tractor driver.]

1346 Hua, To. "Tea Pickers." *Chinese Literature* 1963:10:32–33.

1347 Huang, Lin. "Eight Women Transform an Island." *China Reconstructs* 10(Mar. 1961):9.

1348 *Hung-ch'i* commentator. "The People's Commune Advances Women's Complete Emancipation." *Peking Review* 3(Mar. 8, 1960):6–9.

1349 JPRS, no. 9181 (Sept. 1958). Nan, Ts'ai-ying. "The Dextrous Girls Movement," pp. 91–95. [From *Hongqi*.]

1350 JPRS, no. 14809 (June 6, 1962). "Rural Household Hand Craft Production," pp. 22–26. [From *Dagong bao*.]

1351 JPRS, no. 28766 (Nov. 24, 1964). "Poor Peasant Girl's Fight Against Theft of Collective Property Posed as an Example to be Followed," pp. 113–14. [From *Zhongguo qingnian bao*.]

1352 JPRS, no. 33793 (Dec. 4, 1965). "Subsidiary Household Industry Is Helper of Socialist Economy." [From *Renmin ribao*, p. 1.]

1353 JPRS, no. 34742 (Mar. 28, 1966). "High Political and Ideological Awareness among Tachai Women," pp. 9–13.

1354 "Kiangsi Province Women Mobilized for Revolutionary Action." *China Notes* 9(Spring, 1971):16–17.

1355 Kräuter, Uwe. "Interview with Kuo Feng-lien." *Eastern Horizon* 16(Oct. 1977):31–37. [Interview with a woman leader of Dazhai.]

1356 Lake, Douglas; Kramer Ione; and Epstein, Israel. "Working and Living with Chinese Peasants." *China Reconstructs* 16(Feb. 1967):36–40.

1357 Lee, Tsung-ying. "Eastern Diary." *Eastern Horizon* 14(1975):3:2–10. [About women leaders of Dazhai production brigade.]

1358 Lin, Fan. "A Women Production Team." *Women of China* 1957:6:20–23.

1359 "A Model Woman Farmer." *Peking Review* 2(Mar. 17, 1959):19.

1360 Myrdal, Jan. *Report from a Chinese Village*. N.Y.: Pantheon Books, 1965. [Interviews with men and women of Liu Ling Village, northern Shaanxi in 1962–1963.]

1361 National Women's Federation of the People's Republic of China. *Women in the People's Communes*. Peking: Foreign Languages Press, 1960.

1362 "Pi Ying-lan—Good Daughter of the Communist Party." *Peking Review* 12(Sept. 19, 1969):15–18, 22. [About the director of a credit cooperative.]

1363 Schran, Peter. *The Development of Chinese Agriculture, 1950–1959*. Chicago: University of Illinois, 1959.

1364 SCMM, no. 291 (Nov. 11, 1961). "Respect the Opinions of Women Members, Fix the Quota of Guaranteed Output Rationally," p. 16.

1365 SCMM, no. 291 (Nov. 11, 1961). "Same Pay for Same Work to Men and Women in the Chinghsi Production Brigade," p. 13.

1366 SCMM, no. 474 (May 1, 1965). Wang, Yun-ch'ang; Li, Yueh-ling; and T'ien, Shen-yuan. "'Woman *Hsiu-ts'ai*' Tills Land in Scientific Way," p. 17.

1367 SCMM, no. 502 (Nov. 1, 1965). Chao, Ngo-ni (Chairman of the Women's Committee, Hsiap'ingliang Brigade, Hsiaots'ao Commune, Yu Hsien, Shensi). "All Women of Our Village Emulate Tachai," p. 35. [From *Zhongguo funü*, 1965, no. 11.]

1368 SCMM, no. 552 (May 2, 1966). "Ambitious Women of Yinshi Carry out Revolution for Changing Heaven and Earth," pp. 6–13. [From *Zhongguo funü*, Feb. 1, 1966.]

1369 SCMM, no. 666 (Oct. 31, 1969). "Rural Women Constitute a Tremendous Revolutionary Force," pp. 70–73. [From *Hongqi*, Sept. 30, 1969.]

1370 SCMM, no. 700 (Feb. 1, 1971). "The Revolutionary Women's Will Is Strong—An Investigation Report on the Tungchin Brigade, Huanchiang Hsien, Kwangsi," p. 79.

1371 SCMM, no. 723–724 (Feb. 28–Mar. 6, 1972). Chin, Chi-tsu and Hung, Sung. "Equal Pay for Equal Work for Men and Women—Commenting on a Wrong Tendency on the Question of Distribution in the Rural Areas," pp. 88–92. [From *Hongqi* 1972, no. 2.]

1372 SCMM, no. 725–726 (Apr. 3–10, 1972). "How to Realize Equal Pay for Equal Work for Men and Women—Investigation Report on Ch'enchiafang Brigade, Hsüanhua *hsien*, Hopei," pp. 128–134.

1373 SCMM, no. 749–750 (Mar. 26–Apr. 2, 1973). "Bring Into Fuller Play the Role of Women as a Labor Force—Investigation Report on No. 10 Production Brigade of Lüszu Commune, Ch'itung Hsien, Kiangsu," pp. 51–54.

1374 SCMM, no. 757 (July 1, 1973). P'an Mei-ying (Huangshih Production Brigade, Ho Hsien, Kwangsi). "Persist in Taking Part in Collective Productive Labor," p. 106.

1375 SCMM, no. 762 (Oct. 1, 1973). The "Ten Sisters" Cotton-Planting Team of Wangchien Production Brigade in Lin-i Hsien, Shansi. "Whatever Men Comrades Can Accomplish, Women Comrades Can Too," p. 136.

1376 SCMP, no. 81 (Mar. 8, 1951). "90% of Women in Liberated Areas Take Part in Farm Work."

1377 SCMP, no. 103 (May 10, 1951). "Kwangtung Women to Be Organized for Agrarian Reform," p. 50.

1378 SCMP, no. 142 (July 24, 1951). "More Women in Northeast China Take Part in Tilling This Summer," p. 15.

1379 SCMP, no. 761 (Mar. 4, 1954). "Northwest Cooperative Farm Cited for Good Work in Mobilizing Women," p. 31.

1380 SCMP, no. 1254 (Mar. 9, 1956). "Working Days of Rural Women of Szechwan in Three Years to Surpass Target Set for 7th Year of National Program for Agriculture," p. 22.

1381 SCMP, no. 1258 (Mar. 8, 1956). "National Women's Draft Program for Realizing the National Program for Agriculture," p. 27. [Proposed by All China Democratic Women's Federation on Mar. 8, 1956.]

1382 SCMP, no. 1432 (Dec. 11, 1956). "Labor Protection for Women Peasants," p. 7.

1383 SCMP, no. 1447 (Dec. 26, 1956). "Forum on Work among Women in Rural Areas," p. 8.

1384 SCMP, no. 1772 (May 7, 1958). "Women's Big Role in Honan," p. 34.

1385 SCMP, no. 1779 (May 7, 1958). "Millions of Rural Women in Honan Province Play Important Role in Big Leap Forward," p. 40.

1386 SCMP, no. 1821 (July 13, 1958). "A New Contradiction That Has to Be Solved," p. 4.

1387 SCMP, no. 1901 (Nov. 20, 1958). "700,000 Women Experts Selected in Shansi," p. 25.

1388 SCMP, no. 1914 (Dec. 10, 1958). "Women's Contribution to Agricultural Upsurge," p. 24.

1389 SCMP, no. 1951 (Feb. 3, 1959). "Why Peasant Women Like the Communes," p. 6.

1390 SCMP, no. 1975 (Feb. 24, 1959). "Women's New Life in Rural People's Communes," p. 8.

1391 SCMP, no. 2162 (Dec. 17, 1959). "Women Play Important Part in East China Rural Area," p. 34.

1392 SCMP, no. 2410 (Dec. 29, 1960). "Educated Women Peasants in North China," p. 8.

1393 SCMP, no. 2451 (Mar. 2, 1961). "Energetic Woman Commune Leader in Shansi," p. 14.

1394 SCMP, no. 2456 (Mar. 4, 1961). "Commune Brings Forward New Type of Woman," p. 8.

1395 *SCMP*, no. 2463 (Mar. 8, 1961). "Women, Contribute More to the Effort to Win a Bumper Harvest Crops This Year," p. 13. [*Renmin ribao* editorial.]

1396 *SCMP*, no. 2560 (May 24, 1961). "A Production Brigade in Kwangtung Insists on Same Pay for Men and Women Doing Same Kind of Job," p. 5. [From *Nanfang ribao* (Guangdong), May 24, 1961.]

1397 *SCMP*, no. 2586 (Sept. 3, 1961). "YCL Branch of Linpu Brigade Studies Way to Help Young Women in Acquiring Working Experience," p. 15.

1398 *SCMP*, no. 3408 (Feb. 26, 1965). "Women Directors of Rural Communes in Southwest China," p. 21.

1399 *SCMP*, no. 3413 (Mar. 6, 1965). "An Outstanding Woman Leader in a Northeast China Commune," p. 24.

1400 *SCMP*, no. 3414 (Mar. 7, 1965). "Woman Leads Outstanding Production Team in South China," p. 25.

1401 *SCMP*, no. 4243 (Aug. 15, 1968). "Peasant Women's Study Class," pp. 16–18. [From New China News Agency, Beijing.]

1402 *SCMP*, no. 4359 (Feb. 8, 1969). "An Old Poor Peasant Woman Wholeheartedly Dedicated to Revolution," p. 15. [From New China News Agency, Nanning.]

1403 *SCMP*, no. 4418 (May 13, 1969). "Iron-willed Girls Water Conservancy Team on Northeast China Grassland," p. 16. [From New China News Agency, Harbin.]

1404 *SCMP*, no. 4615 (Mar. 7, 1970). "Woman Production Team Leader Keeps to Socialist Road," p. 138.

1405 *SCMP*, no. 4661 (May 13, 1970). "Coal Miners' Family Members Get Organized for Agriculture and Score Successes," p. 125.

1406 *SCMP*, no. 4841 (Feb. 9, 1971). "Noted Woman Model Peasant Applies Materialist Dialectics in Growing Cotton," p. 143.

1407 *SCMP*, no. 4858 (Mar. 5, 1971). "Peasant Woman Tells How She Studies and Applies Mao Tsetung Thought," p. 57.

1408 *SCMP*, no. 4860 (Mar. 8, 1971). "Women of Central China *Hsien* Help Build Canal," p. 137.

1409 *SCMP*, no. 4863 (Mar. 12, 1971). "Young Chinese Fisherwomen Mature in Struggle," p. 75.

1410 *SCMP*, no. 4863 (Mar. 13, 1971). "Chinese Model Peasant Woman Maintains Close Ties with Masses," p. 71.

1411 *SCMP*, no. 4865 (Mar. 15, 1971). "Outstanding Women in China's Old Revolutionary Base Areas," p. 160.

1412 *SCMP*, no. 4905 (May 15, 1971). "Housewives in Sinkiang PLA Production and Construction Corps Carry out Chairman Mao's May 7 Directive," p. 77.

1413 *SCMP*, no. 4993 (Sept. 27, 1971). Tung, Feng-wen (Tungfeng Brigade, Hsinghuo People's Commune, Peking). "The Brilliant Image of a Revolutionary Old Woman," p. 94.

1414 *SCMP*, no. 5025 (Nov. 17, 1971). "Women of Nanchen Peninsula Are Full of Vigor and Vitality," p. 130.

1415 *SCMP*, no. 5029 (Nov. 29, 1971). "A Plan Suggested by the Old Leader of a Production Team," p. 69.

1416 *SCMP*, no. 5095 (Mar. 6, 1972). "Chinese Women in Old Revolutionary Base Carry on Fine Traditions," p. 186.

1417 *SCMP*, no. 5099 (Mar. 12, 1972). "Twenty Young Women Heroically Fight Sand in Northwest China," p. 140.

1418 *SCMP*, no. 5102 (Mar. 17, 1972). "Women Active in Famous East China Tea Growing Commune," p. 73.

1419 *SCMP*, no. 5110 (Mar. 27, 1972). "Women in Central China Mountains Make Progress in Revolutionary Struggles," p. 71.

1420 *SCMP*, no. 5326 (Feb. 19, 1973). "Chiu Hsiu-ying, Woman Leader of East China Production Team," p. 18.

1421 *SCMP*, no. 5343 (Mar. 17, 1973). "Women—An Important Force in China's Pace-Setting Production Brigade," p. 96.

1422 *SCMP*, no. 5343 (Mar. 17, 1973). "Women Engine Operations in East China Fishing Vessels," p. 20.

1423 *SCMP*, no. 5346 (Mar. 22, 1973). "Girls' Team Active in Oyster Farming in South China," p. 22.

1424 *SCMP*, no. 5352 (Mar. 31, 1973). "Women on East China Islands," p. 108.

1425 *SCMP*, no. 5577 (Mar. 10, 1974). "East China Women's Fishing Team," p. 133.

1426 *SCMP*, no. 5599 (Apr. 11, 1974). "Women Help Build up Northeast China Island," p. 74.

1427 *SCMP*, no. 5603 (Mar. 30, 1974). Ch'en En-nü (Holder of the third class order of merit and female fishery worker). "Women Are a Force for the Defense of the Motherland," p. 56.

1428 *SCMP*, no. 5610 (Apr. 28, 1974). "Women's Cotton Growing Teams in North China," p. 166.

1429 *SPRCP*, no. 5812 (Mar. 4, 1975). "Women Commune Peasants Open up East China Mountain Areas," p. 20.

1430 *SPRCP*, no. 5813 (Mar. 6, 1975). "All-Women Well-Drilling Team in North China Village," p. 59.

1431 *SPRCP*, no. 5814 (Mar. 8, 1975). "Women's Fishing Crew in Northeast China People's Commune," p. 98.

1432 *SPRCP*, no. 5819 (Mar. 15, 1975). "Peasant Women Improve Farmland in East China Mountain Area," p. 131.

1433 *SPRCP*, no. 5820 (Mar. 16, 1975). "Iron Girls Active in Central China County," p. 177.

1434 *SPRCP*, no. 5854 (May 5, 1975). "Lumberwomen Active in Northeast China Forests," p. 249.

1435 *SCMP*, no. 5883 (May 13, 1973). "A Brigade Party Branch in Hopei Helps Women Solve Actual Problem in Labor," p. 19.

1436 *SCMP*, no. 5883 (May 13, 1973). "A *Hsien* Party Committee in Fukien Conscientiously Carries out Policy of Equal Pay for Equal Work Done by Men and Women," p. 7.

1437 *SPRCP*, no. 588 4 (June 17, 1975). "Noted Woman Cotton Grower Makes New Achievement," p. 21.

1438 *SPRCP*, no. 5887 (June 23, 1975). "Women Builders of 'Red Flag Canal,'" p. 147.

1439 *SPRCP*, no. 5925 (Aug. 19, 1975). "Women in Southern China Active in Fishing," p. 155.

1440 *SPRCP*, no. 6170 (Aug. 23, 1976). "East China's Women's Fishing Team Surpasses Catch Quotas," p. 113.

1441 *SPRCP*, no. 6230 (Nov. 22, 1976). "Women Bridge Builders in Northeast China Virgin Forests," p. 135.

1442 Strong, Anne Louise. "Women of the Communes." *China Reconstructs* 8(Mar. 1959):9.

1443 Su, M. "Girl on a Tractor." *People's China* 3(1951):4:19.

1444 Tan, Wen-chen. "Peasant Women Do Scientific Experiments." *China Reconstructs* 24(Oct. 1975):44–46.

1445 Thorborg, Marina. "Chinese Employment Policy in 1949–1978 with Special Emphasis on Women in Rural Production." In U.S. Congress, Joint Economic Committee, *Chinese Economy Post-Mao, A Compendium of Papers Submitted to the Joint Economic Committee*, vol. 1, *Policy and Performance*, pp. 535–604. Washington, D.C.: Government Printing Office, 1978.

1446 Tien, Lin. "Farmer Wu and His Girl Trainees." *China Reconstructs* 12(Nov. 1963):19–21.

1447 "A Visit to Tungting People's Commune (VI) Women Members." *Peking Review* 16(May 5, 1973):12–15.

1448 Wang, Chiao. "Girl Cotton Grower." *China Reconstructs* 15(May 1966):18–19.

1449 Wheeler, Jane E. "Young Women in the Chinese Countryside." In *Learning to Speak: Student Work*, ed. Deborah Silverton Rosenfelt, pp. 144–57. Old Westbury, N.Y.: Feminist Press, 1975.

1450 Whyte, Robert O. and Whyte, Pauline. *Rural Asian Women: Status and Environment*. Research Notes and Discussions Paper, No. 9. Singapore: Institute of Southeast Asian Studies, 1978. [Includes sections on China.]

1451 "Women in a Fishing Village." *China Pictorial* 394(Apr. 1981):24–26. [A portrait of women in Jiaodong Peninsula, China.]

1452 "Women of Tachai." *Women of China* 1965:3:5–7.

1453 "Women on the Farms." *Peking Review* 1(June 10, 1958):4.

1454 "Women Wrest Farmland from Sea." *Peking Review* 16(Feb. 2, 1973):31.

1455 Yang, Y. "The Women of Wu Village." *People's China* 1952:5:25.

1456 "Young Woman Cobbler." *Peking Review* 18(Apr. 4, 1975):30–31.

XIA FANG [URBAN YOUTH IN THE COUNTRYSIDE], THE PEOPLE'S REPUBLIC OF CHINA (1949–)

1457 Bernstein, Thomas. *Up to the Mountainside and Down to the Villages: The Transfer of Youth from Urban to Rural China*. New Haven: Yale University, 1977. [See "Facilitating Marriage," pp. 161–66.]

1458 Chang, Ke and Yang, Ching-hsiang. "City Girl Turns Farmer." *China Reconstructs* 9(Nov. 1960):32.

1459 "A City Girl." *China Pictorial* 376(Oct. 1979):38–40. [A love story about a Chinese woman barefoot doctor.]

1460 "The Deputy Commander's Daughter Put Down Roots in the Countryside." *Chinese Sociology and Anthropology* 11(Winter 1978–1979):53–61. [From New China News Agency.]

1461 "The Good Cadre Sends His Daughter off to Engage in Agriculture and Teaches Her to Put Down Roots in the Countryside." *Chinese Sociology and Anthropology* 11(Winter 1978–1979):62–68. [Translation from *Jiefang ribao* (Liberation Daily).]

1462 Ling, Cheng. "The Commander Sends His Daughter up to a Mountain Village." *Chinese Sociology and Anthropology* 11(Winter 1978–1979):29–36.

1463 "Making Our Home in a Mountain Village." *China Reconstructs* 17(Nov. 1968):19–23.

1464 "The Political Commissar Instructs His Daughter to Become a Stable Worker." *Chinese Sociology and Anthropology* 11(Winter 1978–1979):46–52. [From New China News Agency.]

1465 *SCMP*, no. 1720 (Dec. 29, 1957). "Girls Graduated from Middle Schools Marry Peasants in Shansi," p. 27.

1466 *SCMP*, no. 3411 (Mar. 3, 1965). "Girl Students from North China City Work in Countryside," p. 21.

1467 *SCMP*, no. 3703 (Apr. 12, 1966). "Returned Young Intellectuals of Mukang Commune Dare to Shatter Bad Customs and Create New Trends of Thought," p. 12.

1468 *SCMP*, no. 4430 (May 29, 1969). "Young Girl School Graduate Serves Poor and Lower-Middle Peasants Wholeheartedly," p. 23.

1469 *SCMP*, no. 4639 (Apr. 12, 1970). "Chinese Heroine Dies Saving State Property," p. 15. [About a young doctor in a mountainous village.]

1470 *SCMP*, no. 4679 (June 10, 1970). Shen, Hsiu-chin. "Exemplary Deeds of Outstanding Communist," p. 121. [About an educated woman settled in the countryside.]

1471 *SCMP*, no. 4919 (June 7, 1971). "Chinese Girl Student Matures Politically in Countryside," p. 118.

1472 *SCMP*, no. 5055 (Jan. 5, 1972). "Educated Young Woman Makes Progress in Countryside," p. 14.

1473 *SCMP*, no. 5135 (May 6, 1972). "Chinese Parents Happy about Their Children's Progress in Countryside," p. 119.

1474 *SCMP*, no. 5136 (May 7, 1972). "Daughter of Veteran Red Army Man Works Well in Countryside," p. 166.

1475 *SCMP*, no. 5136 (May 8, 1972). "Educated Young Woman in Chinese Countryside," p. 67.

1476 *SCMP*, no. 5155 (June 5, 1972). "Educated Shanghai Girls in Southwest China Mountainous Area," p. 135.

1477 *SCMP*, no. 5212 (Aug. 29, 1972). Ko, Chih-li (Director of the Neurological Department of the First Hospital Attached to Sian Medical College). "Support and Educate Our Sons and Daughters in Going to Mountain and Rural Areas to Make Revolution," p. 17.

1478 *SCMP*, no. 5245 (Oct. 16, 1972). The Revolutionary Committee of Hsiatao Production Brigade, Ot'ang Commune, Ho *Hsien*, Kwangsi. "Show Greater Concern for Educated Young Women Sent to the Countryside," p. 45.

1479 *SCMP*, no. 5337 (Mar. 8, 1973). "Educated Young Women from Peking in Yenan," p. 63.

1480 *SCMP*, no. 5572 (Mar. 4, 1974). "Well-known Educated Young Women in Chinese Countryside Criticize Lin Piao and Confucius," p. 141.

1481 *SCMP*, no. 5632 (May 30, 1974). "Woman College Graduate Takes Root in North China Countryside,' p. 66.

1482 *SPRCP*, no. 5813 (Mar. 6, 1975). "Educated Young Girl in Leading Cadre in Northwest China Countryside," p. 58.

1483 *SPRCP*, no. 5815 (Feb. 8, 1975). "I Love the Blue Sea of the Motherland," p. 126.

1484 *SPRCP*, no. 6067 (Mar. 25, 1976). "An Educated Girl Settles in a Mountain Village," p. 160.

1485 *SPRCP*, no. 6102 (May 4, 1976). "More Educated Young Women Settle in Border Area," p. 77.

1486 *SPRCP*, no. 6129 (June 25, 1976). "Woman College Graduate Persists in Working in Countryside," p. 19.

1487 Wen, Tzu-pien. "Good Daughter of the Party, Shen Hsiu-chin" (Reportage). *Chinese Literature* 1971:3:3–30.

SOCIAL WELFARE AND THE SOCIALIZATION OF HOUSEWORK

1488 "At Your Service." *Peking Review* 3(Mar. 29, 1960):4. [About collectivization of child care and housework.]

1489 "Best for the Children." *Peking Review* 3(May 24, 1960):5. [About organization of nurseries and kindergartens.]

1490 Chang, Yu. "Community Services in the Communes." *Peking Review* 1(Dec. 16, 1958):9–10.

1491 Chuan, Nung-tiao. "How Commune Dining Rooms Serve the Peasants." *Peking Review* 3(Jan. 12, 1960):16.

1492 "Happy Life for Retired Women Textile Workers." *Peking Review* 18(July 25, 1975):22–23.

1493 Hoffman, Charles. *Work Incentive Practices and Policies in the People's Republic of China, 1953–1965*. N.Y.: State University of New York Press, 1967. [See "Social Insurance," pp. 35–42.]

1494 Huang, Ying. "A Nursery Run Well, and Thriftily Too." *Women of China* 1961:3:11–13.

1495 "Innovation Comes to the Kitchen." *Peking Review* 3(Jan. 19, 1960):5.

1496 JPRS, no. 383D (Sept. 1, 1958). Hu, Sheng. "The Collectivization and Socialization of Domestic Labor," pp. 24–30.

1497 JPRS, no. 5104 (July 7, 1959). "Organization of Health Services under Communist China's Commune System (2)," pp. 1–7. [From *Renmin baojian*.]

1498 JPRS, no. 15445 (May 29, 1962). "Production Team's Arrangements of Labor for Collective Production and Housework Cited," p. 16. [From *Renmin ribao*.]

1499 Kung, Mai. "Collective Welfare Services in a Commune." *Peking Review* 3(May 17, 1960):45–47.

1500 "New Nurseries Everywhere." *China Reconstructs* 2(Mar./Apr. 1953):33.

1501 Prybyla, Jan. "Social Services Supporting the Dictatorship of the Masses." *Far Eastern Economics* 90(Oct. 3, 1975):14–16.

1502 *SCMM*, no. 259 (Apr. 1, 1961). "Proper Labor Protection Stimulates Women's Work Ardor—Introducing Cheng Pi-fang, a Good Production Team Leader who Puts into Practice the Policy of Labor Protection for Women," p. 13.

1503 *SCMM*, no. 261 (Feb. 1, 1961). *Chung-kuo fu-nü* correspondent. "A Good Housekeeper of Commune Members," p. 15.

1504 *SCMM*, no. 280 (Aug. 1, 1961). "Further Improve the Labor Protection Work for Members in Rural Communes," p. 16. [*Zhongguo funü* editorial.]

1505 *SCMM*, no. 384 (Sept. 30, 1963). "The Relationship between Work and Household Chores." [From *Zhongguo funü*, Aug. 1, 1963.]

1506 *SCMP*, no. 1002 (Mar. 7, 1955). "Mother, Children Care Work in China Reviewed," p. 7.

1507 *SCMP*, no. 1273 (Apr. 12, 1956). "Arrangements Must Be Made For the Protection and Living Conditions of Widows, Widowers, the Helpless and Disabled Servicemen," p. 2. [*Renmin ribao* editorial.]

1508 *SCMP*, no. 1358 (Aug. 13, 1956). "The Forsaken Ones Left by the Old Society and New Life for Vagrants, Street Walkers, Waifs, and Aged People in Shanghai," p. 42.

1509 *SCMP*, no. 1747 (Mar. 3, 1958). "Big Progress Achieved in Woman and Child Welfare Enterprises in Szechwan Province," p. 30.

1510 *SCMP*, no. 1841 (Aug. 21, 1958). "Hotel for Women and Children," p. 4.

1511 *SCMP*, no. 1869 (July 13, 1958). "Child Care Organizations Extensively Established in the Rural Areas of Heilungkiang," p. 41.

1512 *SCMP*, no. 1905 (Nov. 27, 1958). "Thousands of Women Model Workers in Commune Service Work," p. 4.

1513 *SCMP*, no. 1935 (Dec. 1, 1958). "Pan *Hsien* Details Large Number of Women Communist Party and Young Communist League Members to Look after Small Children," p. 8.

1514 *SCMP*, no. 1973 (Mar. 7, 1959). "More Child Care Facilities for Peking Women," p. 12.

1515 *SCMP*, no. 2105 (Sept. 22, 1959). "Historic Change of Several Hundred Million Rural Women—From Servant-like Domestic Laborers to Social Laborers," p. 25.

1516 *SCMP*, no. 2212 (Mar. 3, 1960). "Good Facilities for China's Women Workers," pp. 2–3.

1517 *SCMP*, no. 2220 (Mar. 13, 1960). "Working Women Freed of Household Work in Southwest China," p. 37.

1518 *SCMP*, no. 2222 (Mar. 16, 1960). "Harbin Working Women Freed of Household Burdens," p. 19.

1519 *SCMP*, no. 2350 (Sept. 29, 1960). "Urban Communes Set Chinese Women Free," p. 10.

1520 *SCMP*, no. 2651 (Jan. 4, 1962). Liu, Hsi-chun. "Properly Arranging the Life is an Important Task," p. 20. [From *Dagongbao*.]

1521 *SCMP*, no. 2708 (Mar. 8, 1962). "Properly Carry Out '4 Period' Protection for Women Workers," p. 5.

1522 *SCMP*, no. 5137 (May 6, 1972). "Nursery Classes Universally Set up in Hsihsinchuang Brigade, Ku-an *Hsien*, Hopei Province," p. 203.

1523 *SCMP*, no. 5333 (Mar. 2, 1973). "Shanghai Women Workers Benefit from Labor Insurance," p. 92.

1524 *SCMP*, no. 5338 (Mar. 9, 1973). "Welfare Services for Peking Women Textile Workers," p. 100.

1525 *SCMP*, no. 5714 (Sept. 29, 1974). "Residents Committee—Mass Organizations for Urban Populations," p. 266.

1526 "The Service House—a Friend in the Neighborhood." *China Reconstructs* 8(Dec. 1959):38.

1527 Soong, Ching-ling. "Welfare Work and Socialism." *China Reconstructs* 5(Aug. 1956):28.

1528 *SPRCP*, no. 5824 (Mar. 6, 1975). "It is Good to Run Nurseries in the Countryside—an Investigation of the Lichiap'ing Commune in Ch'iyang County, Hunan Province," p. 136.

1529 *SPRCP*, no. 5884 (June 18, 1975). "Socialist System Insures Full Employment for Working Women," p. 18.

1530 *SPRCP*, no. 5899 (July 10, 1975). "Peking Expands Nurseries," p. 68.

1531 Sun, Tan-wei. "A Village Nursery—How It Grew." *China Reconstruction* 5(Aug. 1956):28.

1532 "Training Teachers for Commune Nurseries." *China Reconstructs* 8(Aug. 1959):38.

1533 "What Social Guarantees Do Working Women Have in China?" *Women of China* 1957:1:2–3.

1534 "Working Mothers—Well-Cared-for Children." *China Reconstructs* 24(June 1975):38–43.

1535 Yang, Ching. "Women in a City Commune." *China Reconstructs* 10(Apr. 1961):2–5.

CONSUMER AFFAIRS

1536 *ECMM*, no. 32 (Feb. 16, 1956). New Observer. "Why Our Cotton Prints Do Not Look Pretty," p. 45.

1537 Hou, Yu-chen. "Housewives Step Out." *China Reconstructs* 7(Aug. 1958):24. [About family budgets.]

1538 Kuo, Chung-yi. "Making Shopping Easier." *Peking Review* 1(May 20, 1958):14–15.

1539 "Quality Fabrics for the Villages." *Peking Review* 5(Dec. 21, 1962):4.

1540 *SCMP*, no. 1258 (Mar. 26, 1956). "Shanghai Supplies More Cotton Prints," p. 34.

1541 *SCMP*, no. 1278 (Apr. 25, 1956). "Store Catering to Women and Children Opens in Tientsin," p. 18.

1542 *SCMP*, no. 1279 (Apr. 28, 1956). "Women's Dress Shop Opens in Peking," p. 16.

SLAVERY AND DOMESTIC LABOR

1543 Cable, Emma R. *Little Ah Yee of the Opium Dens*. San Francisco, 1880. [Describes the life of Chinese slave girls in the opium dens of San Francisco's Chinatown.]

1544 Chhodnam, Drolma. "Tibetan Slave Girl." *Chinese Literature* 1966:5:46–56. [Autobiography.]

1545 Davis, John A. (Rev.). *The Chinese Slave-Girl: A Story of Woman's Life in China*. Philadelphia: Presbyterian Board of Publication, 1880.

1546 Dillon, Richard H. *The Hatchet Man: The Story of the Tong Wars in San Francisco's Chinatown.* N.Y.: Coward-MacCann Inc., 1962. [See chapter 9, "Slave Girls."]

1547 *Dragon Stories.* Oakland: Pacific Presbyterian Publishing Co., 1908. [Narratives of the rescues and romances of Chinese slave girls in the United States.]

1548 Gola, H. R. "Slavery in China." *Living Age*, no. 344 (May, 1933), pp. 254–58.

1549 Han, Wen-chou and Yao, Lung-chang. "A Home Given by Chairman Mao." *Chinese Sociology and Anthropology* 4(Spring, 1972):240–62. [A former woman slave's life history. Excerpted from Sidney L. Greenblatt, ed., *The People of Taihang*, pp. 9–32. White Plains, N.Y.: International Arts and Sciences Press, 1972.]

1550 Harris, J. H. "Slave Trading in China." *Contemporary China* 137(Feb. 1930):174–80.

1551 Haslewood, Hugh Lyttleton. *Child Slavery in Hong Kong.* London: Sheldon Press, 1930.

1552 Holder, C. F. "Chinese Slavery in America." *North American Review* 165(July, 1897). [The author accuses the Chinese of tricking or kidnapping girls to be used as household drudges in America.]

1553 Hong Kong, Mui-tsai Committee. *Mui-tsai in Hong Kong: Report of the Committee Appointed by His Excellency the Governor, Sir William Peel.* London: His Majesty's Stationery Office, 1936.

1554 Kao, Feng; Chang, Tso-pin; and Lang, Ch'eng-hsin. "The Story of Selling Oneself." *Chinese Sociology and Anthropology* 4(Summer 1972):287–98. [Excerpt from Sidney L. Greenblatt, ed., *The People of Taihang*, pp. 51–63. White Plains, N.Y.: International Arts and Sciences Press, 1972.]

1555 McLeod, Alexander. *Pigtails and Gold Dust.* Caldwell, Idaho: Caston Printers, 1947. [Chinese slave girls in the United States and the Chinese slave market are discussed in chapter 13.]

1556 "Maidservant Becomes Teacher." *China Reconstructs* 18(Dec. 1969):36.

1557 O'Callaghan, Sean. *The Yellow Slave Trade: A Survey of Traffic in Women and Children in the East.* London: Blond, 1968. [See "Macao: The Cesspool of the Far East," pp. 51–59; "The Mui-tsai: The Child Slaves of Hong Kong," pp. 17–28; "The Traffic in Women and Children in China," pp. 7–16.]

1558 Office of the Chinese Communist Party Committee in Ch'in-shui *hsien*. "A Cave with Two Entrances." *Chinese Sociology and Anthropology* 4(Summer 1972):315–22. [Excerpt from Sidney L. Greenblatt, ed., *The People of Taihang*, pp. 81–88. White Plains, N.Y.: International Arts and Sciences Press, 1972.]

1559 Price, O. "Love-True: Biography of a Chinese Amah." *Asia* [Asia and the Americas] 29(Sept. 1929–Feb. 1930):679–685+.

1560 Pruitt, Ida. *A Daughter of Han: The Autobiography of a Chinese Working Woman.* New Haven: Yale University, 1945.

1561 Russell, J. "Report on Child Adoption and Domestic Service among Hong Kong Chinese. Mui-tsai in Hong Kong: Report (1936)." *British Parliamentary Papers 1935–1936*, vol. 7, pp. 922–31.

1562 Sung, Kuei-sheng and Lang, Chih-jen. "The Fight." *Chinese Sociology and Anthropology* 4(Summer 1972):342–64. [Excerpt from Sidney L. Greenblatt, ed., *The People of Taihang*, pp. 110–133. White Plains, N.Y.: International Arts and Sciences Press, 1972.]

1563 Watson, James L. "Chattel Slavery in Chinese Peasant Society: A Comparative Analysis." *Ethnology* 15(Oct. 1976):361–75. [Mostly on male slavery, but deals with slave family organization also.]

1564 Wilbur, Clarence Martin. *Slavery in China during the Former Han Dynasty, 206 B.C.–A.D. 25.* N.Y.: Russell and Russell, 1967.

1565 Winnington, Alan. *The Slaves of the Cool Mountains; Ancient Social Conditions and Changes Now in Progress on the Remote Southwestern Borders of China.* London: Lawrence and Wishart, 1959.

1566 Yüen, Feng and Wang, Tien-ch'i. "The Land." *Chinese Sociology and Anthropology* 4(Summer 1972):299–314. [Excerpt from Sidney L. Greenblatt, ed., *The People of Taihang*, pp. 64–80. White Plains, N.Y.: International Arts and Sciences Press, 1972.]

PROSTITUTION

1567 The Board of Health. *Chinatown: Declared a Nuisance.* San Francisco, 1880. [An inspection of prostitution problems in San Francisco's Chinatown.]

1568 California Legislature. *Chinese Immigration: The Social, Moral and Political Effect of Chinese Immigration.* Testimony Taken before a Committee of the Senate of the State of California, Appointed April 3, 1836. Sacramento, 1876. [The hearings covered a myriad of topics, including prostitution.]

1569 "Commercialized Vice in China." In *The Christian Occupation of China*, ed. Milton Theobald Stauffer, pp. 396–97. Shanghai: China Continuation Committee, 1922.

1570 "The Demi-monde of Shanghai." *Chinese Medical J.* 37(Sept. 1923):782–88.

1571 Drunken Whiskers [Pseud.]. *That Chinese Woman: The Life of Sai-chin-hua, 1874–1936.* Trans. Henry MacAleavy. N.Y.: Crowell, 1959.

1572 Fenn, William P. *Ah Sin and His Brethren in American Literature.* Peiping: College of Chinese Studies, 1933. [Includes stories of Chinese slave girls and prostitutes in America during the last half of the 19th century.]

1573 Gentry, Curt. *The Madams of San Francisco.* Garden City, N.Y.: Doubleday, 1964. [Story of Ah Toy, the first prostitute in San Francisco Chinatown.]

1574 Glenn, W. "Free and Easy in Taiwan." *Far Eastern Economic Review* 91(Jan. 9, 1976):32. [A discussion on prostitution in Taiwan.]

1575 Heath, F. J. "Venereal Disease in Relation to Prostitution." *Social Pathology* 1(1925):6:278–84.

1576 Henderson, Edward. *A Report on Prostitution in Shanghai.* Shanghai: North China Herald, 1871.

1577 Henriques, Fernando. *Prostitution and Society: A Survey.* London: MacGibbon and Kee, 1962. [See "The Prostitutes of China," in vol. 1, pp. 241–77.]

1578 Hirata, Lucie Cheng. "Free, Indentured, Enslaved: Chinese Prostitutes in Nineteenth-Century America." *Signs* 5(1979):1:3–29.

1579 Hsiao, Kan. "The Return to Daylight: The Reformation of Peking Prostitutes." *People's China* 1(Mar. 16, 1950):12, 22–26.

1580 Hsiao, Wen. "Shanghai Prostitutes Begin Their Lives Anew." *Women of China* 1957:2:24–27.

1581 JPRS, no. 49822 (Dec. 8, 9, 10, 1969). "Article Claims Prostitution Not Dead in Communist China," pp. 7–12. [From *Xingdao ribao*, p. 4.]

1582 Lamson, Herbert Day. *Social Pathology in China: A Source Book for the Study of Problems of Livelihood, Health, and the Family.* Shanghai: Commercial Press, 1934. [For prostitution, see pp. 362-64, 518-19.]

1583 Lee, B. E. "How Can We Honor Women." *Chinese Recorder,* Oct. 1919, pp. 663-64. [A speech calling for the prohibition of girl slaves, concubinage and prostitution in China.]

1584 Lethbridge, Henry James. "Girls in Danger." *Far Eastern Economic Review* 53(Sept. 22, 1966):583-87.

1585 Logan, Lorna E. *Venture in Mission: The Cameron House Story.* San Francisco, 1976. [The story of a group of Christian women who rescued Chinese prostitutes in San Francisco's Chinatown.]

1586 Longstreet, Stephen. *The Wilder Shore: A Gala Social History of San Francisco's Sinners and Spenders, 1849-1906.* Garden City, New York: Doubleday, 1968. [Contains unusually frank statements about Chinese prostitution in San Francisco around the turn of the century.]

1587 McAleavey, Henry. "Sai-chin-hua (1874-1936), the Fortunes of a Chinese Singing Girl." *History Today* 7(Mar. 1959):191-99.

1588 Miller, I. L. *The Chinese Girl.* Tientsin: Peiyang Press, 1932. [Translation from E. de Laberbis' unpublished manuscript in Russian.]

1589 Miller, Ronald Dean. *Shady Ladies of the West.* Los Angeles: Westernlore Press, 1964. [Includes the lives of Chinese prostitutes in the American west.]

1590 Morris, M. C. "Chinese Daughters of the Night." *Missionary Review* 39(Oct. 1916):753-62. [Story of the Door of Hope for women in Shanghai.]

1591 O'Callaghan, Sean. *The Yellow Slave Trade: A Survey in the Traffic in Women and Children in the East.* London: Blond, 1968. [See "Hong Kong: Clearing House of the Far East Vice Trade," pp. 40-50; "The Room Girls of Taiwan," pp. 60-65; "The World of Suzie Wong," pp. 29-39.]

1592 Pan, Margaret Tai-li. "The Attitudes of Taiwan Businessmen toward the Entertaining Girls of the City of Taipei." Ph.D. dissertation, New York University, 1973.

1593 Schlegel, Gustaaf. "A Canton Flower-boat." *Internationales Archiv für Ethnographie* 7(1894):1-9.

1594 *SCMP,* no. 1245 (Mar. 7, 1956). "Taiwan Women Live in Misery," p. 19.

1595 Seward, George. *Chinese Immigration and Its Social and Economical Aspects.* San Francisco: Edward Bosqui, 1881. [Includes discussion on the prostitution problem in California Chinatown.]

1596 Shepherd, Charles R. *The Ways of Ah Sin: A Composite Narrative of Things as They Are.* N.Y.: Fleming H. Revell, 1923. [Includes description of Tong control over Chinese women in American Chinatowns.]

1597 Stanford, Sally. *The Lady of the House: The Autobiography of Sally Stanford.* N.Y.: G. P. Putnam's Sons, 1966. [Contains description of Chinese prostitution establishments in San Francisco Chinatown during the 1920s.]

1598 Wei, W. L. "Sing-song Girls." *Mentor* 18(July 1930):12-15+.

1599 Wicher, Edward Arthur. *The Presbyterian Church in California, 1849-1927.* N.Y.: Frederick H. Hitchcock, 1927. [A story about a group of California Presbyterian women who helped Chinese girls escape a life of prostitution in San Francisco.]

1600 Wiley, James Hundley. "A Study of Chinese Prostitution." M.A. thesis, University of Chicago, 1928.

1601 Wong, Jayce Mende. "Prostitution: San Francisco Chinatown, Mid and Late-Nineteenth Century." *Bridge Magazine* 6(Winter 1978):2328.

1602 Yao, R. "Wild Flowers of Hong Kong." *Far Eastern Economic Review* 91(Jan. 9, 1976):25-26.

LABOR AND PRODUCTION IN MINORITY AREAS, THE PEOPLE'S REPUBLIC OF CHINA (1949-)

1603 "A Good Leader of the Masses." *China Reconstructs* 19(June 1970):39-41. [Biographical sketch of commune chairwoman in Inner Mongolian Autonomous Region.]

1604 "Inner Mongolian Women Progress in Struggle." *China Pictorial* 1977:4:34. [Depiction of shepherds.]

1605 "A Mother and Daughter Save the Commune's Sheep." *China Reconstructs* 17(Sept. 1968):27. [Heroism by commune members in Inner Mongolia.]

1606 Pei, Kuo-hung. "A Girls' Herding Team." *China Reconstructs* 18(Sept. 1969):32-34.

1607 *SCMP,* no. 1854 (Aug. 21, 1958). "New Aspect of Women of All Nationalities in Sinkiang," p. 13. [About women's productive work in the agricultural cooperatives.]

1608 *SCMP,* no. 2403 (Dec. 16, 1960). "People's Commune Provides Wide Opportunities for Women in Inner Mongolia," p. 18.

1609 *SCMP,* no. 2695 (Mar. 6, 1962). "Women of Minority Nationality in China Active in Public Services," p. 33.

1610 *SCMP,* no. 4860 (Mar. 8, 1971). "Women Drillers on Inner Mongolian Grassland," p. 135.

1611 *SCMP,* no. 4895 (Apr. 30, 1971). "Northwest China's Herdswoman Works for the Revolution," p. 82.

1612 *SCMP,* no. 4977 (Sept. 7, 1971). "Outstanding Kazakh Herdswoman," p. 227.

1613 *SCMP,* no. 5151 (May 30, 1972). "Shepherdesses in Inner Mongolia," p. 180.

1614 *SCMP,* no. "Two Tibetan Girls Praised for Protecting Collective Sheep in Blizzard," p. 65.

1615 *SCMP,* no. 5549 (June 14, 1974). The Red Detachment of Women Squad" of Kuchiningjulien Plant, Inner Monogolia. "Women Can Prop Up 'Half the Heaven,'" p. 163.

1616 *SPRCP,* no. 5855 (May 6, 1975). "Tibetan Women in Lhasa Fully Employed," p. 25.

1617 Teng, Yuan-ying. "A Miao Woman's Story." *China Reconstructs* 22(Aug. 1973):42-45. [Includes life and work in a production brigade.]

1618 Wu, Hsiao-ming. "Be a Good Daughter of the Poor Herdsmen" (Reportage). *Chinese Literature* 1968:11:51-59.

1619 Yang, Tse-feng. "Tibet's New Women Electrical Workers." *Women of China,* 1963:3:63-65.

LABOR AND PRODUCTION IN HONG KONG, TAIWAN AND OVERSEAS CHINA

1620 Armbruster, W. "Pressure on Wages in Taiwan." *Far Eastern Economic Review* 93(July 2, 1976):72-77. [The author argues that the shortage of woman power is an effective force in raising wages.]

1621 Arrigo, Linda Gail. "The Industrial Work Force of Young Women in Taiwan." *Bulletin of Concerned Asian Scholars* 12(Apr.-June 1980):25-38.

1622 Butters, H. R. *Report on Labour and Labour Conditions in Hong Kong.* Hong Kong: Government Printer, 1939.

1623 Cather, Helen Virginia. *The History of San Francisco Chinatown.* San Francisco: R. & E. Research Association, 1974. [Includes discussion of Chinese women workers in shoe-tailoring and tobacco businesses.]

1624 Chang, Ching-hsi. "Female Labor Force Participation in Taiwan." Ph.D. dissertation, Ohio State University, 1978.

1625 *Chinese-American Workers: Past and Present—An Anthology of "Getting Together."* N.d. [See chapter 3, "Working Women," pp. 49-66.]

1626 Diamond, Norma. "Women and Industry in Taiwan." *Modern China* 5(July 1979):317-40.

1627 Fong, Patricia M. "The 1938 National Dollar Store Strike," *Asian American Review* 2(1975):1. [Includes discussion of Chinese women workers and their organization in Chinatown.]

1628 Gamarekian, E. "Hong Kong's Forgotten Girls." *United Asia* 15(June 1963):432-35.

1629 Hirata, Lucie Cheng. "Chinese Immigrant Women in Nineteenth Century California." In *Women of America: A History,* ed. Carol Ruth Berkin and Mary Beth Norton. Boston: Houghton Mifflin, 1979. [A discussion of the occupations of the early Chinese immigrant women including working women, housewives, prostitutes, etc.]

1630 Hong Kong, Colonial Secretariat. *Report on Women's Salary Scales in the Public Service.* Hong Kong: S. Young Government Printer, 1962.

1631 Hopkins, Keith. *Hong Kong, the Industrial Colony.* London: Oxford University, 1971. [See pp. 34-42 and *passim.*]

1632 Kung, Lydia. "Factory Work and Women in Taiwan: Changes in Self-image and Status." *Signs* 2(Aug. 1976)35-58.

1633 Kung, Lydia. "Factory Work, Women, and the Family in Taiwan." Ph.D. dissertation, Yale University, 1978.

1634 Kung, Shien-Woo. *Chinese in American Life: Some Aspects of Their History, Status, Problems and Contributions.* Seattle: University of Washington Press, 1962. [Includes discussion on the adjustment of Chinese women to various kinds of occupation.]

1635 Lan, Dean. "The Chinatown Sweatshops: Oppression and an Alternative." *Amerasia J.* 1(Nov. 1971)3. [Includes issue of the oppression and exploitation of Chinese women workers in Chinatown garment industry.]

1636 Loomis, Augustus Ward. "Chinese Women in California." *Overland* 2(Apr. 1869).

1637 "Notes on the Clothing Industry in Hong Kong." *International Labour Review* 92(Dec. 1965):506-511.

1638 Royal Asiatic Society, Hong Kong Branch. *Aspects of Social Organization in the New Territory.* Hong Kong, 1964. [See Ronald Ng, "Economic Life and the Family," pp.32-35.]

1639 Salaff, Janet W. "Hong Kong: Inside the Factory." *Ms.* 3(Feb. 1975):106-107.

1640 Salaff, Janet W. *Working Daughters of Hong Kong.* N.Y.: Cambridge University, 1981.

1641 Soo, Annie. "The Life, Influence and Role of the Chinese Women in the United States, Specifically in the West, 1906-1966." In *The Life, Influence and the Role of the Chinese in the United States, 1776-1960.* Proceedings/Papers of the National Conference Held at the University of San Francisco, July 10, 11, 12, 1975. San Francisco: Chinese History Society of America, 1976.

1642 Sung, Betty Lee. *Chinese American Manpower and Employment.* A Report to Manpower Administration, U.S. Department of Labor, 1975. [Topics covered include working women.]

1643 Wong, Aline K. "Rising Social Status and Economic Participation of Women in Hong Kong: Review of a Decade." *Southeast Asia J. of Social Science* 1(1973):2:11-27.

1644 Wong, Fai-ming. *Maternal Employment and Family Taskpower Differentiation among Lower Income Chinese Families.* Hong Kong: Chinese University of Hong Kong, Social Research Center, 1972.

Literature, Art and Folklore

LANGUAGE AND LINGUISTICS

1645 Arlington, Lewis Charles. "The Chinese Female Names." *China J.* 1(July 1923):316-25; 1(Sept. 1923):454-62; 1(Nov. 1923):561-71.

1646 Chao, Y. R. [Chao, Yuan-jen]. "Chinese Terms of Address." *Language* 32(Jan.-Mar. 1956):217-41.

1647 Chen, Ta [Ch'en, Ta] and Shyrock, John Knight. "Chinese Relationship Terms." *American Anthropologist,* new (2nd) series, 34(Oct.-Dec. 1932):623-99.

1648 Fu, Mao-chi. "The Solo Kinship Terms as Affected by the Sex of the Speaker." *Asia Minor,* new series, 2, Part 1 (Apr. 1951), pp. 68-70.

1649 Hsu, Francis L. K. [Hsü, Lang-kuang]. "On a Technique for Studying Relationship Terms." *American Anthropologist,* new (2nd) series, 49(Oct.-Dec. 1947):618-24.

1650 Scarborough, William. "Chinese Modes of Address: A Chapter in Native Etiquette." *Chinese Recorder* 10(May-June 1879):187-97; 10(July-Aug. 1879):261-69; 10(Sept.-Oct. 1879):337-48.

1651 Wu, Ching-chao [Wu Ching-ch'ao]. "The Chinese Family: Organization, Names and Kinship Terms." *American Anthropologist,* new (2nd) series, 29(July-Sept. 1927):316-25.

FOLKLORE AND FOLKLORE STUDIES

1652 Anderson, Eugene N. Jr. "The Folksongs of the Hong Kong Boat People." *J. of American Folkore* 80(1967):285-96. [Also in his *Essays on China's Boat People,* pp. 21-32. Taipei: Orient Cultural Service, 1972.]

1653 Anon. *The Flower Lover and the Fairies.* Trans. Chi-chen Wang. N.Y.: Archway Press, 1946.

1654 "The Ballad of Meng Chiang Nü Weeping at the Great Wall." Trans. Joseph Needham and Hung-ying Liao. *Sinologica* 1(1948):194-209.

1655 Blake, Fred C. "Death and Abuse in Marriage Laments: The Curse of Chinese Brides." *Asian Folklore Studies* 37(1978):1:13-33.

1656 Carpenter, Frances. *Tales of a Chinese Grandmother.* Rutland, Vt.: C.E. Tuttle, 1973. [Popular folktales from E. T. C. Werner's "Myths and Legends of China," Dr. John C. Ferguson's "Chinese Mythology," etc.]

1657 "The Chastity Arch." (East Shantung folk tale) *China Reconstructs* 2(Mar. 1953):24-25.

1658 "The Cloud Maiden, Yang Mei-ching." *Chinese Literature* 1959:8:3-35. [Folk tales of the Bai minority.]

1659 "The Conch Maiden." *Chinese Literature* 1959:3:49-56. [Tibetan folk tales.]

1660 Eberhard, Wolfram. "The Girl That Became a Bird: A Comparative Study." In *Semitic and Oriental Studies,* ed. Walter J. Fischel, pp. 79-86. Berkeley, 1951.

1661 Eberhard, Wolfram, ed. *Folktales of China,* revised ed. Folktales of the World Series. Chicago: University of Chicago, 1965. [See chapter 3, "Tales of Love," pp. 21-38; chapter 4, "Supernatural Marriages," pp. 41-69.]

1662 Eberhard, Wolfram. *Studies in Taiwanese Folktales.* Taibei: Orient Cultural Service, 1974.

1663 Eberhard, Wolfram. *Chinese Fables and Parables.* Taipei: Oriental Cultural Service, 1974.

1664 Hensman, Bertha and Mack, Kwok-Ping, trans. *Hong Kong Talespinners: A Collection of Tales and Ballads Transcribed and Translated from Story-tellers in Hong Kong.* Hong Kong: Chinese University of Hong Kong, 1968.

1665 Hensman, Bertha, trans. *More Hong Kong Talespinners: Twenty-five Traditional Chinese Tales and Ballads Collected by Tape-recorder and Translated into English by Bertha Hensman.* Hong Kong: Chinese University of Hong Kong, 1971.

1666 Hsu, Yu. *Woman in the Mist and Two Other Tales Set in Hong Kong and China.* Hong Kong: Rainbow Press, 1961.

1667 Hummel, Siegbert. "The Three Sisters in the Ge-Sar Epic." *Bulletin of Tibetology* 11(July 23, 1974):5-12.

1668 Ishida, Euchiro. "The Mother-Son Complex in East Asiatic Religion and Folkore." *Wiener Schuler der Volkerkunde, Festschrift,* 1956, pp. 411-19.

1669 Johnson, Kinchen, trans. *Folksongs and Children's Songs from Peiping.* 2 vols. Asian Folklore and Social Life Monographs 16. Taipei: Orient Cultural Service, 1971. [Chinese and English. Original preface dated 1932.]

1670 Li, Chao-wei. "The Dragon King's Daughter." *Chinese Literature* 1954:2:189-98. [A folk tale.]

1671 Liu, Ching-an. *Women in Folksongs.* Folklore and Folkliterature series, no. 34. Peking: National Peking University and Chinese Association for Folklore.

1672 *Love Under the Willows* [Szechuan opera]. Trans. Hsien-yi Yang and Gladys Yang. Peking: Foreign Language Press, 1956. [Based on the folk story "Liang Shanbo and Zhu Yingtai."]

1673 Lu Hsun [Chou, Shu-jen]. "The Hanging Woman." *Chinese Literature* 1956:3:115-20. [Written in 1936. Discusses a unique kind of ghost in Shaoxing opera.]

1674 *Meng Chiang Nü (Chinese Drum Song), the Lady of the Long Wall, a Ku-shih, or Drum Song of China.* Trans. Genevieve Wimsatt and Geoffrey Chen. N.Y.: Columbia University, 1934.

1675 "The Peacock Maiden." Trans. Alex Young. *Chinese Literature* 1958:4:80-95. [A new version of the Tai legend.]

1676 "A Princess Gets Smacked" [Shansi opera]. *Chinese Literature* 1961:8:83-111. [Local comedy based on folk legend.]

1677 Radin, Paul. *The Golden Mountain: Chinese Tales Told in California.* Taipei: Orient Cultural Service, 1972. [Includes many female ghost stories, such as the ghost wife, the marriage festival of the ghosts, the woman with a long tongue, etc.]

1678 Satoh, May Miki. "Women in Chinese Folksongs." *Eastern Asia* 5(Spring 1941):59-64.

1679 Schaffer, Edward H. *The Vermilion Bird: T'ang Images of the South.* Berkeley: University of California, 1967. [See chapter 4, "Women."]

1680 Schaffer, Edward H. *The Divine Woman: Dragon Ladies and Rain Maidens in T'ang Literature.* Berkeley: University of California, 1973.

1681 Schaffer, Edward H. "Dragon-Women in Medieval Prose Literature." In *Papers of the C.I.C. Far Eastern Language Institute,* 4, ed. Richard B. Mather, pp. 48-62. Ann Arbor: Committee on Institutional Cooperation, 1973.

1682 *The Seven Sisters: Selected Chinese Folk Stories.* Peking: Foreign Languages Press, 1965.

1683 Sheng, Chiang. *The Forsaken Wife (A Chinese Folktale).* Peking: Foreign Languages Press, 1958.

1684 Shephard, Esther. *The Cowherd and the Sky Maiden.* San Jose, Calif.: Pacific Rim Publishers, 1950.

1685 "The Sisters' Festival of the Miaos." *China Pictorial* 393(Mar. 1981):12-14. [A pictorial story of the Miao Sisters' Festival held annually on the 15th day of the 3rd lunar month in Guizhou.]

1686 Soong, Mayling. *Little Sister Su, a Chinese Folk Tale.* N.Y.: John Day, 1942.

1687 Ting, Nai-tung. "The Holy Man and the Snake Woman; A Study of a Lamia Story in Asian and European Literature." *Fabula* 8(1966):3:145-91.

1688 Waley, Arthur. "The Chinese Cinderella Story." *Folk-lore* 58(1947):226-38.

1689 "A Woman's Love." *Chinese Literature* 1956:3:130. [A Uighur folktale.]

1690 Wu, Pei-yi. "The White Snake: The Evolution of a Myth in China." Ph.D. dissertation, Columbia, 1969.

1691 Yang, Mei-ching. "The Cloud Maiden." Trans. Hsien-yi Yang and Gladys Yang. *Chinese Literature* 1959:8:3-35. [Narrative poem, based on the folk legend of the Dali Bai minority in Yunnan.]

ANTHOLOGIES: TRADITIONAL FICTION, POETRY AND DRAMA (TO 1911)

1692 Birch, Cyril. *Stories from a Ming Collection: Translations of Chinese Short Stories Published in the 17th Century.* N.Y.: Grove Press, 1958. [Contains love stories. "The Lady Who Was a Beggar" (pp. 15-36) is a romance. "The Pearl-Sewn Shirt" (pp. 37-96) illustrates the moral standard forced upon women by tradition.]

1693 Birch, Cyril, ed. *Anthology of Chinese Literature,* vol. 1, *From Early Times to the 14th Century;* vol. 2, *From the 14th Century to the Present Day.* N.Y.: Grove Press, 1972. [Includes works on women and by women.]

1694 Chai, Ch'u and Chai, Winberg, trans. and eds. *A Treasury of Chinese Literature: A New Prose Anthology Including Fiction and Drama.* N.Y.: Appleton-Century, 1965. [Includes such works on women as "The Lady Yü-nu: A Beggarchief's Daughter," etc.]

1695 Chang, H. C., trans. *Chinese Literature: Popular Fiction and Drama.* Edinburgh: Edinburgh University Press, 1973. [Includes "Madam White," "Flowers in the Mirror," etc.]

1696 Cornaby, William Arthur. *A String of Chinese Peace-Stones.* London: C.H. Kelly, 1895. [Chinese tales, anecdotes and literary references strung together on a thread of narrative and picturing the village life of central China during the period of the Taiping Rebellion, 1849-67.]

1697 *The Dragon King's Daughter, Ten T'ang Dynasty Stories.* Peking: Foreign Languages Press, 1954.

1698 *Eastern Shame Girl and Other Stories.* N.Y.: Avon Book Co, 1947. [Love stories of the 17th century.]

1699 Edwards, E. D. *Chinese Prose Literature of the T'ang Period.* 2 vols. London: Probsthain, 1937. [Contains some love stories.]

1700 Feng, Meng-lung. *The Perfect Laay by Mistake.* Trans. William Dolby. London: Paul Elek, 1976. [Six stories from Feng Menglong's 17th-century collection *Sanyan.*]

1701 Fisher, Welthy, Mrs. (Honsinger). *A String of Chinese Pearls: Ten Tales of Chinese Girls Ancient and Modern.* N.Y.: Women's Press, 1924.

1702 Howell, E. Butts, trans. *The Inconstancy of Madam Chuang, and Other Stories from the Chinese.* Shanghai: Kelly and Walsh, 19__; London: T.W. Laurie, 1924. [Stories from *Jingu qiguan* by Feng Menglong.]

1703 *The Illusory Flame (Hsiang-yen tsung-shu).* Trans. Howard S. Levy. Tokyo, 1962. [Ten love stories from the Qing anthology *Xiangyan congshu*.]

1704 Kashiwagi, Toshio. *Selected Poems of Chinese Poetesses from the Han to Qing Dynasties.* Trans. Hideho Naka. Tokyo: Japan Federation of Composers, c. 1973.

1705 Lin, Yü-t'ang [Lin, Yü-t'ang], trans. *A Nun of Taishan and Other Translations.* Shanghai: Commercial Press, 1936.

1706 Lin, Yutang [Lin, Yü-t'ang], trans. and adapt. *Widow, Nun, and Courtesan: Three Novelettes from the Chinese.* Reprint of the 1951 ed. Westport, Conn.: Greenwood, 1971. [The second story is a partial translation of *Laocan youji*; the third one is based on a *Sanyan* story]

1707 Liu, Jung-en, trans. *Six Yüan Plays.* Penguin, 1977. [Includes stories about women such as "The Soul of Ch'ien-nü Leaves Her Body," "The Injustice Done to Tou Ngo," etc.]

1708 Ma, Y. W. and Lau, Joseph S. M. *Traditional Chinese Stories: Themes and Variations.* Columbia University Press, 1978. [See stories under the following thematic headings: "The Knight-errant," "The Heartless Lover," "The Dedicated Lover," "The Reunited Couple," "The Femme Fatale," "The Superhuman Maiden," and "The Ghost Wife."]

1709 P'u, Sung-ling. *Strange Stories from a Chinese Studio.* Trans. Herbert Giles. Shanghai: Kelly and Walsh, 1916. [Translation of *Liaozhai*. Many stories about female ghosts.]

1710 Quong, Rose, trans. *Chinese Ghost and Love Stories, a Selection from the Liao-chai by P'u Sung-ling.* N.Y.: Pantheon, 1946.

1711 Rexroth, Kenneth and Chung, Ling, trans. and ed. *The Orchid Boat: Women Poets of China.* N.Y.: McGraw-Hill, 1972.

1712 Souile, Charles George, comp. and trans. *Chinese Love Tales* Garden City, N.Y.: Halcyon House, 1950. [Translation from the original French of George Souile. N.Y.: Three Sirens Press, 1935.]

1713 Waley, Arthur. *Translations from the Chinese.* N.Y.: Random House, 1971. [Contains poems by various Chinese poets, from the 4th century B.C. to the 12th century A.D., some on women.]

1714 Wang, Elizabeth Te-chen. *Ladies of the T'ang: Twenty-two Classical Chinese Stories.* Taipei: Heritage Press, 1961.

1715 Yang, Hsien-yi and Yang, Gladys. *The Courtesan's Jewel Box: Chinese Stories of the 10th–16th Centuries.* Peking: Foreign Languages Press, 1957.

1716 Yen, W. W., trans. *Stories of Old China.* Peking: Foreign Languages Press, 1958. [Covers period from the Tang to the Qing. Includes "Love and Loyalty of a Courtesan," etc.]

TRADITIONAL FICTION, POETRY AND DRAMA: THROUGH THE YUAN DYNASTY (TO 1368)

1717 "The Bride of Chiao Chung-ch'ing." *Chinese Literature* 1959:4:3–15. [A "yuan-fu song," a classical narrative poem written around 3 A.D.]

1718 Chang, Tsu. *The Dwelling of Playful Goddesses: China's First Novelette (Yu-hsien-k'u).* Annotated trans. Howard Levy. Tokyo: Dai Nippon Insatsu, 1965. [A late 7th-century or early 8th-century work, blending poetry with parallel prose, about the romantic encounter of a scholar official with two fairy-goddesses.]

1719 Foster, J. "Love for Yang Kuei Fei, the Ballad of the Eternal Sorrow." *China J. of Science and Art* 4(1926):115–19.

1720 Kao, Ming. *The Two Wives.* N.p, n.d. [Yuan drama about marriage. English translation from the German version by Vincenz Hundhausen. No translator is given.]

1721 Li, Ch'ing-chao*. *The Lady and the Hermit: Thirty Chinese Poems by Li Ch'ing-chao of the Sung and Wang Fan-chih of the T'ang.* A New Translation by Vincent McHugh and C.H. Kwôck. San Francisco: Golden Mountain Press, 1962.

1722 Li, Ch'ing-chao*. *Li Ch'ing-chao, Complete Poems.* Trans. and ed. Kenneth Rexroth and Ling Chung. N.Y.: New Directions, 1979.

1723 Li, Hsing-tao. *The Circle of Chalk.* Trans. James Laver. London: W. Heinemann, 1929. [Yuan drama about marriage. Translation frm a German version by Klabund.]

1724 Li, Hsing-tao. *The Story of the Circle of Chalk.* Trans. Frances Hume. London: Rodale Press, 1954. [Translation from Stanislas Julien's French version.]

1725 Pai, Hsing-chien. "Story of a Singsong Girl." *Chinese Literature* 1954:2:198–207.

1726 Pei, Hsing. "Nieh Yin-niang." Trans. Tze-yen Pan. *China J. of Science and Art* 17(1932):204–207. [Translation of a Tang dynasty short story about a girl knight-errant.]

1727 Po, Chü-i. *The Everlasting Woe.* Trans. Jen Tai. Shanghai: Zhonghua Book Co., 1939. [Ballad of Yang Guifei.]

1728 Po, Hsing-chien. "The Story of Miss Li." Trans. Arthur Waley. In *Anthology of Chinese Literature,* vol. 1, ed. Cyril Birch, pp. 300–313. N.Y.: Grove Press, 1965.

1729 "Scholar Ts'ui and the Fairy Maiden." Trans. Tze-yen Pan. *Chinese J. of Science and Art* 1933:19:284–86. [A fairy love story set in the Tang dynasty.]

1730 Shih, Chung-wen. *Injustice to Tou O (Tou O yüan); a Study and Translation.* Princeton-Cambridge Studies in Linguistics 4. Cambridge, England: Cambridge University Press, 1972. [A Yuan drama.]

1731 Sung, Yüh. "Shen-nü-fu, the Song of the Goddess." Trans. E. Erkes. *T'oung Pao* 25(1928):387–402. [Rhyme-prose written in the Warring States period in which an emperor meets a goddess in a dream.]

1732 Yüan, Chen. "The Story of Ts'ui Ying-ying." Trans. Arthur Waley. In *Anthology of Chinese Literature,* vol. 1, ed., Cyril Birch, pp. 290–99. N.Y.: Grove Press, 1965. [Tang romance.]

TRADITIONAL FICTION, POETRY AND DRAMA: THE MING-QING DYNASTIES (TO 1911)

1733 Anon. *The Adventures of Hsi Men Ching.* Trans. Anon. N.Y.: Privately Printed for the Library of Facetious Lore, 1927. [Translation of *Jin Ping Mei*, erotic novel of the Ming.]

1734 Anon. *Chin P'ing Mei: The Adventurous History of Hsi Men and His Six Wives.* Trans. Bernard Miall. London: John Lane, 1939. [Translation of Franz Kuhn's German abridged version. Another edition: N.Y.: Putnam, 1940; reprint: Capricorn Books, 1962.]

1735 Anon. *The Golden Lotus.* Trans. Clement Egerton. London: Routledge, 1939. 4 vols. [Other editions: N.Y.: Paragon Book Gallery, 1962; London: Routledge & K. Paul, 1972. Unabridged translation of *Jin Ping Mei*.]

1736 Anon. "Hsi Men and the Gold Lotus." Trans. Bernard Miall. In *Chinese Wit and Humor*, ed. George Kao, pp. 126-48. N.Y: Coward-McCann, 1946.

1737 Anon. "Chin P'ing Mei." Trans. Ch'u Chai and Winberg Chai. In *A Treasury of Chinese Literature*, ed. Ch'u Chai and Winberg Chai, pp. 235-48. N.Y.: Appleton-Century, 1965. [Chapter 1 of *Jin Ping Mei*.]

1738 "The Beggar Chief's Daughter." *Chinese Literature* 1955:3:108-119. [Short story of the Ming dynasty.]

1739 "Ch'en Yuan-yuan." Trans. Tze-yen Pan. *China J. Of Science and Art* 17(1932):260-65. [Story about a famous courtesan during the Ming-Qing transition.]

1740 *Ch'un-meng-so-yen, Trifling Tale of a Spring Dream.* Trans. Robert H. van Gulik. Tokyo, 1950. [A Ming erotic story.]

1741 *Dee Goong An.* Trans. Robert H. van Gulik. Tokyo, 1949. [An 18th-century detective story in which several women play notable roles.]

1742 *Eighteen Songs of a Nomad Flute: The Story of Lady Wen-chi; a Fourteenth-Century Handscroll in the Metropolitan Museum of Art.* Trans. Robert A. Rorex and Wen Fong. N.Y.: New York Metropolitan Museum of Art; distributed by Greenwich, Conn.: New York Graphic Society, 1974.

1743 Feng, Menglong. *The Oil Vendor and the Singsong Girl.* Trans. Fritz Ruesch. N.Y.: F. Ruesch, 1938. [Translation from the German version of Vincenz Hundhausen.]

1744 Feng, Menglong. "Eastern Shame Girl." In *Eastern Shame Girl*, trans. Charles George Souile, pp. 7-31. N.Y.: Avon Book Co., 1947. [Ming short story about a courtesan.]

1745 Feng, Menglong. "The Courtesan's Jewel Box." *Chinese Literature* 1955:3:90-107.

1746 Feng, Menglong. *Tse Hiong Hiong Ti, The Two Brothers of Different Sex.* Trans. Frances Hume. London: Rodale Press, 1955. [A late Ming story. Translation from Stanislas Julien's French version.]

1747 Feng, Menglong. "The Clerk's Lady." In *Chinese Literature: Popular Fiction and Drama*, trans. H. C. Chang, pp. 179-204. Edinburgh: Edinburgh University, 1973.

1748 Feng, Menglong. "Madam White." In *Chinese Literature: Popular Fiction and Drama*, trans. H. C. Chang, pp. 205-262. Edinburgh: Edinburgh University, 1973. [A short story of the Ming dynasty based on the white snake legend.]

1749 Feng, Menglong. "The Shrew." In *Chinese Literature: Popular Fiction and Drama*, trans. H. C. Chang, pp. 22-56. Edinburgh: Edinburgh University, 1973.

1750 *The Fortunate Union.* Trans. Sir John F. Davis. London, 1829. [Scholar-beauty novel of the Ming dynasty.]

1751 Hung, Sheng. "The Palace of Eternal Youth." *Chinese Literature* 1954:4:69-105. [Excerpt from a Qing drama on Yang Guifei.]

1752 Hung, Sheng. *The Palace of Eternal Youth.* Trans. Hsien-yi and Gladys Yang. Peking: Foreign Languages Press, 1955. [A Qing drama on Yang Guifei.]

1753 "The Lady in the Picture." Trans. Tao Cheng and Tang Sheng. *Chinese Literature* 1955:4:145-50.

1754 Li, Ju-chen. "A Journey into Strange Lands." *Chinese Literature* 1958:1:76-122. [Excerpt from *Jinghua yuan*, the Qing novel set in the court of the Tang Empress Wu.]

1755 Li, Ju-chen. *Flowers in the Mirror (Ching-hua-yuan).* Trans. Tai-yi Lin. Berkeley: University of California Press, 1965.

1756 Li, Ju-chen. "In the Country of Women." Trans. Cyril Birch. In *Anthology of Chinese Literature*, vol. 2, ed. Cyril Birch, pp. 187-88. N.Y.: Grove Press, 1972. [Translation of Chapter 33 of *Jinghua yuan*.]

1757 Li, Ju-chen. "The Women's Kingdom." In *Chinese Literature: Popular Fiction and Drama*, trans. H. C. Chang, pp. 405-466. Edinburgh: Edinburgh University Press, 1973. [Translation of chapters 32-37 of *Jinghua yuan*.]

1758 Li, Yü. *Jou P'u T'uan: The Prayer Mat of Flesh.* Trans. Richard Martin. N.Y.: Grove Press, 1963. [17th-century pornographic novel. Translation from Franz Kuhn's German version.]

1759 Li, Yü. *Twelve Towers.* Trans. Nathan Mao. Hong Kong: Chinese University Press, 1979. [Sex relations are predominant themes in these 17th-century stories.]

1760 Lin, Yutang. *Widow Chuan Retold by Lin Yutang.* London and Melbourne: W. Heinemann, 1952. [Translation based on *Zhuan Jia Zhun* by Lao Xiang.]

1761 Liu, T'ieh-yün. "The Singing Girl." Trans. Arthur Waley. *Asia* [Asia and the Americas] 19(1929):876-77, 904-906. [Selections from *Laocan youji*.]

1762 "The Mandarin Duck Girdle." In Acton, H. and Lee Yi-hsieh, *Four Cautionary Tales*. N.Y.: A. A. Wyn, 1948. [A Ming tale about licentious Buddhist nuns.]

1763 Mo, Shih-lung. "Saying Goodbye to a Singing Girl." Trans. Jonathan Chaves. *Asia* 1(Nov.-Dec. 1978):14-17. [Mo Shilong (1540-1587) was a Ming poet.]

1764 P'u, Sung-ling. "A Crow Wife." Trans. Tze-yen Pan. *China J. of Science and Art* 1933:18:175-78. [Translation from *Liaozhai jiyi*.]

1765 P'u, Sung-ling. *The Painted Skin.* Trans. Fan-chin Yu. Peking: Foreign Languages Press, 1957.

1766 "The Resourceful Woman." Trans. Tze-yen Pan. *China J. of Science and Art* 1933:19:55-56. [A short story about a woman warrior.]

1767 *The Runaway Maid.* Revised by The Cantonese Opera Company of Kwangtung. Trans. Gladys Yang. Peking: Foreign Languages Press, 1958.

1768 T'ang, Hsien-tsu. "Ch'un-hsiang Nao Hsüeh ...." Trans. H. Acton. *T'ien-hsia Monthly* 8(Apr. 1939):357-72. [A Ming comedy in which a girl is revived by her dream lover.]

1769 Ting, Yao-k'ang. *Flower Shadows behind the Curtain.* (Ko Lien Hua Ying) Trans. Vladimir Kean. N.Y.: Pantheon Books, 1959. [Translation of *Xu Jin Ping Mei* (sequel to *Jin Ping Mei*.) from Franz Kuhn's German version.]

1770 Ts'ao Hsüeh-ch'in. *Dream of the Red Chamber.* Trans. Chi-chen Wang. Garden City, N.Y.: Doubleday, Doran, 1929. [Another edition: N.Y.: Anchor Doubleday, 1958. Abridged translation of *Hong lou meng*, renowned 18th-century novel of gentry domestic life. Its leading female characters are considered archetypical.]

1771 Ts'ao Hsüeh-ch'in. *The Dream of the Red Chamber.* Trans. Florence and Isabel McHugh. N.Y.: Pantheon, 1958. [Translation of Franz Kuhn's abridged German version.]

1772 Ts'ao Hsüeh-ch'in. "Dream of the Red Chamber." Trans. Hsien-yi Yang and Gladys Yang. *Chinese Literature* 1964:6:38-82; 1964:7:44-75; 1964:8:41-95. [Translation of chapters 18, 19, 20, 32,33, 34, 74, 75, 77 of the novel.]

1773 Ts'ao Hsüeh-ch'in. "A Burial Mound for Flowers." Trans. H. C. Chang. In *Chinese Literature: Popular Fiction and Drama,* pp. 383–403. Edinburgh: Edinburgh University Press, 1973.

1774 Ts'ao, Hsüeh-ch'in [Cao, Xueqin]. *The Story of the Stone,* vol. 1, *The Golden Days.* Trans. David Hawkes. Baltimore: Penguin Books, 1973. [Unabridged translation of chapters 1–26 of *Hong lou meng.*]

1775 Ts'ao, Hsüeh-ch'in [Cao, Xueqin]. *The Story of the Stone,* vol. 2, *The Crabtree Club.* Trans. David Hawkes. Baltimore: Penguin Books, 1973. [Unabridged translation of chapters 27–53 of *Hong lou meng.*

1776 Wang, Shih-fu. *The Romance of the Western Chamber.* Trans. S. I. Hsiung. London: Methuen, 1935. [A Ming romantic drama based on the Tang story "Story of Ts'ui Ying Ying."]

1777 Wang, Shih-fu. *The West Chamber.* Trans. Henry H. Hart. Stanford: Stanford University, 1936.

1778 Wang, Shih-fu. "The Romance of the Western Chamber." Trans. Chieh-yuan Tung. *Renditions: A Chinese-English Translation Magazine,* no. 7 (Spring 1977), pp. 115–31. [Excerpt from the Ming drama.]

CRITICAL STUDIES: TRADITIONAL LITERATURE

1779 Brandauer, Frederick P. "Women in the Ching-hua yüan: Emancipation toward a Confucian Ideal." *J. of Asian Studies* 36(Aug. 1977):647–60.

1780 Ch'en, Toyoko Yoshida. "Women in Confucian Society—a Study of Three T'an-tz'u Narratives." Ph.D. dissertation, Columbia University, 1974.

1781 Cheng, Stephen H. L. "Some Aspects of *Flowers of Shanghai.*" *Tamkang Review* 9(Fall 1978):51–65. [A study of *Hai shang hua liezhuan,* a late Qing courtesan novel.]

1782 Cheng, Stephen H. L. "*Flowers of Shanghai* and the Late Ch'ing Courtesan Novels." Ph.D. dissertation, Harvard University, 1980.

1783 Chuang, Hsin-cheng. "Themes of Dream of the Red Chamber: A Comparative Interpretation." Ph.D. dissertation, University of Indiana, 1966.

1784 Chuang, Shen. "Ming and Ch'ing Exotica: A Reflection of Literary Taste." *J. of Oriental Studies* 9(Jan. 1971):92–131.

1785 Crawford, William Bruce. "Beyond the Garden Wall: A Critical Study of Three Ts'ai-tzu Chia-jen [scholar-beauty] Novels." Ph.D. dissertation, Indiana University, 1972.

1786 Eberhard, Wolfram. "Ideas about Social Reform in the Novel Ching-hua yüan." In *Festschrift für A Jensen,* pp. 113–21. Munich, 1964.

1787 Evans, Nancy Jane Francis. "Social Criticism in the Ch'ing: The Novel Ching-hua yüan." *Papers on China,* 23(July 1970):52–66.

1788 Fish, Michael B. "Yang Kuei-fei as the Hsi Wang Mu: Secondary Narrative in Two T'ang Poems." *Monumenta Serica* 32(1976):337–54.

1789 Fu, James S. "Liu Lao-lao and the Garden of Takuanyüan." *Literature East and West* 17(1973):305–314.

1790 Giles, H. A. "Women in Chinese Literature." *19th Century* 56(Nov. 1904):820–32. [Also appears in *Living Age,* no. 243 (Dec. 24, 1904), pp. 810–820.]

1791 Giles, H. A. "Mr. Waley and the 'Lute Girl's Song.'" *New China Review* 3(1921):281–88. [Mr. Waley's reply is on pp. 376–77 of the same issue.]

1792 Grieder, Jerome B. "The Communist Critique of *Hung Lou Meng.*" *Papers on China,* 10, pp. 142–68. Harvard University Committee on Regional Studies, 1956.

1793 Hanan, Patrick. "The Making of the Pearl-Sewn Shirt and the Courtesan's Jewel Box." *Harvard J. of Asiatic Studies* 33(1973):124–53.

1794 Hawkes, David. "The Quest of the Goddess." *Asia Major* 13(1967):71–94. [On the Chu poems. Also appears in *Studies in Chinese Literary Genres,* ed. Cyril Birch, pp. 42–68. Berkeley, 1974.]

1795 Hegel, Robert E. "Dream of the Red Chamber." *Orientations* 3(Sept. 1972):51–58.

1796 Hessney, Richard Charles. "Beautiful, Talented, and Brave: Seventeenth-Century Chinese Scholar-Beauty Romances." Ph.D. dissertation, Columbia University, 1979.

1797 Heyer, Virginia. "Relations between Men and Women in Chinese Stories." In *The Study of Culture at a Distance,* ed. Margaret Mead and Rhoda Metraux, pp. 211–34. Chicago: University of Chicago, 1953.

1798 Hightower, James R. "Yüan Chen and the Story of Yingying." *Harvard J. of Asiatic Studies* 33(1973):90–123. [A discussion of Yuan Zhen's "The Story of Yingying," a Tang love story.]

1799 Hsia, C. T. [Hsia, Chih-ch'ing]. "Love and Compassion in Dream of the Red Chamber." *Criticism* 5(Summer 1963):261–71.

1800 Hsia, C. T. [Hsia, Chih-ch'ing]. *The Classical Chinese Novel.* N.Y. and London: Columbia University, 1968. [See the section "Dream of the Red Chamber," pp. 245–97.]

1801 Hsia, C. T. [Hsia, Chih-ch'ing]. "The Military Romance." In *Studies in Chinese Literary Genres,* ed. Cyril Birch, pp. 339–90. Berkeley: University of California Press, 1974.

1802 Hsia, C. T. [Hsia, Chih-ch'ing]. "The Scholar-Novelist and Chinese Culture: A Reappraisal of *Ching-hua yüan* [Flowers in the Mirror]." In *Chinese Narrative: Critical and Theoretical Essays,* ed. Andrew H. Plaks, pp. 266–308. Princeton: Princeton University, 1977.

1803 Hu, Shih. "A Chinese Declaration of the Rights of Women." *Chinese Social and Political Review* 8(1924):2:100–109. [On the *Jinghua yuan* by Li Ruzhen.]

1804 Hu, Shih. "A Chinese Gulliver on Woman's Rights." *People's Tribune,* new series 7(1934):121–127; *China Review* 4(1935):1:31–33. [On the *Jinghua yuan.*]

1805 Ingalls, Jeremy. "Mr. Ch'ing-yin and the Chinese Erotic Novel." *Yearbook of Comparative and General Literature* 13(1964):60–63. [Review of Franz Kuhn's translation of *Rou putuan.* Reviewer's remarks are based on Richard Martin's English version of Kuhn's German translation.]

1806 Knoerle, Jeanne. *The Dream of the Red Chamber: A Critical Study.* Bloomington: Indiana University, 1972.

1807 Levy, Howard S. "Love Themes in T'ang Literature." *Orient/West* 7(Jan. 1962):67–78.

1808 Li, Chang-chih. "Some Notes on *Flower in the Mirror.*" *Chinese Literature* 1958:1:144–48.

1809 Lin, Yutang. "Appreciation of the Red Chamber Dream." *Renditions: A Chinese-English Translation Magazine,* no. 2 (Spring 1974), pp. 23–30.

1810 Liu, James J. Y. *The Chinese Knight Errant.* Chicago: University of Chicago, 1967. [Includes discussion of female knight errants: "The Maiden of Yüeh," "Hung-hsien," "Nieh Yin-niang," and "Ts'ui Shen-ssu's Wife," pp. 85–97, 164–66.]

1811 Lu Hsün [Chou, Shu-jen]. *A Brief History of Chinese Fiction.* Peking Foreign Languages Press, 1959. [Contains material on women both as writers and as subjects of fiction.]

1812 McAleavy, Henry. "Tseng P'u and the *Nieh Hai Hua.*" *St. Antony's Papers,* 7, pp. 88-137. London: Chatto & Windus, 1960. [A study of a biographical novel of Sai Jinhua (1874-1936), a famous Chinese courtesan.]

1813 Mao, Nathan K. "The Tradition of Seduction in Chinese Literature." *Enquiry* 1(1967):3:1-11.

1814 Miller, Lucien M. *Masks of Fiction in Hung-lou Meng: Myth, Mimesis, and Persona.* Association for Asian Studies Monograph, no. 28. Tucson: University of Arizona, 1975.

1815 Palandri, Angela Jung. "Women in Dream of the Red Chamber." *Literature East and West* 12(Dec. 1968):226-38.

1816 Partington, T. B. "Women and the Chinese Poets." *Asiatic Review* 19(1923):173-77.

1817 Schurmann, H. F. "On Social Themes in Sung Tales." *Harvard J. of Asiatic Studies* 20(June 1957):239-61. [Analysis of some Song love stories.]

1818 Sun, Phillip S. Y. "The Seditious Art of the Water Margin: Misogynists or Desperadoes?" *Renditions, a Chinese-English Translation Magazine,* no. 1 (1973), pp. 99-106.

1819 Waley, Arthur. "Notes on the 'Lute-girl's Song.'" *New China Review* 2(1920):591-97.

1820 Waley, Arthur. "Courtship and Marriage in Early Chinese Poetry." *Asia* 36(1936):403-406.

1821 West, Anthony. "Through a Glass, Darkly." *New Yorker,* Nov. 22, 1958, pp. 223-32. [Review of Florence and Isabel McHugh's *The Dream of the Red Chamber.*]

1822 Willis, Donald S. "The *Nieh-hai-hua* and Its Place in the Late Ch'ing Social Novel of Protest." Ph.D. dissertation, University of Washington, Seattle, 1951.

ANTHOLOGIES: MODERN SHORT STORIES (1911-PRESENT)

1823 Ai, Wu. *Wild Bull Villages: Chinese Short Stories by Ai Wu and Others.* Peking: Foreign Languages Press, 1965.

1824 Chao, Shu-li. *Rhymes of Li Yu-tsai and other Stories.* Trans. Sidney Shapiro, et al. Peking: Foreign Languages Press, 1955. [Stories of the marriage reform.]

1825 *City Cousin and Other Stories.* Peking: Foreign Languages Press, 1973. [Includes the story of a woman storekeeper in a mountain area.]

1826 Contemporary Chinese Women Writers. *The Muse of China: A Collection of Prose and Short Stories,* trans. Anna Chennault, Liu-li Mi, et al. Taibei, Taiwan: Chinese Women Writers' Association, 1974.

1827 *Dawn on the River and Other Stories by Contemporary Chinese Writers.* Peking: Foreign Languages Press, 1957. [See "Marriage" by Li Wen-yuan and "The Newlyweds" by Hai Mo.]

1828 Hsia, C. T., ed., with the assistance of Joseph S. M. Lau. *Twentieth Century Chinese Stories.* N.Y.: Columbia University, 1971. [See "Li T'ung: A Chinese Girl in New York," pp. 218-239. Works by Eileen Chang and Nieh Hua-ling, two women writers, are also included.]

1829 Hsu, Vivian Ling, ed. *Born of the Same Roots: Stories of Modern Chinese Women.* Bloomington: Indiana University, 1981. [Collection of modern Chinese short stories on Chinese women on the mainland, on Taiwan, and in the United States, and the problems they faced from 1919 through the 1960s.]

1830 Isaacs, Harold Robert, ed. *Straw Sandals: Chinese Short Stories, 1918-1933.* Cambridge, Mass.: M.I.T. Press, 1974.

1831 Jenner, W. F., ed. *Modern Chinese Stories.* Trans. W. E. Jenner and Gladys Yang. London: Oxford University, 1970. [Includes Lu Xun's "The New Year Sacrifice," depicting the wretched lot of a woman; Rou Shi's "Slaves' Mother"; and Zhao Shuili's "Meng Xiangying Stands Up," concerning village women and politics.]

1832 Katz, Naomi and Milton, Nancy, eds. *Fragments from a Lost Diary and Other Stories: Women of Asia, Africa and Latin America.* Random House, 1973. [Another edition: Boston: Beacon Press, 1975.]

1833 Lau, Joseph S. M., ed. *Chinese Stories from Taiwan: 1960-1970.* N.Y.: Columbia University, 1976. [Women in traditional Chinese society is the major theme in Ch'en Jo-hsi*, "The Last Performance"; Yü Li-hua*, "In Liu Village"; Huang Chun-ming, "A Flower in the Rainy Night"; Lin Huai-min, "Cicada"; and Yang Ch'ing-chu, "Enemies."]

1834 Munro, Stanley R., trans. *Genesis of a Revolution: An Anthology of Modern Chinese Short Stories.* Writing in Asia Series. Kuala Lumpur & Hong Kong: Heinemann Educational Books (Asia) Ltd., 1979. [Includes Lao She's "The Woman from Liu Tun," and others.]

1835 *A New Home and Other Stories by Contemporary Chinese Writers.* Peking: Foreign Languages Press, 1955. [See "Mother Wang," by Lo Pin-chi.]

1836 Nieh, Hua-ling,* ed. *Eight Stories by Chinese Women.* Taipei: Heritage Press, 1962.

1837 *Registration and Other Stories by Contemporary Chinese Authors.* Peking, 1954. [Contains: "Registration of Marriage," "Sacrifice to the Kitchen God," "I Want to Study," and other stories about women.]

1838 Snow, Edgar, comp. and ed. *Living China: Modern Chinese Short Stories.* Peking, 1936. [Includes Lu Hsün's "Divorce," and Jou Shih's "Slave Mother."]

1839 Wang, Chi-chen, trans. *Contemporary Chinese Stories.* N.Y.: Columbia University, 1944. [Includes "Grandma Takes Charge" by Lao She and "Little Sister" by Feng Wen-ping.]

1840 *The Young Coal-Miner and Other Stories by Contemporary Chinese Writers.* Peking: Foreign Languages Press, 1958. [Includes Fu Tse's "The Little Sisters," Li Chun's "Soldier's Wife," and "Father and Daughter" by Lo Pin-chi.]

REPUBLICAN FICTION, POETRY, AND DRAMA (1911-1949)

1841 Ah-mei. "My Sister." Trans. Chi-chen Wang. *Far Eastern Magazine* 2(1938):1:32-37. [Reprinted as "Little Sister" in Chi-chen Wang's *Contemporary Chinese Stories,* pp. 127-34. N.Y.: Columbia University, 1944.]

1842 Ai Wu. "Mrs. Shih Ching." *Chinese Literature* 1954:3:84-97. [Written in 1947.]

1843 Ch'ien, Chung-shu. *Fortress Besieged.* Trans. Jeanne Kelly and Nathan K. Mao. Chinese Literature in Translation Series. Bloomington & London: Indiana University, 1980. [With satiric commentary on courtship and marriage.]

1844 Der Ling, (Princess).* *Two Years in the Forbidden City.* N.Y.: Dodd, Mead, 1928.

1845 Der Ling, (Princess).* *Lotus Petals.* N.Y.: Dodd, Mead, 1930.

1846 Der Ling, (Princess).* *Golden Phoenix.* N.Y.: Dodd, Mead, 1932.

1847 Der Ling, (Princess).* *Jade and Dragons.* N.Y.: Mohawk Press, 1932.

1848 Fisher, Welthy, Mrs. [Honsinger]. *A String of Chinese Pearls: Ten Tales of Chinese Girls Ancient and Modern.* N.Y.: Women Press, 1924.

1849 Gamble, Sidney D. *Chinese Village Plays from the Ting Hsien Region (Yang Ke Hsuan).* Amsterdam: Philo Press, 1970. [A collection of 48 Chinese plays staged by villagers from Ding xian in northern China around 1920.]

1850 Han, Suyin.* *Destination Chungking.* Boston: Little, Brown, 1942. [Another edition: London: Cape, 1943. New edition: London: Cape; N.Y.: Clark, Irwin, 1953.]

1851 Han, Suyin.* *A Many-Splendored Thing.* Boston: Little, Brown, 1952. [Another edition: London: Cape, 1952.]

1852 Han, Suyin.* *...And the Rain My Drink.* Boston: Little, Brown, 1956. [Another edition: London: Cape, 1956.]

1853 Han, Suyin.* *The Crippled Tree.* London: J. Cape, 1965. [Fictionalized autobiography and family history covering period from 1886 to 1928.]

1854 Han, Suyin.* *A Mortal Flower.* N.Y.: Putnam, 1966. [Continuation of autobiography.]

1855 Han, Suyin.* *Birdless Summer.* N.Y.: Putnam, 1968. [Continuation of autobiography.]

1856 Ho, Ro-se.* *Love and Duty: The Love Story of a Chinese Girl.* Shanghai: Commercial Press, 1932. [c. 1926.]

1857 Hsiao Hung [Chang, Nai-ying].* "Hands." Trans. R. L. Jen. *T'ien-hsia Monthly* 4(May 1937):498–518.

1858 Hsiao Hung [Chang, Nai-ying].* "A Night in a Stable." *Asia* 41(1941):487–89.

1859 Hsiao Hung [Chang, Nai-ying].* "Hands." *Chinese Literature* 1959:8:36–52.

1860 Hsiao Hung [Chang, Nai-ying].* "Spring in a Small Town." *Chinese Literature* 1961:8:59–82.

1861 Hsiao Hung [Chang, Nai-ying].* "Harelip Feng." *Chinese Literature* 1963:2:3–24. [Excerpt from *The Hulan River.*]

1862 Hsiao Hung [Chang, Nai-ying].* *The Field of Life and Death and Tales of Hulan River.* Bloomington: Indiana University, 1979. [Includes sensitive memoir of author's girlhood in rural Manchuria in the 1920s. An important modern Chinese feminist writer.]

1863 Hsieh, Wan-ying [pseud.: Hsieh Ping-hsin].* *Spring Water.* Trans. Grace M. Boynton. Peking (?), 1929 (?).

1864 Hsiung, Shih-i, trans. *Lady Precious Stream* (Wang Pao-ch'uan). London: Methuen, 1934. [Modern Chinese version of a Peking Opera. Acting edition: 1936.]

1865 Hsiung, Shih-i. *The Story of Lady Precious Stream.* London: Hutchinson, 1950.

1866 Hsu, Ti-shan. "Big Sister Lin." *Chinese Literature* 1957:1:79–96.

1867 Huang, Lu-yin.* [Excerpts from several short stories and essays] Trans. J. Häringorá and L. Doležalavá. *New Orient* 4(1965):6:187–89.

1868 Jou Shih [Chao, P'ing-fu]. "Slave Mother." Trans. George A. Kennedy. *China Forum* (Shanghai) 1(1932):8:7–8. [Reprinted in *Living China, Modern Chinese Short Stories,* ed. Edgar Snow, pp. 100–126. London: George G. Harrap and Co., 1936.]

1869 Jou Shih [Chao, P'ing-fu]. "A Slave Mother." Trans. Pei-chi Chang. *Chinese Literature* 1955:1:107–124.

1870 Jou Shih [Chao, P'ing-fu]. "Slave Mother." Trans. W. J. F. Jenner. In *Modern Chinese Stories,* ed. W. J. F. Jenner, pp. 47–67. London: Oxford University, 1970.

1871 Kuo, Mo-jo. "Cho Wen-chün." In *Straw Sandals, Chinese Short Stories, 1918–1933,* ed. Harold R. Isaacs, pp. 45–67. Cambridge, Mass.: M.I.T. Press, 1974. [Abridged.]

1872 Lin, Adet.* *Flame from the Rock.* N.Y.: John Day, 1943. [Another edition: London, Toronto: W. Heinemann, 1944.]

1873 Lin, Adet and Lin, Anor.* *Our Family.* N.Y.: John Day, c. 1939.

1874 Lin, Anor [Lin, Tai-yi].* *War Tide.* N.Y.: John Day, 1943.

1875 Lin, Anor [Lin, Tai-yi].* *The Golden Coin.* N.Y.: John Day, 1946.

1876 Lin, Yutang. *Confucius Saw Nancy and Essays about Nothing.* Shanghai: Commercial Press, 1937. [See "Confucius Saw Nancy," pp. 1–46.]

1877 Lin, Yutang. *The Importance of Living.* N.Y.: Reynal and Hitchcock, 1938. [See chapter 10, "Two Chinese Ladies," which includes a translation of a Qing scholar's account of his favorite concubine.]

1878 Lin, Yutang. *Moment in Peking.* N.Y.: Sun Dial Press, 1942. [Chief figures are traditional and emancipated heroines.]

1879 Lin, Yu-t'ang [Lin Yutang]. *Miss Tu.* London: W. Heinemann, 1950.

1880 Lin, Yutang, trans. *Widow, Nun, and Courtesan.* N.Y.: John Day, 1951. [Three novelettes set in various periods, from the late Ming to modern times. The story of the widow was written in the modern period.]

1881 Ling, Hsu-hua [Ling, Shu-hua].* "What's the Point of It?" Trans. the author and J. Bell. *T'ien-hsia Monthly* 3(Aug. 1936):53–62.

1882 Ling, Shu-hua.* "A Poet Goes Mad." Trans. the author and Julian Bell. *T'ien-hsia Monthly* 4(Apr. 1937):401–421.

1883 Ling, Shu-hua.* "Under the Iron Heel." *Voice of China* 2:(1937):11:2–3, 14.

1884 Ling, Hsu-hua [Ling, Shu-hua].* "Writing a Letter." *T'ien-hsia Monthly* 5(Dec. 1937):508–513.

1885 Ling, Shu-hua.* "The Helpmate." Trans. Chi-chen Wang. In *Contemporary Chinese Stories,* by Chi-chen Wang, pp. 135–42. N.Y.: Columbia University, 1944.

1886 Ling, Shu-hua.* *Ancient Melodies.* London: Hogarth Press, 1953. [Autobiographical novel.]

1887 Lu Hsün [Chou, Shu-jen]. "Benediction." Trans. Edgar Snow and Hsin-nung Yao. In *Living China, Modern Chinese Short Stories,* ed. Edgar Snow, pp. 51–74. London: George G. Harrap and Co., 1936.

1888 Lu Hsün [Chou, Shu-jen]. "Divorce." In *Living China, Modern Chinese Short Stories,* ed. Edgar Snow, pp. 85–96. London: George G. Harrap and Co., 1936.

1889 Lu Hsün [Chou, Shu-jen]. "The New Year Blessing." Trans. Yi-chin Lin. *People's Tribune,* new series 12(1936):35–50. [Story about the suffering of a lower-class woman.]

1890 Lu Hsün [Chou, Shu-jen]. "A Rustic Divorce." *People's Tribune,* new series 13(1936):45–53.

1891 Lu Hsün [Chou, Shu-jen]. "Sister Sianglin." Trans. C. C. Wang. *Far Eastern Magazine* 2(1938):4:182–87; 2(1939):5:238–43.

1892 Lu Hsün [Chou, Shu-jen]. "Dawn." Trans. C. C. Wang. *Far Eastern Magazine* 3(1940):3:14–17. [A short story about a woman who tries to save the life of her child.]

1893 Lu Hsün [Chou, Shu-jen]. "Remorse." Trans. C. C. Wang. *T'ien-hsia Monthly* 11(Aug.–Sept. 1940):68–86. [Depicts a failed love affair between two 1920s intellectuals.]

1894 Lu Hsün [Chou, Shu-jen]. "The Divorce." Trans. C. C. Wang. In *Ah Q and Others: Selected Stories of Lusin*, trans. C. C. Wang, pp. 31-34. N.Y.: Columbia University, 1941.

1895 Lu Hsün [Chou, Shu-jen]. "The Widow." Trans. C. C. Wang. In *Ah Q and Others: Selected Stories of Lusin*, trans. C. C. Wang, pp. 184-204. N.Y.: Columbia University, 1941.

1896 Lu Hsün [Chou, Shu-jen]. "At Dawn." Trans. Joseph Kalmer. *Life and Letters* 60(1949):137:13-19.

1897 Lu Hsün [Chou, Shu-jen]. "The New Year's Sacrifice." In *Selected Stories of Lu Hsun*, pp. 95-118. Peking: Foreign Languages Press, 1954.

1898 Lu Hsün [Chou, Shu-jen]. "Regret for the Past." In *Selected Stories of Lu Hsun*, pp. 173-196. Peking: Foreign Languages Press, 1954. [Depicts a failed love affair.]

1899 Lu Hsün [Chou, Shu-jen]. "The New-year Sacrifice." Trans. Gladys Yang. In *Modern Chinese Stories*, ed. W. J. F. Jenner, pp. 29-45. London: Oxford University, 1970.

1900 Lu Hsün [Chou, Shu-jen]. "Remorse." Trans. George A. Kennedy. In *Straw Sandals, Chinese Short Stories, 1918-1933*, ed. Harold R. Isaacs, pp. 107-128. Cambridge, Mass.: M.I.T. Press, 1974.

1901 Nieh, Kan-nu. *Sister*. Trans. Chin Chung. Guilin: Yuanfang shudian, 1944.

1902 Pa Chin [Li, Fei-kan]. *The Family*. Peking: Foreign Languages Press, 1958. [Another edition: Garden City, N.Y.: Doubleday, 1972. Famous novel of family revolution in Republican China, originally published in 1931.]

1903 Pa Chin [Li, Fei-kan]. "The Landlady." Trans. Diana Granat. In "Three Stories of France: Pa Chin and His Early Short Stories," pp. 34-55. M.A. thesis, University of Pennsylvania, 1972.

1904 Ping Hsin [Hsieh, Wan-ying].* "The First Home Party." Trans. R. L. Jen. *T'ien-hsia Monthly* 4(Mar. 1937):294-306.

1905 Shen, Ts'ung-wen. "Green Jade." Trans. E. Hahn and Mo-lei Shing. *T'ien-hsia Monthly* 2(Jan. 1936):87-107, 2(Feb. 1936):174-96, 2(Mar. 1936):271-99, 360-390. [Novel of the life of a girl living in a border area.]

1906 Shen, Tseng-wen [Shen, Ts'ung-wen]. "The Frontier City." Trans. Ching Ti and R. Payne. In *The Chinese Earth*, trans. Ching Ti and Robert Payne, pp. 190-289. London: George Allen and Unwin, 1947. [Love story.]

1907 Shen, Ts'ung-wen. "The Border Town." *Chinese Literature* 1962:10:3-46; 1962:11:38-69.

1908 Shun, Chung-wen. "Old Mrs. Wang's Chickens." Trans. Shih Ming. *T'ien-hsia Monthly* 11(Dec.-Jan. 1940-41):274-80.

1909 Sze, Mai-mai.* *Echo of a Cry*. N.Y.: Harcourt, Brace, 1945. [Another edition: London: Cape, 1947.]

1910 Sze, Mai-mai.* *Silent Children*. N.Y.: Harcourt, Brace, 1948.

1911 Ting Ling [Chiang, Ping-chih].* "One Certain Night." Trans. George A. Kennedy. *China Forum* (Shanghai) 1(1932):21:9. [Ding Ling is China's best known feminist revolutionary writer.]

1912 Ting Ling [Chiang, Ping-chih].* "Flood!" Trans. Jolin Huang. *People's Tribune*, new series 7(1934):12:583-91.

1913 Ting Ling [Chiang, Ping-chih].* "Flood." *Asia* [Asia and Americas] (New York) 35(1935):10:631-34. [Incomplete.]

1914 Ting Ling [Chiang, Ping-chih].* "The Flood." In *Living China: Modern Chinese Short Stories*, ed. Edgar Snow, pp. 154-64. Peking, 1936.

1915 Ting Ling [Chiang, Ping-chih].* "News." In *Living China: Modern Chinese Short Stories*, ed. Edgar Snow, pp. 165-72. Peking, 1936.

1916 Ting Ling [Chiang, Ping-chih].* "One Day." *New Writing* 5(1938):236-40.

1917 Ting Ling [Chiang, Ping-chih].* *Our Children and Others*, ed. and annotated by Meng Tsiang. Shanghai: Ying-wen hsüeh-hui, 1941. [Chinese and English. See "Our Children," pp. 2-15 and "The Flood," pp. 16-43.]

1918 Ting Ling [Chiang, Ping-chih].* *When I Was in Sha Chuan and Other Stories*. Trans. Pu-sheng Kung. Bombay: Kutub, 1945. [Another edition: Poona, India: Kutub Publishers, n.d.]

1919 Ting Ling [Chiang, Ping-chih].* "The Soldier and the Journalist." Trans. G. Begley. *Life and Letters* 60(1949):137:75-80. [Excerpt.]

1920 Ting Ling [Chiang, Ping-chih].* "The Diary of Miss Sophia." Trans. A. L. Chin. In *Straw Sandals, Chinese Short Stories, 1918-1933*, ed. Harold R. Isaacs, pp. 129-69. Cambridge, Mass.: M. I. T. Press, 1974. [Famous story of a young emancipated woman's sexual temptations.]

1921 Ting Ling [Chiang, Ping-chih].* "Sophia's Diary." Trans. Joseph Lau. *Tamkang Review* 5(1974):1:57-96.

1922 Ting Ling [Chiang, Ping-chih].* "When I Was in Sha Chuan." In Yi-tsi Feuerwerker, "Ting Ling's 'When I Was in Sha Chuan (Cloud Village).'" *Signs* 2(Aug. 1976):255-279.

1923 Ting Ling [Chiang, Ping-chih].* "In the Hospital." Trans. Susan M. Vacca. *Renditions: A Chinese-English Translation Magazine*, no. 8 (Autumn 1977), pp. 123-137.

1924 Yang, Chen-sheng. "Three Stories." Trans. Sidney Shapiro. *Chinese Literature* 1964:2:79-88. [Contains: "One-sided Wedding," "Wang the Miller," and "Li Sung's Crime."]

1925 Yao, Hsin-nung. "When the Girls Come Back." *T'ien-hsia Monthly* 7(Aug. 1938):94-120. [One act play about student life during the Anti-Japanese War.]

1926 Yao, Hsin-nung. *The Malice of Empire*. Trans. Jeremy Ingalls. Berkeley: University of California, 1970. [Historical novel about the Empress Dowager Cixi.]

1927 Yin Fu [Hsü, Yin-fu]. "Little Mother." Trans. George A. Kennedy. *China Forum* (Shanghai) 1(1932):17:5-6.

Note: Works written by overseas Chinese may also concern situations in the Republican period. See also the section on "Hong Kong, Taiwan and Overseas China: Fiction, Poetry and Drama."

CRITICAL STUDIES: REPUBLICAN LITERATURE

1928 Bjorge, Gray J. "Sophia's Diary: An Introduction." *Tamkang Review* 5(1974):1:97-110.

1929 Boušková, Marcela. "On the Origin of Modern Chinese Prosody: An Analysis of the Prosodic Components in the Works of Ping Hsin." *Archiv Orientální* 32(1964):4:619-43.

1930 Boušková, Marcela. "The Stories of Ping-Hsin." In *Studies in Modern Chinese Literature*, ed. Jarolslav Průšek, pp. 113-29. Berlin: Akademie-Verlag, 1964.

1931 Chin, Ai-li S. "Family Relations in Modern Chinese Fiction." In *Family and Kinship in Chinese Society*, ed. Maurice Freedman, pp. 87-121. Stanford: Stanford University, 1970.

1932 Chung, Wen. "On Lu Hsun's Story *The New-Year Sacrifice*." *Chinese Literature* 1975:11:63-68.

1933 Feuerwerker, Yi-tsi. "Ting Ling's 'When I Was in Sha Chuan (Cloud Village).'" *Signs* 2(Aug. 1976):255-79.

1934 Feuerwerker, Yi-tsi Mei. "Ideology and Narrative: A Study of Ding Ling's Fiction." Ph.D. dissertation, Harvard University, 1979.

1935 Hsu, Kai-yu. "The Moon and the Beautiful Woman in Modern Chinese Poetry." *East-West Review* 2(Spring/Summer 1966):261-68.

1936 Kobayashi, T. "The Russian Populists in a 1902 Chinese Novel." *J. of the Oriental Society of Australia* 10(1975):26-44. [Study of a Chinese translation of a Russian novel, *Heroic Women of Eastern Europe*.]

1937 Liu, Chun-jo. "The Heroes and Heroines of Modern Chinese Fiction: From Ah Q to Wu Tzu-hsü." *J. Asian Studies* 16(1957):2:201-211.

1938 Pa Chin [Li, Fei-kan]. "How I Wrote the Novel 'The Family.'" *China Reconstructs* 7(Jan. 1958):15-17.

1939 Tang, Tao. "Two Portrayals of Chinese Women in Lu Hsün's Stories." *Chinese Literature* 1973:9:83-90.

THE PEOPLE'S REPUBLIC OF CHINA: FICTION, POETRY AND DRAMA (1949-)

1940 Chalakahu. "A Fine Old Woman." *Chinese Literature* 1978:9:35-43. [Story of an old woman revolutionary in Mongolia.]

1941 Chang, Chi. "Nets." *Chinese Literature* 1973:8:77-83. [Story of women in a fishing collective.]

1942 Chang, Chun. "Her House Has to Wait." Trans. Gladys Yang. *Chinese Literature* 1965:2:61-70.

1943 Chang, Lihan. "A Chinese Love Story." *China Now*, no. 84 (May/June 1979), pp. 6-7. [A love story told by a young woman factory worker in the PRC.]

1944 Chang, Mo-yuan. "The Secret Packet the Little Girl Sent." *Chinese Literature* 1966:12:57-60.

1945 Chang, Yu-teh. "The Country School-teacher." *Chinese Literature* 1958:4:115-122. [Story of a woman teacher.]

1946 Chang, Yung-mei. "Woman Coastguards." *Chinese Literature* 1973:4:91-93.

1947 Chao, Cheng-min. "The Girl on the Raft." *Chinese Literature* 1975:9:85-86.

1948 Chao, Pao-chi. "Sister Autumn." *Chinese Literature* 1977:4:19-35. [About a woman guerrilla leader in revolutionary war.]

1949 Chao, Wen. "Never-Give-Way." *Chinese Literature* 1973:3:99-105. [Story of a women's team in the militia.]

1950 Chen, Hui. "The Girl." *Chinese Literature* 1962:2:88. [Poem.]

1951 Chen, Pei. "Aunt Tangerine." *Chinese Literature* 1971:10:68-70.

1952 Chen, Pi. "Woman Doctor in the Mountains." *Chinese Literature* 1970:12:76-77. [Poem.]

1953 Ch'en, Teng-k'e. "Living Hell." *Chinese Literature* 1952:2:34-116. [Story of a peasant woman partisan in revolutionary war.]

1954 Chen, Yuan-tsung.* *Dragon's Village: An Autobiographical Novel of Revolutionary China*. N.Y.: Pantheon, 1980.

1955 Cheng, Fan and Chuan, Yeh. "Militia Women on Tungting Lake." *Chinese Literature* 1972:1:55-56. [Poem.]

1956 Cheng, Hsuan. "A New Teacher." *Chinese Literature* 1973:10:51-63. [Story of a woman teacher.]

1957 Chi, Wen. "The Fisher-girl." *Chinese Literature* 1972:6:75. [Poem.]

1958 Chiang, Tzu-lung. "Swallow and Dawn." *Chinese Literature* 1973:8:3-9. [Story of a woman worker.]

1959 Chien, Pei-heng. "Snow Lotus." *Chinese Literature* 1972:2:81-88. [Story-sketch of a woman meteorologist.]

1960 Chin, Chao-yang. "Village Vignettes: The Young Wife; Noon; Sacrifice to the Kitchen God." *Chinese Literature* 1954:1:146-63.

1961 Ching, Chih. "Cotton-Boll Galore." *Chinese Literature* 1973:3:81-92. [On a woman production team leader.]

1962 Ching, Lin. "Yuan-yuan and Her Friend." Trans. Sidney Shapiro. *Chinese Literature* 1964:7:10-31.

1963 Chou, Ke-chin. "Li Hsiu-man." *Chinese Literature* 1974:2:94-103. [About a woman party secretary.]

1964 Chou, Tsung-chi. "A Ball of Fire." *Chinese Literature* 1974:6:50-66. [About a woman worker in a coal mine.]

1965 Chou, Yung-chuang. "Out to Learn." *Chinese Literature* 1973:10:16-29. [A girl worker in a generator works.]

1966 Chu, Yu-yuan. "The Young Herdswoman." *Chinese Literature* 1974:3:85-86. [Poem.]

1967 Fang, Nan. "Just Call Me Sea Girl." *Chinese Literature* 1975:12:32-46.

1968 Feng, Chang. "Morning Clouds." *Chinese Literature* 1973:6:13-23. [A woman group leader in a mill.]

1969 Feng, Teh-ying. "Bitter Herb." *Chinese Literature* 1966:4:3-65; 5:57-99; 6:39-89. [Excerpts from the story of a woman leader in the revolutionary war.]

1970 Fu, Chou. "The Girl Driving Yaks." *Chinese Literature* 1966:6:90-92. [Poem.]

1971 Fu, Tse. "The Little Sisters." Trans. Su-chu Chang. *Chinese Literature* 1958:1:19-29.

1972 Hai, Mo. "The Newlyweds." *Chinese Literature* 1956:2:155-63.

1973 Hai, Mo. "Fourth Sister." *Chinese Literature* 1959:9:34-49.

1974 Han, Tzu.* "Foster Daughter." *Chinese Literature* 1961:11:63-77.

1975 Hao Jan. "Sisters-in-law." Trans. Gladys Yang. *Chinese Literature* 1965:2:48-60.

1976 Hao Jan. "The Eve of Her Wedding." Trans. Gladys Yang. *Chinese Literature* 1965:6:20-33.

1977 Hao Jan. "Aunt Hou's Courtyard." *Chinese Literature* 1972:7:75-84.

1978 Hao Jan. "First and Last." *Chinese Literature* 1973:12:3-21. [About dual roles of a woman as party secretary and wife.]

1979 Hao Jan. *Bright Clouds*. Peking: Foreign Languages Press, 1974. [Depiction of women who have shaken off old ways of thinking.]

1980 "A Happy Event in Our Village." *China Reconstructs* 19(May 1970):35-65. [Story about women who deliver babies while traveling.]

1981 Ho, Ching-chih. *The White-Haired Girl: An Opera in 5 Acts*. Peking: Foreign Languages Press, 1954. [Famous opera based on the true story of the sufferings of a peasant girl during the revolutionary war.]

1982 Ho, Shu-yu. "Sister Red Plum." *Chinese Literature* 1978:4:65-83. [About a girl farm worker.]

1983 Ho, Wei. "Two Sisters." *Chinese Literature* 1962:10:65-68.

1984 Hsi, Yung. "The New Member of the Family." Trans. Fan-chin Yu. *Chinese Literature* 1959:2:14-28.

1985 Hsiao, Kuan-hung. "A Young Pathbreaker." *Chinese Literature* 1973:10:3-15. [About a girl assistant in a generator factory.]

1986 Hsiao, Yu-hsuan. "The Girl Warehouse Keeper." *Chinese Literature* 1978:3:3-17.

1987 Hsu, Huai-chung. "The Girl Who Sold Wine." *Chinese Literature* 1962:2:3-12.

1988 Hsueh, Yen. "The Old Accountant's Sister-in-law." *Chinese Literature* 1962:8:82-88.

1989 Ju, Chih-chüan.* *Lilies*. Peking: Jen-min Wen-hsüeh Press, 1959. [See "Lilies," pp. 1-15.]

1990 Ju, Chih-chüan.* "The Maternity Home." *Chinese Literature* 1960:8:6-21.

1991 Ju, Chih-chüan.* "A Promise is Kept." *Chinese Literature* 1960:12:50-60. [About the life of a woman worker before and after liberation.]

1992 Ju, Chih-chüan.* "A Third Visit to Yen Chuang." *Chinese Literature* 1961:4:87-111. [About a girl militia leader.]

1993 Ju, Chih-chüan.* "The Warmth of Spring." *Chinese Literature* 1961:7:67-81.

1994 Ju, Chih-chüan.* "The Beginning of Tomorrow." *Chinese Literature* 1962:4:76-91.

1995 Ju, Chih-chüan.* "Comradeship." *Chinese Literature* 1963:3:50-62.

1996 Ju, Chih-chüan.* "On the Banks of the Ch'eng." *Chinese Literature* 1963:7:3-15.

1997 Ju, Chih-chüan.* "Between Two Seas." *Chinese Literature* 1965:6:76-81.

1998 Kao, Hsiao-sheng. "Breaking Off the Engagement." Trans. Tso Cheng. *Chinese Literature* 1956:4:82-93.

1999 Kao, Hung. "Storm Warning." *Chinese Literature* 1973:8:35-60. [About a woman weather forecaster in a PLA weather station.]

2000 Kao, Yin. "Dajee and Her Father." Trans. Tang Sheng. *Chinese Literature* 1959:11:20-40.

2001 Ku, Yü. "New Times, New Methods." In *Registration and Other Stories by Contemporary Chinese Authors*, pp. 45-54. Peking: Foreign Languages Press, 1954. [A story of marriage reform in rural China.]

2002 K'ung, Chueh and Yuan, Ching*. "Daughters and Sons." *Chinese Literature* 1951:1:19-202.

2003 K'ung, Chueh and Yuan, Ching*. *Daughters and Sons*. Trans. Po-li Sha. N.Y.: Liberty Press, 1952.

2004 Kuo, Ning. "The Daughter of a Revolutionary." *Chinese Literature* 1974:7:3-22. [About a girl secretary of a Youth League branch.]

2005 Kuo, Po. "Spring Showers." *Chinese Literature* 1974:2:104-110. [About two girls, one the village storekeeper and the other the village accountant.]

2006 Lee, Yu-hwa. "Stories of My Sisters." *New China* 4:1(Sept. 1978):14-16.

2007 Li, Chi. *Wang Kuei and Li Hsiang-hsiang*. Trans. Hsien-yi Yang and Gladys Yang. Peking: Foreign Languages Press, 1954. [Narrative poem of anti-landlord revolution and marriage reform.]

2008 Li, Chun. "Mother and Daughter." *Chinese Literature* 1959:12:72-85.

2009 Li, Chun. "The Story of Li Shuang-shuang." *Chinese Literature* 1960:6:3-26. [About a young village woman during the Great Leap Forward.]

2010 Li, Chun. "Sowing the Cloud." *Chinese Literature* 1961:1:58-92. [Village girl studies meteorology and returns home to set up commune weather station.]

2011 Li, Hui-hsin. "The Girl in the Mountains." *Chinese Literature* 1973:10:30-38.

2012 Li, Ju-ching. *Island Militia Women*. Peking: Foreign Languages Press, 1975.

2013 Lin, Chi. "A Slip of a Girl." *Chinese Literature* 1972:8:74-84.

2014 Lin, Chin-lan. "Taiwan Girl." *Chinese Literature* 1957:4:3-19. [A teacher encounters a little girl in Taiwan before liberation.]

2015 Lin, Yin-ko. "Daughter of the People." *Chinese Literature* 1971:4:77-83. [About a girl "sent down" to the countryside to live.]

2016 Little Sisters of the Grassland Compiling and Drawing Group. *Little Sisters of the Grassland*. Peking: Foreign Languages Press, 1973.

2017 Liu, Chen.* "Long Flows the Stream." In *Wild Bull Village, Chinese Short Stories*, pp. 88-108. Peking: Foreign Languages Press, 1965. [About a women's association leader.]

2018 Liu, Teh-chang. "The Girl Taking Lunch to the Lumberman." *Chinese Literature* 1966:8:105-106.

2019 Liu, Xinwu. "The Place of Love." Trans. C. C. Chew. *Eastern Horizon* 18(June 1979):37-48.

2020 Lo, Kuang-pin. "Red Crag." *Chinese Literature* 1962:5:3-32; 1962:6:3-57; 1962:7:4-95. [About a woman revolutionary.]

2021 Lo, Pin-chi [Chang P'u-chün]. "Mother Wang." *Chinese Literature* 1955:1:3-15. [An old woman runs a peasants' child care center.]

2022 Lo, Shu. "Twice-Married Woman." *Chinese Literature* 1961:11:37-52.

2023 Li, Chun-chao. "A Woman Captain." *Chinese Literature* 1974:5:55-70.

2024 Lu, Fei.* "Spring on the Sungari." *Chinese Literature* 1955:4:120-28. [About a young woman teacher in a mining community.]

2025 Lu, Fei.* "Forest Girls." *Chinese Literature* 1957:3:158-68.

2026 Ma, Feng. "Marriage." *Chinese Literature* 1952:2:218-25.

2027 Ma, Feng. "Han Mei-mei." In *The Sun Has Risen*, pp. 73-97. Peking: Foreign Languages Press, 1961. [About a woman worker.]

2028 Ma, Ke. "A Man and Wife Learn to Read." Trans. David Holm. *Bulletin of Concerned Asian Scholars* 8(April/June 1976):5-11. [One-act Yangge play.]

2029 Malchinhu. "In the Snow Storm." *Chinese Literature* 1959:10:80-89. [About a Mongolian nurse.]

2030 Malchinhu. "Woman Basketball Player No. 6." *Chinese Literature* 1978:9:3-21.

2031 Mo, Ying-feng. "A Conversation Overheard at Night." *Chinese Literature* 1973:7:3-9. [Women struggle for equal pay for equal work.]

2032 Nai, Chi-chang. "An Assistant after His Own Heart." *Chinese Literature* 1963:6:3-12. [A girl takes charge of a factory store-room.]

2033 Peking People's Art Theatre. *Between Husband and Wife: A Play in One Act*. Trans. Sidney Shapiro. Peking, 1953. [Reprinted in a supplement to *China Reconstructs* 1953, no. 6.]

2034 Pien, Feng-hao. "New Masters of the Steel Plant." *Chinese Literature* 1974:7:23-42. [Depicts girls working in a steel plant.]

2035 "Red Detachment of Women." *Chinese Literature* 1969:5:3-14. [A play.]

2036 "Red Detachment of Women." *Chinese Literature* 1971:1:2-81. [Ballet script with photos.]

2037 Sha, Hung-ping. "A Soldier and an Old Woman." *Chinese Literature* 1969:6:89-90.

2038 Shih, Min. "Hidden Reef." *Chinese Literature* 1973:9:33-50. [A woman worker on a ship.]

2039 Sun, Ching-jui. "Mother." *Chinese Literature* 1972:11:15-21. [Sketch of a PLA mother.]

2040 Sun, Lai-chin. "A Girl Mail Carrier." *Chinese Literature* 1971:3:53-54. [Poem.]

2041 Sun, Li. "Lotus Creek." *Chinese Literature* 1959:10:70-78. [About a woman in the anti-Japanese war.]

2042 Sun, Li. "Parting Advice." *Chinese Literature* 1962:5:33-42. [About a woman in the anti-Japanese war.]

2043 Sun, Li. "Stormy Years." *Chinese Literature* 1963:8:11–71; 1963:9:3–47. [Excerpts from a novel about a woman leader in the revolutionary war.]

2044 Sun, Li. "Honor." *Chinese Literature* 1965:10:23–38. [About women in the anti-Japanese war.]

2045 Sun, Li. "Country Song." *Chinese Literature* 1966:1:18–64. [A young actress becomes a production team leader.]

2046 Sun, Wei-shih. "A New Dawn." *Chinese Literature* 1977:10:3–83. [Play dramatizing housewives' production at Daqing oilfield.]

2047 Sun, Y. *The Women's Representative: Three One-Act Plays.* Peking: Foreign Languages Press, 1956. [Translation of *Funü daibiao.*]

2048 Sun, Yung. "Generation after Generation." *Chinese Literature* 1974:11:3–32. [About a young woman political instructor.]

2049 Sung, An-na. "Granny Chin." *Chinese Literature* 1974:11:47–54. [An old woman in a production brigade.]

2050 Tang, Tien-yüan. "The Iron-Armed Girl." *Chinese Literature* 1978:9:22–34. [About a woman construction worker.]

2051 "Third Sister Liu." *Chinese Literature* 1961:2:52–110. [A collectively composed opera. Also published by Peking: Foreign Languages Press, 1962.]

2052 Tien, Chien. "The Girl." *Chinese Literature* 1959:6:117–18. [Poem.]

2053 Tien, Han. "Princess Wen Cheng." *Chinese Literature* 1962:6:116–18. [Publication notice of a historical play in ten scenes.]

2054 Tien, Leng. "Mrs. Ma's Tea-house." *Chinese Literature* 1959:12:86–94.

2055 Ting, Yi and Ho, Ching-chih. "The White-haired Girl." *Chinese Literature* 1953:2:38–109. [Opera based on play of the same name.]

2056 Ting Ling [Chiang, Ping-chih].* "Sun Over the Sangkan River." *Chinese Literature* 1953:1:26–296. [Novel of land reform; winner of Stalin Prize in 1952.]

2057 Ting Ling [Chiang, Ping-chih].* *The Sun Shines over the Sangkan River.* Trans. Hsien-yi Yang and Gladys Yang. Peking: Foreign Languages Press, 1954.

2058 Ting, Tzu-ping. "Cipher Officer." *Chinese Literature* 1973:2:3–12. [Story of a female cipher officer.]

2059 Ts'ao Ming [Lo, Ts'ao-ming].* *The Moving Force.* Peking: Cultural Press, 1950.

2060 Ts'ao Ming [Lo, Ts'ao-ming].* "New Problems." *Chinese Literature* 1957:4:163–68.

2061 Ts'ao Ming [Lo, Ts'ao-ming].* "The Peaceful Dike Orchard." *Chinese Literature* 1964:3:59–77.

2062 Ts'ao Ming [Lo, Ts'ao-ming].* "Peasant Woman." *Chinese Literature* 1964:3:51–59.

2063 Tsin, Ching. "Liu Hu-lan." *Chinese Literature* 1972:2:15–43. [Reminiscences about a guerrilla heroine.]

2064 Tsung, Pu. "The Marriage of Late Sister." Trans. Sidney Shapiro. *Chinese Literature* 1964:1:3–21.

2065 Tu, P'eng-ch'eng.* *In Days of Peace.* Peking: Foreign Languages Press, 1962.

2066 Tung, Chun-lun and Chiang, Yuan. "The Silkworm Maid." Trans. Gladys Yang. *Chinese Literature* 1959:8:111–19.

2067 Wang, An-yu. "Sister-in-law Remarries." *Chinese Literature* 1959:8:78–110. [About a widow's romance.]

2068 Wang, Ho-ho. "My Future Daughter-in-law." *Chinese Literature* 1973:7:53–65.

2069 Wang, Shan-hung and Hung, Tieh-shan. "The Iron Girl." *Chinese Literature* 1971:5:59–66.

2070 Wang, Shu-yuan, et al. "Azalea Mountain; a Revolutionary Modern Peking Opera." *Chinese Literature* 1974:1:3–69. [Heroine is a party representative of peasants' self-defense corps.]

2071 Wang, Yüan-chien. "The Mother." *China Reconstructs* 9(June 1960):34.

2072 Wang, Yüan-chien. "Party Membership Dues." In *An Ordinary Laborer*, pp. 1–17. Peking: Foreign Languages Press, 1961. [About a woman revolutionary in the anti-Japanese war.]

2073 Wei, Chin-chih. "Wet Nurse." *Chinese Literature* 1960:7:110–123.

2074 Wen, Chieh. "Boosara, an Uighur Girl." *Chinese Literature* 1958:2:86–90.

2075 *The Women's Representative: Three One-act Plays.* Peking: Foreign Languages Press, 1956. [Plays dealing with love and family life of the new Chinese woman.]

2076 Wu, Yen-ko. "The Women's Team Leader." *Chinese Literature* 1974:8:3–22.

2077 Yang, Mo.* "The Song of Youth." *Chinese Literature* 1960:3:3–48; 1960:4:46–105; 1960:6:80–137.. [Abridgement of a best-selling novel published in 1958 about young women in the patriotic student movement in the 1930s.]

2078 Yang, Yun-shen. "Two Young Women." *Chinese Literature* 1959:3:35–40.

2079 Yao, Keh-ming. "When the Party Secretary Showed Up." *Chinese Literature* 1973:2:36–45. [A woman worker becomes deputy secretary of a district party committee.]

2080 Yeh, Mien. "A Lecture on History." *Chinese Literature* 1974:11:33–46. [A young woman political instructor.]

2081 Yin, Yi-ping. "Half the Population." *Chinese Literature* 1971:7:62–68. [About women who want jobs.]

2082 Yu, Jen. "Aunt Liang's Dinner Party." *Chinese Literature* 1968:12:83–89.

2083 Yu, Tsung-hsin. "Our Olunchun Girl." *Chinese Literature* 1971:4:58–60. [Poem.]

2084 Yu, Yu. "Sister Lung." *Chinese Literature* 1972:12:46–52. [About a young woman commune worker.]

2085 Yu, Yun-chuan. "Hidden Potential." *Chinese Literature* 1974:7:55–65. [About a young woman secretary of a party branch.]

2086 Yueh, Wen. "The Cave Hospital." *Chinese Literature* 1977:7:45–55. [A young woman party branch secretary works in a hospital.]

2087 Yusuf, Alieas. "A Mother's Heart." *Chinese Literature* 1956:4:120–23.

Note: Works written by overseas Chinese may also concern situations in the People's Republic. See also "Hong Kong, Taiwan, and Overseas Chinese: Fiction, Poetry and Drama."

CRITICAL STUDIES: LITERATURE OF THE PEOPLE'S REPUBLIC OF CHINA

2088 "An Appreciation of the Ballet 'White-Haired Girl.'" *Chinese Literature* 1969:4:75–86.

2089 Braga, Anthony. "Aijiguli—a new Operatic Heroine." *Eastern Horizon* 5(July 1966):23–34.

2090 Chin, Ai-li Sung. *Modern Chinese Fiction and Family Relations, Analysis of Kinship, Marriage and the Family in Contemporary Taiwan and Communist Stories.* Cambridge, Mass.: M.I.T. Center for International Studies, 1966.

2091 "Comments on the Ballet 'White Haired Girl.'" *Chinese Literature* 1966:8:133–146.

2092 Croizier, Ralph. "Chinese Art in the Chiang Ch'ing Era." *J. of Asian Studies* 38(Feb. 1979):303-311.

2093 Eber, Irene. "Images of Women in Recent Chinese Fiction: Do Women Hold up Half the Sky?" *Signs* 2(Autumn 1976):24-34.

2094 Feuerwerker, Yi-tsi Mei. "Ideology and Narrative: A Study of Ding Ling's Fiction." Ph.D. dissertation, Harvard University, 1979.

2095 Hsia, C. T. [Hsia, Chih-ch'ing]. "Residual Femininity: Women in Chinese Communist Fiction." *China Quarterly*, no. 13 (Jan.-Mar. 1963), pp. 158-79. [Also in *Communist Chinese Literature*, ed. Cyril Birch, pp. 158-79. N.Y., 1963.]

2096 Hsiao, Yun-peng. "Women Fliers." *Chinese Literature* 1965:6:101-106. [Criticism of a modern play.]

2097 Hsieh, Frances Mei-huei Yang [Hsieh, Yang Mei-hui]. "The Normative Pattern of Family Life in Chinese Communist Society: A Content Analysis of 120 Magazine Short Stories." M.A. thesis, Tufts University, 1965.

2098 Huang, Chao-yen. "On *The Song of Youth.*" *Chinese Literature* 1960:6:138-41.

2099 Mei, Lan-fang. "My New Opera." *Chinese Literature* 1959:10:133-39. [Mei was a famous star of Peking opera who specialized in female roles.]

2100 "'The Red Detachment of Women'—China's First Revolutionary Ballet." *Peking Review* 11(Mar. 22, 1968):37-38.

2101 Sang, Hu. "About the Film 'The White Haired Girl.'" *Chinese Literature* 1972:7:96-99.

2102 *SCMM*, no. 728 (Apr. 1, 1972). Sung, Hung-hua. "A Remarkable Achievement of Theatrical Transplanting—comment on the Revolutionary Modern Opera 'Red Detachment of Women,'" p. 105. [*Hongqi* 1972, no. 4.]

2103 *SCMP*, no. 183 (Sept. 21, 1951). "*White Haired Girl* on the Screen," p. 19.

2104 *SCMP*, no. 381 (July 17, 1952). "*White Haired Girl*--New Folk Opera," p. 30.

2105 *SCMP*, no. 4931 (June 27, 1971). "Chinese Color Film 'The Red Detachment of Women' Shown in Japan," p. 110.

2106 *SCMP*, no. 4976 (Sept. 4, 1971). "Chinese Color Film 'The Red Detachment of Women' Warmly Welcomed at Venice International Film Festival," p. 200.

2107 *SCMP*, no. 5048 (Dec. 25, 1971). "Chinese Film 'The Red Detachment of Women' Shown in Norway," p. 157.

2108 *SCMP*, no. 5100 (May 13, 1972). "Chinese Film 'The Red Detachment of Women' Televised by US National Broadcasting Company," p. 186.

2109 *SCMP*, no. 5187 (July 22, 1972). "Shanghai Dance Drama Troupe of China Presents Ballet 'The Red Detachment of Women' in Tokyo," p. 127.

2110 "A Shining Example from the Great Proletarian Cultural Revolution—on the Ballet 'White Haired Girl.'" *China Reconstructs* 15(Aug. 1966):28-36.

2111 Tannenbaum, Gerald. "Another Triumph in Chinese Ballet: the White Haired Girl." *Eastern Horizon* 5(Dec. 1966):21-29.

2112 Tung, Feng-wen. "A Revolutionary Mother." *Chinese Literature* 1971:12:105-106. [About Aunt Sha in the screen version of the Peking opera "Sha jia bang."]

2113 Weakland, John H. "Chinese Film Images of Invasion and Resistance." *China Quarterly*, no. 47 (1971), pp. 439-470. [Also includes discussion of women's roles in Chinese films.]

2114 "What 'The White Haired Girl' Teaches Us." *China Reconstructs* 15(Aug. 1966):47-50.

2115 "The 'White Haired Girl,' a New Revolutionary Ballet." *Peking Review* 9(May 20, 1966):25.

2116 Wilhelm, Hellmut. "The Image of Youth and Age in Chinese Communist Literature." *China Quarterly*, no. 13 (Jan.-Mar. 1963), pp. 180-94.

2117 "'Yang K'ai-hui'—a New Play." *China Pictorial* 1978:12:20.

2118 Yang, Yang. "On the Stage: Liu Hu-lan." *Chinese Literature* 1965:6:10711.

2119 Yeh, Lin. "The Ballet: 'The Red Detachment of Women.'" *Chinese Literature* 1964:12:9604.

WOMEN WRITERS AND ARTISTS

2120 Anderson, Colena M. "Two Modern Chinese Women: Ping Hsin and Ting Ling." Ph.D. dissertation, Claremont Graduate School, 1954.

2121 Bao, Wenqing. "A Woman Painter's Story." *China Reconstructs* 30(Jan. 1981):62-63.

2122 Bernard, Suzanne. "An Interview with Ru Zhijuan." *Chinese Literature* 1980:3:92-98. [Ru is a woman writer and soldier.]

2123 Chang, Jun-mei. *Ting Ling: Her Life and Her Work.* Taibei, 1978.

2124 Chao, Pu-wei (Yang). *Autobiography of a Chinese Woman, by Buwei Yang Chao.* Trans. Yuenren Chao. N.Y.: John Day, 1947. [Author was one of the early "emancipated" college-educated women in the 1920s.]

2125 Ch'i-chun. "Mother's Books." *Chinese Studies in History* 14(1980):1:79-84.

2126 Chong, Lily Pao-hu. "Li I-an, Eleventh Century Poetess." *J. of Oriental Literature* 6(1953):59-64. [On a poetess of the Northern Song dynasty.]

2127 Chow, Ching Lie. *Journal in Tears: Memory of a Girlhood in China.* N.Y.: McGraw-Hill, 1978.

2128 Chow, Chung-cheng. *The Lotus Pool.* Trans. Joyce Emerson. N.Y.: Appleton-Century-Crofts, 1960. [Autobiography of a woman in the 1930s. See also Chow, Chung-cheng, *The Lotus Pool of Memory*. London: Michael Joseph, 1961.]

2129 Colby, Venetta. "Han Su-yin." *Wilson Library Bulletin* 31(May 1957):690.

2130 Davies, Derek. "Interview with Han Suyin." *Far Eastern Economic Review* 54(Nov. 24, 1966):430-34.

2131 Der Ling (Princess). *Kowtow.* N.Y.: Dodd Mead, 1930. [Autobiography.]

2132 Ding Ling [Ting Ling]. "A Few Words from My Heart." *Chinese Literature* 1980:4:106-109. [A speech made by the Chinese woman writer at the 4th Congress of Chinese Writers and Artists held in Beijing in 1979.]

2133 "Ding Ling to Publish New Books." *Beijing Review* 22(July 6, 1979):45-46.

2134 Fang, Jufen. "My Life as an Actress." *China Pictorial* no. 377 (Nov. 1979), pp. 38-39.

2135 Fang, Wen-jen. "A Woman Writer of Distinction—an Interview." *Chinese Literature* 1963:7:104-106. [Biographical sketch and interview with Ru Zhijuan.]

2136 Feng, Xiaxiong. "Ding Ling's Reappearance on the Literary Stage." *Chinese Literature* 1980:1:3-16.

2137 Feuerwerker, Yi-tsi. "Women as Writers in the 1920s and 1930s." In *Women in Chinese Society*, ed. Margery Wolf and Roxane Witke, pp. 143-168. Stanford: Stanford University, 1975.

2138 Gigliesi, Primrose. "The Art of Hsiao Shu-fang." *Orientations* 10(Oct. 1979):60-65. [Introduces Chinese woman artist Xiao Shufang.]

2139 Goldblatt, Howard Charles. "A Literary Biography of Hsiao Hung (1911-1942). Ph.D. dissertation, Indiana University, 1974.

2140 Goldman, Merle. *Literary Dissent in Communist China.* Cambridge, Mass.: Harvard University, 1967. [Contains material on female writers.]

2141 Guo, Linxiang. "Zhang Jie, a New Woman Writer." *Chinese Literature* 1979:9:103-104.

2142 Herdan, Innes. "Li Feng-lan: Peasant Painter." *China Now*, no. 40 (Mar. 1974), pp. 6, 13. [Li is a woman painter.]

2143 Hsieh, Ping-ying. *Autobiography of a Chinese Girl: A Genuine Autobiography by Hsieh Ping-ying.* Trans. Tsui Chi. London: G. Allen and Unwin, 1943.

2144 Hsieh, Ping-ying. *Girl Rebel: The Autobiography of Hsieh Pingying with Extracts from Her "New World Diaries."* N.Y.: DaCapo, 1975. [Reprint of 1940 ed.]

2145 Hsieh, Ping-ying. "My Life as a Writer." *Chinese Studies in History* 14(Fall 1980):42-56. [Article selected from *Nü zuojia zizhuan* (Autobiographical sketches of Chinese women writers), comp. by Wu Yumin. Taibei: Lianhe, 1972.]

2146 Hsu, Pang-ta. "Women Painters' Works in the Palace Museum." *Chinese Literature* 1959:7:165-67.

2147 Hu, Pin-ching. *Li Ch'ing-chao.* N.Y.: Twayne, 1966. [China's best known traditional woman poet, of the Northern Song dynasty.]

2148 Hu, Pin-ching. "Courtesan Poetess Hsueh T'ao." *Free China Review* 22(May 1972):23-25. [On a Tang poet who was also a Taoist nun.]

2149 "Jin Yueling, a Composer." *China Pictorial* 1979:2:35.

2150 Kräuter, Uwe and Wilson, Patricia. "Films in China, Part 1." *China Reconstructs* 28(Aug. 1979):4-17. [On Yu Lan and Zhang Ruifang, actress and film director.]

2151 Leaf, E. H. "Ting Ling, Herald of a New China." *T'ienhsia Monthly* 5(Oct. 1937):225-36.

2152 Liao, Chengzhi. "My Mother and Her Paintings." *China Reconstructs* 28(June 1979):46-55.

2153 Luo, Binji. "A Brief Biography of Xiao Hong." *Chinese Literature* 1980:11:73-85. [A biography of Chinese woman writer Xiao Hong (Zhang Naiying).]

2154 Mao Tun [Shen, Yen-ping]. "Ting Ling—Girl Herald of the New China." *China Forum* (Shanghai) 2(1933):7:6-7.

2155 *SCMP*, no. 183 (Sept. 21, 1951). "I Played the White Haired Girl," p. 21.

2156 *SCMP*, no. 4250 (July 28, 1968). "Stem the Evil Wind of Falling in Love and Getting Married Early among Literary and Art Circles—Letters from the Revolutionary Masses," p. 17. [From *Wenhui bao*.]

2157 "She Sings on the University Platform." *Chinese Literature* 1971:8:112-17.

2158 "Stage Left, Stage Right." *New China* 1(Winter 1976):32-35. [On the Shanghai actress Chen Yuanji.]

2159 "Standing Room Only." *Peking Review* 3(April 19, 1960):28. [On the successes of opera actresses.]

2160 Swann, Nancy Lee. *Pan Chao: Foremost Woman Scholar of China, 1st Century A.D.* N.Y.: Century, 1932.

2161 Teh, Yung. "The Story of a Ballad-Singer." *Chinese Literature* 1979:9:49-53.

2162 Ting Ling [Chiang, Ping-chih]. "My Creative Work Life." *China Forum* (Shanghai) 2(1933):8:2-3.

2163 Ting Ling [Chiang, Ping-chih]. "Life and Creative Writing." *Chinese Literature* 1954:3:152-58.

2164 Walls, Jan Wilson. "The Poetry of Yü Hsüan-chi: A Translation, Annotation, Commentary, and Critique." Ph.D. dissertation, Indiana University, 1972. [On a woman poet of the Tang dynasty.]

2165 Wimsatt, Genevieve. *Selling Wilted Peonies; Biography and Songs of Yü Hsüan-chi, T'ang Poetess.* N.Y.: Columbia University, 1936.

2166 Wu, Yang. "Yang Mo and Her Novel *The Song of Youth.*" *Chinese Literature* 1962:9:111-16. [An interview.]

2167 Yang, Gladys. "A New Woman Writer Shen Rong and Her Story 'At Middle Age.'" *Chinese Literature* 1980:10:64-70.

2168 Yang, Minru. "Xue Tao: A Tang-Dynasty Woman Poet." Trans. Shiguang Hu. *Chinese Literature* 1981:8:113-20.

2169 Yao, Hsin-nung. "When Sing-Song Girls Were Muses." *T'ien-hsia Monthly* 4(May 1937):474-83.

2170 Yeh, Ch'an-chen. "Writing and Me." *Chinese Studies in History* 14(1980):1:106-117. [Describes the author's mother, and life and literature during a turbulent age from a woman writer's point of view.]

2171 Zhou, Yixing. "In the Limelight: Interview with Chen Chong." *China Now*, no. 93 (Nov./Dec. 1980), pp. 10-11. [An interview with actress Chen Chong, winner of the "Hundred Flower Awards."]

CHINESE WOMEN THROUGH WESTERN EYES: LITERARY REPRESENTATIONS

2172 Anson, Robert Sam. "Portraits of Four Chinese." *Saturday Review* 7(March 15, 1980):20-23. [Report by an American writer on some encounters in the People's Republic. One of the stories is about a Chinese woman, Mrs. Yi Hsiao-li.]

2173 Applegarth, Margaret Tyson. *A China Shepherdess.* Philadelphia: Judson Press, 1924.

2174 Atherton, Gertrude. *My San Francisco: A Wayward Biography.* N.Y.: Bobbs-Merrill, 1946. [The author writes of one of her favorite California Chinese women: Dr. Margaret Chung, founder of the World War II WAVES and leader in other patriotic pursuits.]

2175 Brown, Karen. *The Shanghai Lady.* N.Y.: Efrus and Bennet, 1929.

2176 Buck, Pearl S. *The Good Earth.* N.Y.: John Day, 1931. [Story of a Chinese farmer and his wife, a former servant sold by parents during a famine to a rich family. About her struggle to maintain the family and her reaction to her husband taking a concubine. Other eds.: London: Methuen, 1931; Leipzig: B. Tauchnitz, 1932; N.Y.: Modern Library, 1934, etc.]

2177 Buck, Pearl. *Sons.* N.Y.: John Day, 1932. [Also published by: London: Methuen, 1932. A continuation of *The Good Earth.*]

2178 Buck, Pearl. *The Mother.* N.Y.: John Day, 1934. [Also published by: London: Methuen, 1934.]

2179 Buck, Pearl S. *Of Men and Women.* N.Y.: John Day, 1941.

2180 Buck, Pearl S. *Pavilion of Women.* N.Y.: John Day, 1946. [Appeared in part in serial form in *The Woman's Home Companion.*]

2181 Buck, Pearl S. *Peony.* N.Y.: John Day, 1948. [A novel about a rich merchant, son of a Jewish father and a Chinese mother, and their Chinese bondmaid, Peony.]

2182 Buck, Pearl S. *The Bondmaid.* London: Methuen, 1949.

2183 Buck, Pearl S. *My Several Worlds.* N.Y.: John Day, 1954. [Autobiography, giving a foreign woman resident's view of the transitional position of Chinese women during the Republican era.]

2184 Buck, Pearl S. *Imperial Woman.* N.Y.: John Day, 1956. [Based on the life of Empress Dowager Cixi.]

2185 Collis, Maurice. *The Motherly and Auspicious.* London: Faber and Faber, 1943. [Drama based on the life of Empress Dowager Cixi.]

2186 Daggett, Mary (Stewart) [Mrs.] *The Yellow Angel.* Chicago: Browne & Howell, 1914. [Includes depiction of Chinese women in America, e.g., slave girls.]

2187 Duffield, Anne. *Miss Mayhew and Ming Yun, a Story of East and West.* N.Y.: Frederick A. Stokes, 1928.

2188 Forsythe, Irene. *Cheng's Mother.* N.Y.: Friendship Press, 1948.

2189 Gardner, M. "Shoes Are So Difficult." *Asia* [Asia and the Americas] 35(April 1935):254–56

2190 Graham, Dorothy and Bennet, James W. *Brush Strokes on the Fan of a Courtesan; Verse Fragments in the Manner of the Chinese.* N.Y.: H. Vindal, 1927.

2191 Grantham, Alexandra Ethelred. *The Twilight Hour of Yang Kuei-fei.* Shanghai: Kelly and Walsh, 1923.

2192 Haden, Allen. *My Enemy, My Wife.* N.Y.: Putnam, 1951.

2193 Hibbert, Eloise Talcott. *Embroidered Gauze.: Portraits of Famous Chinese Ladies.* Freeport, N.Y.: Books for Libraries Press, 1969.

2194 Huggins, Alice Margaret. *Fragrant Jade.* Nashville: Broadman Press, 1948.

2195 Huggins, Alice Margaret. *The Red Chair Waits.* Philadelphia: Westminster Press, 1948.

2196 Huggins, Alice Margaret and Robinson, Hugh. *Wan-fu; Ten Thousand Happinesses.* N.Y.: Longmans Green, 1957.

2197 Jernigan, Muriel M. *The Two Lives of An-marie.* N.Y.: Crown, 1957.

2198 Keyte, John Charles. *A Daughter of Cathay.* London: A. Rivers, 1926.

2199 Lancing, George. *Imperial Motherhood.* London: R. Hale, 1945.

2200 Lane, Kenneth Westmacott [Keith West]. *Ma Wei Slop.* London: Cresset Press, 1944. [Novel of Tang dynasty imperial concubine Yang Guifei.]

2201 Leavelle, Elizabeth. *Lustrous Heroine.* London: Hurst and Blackett, 1934.

2202 Lewis, Elizabeth F. *Ho-Ming: Girl of New China.* Philadelphia: Quaker City Books, 1934. [The story of a girl who was encouraged by her father against her mother's wishes to pursue education for a medical career.]

2203 Mackay, Margaret. *Lady with Jade.* N.Y.: John Day, c. 1939.

2204 Mackay, Margaret. *Great Lady.* N.Y.: John Day, 1946.

2205 Mason, Richard L. *The World of Suzi Wong.* Cleveland: World Publishing Co., 1957.

2206 Miln, Louise. *Mr. and Mrs. Sên.* N.Y.: Frederick A. Stokes, 1923.

2207 Miln, Louise. *Ruben and Ivy Sên.* N.Y.: Frederick A. Stokes, 1926.

2208 Owen, Frank. *Della-Wu, Chinese Courtesan, and Other Oriental Love Tales.* N.Y.: Lantern Press, 1931.

2209 Pettit, Charles. *The Unfaithful Lady.* N.Y.: Avon Book Co., 1948.

2210 Poston, Martha Lee. *The Girl Without a Country.* N.Y.: Edinburgh T. Nelson, 1944.

2211 Sanford, Agnes Mary (White). *The 2nd Mrs. Wu.* Philadelphia: Lippincott, 1965.

2212 Simpson, Bertram Lenox [Putnam Weale]. *Her Closed Hands.* N.Y.: MacMillan, 1927.

2213 Una, Lady Troubridge, trans. *The Woman Who Commanded 500,000,000 Men.* N.Y.: H. Liveright, 1929. [Translation from the French of Charles Pettit.]

2214 Ward, Arthur Sarsfield. *Fu Manchu's Bride.* N.Y.: Doubleday, 1933.

2215 Wimsatt, Genevieve Blanche. *A Lady Like the Moon.* N.Y.: B. Ackerman, 1945.

HONG KONG, TAIWAN AND OVERSEAS CHINA: FICTION, POETRY AND DRAMA

2216 Chang, Eileen.* *The Rice-Sprout Song.* N.Y.: Scribner, 1955.

2217 Chang, Eileen.* "Stalemates." Trans. by the author. *The Reporter* 15(Sept. 20, 1956):34–38.

2218 Chang, Eileen.* *Naked Earth.* Trans. by the author. Hong Kong: Union Press, n.d. [c. 1956].

2219 Chang, Eileen.* "The Golden Cangue." Trans. by the author. In *Twentieth-Century Chinese Stories,* ed. C. T. Hsia, pp. 138-91. N.Y.: Columbia University, 1971.

2220 Chen, Jo-hsi.* *The Execution of Mayor Yin and Other Stories from the Great Proletarian Cultural Revolution.* Trans. Nancy Ing and Howard Goldblatt. Bloomington: Indiana University, 1978. [Another ed.: London: Allen and Unwin, 1979.]

2221 Chen, Ying-chieh. "Love by Arrangement." *Free China Review* 22(Feb. 1972):27–32.

2224 Chi, Pang-yuan, et al., eds. *Anthology of Contemporary Chinese Literature: Taiwan, 1960-1974.* Taibei: National Institute for Compilation and Translation, 1975.

2224 Fang, Hao. "My Mother." Trans. Wu Wang Heng-ling. *Chinese Pen,* Spring 1978, pp. 106-114. [From Taiwan.]

2224 Hsu, Yu. "Sister Tsui-ling." Trans. George Kao. *Renditions: A Chinese-English Translation Magazine,* no. 2 (Spring 1974), pp. 99-114.

2225 Kingston, Maxine Hong. *The Woman Warrior.* N.Y.: Alfred A. Knopf, 1976. [A work by a Chinese-American woman writer.]

2226 Lau, Joseph S. M., ed. *Chinese Stories from Taiwan, 1960-1970.* N.Y.: Columbia University, 1976. [Yang Ch'ing-ch'u's "Enemies" concerns an unmarried woman in Japanese occupied Taiwan.]

2227 Lee, Yu-hua.* *The Last Rite and Other Stories.* San Francisco: Chinese Materials Center, 1979.

2228 Li, He. "Mother's New Year's Eve Money." Trans. Y. T. Chen. *Chinese Pen,* Winter 1978, pp. 52-67. [Story from Taiwan.]

2229 Liu, Ts'un-yan. "Ying Niang." Trans. Susan MacDougall. *Renditions: A Chinese-English Translation Magazine,* no. 3 (Fall 1974), pp. 19-27.

2230 MacCunn, Ruthann Lum. *Thousand Pieces of Gold.* San Francisco: Design Enterprises of San Francisco, 1981. [A biographical novel about Polly Bemis, a pioneer Chinese American woman in Idaho.]

2231 *The Muse of China: A Collection of Prose and Short Stories by Contemporary Chinese Women Writers.* Taibei: Chinese Women Writers' Association, 1974.

2232 Nieh, Hua-ling.* *The Purse.* Taibei, 1971.

2233 Sansan.* *Eight Moon: The True Story of a Young Girl's Life in Communist China by Sansan as Told to Betty Lord.* London: Robert Hale, 1966.

2234 Wong, Jade Snow. *Fifth Chinese Daughter.* N.Y.: Harper & Rowe, 1950. [Autobiography of a 24 year-old Chinese American woman.]

2235 Wang, Wen-hsing. "The Two Women." Trans. Li-fen Chen. *Chinese Pen*, Summer 1978, pp. 79–90. [By a writer in Taiwan.]

CRITICAL STUDIES: LITERATURE OF HONG KONG, TAIWAN AND OVERSEAS CHINA

2236 Bohlmeyer, Jeannine. "Eileen Chang's 'Bridges to China.'" *Tamkang Review* 5(1974):1:111–28.

2237 Chiang, Kui-ching. "Last Curtain Call for an Actress." *Free China Review* 22(Nov. 1972):29–32.

2238 Chin, Ai-li Sung. *Modern Chinese Fiction and Family Relations, Analysis of Kinship, Marriage and the Family in Contemporary Taiwan and Communist Stories.* Cambridge, Mass.: M.I.T. Center for International Studies, 1966.

2239 Faurot, Jeannette L. *Chinese Fiction from Taiwan: Critical Perspectives.* Bloomington: Indiana University, 1980.

2240 Liang, Shih-chiu. "Dimensions of Women." Trans. Chao-ying Shih. *Free China Review* 23(July 1973):22–24.

2241 Rexroth, Kenneth and Chung, Ling, trans. "From the Orchid Boat—3 Women Poets of Today." *Renditions: A Chinese-English Translation Magazine*, no. 1 (Fall 1973) pp. 121–24.

Marriage and the Family

COURTSHIP, MARRIAGE, DIVORCE AND WIDOWHOOD: TRADITIONAL CHINA (TO 1911)

2242 American Academy of Political and Social Science, Philadelphia. *China, Social and Economic Conditions.* 1912. [See "The Life of a Young Girl" by Li Yieni Tsao and "A Wedding in South China" by Ying-mei Chun.]

2243 Bismark, Karl. "The Marriage of the Emperor of China." *Galaxy* 19(Jan.–June 1875):182–93.

2244 Buxbaum, David C., ed. *Chinese Family Law and Social Change in Historical and Comparative Perspective.* Seattle: University of Washington, 1978. [See Jack L. Dull, "Marriage and Divorce in Han China: A Glimpse at 'Pre-Confucian' Society," pp. 23–74.]

2245 Chiao, Chien. "Female Chastity in Chinese Culture." *Bulletin of the Institute of Ethnology, Academia Sinica,* no. 3 (Spring 1971), pp. 205–211.

2246 Chiu, Vermier Yantak [Chao P'ing]. "Some Notes on Chinese Customary Marriage." In *Family Law and Customary Law in Asia: A Contemporary Legal Perspective,* ed. David Charles Buxbaum, pp. 45–49. The Hague: Nijhoff, 1968.

2247 Ch'ü, T'ung-tsu. *Law and Society in Traditional China.* Paris: Mouton, 1965. [See chapter 2, "Marriage," pp. 91–127.]

2248 Collins, Leslie E. "Death in the Life of Chinese Women: Marriage." *China Notes* 10(Winter 1971/72):8–10. [About the Chinese woman in late traditional times (1860–1930).]

2249 De Groot, Jan Jakob Maria. "The Wedding Garments of a Chinese Woman." *Internationales Archiv für Ethnographie,* no. 4 (1891), pp. 182–84.

2250 De Groot, Jan Jakob Maria. "Adoption (Chinese)." In *Encyclopedia of Religion and Ethics,* ed. James Hastings, vol. 1, p. 107. N.Y.: Scribner, 1908.

2251 De Groot, Jan Jakob Maria. "Sutteeism: Widowhood." In *The Religious System of China,* vol. 2, pp. 735–69. Leiden: E.J. Brill, 1892–1910.

2252 Doré, Henry, S.J. *Researches into Chinese Superstitions,* vols. 1–8. Trans. M. S. J. Kennelly. Shanghai: T'usewei Printing Press, 1914. [Translated from the French with historical and explanatory notes. See "Birth and Childhood," vol. 1, pp. 1–28; "Betrothal and Marriage," vol. 1, pp. 29–40.]

2253 Dull, Jack L. "Marriage and Divorce in Han China: A Glimpse at 'Pre-Confucian' Society." In *Chinese Family Life and and Social Change in Historical and Comparative Perspective,* ed. David C. Buxbaum, pp. 23–74. Seattle: University of Washington Press, 1978.

2254 Eberhard, Wolfram. "Auspicious Marriages: A Statistical Study of a Chinese Custom." *Sociologus,* neue (2.) Folge 13, 1 (1963), pp. 49–55. [Reprinted in *Studies in Chinese Folklore and Related Essays,* by Wolfram Eberhard, pp. 201–207. Indiana University, Folklore Institute Monograph Series, 23. Bloomington: Indiana University, Research Center for the Language Sciences, 1970.]

2255 Feifel, Eugene. "The Marriage of Po Chü-i's Parents." *Monumenta Serica,* 15, fasc. 2 (1956), pp. 344–55.

2256 Fielde, Adele Marion. "Chinese Marriage Customs." *Popular Science Monthly* 34(Dec. 1888):241–46.

2257 Freedman, Maurice. *Rites and Duties: Or, Chinese Marriage.* London: Bell, 1967. [Also in *The Study of Chinese Society: Essays by Maurice Freedman,* pp. 255–72. Stanford: Stanford University, 1979.]

2258 Freedman, Maurice. "Ritual Aspects of Chinese Kinship and Marriage." In *Family and Kinship in Chinese Society,* ed. Maurice Freedman, pp. 163–87. Stanford: Stanford University, 1970. [Also in *The Study of Chinese Society: Essays by Maurice Freedman,* pp. 273–95. Stanford: Stanford University, 1979.]

2259 Hsu, Francis L. K. [Hsü, Lang-kuang]. "Observations on Cross-Cousin Marriage in China." *American Anthropology,* new (2nd) series 47(Jan.–Mar. 1945):83–103.

2260 K'in Sin. "Divorce for Women in Ancient China." *Asia* [Asia and the Americas] 2(1952):34–36.

2261 Liu, Francis S. F. [Liu, Shih-fang]. "Adultery as Crime in China." *China Law Review* 7(Feb. 1935):144–47.

2262 Lo, Tung Fan [Lo, Tung-hsün]. "The Institution of Marriage in China: A Historical Study." *Hong Kong University Law J.* 1:2(Jan. 1927):131–49.

2263 MacCreery, J. "The Gift of the Bride: A Critical Note on Maurice Freedman's Interpretation of Traditional Chinese Marriage." *Kroeber Anthropological Society Papers* 45–76(1972):56–71.

2264 Mace, David and Vera. *Marriage: East and West.* N.Y.: Doubleday, 1960.

2265 Medhurst, Walter Henry. "Marriage, Affinity and Inheritance in China." *Transactions of the China Branch of the Royal Asiatic Society,* no. 4(1853/1854), pp. 1–32.

2266 "A Posthumous Marriage." *T'oung Pao* 10(1899):1:114.

2267 Tjan, Tjoe-som. *Po-hu-t'ing: The Comprehensive Discussions in the White Tiger Hall.* 2 vols., Sinica Leidensia. Leiden: Brill, 1949. [See "Han Marriage Regulations," vol. 1, pp. 244–63.]

2268 Topley, Marjorie. "Marriage Resistance in Rural Kwangtung." In *Studies in Chinese Society,* ed. Arthur P. Wolf, pp. 247–68. Stanford: Stanford University, 1978. [Discusses the situation from the early 19th to the early 20th century.]

2269 Tso, S. W. "Ceremonies and Customs of the Chinese." In *Twentieth Century Impressions of Hong Kong, Shanghai, and Other Treaty Ports of China: Their History, People, Commerce, Industries and Manners,* ed. Arnold Wright and H. A. Cartwright, pp. 307-318. London: Lloyd's Greater Britain Publishing Co., 1908.

2270 Van Wettum, B. A. J. "A Pair of Chinese Marriage Contracts." *T'oung Pao* 5(Dec. 1894):371-85.

2271 Walshe, William Gilbert. *Ways That Are Dark: Some Chapters on Chinese Etiquette and Social Procedure.* Shanghai: Kelly and Walsh, 1906(?).

2272 Wilhelm, Richard. "The Chinese Conception of Marriage." Trans. W. H. Hilton-Brown. In *The Book of Marriage,* ed. H. A. Keyserling, pp. 123-37. N.Y.: Harcourt, Brace, 1926.

2273 Wilkinson, William Henry. "The Marriage of the Chinese Emperor." *Asiatic Quarterly Review* 8(July-Oct. 1889):82-93.

2274 Wolf, Arthur Paul and Huang, Chieh-shan. *Marriage and Adoption in China, 1845-1945.* Stanford: Stanford University Press, 1980.

2275 Wong, C. M [Wang, Mei-ch'ih]. "The Ancient Custom of Cantonese Marriage." *Annual of the China Society* (Singapore) 1960/1961:60-65.

2276 Wong, Sun-ming. "Confucian Ideal and Reality: The Transformation of the Institution of Marriage in T'ang China (A.D. 618-907)." Ph.D. dissertation, University of Washington (Seattle), 1979.

2277 Yang, Pi-wang. "Ancient Bridal Laments." *China Reconstructs* 12(Oct. 1963):42-44. [Collection of sayings from pre-liberation days.]

COURTSHIP, MARRIAGE, DIVORCE AND WIDOWHOOD: THE CHINESE REPUBLIC (1911-1949)

2278 Bryan, Robert Thomas. "Divorce Law of China." *Chinese Social and Political Science Review* 4(June 1919):126-32.

2279 Buck, Pearl Sydenstricker. "New Modes of Chinese Marriage." *Asia* [Asia and the Americas] 27(Aug. 1927):650-53.

2280 Chang, Hsi-ch'eng. *Problems of Divorce: A Special Issue of the Ladies Journal.* Folklore & Folkliterature Series, no. 125. Peking: National Peking University and Chinese Association for Folklore.

2281 Chang, Shao-wei. "Divorce Plague in China." *China Critic* 6(Apr. 27, 1933):426-29.

2282 Chao, Chi-chen. "Being an Old Maid in China." *Asia* [Asia and the Americas] 41(Sept. 1941):492-96.

2283 Cheng, Hawthorne [Cheng, Chün]. "Marriage in Chungking." *Asia and the Americas* 44(July 1944):308-311.

2284 Chin, Ai-li Sung [Ch'en, Shen Ai-li]. "Some Problems of Chinese Youth in Transition." *American J. of Sociology* 54(July 1948):1-9.

2285 "China's New Wedding Ceremony Takes Only Fifteen Minutes." *Literary Digest* 60(Mar. 15, 1919):48.

2286 Close, V. "Mating and Marriage in China." *Forum* 78(Nov. 1927):673-84.

2287 Cormack, Mrs. J. G. *Chinese Birthday, Wedding, Funeral and Other Customs.* London-Peking: Kegan Paul, 1923.

2288 "Divorce Statistics in Shanghai, 1929-1930." *China Critic* 4(March 11, 1931):257.

2289 Eskelund, Karl. *My Chinese Wife.* London: George G. Harrap, 1947. [Published in New York by Doubleday, Doran & Co., 1945.]

2290 Feng, Han-yi and Shryock, J. K. "Marriage Customs in the Vicinity of I Ch'ang." *Harvard J. of Asiatic Studies* 13(Dec. 1950):362-430.

2291 Frey, W. "Do You Solemnly Swear? Chinese Marriage Customs." *Country Life* 72(June 1937):41-42+.

2292 [Ginling] college girls. "Students and Marriage Customs in China." *Chinese Recorder,* July 1926, pp. 493-97.

2293 Kahn, Ida. "Daughters of Cathay." *Asia* [Asia and the Americas] 21(Jan. 1921):66-69.

2294 Komor, M. "Chinese Wedding." *Living Age,* no. 346 (July 1934), pp. 421-23.

2295 MacKinnon, Catherine. "Chinese Women and Marriage." *Chinese Recorder,* Dec. 1923, pp. 709-712.

2296 "Marriage beyond the Grave." *China J.* 35(Aug. 1941):45-46.

2297 Mossman, Mereb E. "The Changing Marriage Customs in China." *Sociology and Social Research* 29(Nov.-Dec. 1944):104-112.

2298 "No Doll or Dumb-bell Is the Chinese Wife." *Literary Digest* 92(Feb. 19, 1927):36+.

2299 Reber, Calvin H., Jr. "Protestant Christianity and Marriage in China." Ph.D. dissertation, Columbia University, 1958.

2300 Serruys, Paul. "Christian Adaptation of Wedding Ceremonies." *China Missionary* 1(1948):1-2:28-45, 166-76.

2301 Smedley, Agnes. "Hsu Mei-ling." *New Republic* 62(Apr. 9, 1930):219-20. [About husband-wife relationships under Western influence.]

2302 Spencer, Robert F. and Barnett, S. A. "Notes on a Bachelor House in the South China Area." *American Anthropologist,* new (2nd) series 50(July-Sept. 1948):463-78.

2303 Waln, N. "House of Exile." *Atlantic* 151(Feb.-Apr. 1933):129-41, 336-46, 425-34.

2304 Wei, T. F. "Chinese Wedding." *China J. of Science and Art* (Shanghai) 34(Feb. 1941):56-58.

2305 "Widow Chang of China." *Literary Digest* 108(Mar. 28, 1931):16.

2306 Young, T. S. "Cupid in China." *Living Age,* no. 352 (Aug. 1937), pp. 536-39.

COURTSHIP, MARRIAGE, DIVORCE AND WIDOWHOOD: THE PEOPLE'S REPUBLIC OF CHINA (1949-)

2307 Bender, Peter. "Divorce, Chinese Style." *Atlas* 9(June 1965):348-52.

2308 Blake, Fred C. "Love Songs and the Great Leap: The Role of a Youth Culture in the Revolutionary Phase of China's Economic Development." *American Ethnologist* 6(1979):1:41-54.

2309 Chang, Ching-wen. "The Youth Problem on the Chinese Mainland." *Issues and Studies* 2(Apr. 1966):21-29.

2310 Chang, Li-han. "A Chinese Love Story." *China Reconstructs* 28(Jan. 1979):10-12.

2311 Chen, Hsu. "How Wang Kwei-lan Married the Man of Her Choice." *Chinese Studies in History* 5(1971-1972):2-3:189-92.

2312 Chu, Godwin C. and Hsu, Francis L. K., eds. *Moving a Mountain: Cultural Change in China.* Honolulu: University of Hawaii, 1979. [In the third section Hsu analyzes changes in China's marriage patterns.]

2313 Croll, Elisabeth Joan. "The Negotiation of Marriage in the People's Republic of China." Ph.D. dissertation, London University, 1978.

2314 Croll, Elisabeth Joan. *The Politics of Marriage in Contemporary China.* N.Y.: Cambridge University Press, 1981.

2315 Crook, David. "Marriage, Housing, Smuggling, Seafood and Scenery." *Eastern Horizon* 20(May 1981):22. [While touring, the author observes marriage in China among other things.]

2316 Dorros, Sybilla. "The Theoretical Basis of Sexual Equality and Marriage Reform in China." *Asian Studies* 13(Aug. 1975):13–25.

2317 *ECMM*, no. 22 (Nov. 16, 1955). Chou, K'e-hsien. "How I Handle My Love Problem," p. 3.

2318 *ECMM*, no. 22 (Nov. 16, 1955). Liu, Lo-ch'un. "Why Our Marital Relations Become Strained," p. 5.

2319 *ECMM*, no. 22 (Nov. 16, 1955). Yu, Li. "How to Deal with the Shortcomings of your Husband," p. 1. [From *Zhongguo qingnian.*]

2320 *ECMM*, no. 23 (Jan. 1, 1956). "Comments on the Marital Relations of Liu Lo-chun and Lo Pao-yi," p. 46.

2321 *ECMM*, no. 28 (Nov. 24, 1955). Ai, Nan. "How I Deal with My Counter-Revolutionary Husband," p. 23.

2322 *ECMM*, no. 41 (Apr. 3, 1956). "Do Not Start Making Love Too Early," p. 23.

2323 *ECMM*, no. 41 (May 16, 1956). "Respect the Principle of Voluntariness in Love Life," p.27.

2324 *ECMM*, no. 57 (Oct. 1956). "Principles for Handling Divorce Cases during the Years Since Promulgation of Marriage Law," p. 15.

2325 *ECMM*, no. 65 (Dec. 15, 1956). "In the Handling of Divorce Cases We Must Struggle against Bourgeois Ideology," p. 5.

2326 *ECMM*, no. 66 (Nov. 1, 1956). "Give Correct Guidance to the Marriage and Love Problems of Rural Youth," p. 13.

2327 *ECMM*, no. 66 (Nov. 16, 1956). "Do Not Make Love to Middle School Students Who Are Still Young," p. 16.

2328 *ECMM*, no. 85 (Apr. 1, 1957). Lim, Kha-ti. "The Best Marriage Age from the Physiological Standpoint," p. 31.

2329 *ECMM*, no. 134 (July 7, 1958). Chi, Feng. "How to Handle Your Spouse and Teachers If They Are Rightists," pp. 15–17. [From *Zhongguo qingnian.*]

2330 *ECMM*, no. 182 (Apr. 16, 1959). "Who Is to Blame?" p. 34. [Letters from readers concerning love and marriage.]

2331 *ECMM*, no. 1132 (Aug. 29, 1955). Jen, Hsi-lien. "I am the Fiancee of a Revolutionary Soldier," p. 42.

2332 Fei, Chih. "Brother and Sister." Trans. Ian MacLaughlin and T. Y. Lee. *Eastern Horizon* 2:(Nov. 1963):57–65.

2333 "Freedom to Marry." *China Reconstructs* 1(Jan.–Feb. 1952):40.

2334 Han, Suyin. "Down with the Meal-ticket Husband!" *Atlas* 19(Mar. 1970):49–50.

2335 "A Handbook on Daily Living for Residents of Streets and Neighborhoods (Excerpt): How to Deal with the Question of Love and Marriage." *Chinese Sociology and Anthropology* 8(Summer 1976):11–18. [From *A Handbook of Daily Living*, originally published in 1951.]

2336 *How to Manage Marriage Registration Work Well.* Peking: Village Reader Publication House, 1963.

2337 Huang, Jen L. "Notes on Official View with Regard to Mate Selection and Marital Happiness in Family in People's Republic of China." *J. of Comparative Family Studies* 3(1972):2:283–91.

2338 Huang, Lucy Jen. "The Communist Chinese Attitude towards Inter-Class Marriage." *China Quarterly*, no. 12 (Oct.–Dec. 1962), pp. 183–90. [Also in *Marriage and Family Living* 24(Nov. 1962):389–92.]

2339 "Journey to Tungting Lake, Part 3: 'Widows' Village.'" *China Reconstructs* 22(Nov. 1973):20–23.

2340 JPRS, no. 5345 (Feb. 12, 1960). Lin Lieh-hui. "Views on Marriage, Communist China." [From *Zhongguo gongren.*]

2341 JPRS, no. 14502 (1962). "Should There be a Dowry?" pp. 36–42. [From *Zhongguo funü*, no. 4]

2342 JPRS, no. 14533 (May 10, 1962). "The Attack on Marriage," pp. 102–105. [From *Zhongguo qingnian bao.*]

2343 JPRS, no. 15251 (1962). "Letters to the Editor Opposing Early Marriage," pp. 1–11. [From *Zhongguo funü.*]

2344 JPRS, no. 28413 (Jan. 6, 1965). "Before and After My Wedding Arrangements." [From *Gongren ribao.*]

2345 JPRS, no. 28413 (Jan. 6, 1965). "Do Not Bow Before Old Customs," pp. 36–37. [From *Gongren ribao.*]

2346 JPRS, no. 28543 (Oct. 14, 1964). "What Attitude Should a Husband Take Toward His Wife?" [From *Renmin ribao.*]

2347 JPRS, no. 28766 (Nov. 19, 1965). "Young People Should Take the Lead in Getting Rid of the Outmoded Practice of Asking for 'Betrothal Gifts.'" [From *Zhongguo qingnian bao.*]

2348 JPRS, no. 37161 (Jan. 16, 1966). "Changing Undesirable Wedding Customs and Practices," pp. 134–37. [*Zhongguo qingnian*, no. 2.]

2349 Kan, Aline. "The Marriage Institution in Present-day China." *China Mainland Review* 1(Dec. 1965):1–11.

2350 Kong, Jiesheng. "Marriage." *China Now*, no. 92 (Sept./Oct. 1980), pp. 15–1.

2351 Lihan, Chang. "A Chinese Love Story." *China Now*, no. 84 (May/June 1979), pp. 6–7.

2352 Ling, M. L. "The Growth of a New Outlook on Marriage." *People's China* 3(1951):11:14.

2353 Liu, Hongfa. "Between Husband and Wife." *China Reconstructs* 28(June 1979):16–17.

2354 Liu, M. "Letter from Shunde." *Far Eastern Economic Review* 105(July 6, 1979):58. [On marriage customs and rites.]

2355 McAleavy, Henry. "Some Aspects of Marriage and Divorce in Communist China." In *Family Law in Asia and Africa*, ed. James Norman Dalrymple Anderson, pp. 73–89. N.Y.: Praeger, 1968.

2356 Pasternak, Burton. "Season of Birth and Marriage in Two Chinese Localities." *Human Ecology* 6(1978):3:299–323.

2357 Pollard, R. S. "Marriage and Divorce in China Now." *Plain View* 11(1956):54–64.

2358 "Red Chinese Exploit Love." *Science Newsletter* 78(Sept. 10, 1960):167.

2359 Salaff, Janet W. "The Emerging Conjugal Relationship in the People's Republic of China." *J. of Marriage and the Family* 35(Nov. 1973):4:705–717.

2360 Schell, Orville. "Seeking 'Love's Proper Place' in China." *Asia* 2(May/June 1979):30–37.

2361 SCMM, no. 357 (Mar. 25, 1963). "Readers' Opinions on Consequence of Love at First Sight," p. 41–44. [From *Zhongguo funü.*]

2362 SCMM, no. 370 (May 1, 1963). "What Concepts of Happiness Should Youths Cultivate? An Important Question that Should be Solved When Learning from Comrade Lei Feng," p. 6. [From *Zhongguo qingnian.*]

2363 SCMM, no. 383 (Sept. 23, 1963). Yuan, Tzu-jen. "Yi Shi-chuan Gets Married," pp. 39–41.

2364 SCMM, no. 384 (Aug. 1, 1963). "I Don't Want to Get Married Early," pp. 25–26. [Editorial from *Zhongguo funü.*]

2365 SCMM, no. 386 (Sept. 1, 1963). "What Do Women Live For?" p. 12. [From *Zhongguo funü.*]

2366 *SCMM*, no. 386 (Sept. 16, 1963). Yao, Li-kung. "Fight Resolutely against Bourgeois Thought When It Comes to the Problem of Marriage and Love," p. 18. [From *Zhongguo qingnian*.]

2367 *SCMM*, no. 392 (Oct. 1, 1963). Ch'en, Mei-ying. "How I Fight for Freedom of Marriage," p. 22. [From *Zhongguo funü*.]

2368 *SCMM*, no. 421 (June 15, 1964). "What Is the Criterion for Choosing a Husband?" pp. 23–28. [From *Zhongguo funü*.]

2369 *SCMM*, no. 438 (Oct. 12, 1964). "What Are the Criteria for Choosing a Husband?" pp. 29–32. [From *Zhongguo funü*.]

2370 *SCMM*, no. 452 (Jan. 18, 1965). "What Attitude Should a Husband Take Towards His Wife?" pp. 28–30. [From *Zhongguo funü*, Oct. 1, 1964.]

2371 *SCMM*, no. 475 (May 1, 1965). "How Can the Problem of Love and Marriage Be Correctly Handled for Young People from Families of the Exploiting Classes?" p. 19. [From *Zhongguo funü*.]

2372 *SCMM*, no. 515 (Jan. 16, 1966). Chang, Chi (Yunghuang-ts'un Brigade, Chashan Commune, Ch'angyi *hsien*, Shantung province). "Doing away with Betrothal Money," p. 1.

2373 *SCMM*, no.515 (Jan. 16, 1966). Kao, Shou-ch'eng (Ch'enchi Commune, Huaiying *hsien*, Kiangsu). "Getting Married without a Dowry and Bridal Sedan Chair," p. 3.

2374 *SCMM*, no. 515 (Mar. 14, 1966). "Changing Undesirable Wedding Customs and Practices," pp. 1–5. [From *Zhongguo qingnian*, Jan. 16, 1966.]

2375 *SCMM*, no. 606 (Dec. 18, 1967). "Carry out the Activity of 'One Helping Another to Form a Red Pair,' Develop and Consolidate the Revolutionary Great Alliance," pp. 8–10. [From *Hongqi*.]

2376 *SCMP*, no. 300 (Mar. 8-10, 1952). "He Is Not My Husband But a Robber," p. 28.

2377 *SCMP*, no. 436 (Oct. 18, 1952). Shih, Lu. "Chinese Farm Girls Now Prefer to Marry Workers," p. 34.

2378 *SCMP*, no. 527 (Mar. 5, 1953). "My Happy Life Begins," p. 16.

2379 *SCMP*, no. 535 (Mar. 17, 1953). "Experience in Dealing with Marital Disputes," pp. 9–10.

2380 *SCMP*, no. 966 (Jan. 4, 1955). Lin, Hua. "Illicit Love in Communist China—It's Right That This Affair of Blind Love Should Be Considered As Closed," p. 25.

2381 *SCMP*, no. 1052 (Apr. 1, 1955). Hsu, Ming-chiang. "Several Problems Concerning the Education of the Youth on the Marriage and Love Problem Conducted by the Youth League Organization," p. 25.

2382 *SCMP*, no. 1132 (Aug. 29, 1955). Jen, Hsi-lien. "I Am the Fiancee of a Revolutionary Soldier," p. 42.

2383 *SCMP*, no. 1306 (May 24, 1956). "Don't Interfere with Legal Marriage," p. 12.

2384 *SCMP*, no. 1306 (May 24, 1956). "Why Can't We Get Married?" p. 11.

2385 *SCMP*, no. 1366 (Aug. 23, 1956). "'Man Selects Woman' and 'Woman Selects Man,'" p. 3.

2386 *SCMP*, no. 1372 (Aug. 30, 1956). "Arranged Marriages Getting Serious in Rural Areas in Shensi Province," p. 14.

2387 *SCMP*, no. 1389 (Sept. 4, 1956). "Problems Concerning Snarled Matrimonial Cases," p. 9.

2388 *SCMP*, no. 1389 (Sept. 6, 1956). "Early Marriage Is Not Advisable," p. 7. [*Zhongguo qingnian bao* editorial.]

2389 *SCMP*, no. 1389 (Sept. 6, 1956). "A Survey of Early Marriages Among Young Factory Workers," p. 5.

2390 *SCMP*, no. 1422 (Nov. 15, 1956). "Show Concern for Young People's Happiness in Love and Marriage," p. 6.

2391 *SCMP*, no. 1424 (Nov. 25, 1956). "Evil Daughter-in-law Arrested in Shanghai for Causing Death of Mother-in-law," p. 18.

2392 *SCMP*, no. 1462 (Jan. 12, 1957). "Marriage of Party Members Need Not Be Approved by Party." p. 4.

2393 *SCMP*, no. 1466 (Dec. 22, 1956). "We Must Adopt a Solemn Attitude toward the Problem of Love and Marriage," p. 5.

2394 *SCMP*, no. 1485 (Feb. 20, 1957). "A Case of Matrimonial Fraud in Szechwan," p. 28.

2395 *SCMP*, no. 1487 (Feb. 5, 1957). "Changchun Mobilizes for Implementation of Marriage Law," p. 20

2396 *SCMP*, no. 1509 (Feb. 27, 1957). "The Principle of 'Freedom of Marriage' Should Not Be Abused," p. 7.

2397 *SCMP*, no. 1509 (Mar. 9, 1957). "Some Young People in Tientsin Involved in Hasty Marriage, Divorce," p. 9.

2398 *SCMP*, no. 1569 (July 2, 1957). "How to Tackle the Problem of Love," p. 26. [From *Hunan nongmin bao*.]

2399 *SCMP*, no. 1720 (Dec. 2, 1957). "Girls Graduated from Middle Schools Marry Peasants in Shansi," p. 27.

2400 *SCMP*, no. 1789 (Mar. 8, 1958). "A Talk to Young Comrades on Love and Marriage," p. 23.

2401 *SCMP*, no. 2034 (May 29, 1959). "Treat Marriage Seriously," p. 1.

2402 *SCMP*, no. 2456 (Mar. 8, 1961). "A Village Wedding Near Peking," p. 14.

2403 *SCMP*, no. 3168 (Jan. 30, 1964). Shen, Lien-ting. "Abandon the Old and Establish the New in Arranging Weddings—China Youth League Branch of Hsin-hua Brigade Helps Youths Arrange Weddings Frugally," p. 13. [From *Zhongguo qingnian bao*.]

2404 *SCMP*, no. 3381 (Dec. 25, 1964). "Is a Betrothal Present a Means of Showing Gratitude for Parental Upbringing?" p. 14.

2405 *SCMP*, no. 3469 (May 6, 1965). "Does One Lose One's Stand by Marrying a Person Born of a Family of the Exploiting Class?" p. 14.

2406 *SCMP*, no. 4352 (Jan. 18, 1969). "A New Custom in Marrying off Daughters," p. 10.

2407 *SCMP*, no. 4831 (Jan. 30, 1971). "Vigorously Encourage Late Marriage for the Revolutionary Cause," p. 122.

2408 *SCMP*, no. 5268 (Nov. 20, 1972). "Returning the Present," p. 14.

2409 *SCMP*, no. 5268 (Nov. 20, 1972). "Revolutionary Young People Should Set the Pace in Changing Customs and Traditions," p. 13.

2410 *SCMP*, no. 5400 (June 12, 1973). Chunglou, Commune, P'ingt'an *hsien*, Fukien. "The Custom of Marrying Late," p. 226.

2411 *SCMP*, no. 5435 (July 30, 1973). Ch'ien Shih-lung (Deputy Secretary of the China Youth League Branch and Deputy Commander of the Militia Battalion of the No. 16 Brigade of Chüehchiao Commune in Jutung *hsien*, Kiangsu). "Practice Late Marriage for the Revolutionary Cause," p. 63.

2412 Shapiro-Perl, Nina. "Divorce Trial." *New China* 3(Summer 1977):35–49.

2413 "Since the Criticism of Lin Piao and Confucius Began...: Between Husband and Wife; Listen If It Is Right." *China Reconstructs* 24(June 1975):17–18.

2414 *SPRCP*, no. 6033 (Feb. 2, 1976). "Wedding Ceremony in Rural China," p. 164.

2415 *SPRCP*, no. 6048 (Feb. 26, 1976). "New Life in 'Widow Village.'" p. 194.

2416 Su, Feng. "Changing Times: How Three Generations Married." *Women of China* 1980:5:13-17.

2417 Veneris, Jim. "Deep Roots in Both Countries." *New China* 3(Fall 1977):39-42. [About interracial marriage.]

2418 "Why Our Marital Relationship Has Broken Down." *Chinese Sociology and Anthropology* 7(Spring 1975):5-67. [Including 16 articles originally appearing in the journal *Women of New China* (Nov. 1955-June 1956), later published by the editors of *Chinese Women* under a separate title.]

2419 Whyte, Martin King. "Rural Marriage Customs." *Problems of Communism*, no. 26 (July 1977), pp. 41-55.

2420 Whyte, Martin King. "Revolutionary Social Change and Patrilocal Residence in China." *Ethnology* 18(July 1979):211-227. [Considers whether the revolutionary changes in Chinese society since 1949 have altered the traditional custom of uprooting women from their families at marriage.]

2421 Wong, Alice (Kan). "Changes in Marriage, Family Institutions in China, 1949-1969." In *Selected Seminar Papers on Contemporary China*, 1, ed. Steve Chin and Frank King, pp. 149-78. Hong Kong: University of Hong Kong, 1971.

2422 Yan, Qing. "More Marriage in Zhongshahai." *China Reconstructs* 30(June 1981):13.

2423 Yang, Liu. "Reform of Marriage and Family Systems in China." *Peking Review* 7(Mar. 13, 1964):17-19.

COURTSHIP, MARRIAGE, DIVORCE, WIDOWHOOD AND CELIBACY: HONG KONG, TAIWAN AND OVERSEAS CHINA

2424 Barclay, George Watson. *Colonial Development and Population in Taiwan*. Princeton: Princeton University, 1954. [Includes data on divorce rate, age at marriage.]

2425 Brugger, Florence. "The Chinese-American Girl: A Study in Cultural Conflicts." M.A. thesis, New York University, 1935. [Includes problems of courtship.]

2426 Casterline, John Bernt. "The Determinants of Rising Female Age at Marriage: Taiwan, 1905-1976." Ph.D. dissertation, University of Michigan, 1980.

2427 Chang, Denis K. L. "The New Law of Divorce in Hong Kong." *Hong Kong Law J.* 3(Jan. 1973):51-66.

2428 Chen, Chiyen [Ch'en Chi-yen]. "The Foster Daughter-in-law System in Formosa." *American J. of Comparative Law* 6(Summer 1957):302-314.

2429 Chin, James J. "How I Met My Wife." *Chinese Studies in History* 6(Summer 1973):44-47.

2430 Eberhard, Wolfram. *Moral and Social Values of the Chinese: Collected Essays*. Chinese Materials and Research Aids Service Center Occasional Series 6. Taibei: Chinese Materials and Research Aids Service Center, 1971. [See "Aspirations Concerning Married and Married Life among Contemporary Taiwanese," pp. 235-69.]

2431 Evans, David Meurig Emrys. "The New Law of Succession in Hong Kong." *Hong Kong Law J.* 3(Jan. 1973):7-50. [See especially pp. 35-38 on widows.]

2432 Far, Sui Seen. "The Chinese Woman in America." In *The Land of Sunshine*, Jan. 1897, pp. 59-64. [Describes Chinese women who came to America as brides.]

2433 Gallin, Bernard. "Cousin Marriage in China." *Ethnology* 2(Jan. 1963):104-108.

2434 Greenfield, D. E. "Marriage by Chinese Law and Custom in Hong Kong." *International and Comparative Law Quarterly* 7(1958):437-51.

2435 Hong Kong, Attorney General. *The McDouall-Heenan Report, 1965*. Hong Kong: J. R. Lee Government Printer, 1967. [A report by the Attorney General on "Chinese Marriage in Hong Kong: New Recommendations."]

2436 Hong Kong, Colonial Secretariat. *The 1967 White Paper on Chinese Marriage in Hong Kong*. Hong Kong: J. R. Lee Acting Government Printer, 1967.

2437 Hong Kong, Land Office. *Annual Departmental Report by the Land Officer and Registrar of Marriages, 1946/47-1948/49*. Hong Kong, 1947-1949.

2438 Hong Kong Bar Association, Sub-committee on Chinese Marriages. *Chinese Marriages in Hong Kong: A Report by the Sub-Committee of the Hong Kong Bar Association on Chinese Marriages*. Hong Kong: Hong Kong Bar Association, 1967.

2439 Huang, Lucy Jen [Huang, Jen-hua]. "Dating and Courtship: Innovations of Chinese Students in America." *Marriage and Family Living* 18(Feb. 1956):25-29.

2440 Jarvie, Ian C., ed. *Hong Kong: A Society in Transition: Contributions to the Study of Hong Kong Society*. London: Routledge, 1969. [Includes discussion of marriage.]

2441 Jordan, David Kinsey. "Two Forms of Spirit Marriage in Rural Taiwan." *Bijdragen Tot de taal-, Land-en Volkenkunde van Naderlandsch-Indië* 127(1971):1:181-89.

2442 Lin, Robert. "Marital Composition of the Taiwan Population." *National Taiwan University J. of Sociology*, vol. 10, pp. 96-110. [English summary.]

2443 Lo, Rong-rong. "Marriage Patterns and Modernization in Taiwan." Ph.D. dissertation, University of Minnesota, 1972.

2444 Lyman, Stanford M. "Marriage and the Family among Chinese Immigrants to America, 1850-1960." *Phylon* 29(Winter 1968).

2445 Marsh, Robert M. and O'Hara, Albert R. "Attitudes towards Marriage and the Family in Taiwan." *American J. of Sociology* 67(July 1961):1-8.

2446 O'Hara, Albert Richard. "Changing Attitudes toward Marriage and the Family in Free China." *J. of the China Society* 1962:57-59. [Reprinted in Albert Richard O'Hara, *Research on Changes of Chinese Society*, pp. 9-19. Asian Folklore and Social Life Monographs 20. Taibei: Orient Cultural Service, 1971.]

2447 O'Hara, Albert Richard. "Comparative Values of American and Chinese University Students Choosing a Mate." *J. of China Society* 5(1967):93-100. [Reprinted in Albert Richard O'Hara, *Research on Changes of Chinese Society*, pp. 27-34. Asian Folklore and Social Life Monographs 20. Taibei: Orient Cultural Service, 1971.]

2448 O'Hara, Albert R. "Actual Changes Follow Attitudinal Changes toward Marriage and the Family in the Republic of China." *J. of the China Society* 13(1976):2-15. [Based on data for students from two Taiwan universities. Taiwanese and Mainlanders are compared.]

2449 Pegg, Leonard. "Legitimacy Ordinance and Affiliation Proceedings Ordinance (Nos. 28 and 29 of 1971)." *Hong Kong Law J.* 2(Sept. 1972):348-60. [Discussion of marriage law.]

2450 Podmore, D. and Chaney, D. "Attitudes towards Marriage and the Family amongst Young People in Hong Kong, and Comparisons with the United States and Taiwan." *J. of Comparative Family Studies* 3(1972):2:228-38.

2451 Pratt, Jean. "Emigration and Unilateral Descent Groups: A Study of Marriage in a Hakka Village of the New Territories, Hong Kong." *Eastern Anthropologist* 13(1960):147-58.

2452 Ridehalgh, A. and McDouall, J. C. *Chinese Marriages in Hong Kong.* Hong Kong: Government Printer, 1960.
2453 Rishi, W. R. "Marriage of Orient." *Singapore Chopmen Enterprises.* 1970.
2454 Rosen, Sherry. "Sibling and In-law Relationships in Hong Kong: The Emergent Role of Chinese Wives." *J. of Marriage and the Family* 40(Aug. 1978):621-28.
2455 Ryan, E. "Some Chinese Marriage Recipes." *Catholic World* 171(June 1950):206-211. [An interview with Sir Robert Ho Tung and his wife.]
2456 Salaff, Janet Weitzner. *Social and Demographic Determinants of Marriage in Hong Kong.* IASR Working Papers 2. Vancouver: University of British Columbia, Institute of Asian and Slavonic Research, 1972.
2457 Salaff, Janet Weitzner. "The Status of Unmarried Hong Kong Women and the Social Factors Contributing to Their Delayed Marriage." *Population Studies* 30(Nov. 1976):391-412.
2458 Schak, David Carl. "From *Mang-hun ya-chia* to *tzu-yu lien-ai*: The Evolution of Dating and Free Courtship in Modern China as Manifested in Taipei, Taiwan." Ph.D. dissertation, University of California, Berkeley, 1973.
2459 Smith, Peter C. "Asian Marriage Patterns in Transition." *J. of Family History* 5(Spring 1980):58-96. [Includes situation in Hong Kong and Taiwan.]
2460 Topley, Marjorie D. "Chinese Women's Vegetarian Houses in Singapore." *J. of Malayan Branch of Royal Asiatic Society* 27(1954):1:51-67.
2461 Topley, Marjorie D. "Ghost Marriages among the Singapore Chinese." *Man* 56(1956):71-72.
2462 Topley, Marjorie D. *The Organisation and Social Function of Chinese Women's Chai T'ang [vegetarian halls] in Singapore.* London, 1958.
2463 Tsung, T. "Women Who Do Not Marry." *Orient* (Hong Kon) 2(1952):12:41-43.
2464 Westland, A. B. "A Chinese Misalliance." *Overland Monthly*, 2nd series 37(Jan. 1901), pp. 611-615. [Story about a marriage in Hong Kong.]
2465 Wolf, Arthur Paul. "Marriage and Adoption in a Hokkien Village [Hsia-chi-chou, T'ai-pei *hsien*, Taiwan]." Ph.D. dissertation, Cornell University, 1964.
2466 Wolf, Arthur Paul. "Adopt a Daughter-in-law, Marry a Sister." *American Anthropologist* 70(Oct. 1968):864-74. [Discusses infant betrothal practices in Taiwan.]
2467 Wolf, Arthur Paul. "Marriage and Adoption in Northern Taiwan." In *Social Organization and the Applications of Anthropology: Essays in Honor of Lauriston Sharp*, ed. Robert J. Smith, pp. 128-60. Ithaca: Cornell University Press, 1974.
2468 Wolf, Arthur Paul and Huang, C. T. *Marriage and Adoption in China, 1845-1945.* Stanford: Stanford University, 1979. [Based on research in Taiwan.]
2469 Yuan, D. Y. "Marital Characteristics in Relation to the Rural-Urban Continuum in Taiwan." *Demography* 5(1968):1:93-103.

SOCIOLOGY AND ANTHROPOLOGY OF THE FAMILY: GENERAL WORKS

2470 Baker, Hugh D. R. *Chinese Family and Kinship.* N.Y.: Columbia University, 1969.
2471 Chen, I-fu. "The Old Chinese Family: A Study in Familial Control." M.A. thesis, University of Chicago, 1934.
2472 Cheng, Ch'eng K'un. "Familism, the Foundation of Chinese Social Organization." *Social Forces* 23(Oct. 1944):50-59.
2473 Choi, Jai-seuk. "Comparative Study on the Traditional Families in Korea, Japan and China." In *Families East and West: Socialization Process and Kinship Ties*, ed. Reuben Hill and Rene Konig, pp. 202-210. The Hague: Mouton, 1970.
2474 Cohen, Myron L. "Variations in Complexity among Chinese Family Groups: The Impact of Modernization." New York Academy of Sciences. *Transactions*, series 2, 29(Mar. 1967):638-44.
2475 Cohen, Myron L. "Development Process in the Chinese Domestic Group." In *Family and Kinship in Chinese Society*, ed. Maurice Freedman, pp. 21-36. Stanford: Stanford University, 1970.
2476 Eberhard, Wolfram. "Research on the Chinese Family." *Sociologus* neue (2.) Folge 9, 1(1959):1-11. [Reprinted in: Wolfram Eberhard, *Settlement and Social Change in Asia*, pp. 28-42. Hong Kong University Press, 1967.]
2477 Freedman, Maurice. "The Chinese Domestic Family: Models." In *VIe Congrès international des sciences anthropologiques et ethnologiques, Paris, 30 juillet-6 août 1960*. vol. 2, part 1, pp. 97-100. Paris: Musée de l'homme, 1963. [Also in *The Study of Chinese Society: Essays by Maurice Freedman*, pp. 235-39. Stanford: Stanford University, 1979.]
2478 Freedman, Maurice. "Problems in the Analysis of the Chinese Family." *Philadelphia Anthropological Society Bulletin* 14(Mar. 1961):21-23.
2479 Freedman, Maurice. "The Family in China, Past and Present." *Pacific Affairs* 34(Winter 1961/1962):323-36. [Reprinted in *Modern China*, ed. Albert Feuerwerker, pp. 27-40. Englewood Cliffs, N.J.: Prentice Hall, 1964. Also in *The Study of Chinese Society: Essays by Maurice Freedman*, pp. 250-54. Stanford: Stanford University, 1979.]
2480 Freedman, Maurice, ed. *Family and Kinship in Chinese Society.* Stanford: Stanford University, 1970.
2481 Fried, Morton H. "Trends in Chinese Domestic Organization." In *Proceedings of Symposium on Economic and Social Problems in the Far East*, University of Hong Kong, 1961, pp. 405-414. Hong Kong, 1962.
2482 Fried, Morton H. *Fabric of Chinese Society; a Study of the Social Life of a Chinese Country Seat.* N.Y.: Octagon Books, 1963. [Includes discussion on kinship, the extended family, extra-familial relationships, etc.]
2483 Goode, William Josiah. *World Revolution and Family Patterns.* N.Y.: Free Press of Glencoe, 1963. [See "China," pp. 270-320.]
2484 Ho, Ping-ti. "An Historian's View of the Chinese Family System." In *Man and Civilization: The Family's Search for Survival*, ed. Seymour M. Faber, Piero Mustacchi and Roger H. L. Wilson, pp. 15-30. N.Y.: McGraw Hill, 1965.
2485 Hsu, Francis L. K. [Hsü, Lang-kuang]. "The Myth of Chinese Family Size." *American J. of Sociology* 48(Mar. 1943):555-62.
2486 Hsu, Francis L. K. [Hsü, Lang-kuang]. "The Family in China: The Classical Form." In *The Family: Its Function and Destiny*, revised edition, ed. Ruth Nanda Anshen, pp. 123-45. N.Y.: Harper, 1959.
2487 Hsu, Francis L. K. [Hsü, Lang-kuang]. *Clan, Caste and Club: A Comparative Study of Chinese, Hindu, and American Ways of Life.* Princeton: Van Nostrand, 1963. [See especially pp. 32, 50, on concubinage, and pp. 28, 32-34, on widowhood.]

2488 Johnson, Kay Ann. "The Politics of Women's Rights and Family Reform in China." Ph.D. dissertation, University of Wisconsin, Madison, 1976.

2489 Kao, Ta-kuan. *Changes in Family and Society*. National Peking University and Chinese Association for Folklore and Folkliterature Series, no. 124.

2490 Kiang, Kang-hu. "Chinese Family System." *Annals of American Academy of Political and Social Science* 152(Nov. 1930):39-46.

2491 Lang, Olga. *Chinese Family and Society*. New Haven: Yale University, 1946. [Reprint: Hamden, Conn.: Archon Books, 1968.]

2492 Lee, Shu-ching [Li, Shu-ch'ing]. "China's Traditional Family: Its Characteristics and Disintegration." *American Sociological Review* 18(June 1953):272-80.

2493 Leslie, Gerald R. *The Family in Social Context*. N.Y.: Oxford University, 1967. [See "The Family System of China," pp. 81-124.]

2494 Levy, Marion Joseph, Jr. *The Family Revolution in Modern China*. Cambridge, Mass.: Harvard University, 1949. [Revision of "Some Aspects of Family Structure and the Problem of Industrialization in China." Ph.D. dissertation, Harvard University, 1947. Reprint: N.Y.: Octagon Books, 1963.]

2495 Lin, Yueh-hwa [Lin, Yüeh-hua]. *The Golden Wing: A Sociological Study of Chinese Familism*. N.Y.: Oxford University Press, 1948.

2496 Mai, Hui-ting. *Problems of Change of the Chinese Family*. Folklore and Folkliterature Series, nos. 82 and 83. Peking: National Peking University and Chinese Association for Folklore.

2497 Nee, Victor. "Toward a Social Anthropology of the Chinese Revolution." *Bulletin of Concerned Asian Scholars* 11(July-Sept. 1979):40-51. [Discusses marriage and the social status of women in rich, middle and poor peasant families.]

2498 P'an, Kuang-tan. *Problems of the Chinese Family*. Folklore and Folkliterature Series, no. 123. Peking: National Peking University and Chinese Association for Folklore. [By a famous social scientist of the 1930s.]

2499 Queen, Stuart Alfred; Habenstein, Robert Wesley; and Adams, John B. *The Family in Various Cultures*. Philadelphia: Lippincott, 1961. [See "The Chinese System of Familism," pp. 88-115.]

2500 Stacey, Judith. "Toward a Theory of Family and Revolution: Reflection on the Chinese Case." *Social Problems* 26(June 1979):499-508.

2501 Stacey, Judith. "Toward a Theory of Women, the Family and Revolution: An Historical and Theoretical Analysis of the Chinese Case." Ph.D. dissertation, Brandeis University, 1979.

2502 Su, Sing Ging [Hsü, Sheng-chin]. *The Chinese Family System*. N.Y.: International Press, 1922.

2503 Tamney, Joseph B. "Chinese Family Structure and the Continuation of Chinese Religions." *Asian Profile* 6(June 1978):211-217.

2504 Tao, L. K. [Tao, Meng-ho]. "Some Chinese Characteristics in the Light of the Chinese Family." In *Essays Presented to G. G. Seligman*, ed. Edward Evans-Pritchard, et al., pp. 335-44. London: Kegan Paul, Trench, Trübner, 1934.

2505 Tao, P. L. K. "The Family System in China." *Sociological Review* 6(Jan. 1913):47-54.

2506 *Transactions of the Third World Congress of Sociology*, vol. 4, *Changes in the Family*. London: International Sociological Association, 1956. [See Kizaemon Airga, "Introduction to the Family System in Japan, China and Korea," pp. 199-207; and Tatsumi Makino, "The Family System in China," pp. 208-214.]

2507 Walstedt, Joyce Jennings. "Reform of Women's Roles and Family Structure in the Recent History of China." *J. of Marriage and the Family* 40(May 1978):379-92.

2508 Yang, C. K. [Yang, Ch'ing-k'un]. *Chinese Communist Society: The Family and the Village*. Cambridge, Mass.: M.I.T. Press, 1959. [Deals with transition under socialism.]

CLAN AND LINEAGE

2509 Anderson, Eugene N. "Lineage Atrophy in Chinese Society." *American Anthropologist* 72(April 1970):363-65.

2510 Baker, Hugh David Roberts. "Clan Organization and Its Role in Village Affairs: Some Differences Between Single-Clan and Multiple-Clan Villages." In *Aspects of Social Organization in the New Territories*, ed. Hong Kong Branch, Royal Asiatic Society, pp. 4-5. Hong Kong: Cathay Press, 1964.

2511 Baker, Hugh David Roberts. *A Chinese Lineage Village: Sheung-shui*. London: Frank Cass, 1968.

2512 Baker, Hugh David Roberts. *Chinese Family and Kinship*. N.Y.: Columbia University, 1979.

2513 Beattie, Hilary J. *Land and Lineage in China: A Study of T'ung-ch'eng County, Anhwei, in the Ming and Ch'ing Dynasties*. Cambridge: Cambridge University, 1979.

2514 "Chinese Clans and Their Customs." *Chinese and Japanese Repository* 3(June 1, 1865):281-84.

2515 Chu, Solomon Shu-ping. "Family Structure and Extended Kinship in a Chinese Community." Ph.D. dissertation, University of Michigan, 1969.

2516 "Clanship among the Chinese." *Chinese Repository* 4(Jan. 1836):411-415.

2517 Eberhard, Wolfram. "Chinese Genealogies as a Source for the Study of Chinese Society." In *Studies in Asian Genealogy*, ed. Spencer John Palmer, pp. 27-37. Provo: Brigham Young University, 1972.

2518 Fei, Hsiao-tung [Fei Hsiao-t'ung]. "The Problem of Chinese Relationship System." *Monumenta Serica* 2(1936):1:125-48.

2519 Feng, Han-yi [Feng, Han-chi]. *The Chinese Kinship System*. Philadelphia, 1937. [Ph. D. dissertation, University of Pennsylvania, 1936; reprinted in *Harvard J. of Asiatic Studies* 2(July 1937):141-275.]

2520 Freedman, Maurice. *Chinese Lineage and Society: Fukien and Kwangtung*. N.Y.: Humanities Press, 1966.

2521 Fried, Morton H. "Kin and Non-Kin in Chinese Society, an Analysis of Extra-Kin Relationships in Chinese Society." Ph.D. dissertation, Columbia University, 1951.

2522 Hsu, Francis L. K. [Hsü Lang-kuang]. *Clan, Caste and Club: A Comparative Study of Chinese, Hindu, and American Ways of Life*. Princeton: Van Nostrand, 1963.

2523 Hu, Hsien-chin. *The Common Descent Group in China and Its Functions*. N.Y.: The Viking Fund, 1948.

2524 Kroeber, Alfred Louis. "Process in the Chinese Kinship System." *American Anthropologist*, new (2nd) series 35(Jan.-Mar. 1933):151-57.

2525 Liu, Hui-chen (Wang). *The Traditional Chinese Clan Rules*. Monographs of the Association for Asian Studies, 7. Locust Valley, N.Y.: J. J. Augustin, published for the Association of Asian Studies, 1959.

2526 Skinner, G. William, ed. *The Study of Chinese Society: Essays by Maurice Freedman.* Stanford: Stanford University, 1979. [See part 4, "Kinship and Religion in China."]

2527 Wang, Jen-ying. "Lineage Development and Social Change; a Case Study of Li Lineage in the Southern Taiwan." *Bulletin of the Institute of Ethnology, Academia Sinica* 35(Spring 1973):110. [English abridgement.]

2528 Watson, James Lee. *Emigration and the Chinese Lineage: The Mans in Hong Kong and London.* Berkeley: University of California, 1975.

2529 Yu, Elena S. H. "Kinship Structure, Post-Marital Residence and Sex-Role Equality in China." *Sociological Focus* 10(Apr. 1977):175-88.

FAMILY IN TRADITIONAL CHINA (TO 1911)

2530 Blitsten, Dorothy R. *The World of the Family.* N.Y.: Random House, 1963. [See "The Corporate Family in Confucian China: Its Phases and Functions," pp. 104-131.]

2531 Bridgman, Mrs. Eliza Jane (Gillet). *Daughters of China; or, Sketches of Domestic Life in the Celestial Empire.* N.Y.: R. Carter & Brothers, 1853.

2532 Brown, Carrie Chu. "The Position of a Wife in Late Traditional China." M. A. thesis, Cornell University, 1966.

2533 Bryson, Mary Isabella. *Child Life in Chinese Homes.* London: Religious Tract Society, 1885.

2534 Bryson, Mary Isabella. *Home-Life in China.* N.Y.: American Tract Society, 1886.

2535 Chu, Po-lu. "Maxims for the Well-Governed Household." Trans. Edward H. Kaplan. WWSC Program in East Asian Studies, Occasional Papers, no. 1. Bellingham, 1971. [A famous 17th-century essay illustrating the ideal of family morality during the late imperial period.]

2536 Ch'ü, T'ung-tsu. *Law and Society in Traditional China.* Paris: Mouton, 1965. [See chapter 1, "Family and Tsu," pp. 15-90.]

2537 "Concubines in China." *Literary Digest* 105(Apr. 19, 1930):16.

2538 Cornaby, William Arthur. "The Chinese Maiden at Home." *East of Asia Magazine* 3(1904):137-47.

2539 Douglas, Sir Robert Kennaway. *Society in China.* London: A.D. Innes & Co., 1895. [See chapter 10, "Filial Piety and the Position of Women," pp. 180-91; and chapter 11, "Marriage," pp. 192-218.]

2540 Eberhard, Wolfram. "The Upper Class Family in Traditional China." In *The Family in History,* ed. Charles Rosenberg, pp. 59-94. Pennsylvania: University of Pennsylvania, 1975. [Good introduction by a sociologist.]

2541 Goodrich, L. Carrington. "Maternal Influence: A Note." *Harvard J. of Asiatic Studies* 12(June 1949):226-30.

2542 Headland, Isaac Taylor. "Chinese Nursery Rhymes. *Chinese Recorder* 31(Jan. 1900):1-10.

2543 Headland, Isaac Taylor. *The Chinese Boy and Girl.* N.Y.: Revell, 1901.

2544 Headland, Isaac Taylor. "Chinese Children's Games." *J. of the North China Branch of the Royal Asiatic Society,* new (2nd) series 37(1906):150-84.

2545 Headland, Isaac Taylor. "Chinese Women at Home." *Putnam's* 7(Oct. 1909):20-32.

2546 Headland, Isaac Taylor. *Home Life in China.* N.Y.: Macmillan, 1914. [Reprinted: Detroit: Grand River Books, 1971.]

2547 Hosie, Dorothea. *Two Gentlemen of China.* 5th ed. London: Seeley, Service, 1929. [Late imperial Chinese upper-class home life from a feminine point of view.]

2548 Hsiao, Kung-ch'üan. "My Hometown and Family." *Chinese Studies in History* 10(Summer 1977):6-22. [Recollections of a gentry boyhood in the late Qing period.]

2549 Hsu, Francis L. K. [Hsü, Lang-kuang]. "Filial Piety in Japan and China: Borrowing, Variation and Significance." *J. of Comparative Family Studies* 2(Spring 1971):67-74.

2550 Hu, Shih. "An Autobiographical Account at Forty." *Chinese Studies in History* 11(Summer 1978). [See "Nine Years a Home Village Education," pp. 3-25. Reminiscences of the author's mother in the late Qing.]

2551 Jacobs, Fang-chih Huang. "The Origin and Development of the Concept of Filial Piety in Ancient China." *Chinese Culture* 14(Sept. 1973):15-55.

2552 M. F. C. "The Chinese Daughter-in-Law." *Chinese Recorder* 5(July-Aug. 1874):207-214. [Reprinted by the Ladies Board of Mission of the Presbyterian Church, New York, 1875.]

2553 Macgowan, Rev. John. *Sidelights on Chinese Life.* London: Paul, Trench, Trübner, 1907. [See chapter 2, "Family Life," and chapter 3, "Child Life," pp. 21-64.]

2554 Mariya, Mitsuo. "A Study of the Chinese Family System during the Han Dynasty." *Habado-Enkei-Doshisha Toyo Bunka Koza* 2(1956). [In Japanese with English summary.]

2555 May, Alfred J. "Chinese Relationships." *China Review* 21(July-Aug. 1894):15-39.

2556 Mayers, William Frederick. "The Chinese Imperial Family." *T'oung Pao* 6:3(1895):333-41. [Reprinted from *North China Herald and Supreme Court and Consular Gazette* (Jan. 1895).]

2557 Monroe, Harriet. "The Training of Chinese Children." *Century Magazine* 83(Mar. 1912):643-52.

2558 Nelson, Howard George Horatio. "An Anthropological Study of Inheritance and Succession in Traditional China." M.A. thesis, University of London [London School of Economics and Political Science], 1966.

2559 Osgood, E. I. "Do Little Girls Count in China?" *Missionary Review* 30(Nov. 1907):843-46.

2560 Simon, G. E. "The Family." In *China: Its Social, Political, and Religious Life,* pp. 1-69. London: Sampson, Low, Marston, Searle, and Rivingston, 1887.

2561 Titiev, Mischa and Tien, Hsing-chih [T'ien Hsing-chih]. "A Primer of Filial Piety." *Papers of the Michigan Academy of Science, Arts, and Letters* 33(1947):259-67.

2562 Tsao, Li Yieni. "The Life of a Girl in China." *Annals of the American Academy of Political and Social Sciences* 39(Jan. 1912):62-70.

2563 Wieman, Earl. "The Culture of Concubines." *Orientations* 2(Nov. 1971):37-39.

2564 Wilkinson, Hiram Pardes. *The Family in Classical China.* London: Macmillan, 1926. [Also published by: Shanghai: Kelly & Walsh, 1926. Primarily on the era before 221 B.C.]

2565 Wood, Edith Elmer. "Notes on Oriental Babies." *American Anthropologist,* new (2nd) series 5(Oct.-Dec. 1903):659-66.

2566 Yen, Chih-t'ui. *Family Instructions for the Yen Clan (Yen-shih chia-hsun).* Annotated trans. Ssu-yu Teng. Leiden: Brill, 1968. [From a 7th century A.D. original. See chapter 4, "Remarriage," pp. 12-15; and chapter 5, "Family Management," pp. 16-21.]

FAMILY IN REPUBLICAN CHINA (1911-1949)

2567 Buck, P. S. [Buck, Pearl S.] "In China, Too." *Atlantic* 131 (Jan. 1923):68-72. [About status of housewives.]

2568 Buck, Pearl S. "The First Wife." *Asia* [Asia and the Americas] 31(1931):747-53+.

2569 Cheng, C. K. "Chinese Family." *The China Monthly* 9(Feb. 1948):58-61.

2570 Chiang, Yee [Chiang, I]. *A Chinese Childhood.* N.Y.: Norton, 1963. [Autobiography. About a gentry boyhood.]

2571 Chu, Shih-ming (Mrs.). "Family Living in China." *J. of Home Economics* 35(Sept. 1943):408.

2572 Derling, Princess. "Quiet Day with a Chinese Family." *Mentor* 18(Feb. 1930):17-20. [The author was a Manchu noblewoman.]

2573 Fei, Hsiao-t'ung. *Peasant Life in China, a Field Study of Country Life in the Yangtze Valley.* London: Routledge & K. Paul, 1962. [Study by a leading Chinese anthropologist, originally published in 1939. See chapter 3, "The Chia," pp. 27-55, and *passim.*]

2574 Gamble, Sidney David. *The Household Accounts of Two Chinese Families.* N.Y.: China Institute of America, 1931. [A well-known sociologist's research based on fieldwork in north China in the 1920s.]

2575 Gamble, Sidney David. *How Chinese Families Live in Peiping.* N.Y.: Funk and Wagnalls, 1933.

2576 Gamble, Sidney David. *Ting Hsien: A North China Rural Community.* Stanford: Stanford University, 1954. [Includes illustration of farm families during the 1920s and 1930s.]

2577 Goodman, R. "Chinese Mother." *Living Age,* no. 354 (May 1938), p. 246.

2578 Hamilton, Pauline Ernst. "Home Life in China." *Missionary Review of the World* 66(June 1923):439-44.

2579 Headland, Isaac T. *Home Life in China.* London: Methuen, 1914. [Chinese home life is described by a Peking University Professor. Chapters 6-11 discuss girls, marriage, womanhood, housewives and motherhood.]

2580 Highbaugh, Irma. "Effects of the War on Rural Homes." In *Wartime China, as Seen by Westerners,* pp. 140-51. Chungking: China Publishing Co., 1942.

2581 Highbaugh, Irma. *Family Life in West China.* N.Y.: Agricultural Missions, 1948.

2582 Hirabayashi, Jo Anne and Tang, Peter S. H. [T'ang Shenghao]. "Family." In *A Regional Handbook on Northeast China.* Human Relations Area Files Subcontractor's Monographs, 61. Compiled by Far Eastern and Russian Institute, University of Washington. New Haven: Human Relations Area Files, 1956.

2583 Hosie, Dorothea Soothill. *Two Gentlemen of China: An Intimate Description of the Private Life of Two Patrician Chinese Families...* London: Seeley, Service, 1924.

2584 Hsiung, Yana. "A Study of the Family Life of Preschool Children in a Chinese Rural Town." M.A. thesis, Cornell University, 1947.

2585 Hsu, Francis L. K. [Hsü, Lang-kuang]. "The Functioning of a North China Family (in Mu-erh-shan-li, Ta-ku-shan chen, Chuang-ho *hsien,* Liaoning)." Ph.D. dissertation, University of London [London School of Economics and Political Science], 1940.

2586 Hsu, Francis L. K. [Hsü, Lang-kuang]. *Under the Ancestor's Shadow.* N.Y.: Doubleday, 1967. [A well-known anthropologist's work based on research in rural Yunnan, 1941-43.]

2587 Kulp, Daniel H. *Country Life in South China.* Vol. 1. N.Y.: Teachers College, 1925. [An important study based on first-hand observation. See chapter 6, "Family," pp. 135-189, and *passim.*]

2588 "Latest Statistics on the Size of Urban and Rural Families in China." *Nankai Weekly Statistical Service* 2(1929):2:1, 4.

2589 Newell, Jane I. "The Chinese Family: An Arena of Conflicting Cultures." *Social Forces* 9(June 1931):564-71.

2590 Ni, Ernest [Ni, Yin-hsin]. "Marital Status and Family Size in China." M.A. thesis, University of Chicago, 1945.

2591 Ni, Ernest [Ni, Yin-hsin]. "The Family in China." *Marriage and Family Living.* 16(Nov. 1954):315-18. [Based on research in wartime Yunnan.]

2592 Pruitt, Ida. *Old Madam Yin: A Memoir of Peking Life, 1926-1938.* Stanford: Stanford University, 1979. [Autobiography of a mistress of a large household, as told to the author. Provides information about family system.]

2593 Smythe, Lewis Strong Casey. "The Composition of the Chinese Family." *Nanking J.* 5(1935):2:371-93.

2594 Smythe, Lewis Strong Casey. "Factors Associated with the Success of Chinese Families as Families." *Marriage and Family Living* 14(Nov. 1952):286-94. [Fieldwork carried out in 1940-44.]

2595 Taeuber, Irene Barnes. "The Families of Chinese Farmers." In *Family and Kinship in Chinese Society,* ed. Maurice Freedman, pp. 63-85. Stanford: Stanford University, 1970. [Based on research done in the 1930s.]

2596 Tao, Li-kung. *Livelihood in Peking; an Analysis of the Budgets of 60 Families.* Peking: Social Research Department, China Foundation for the Promotion of Education and Culture, 1928.

2597 Treudley, Mary B. *The Men and Women of Chung Ho Ch'ang* (Szechwan Province). Asian Folklore and Social Life Monographs 14. Taibei: Orient Cultural Service, 1971. [Based on research done in the 1940s.]

2598 Wang, Cheng. "A Preliminary Study of the Disintegration of the Chinese Family under the Impact of Western Ideologies." M.A. thesis, Standford, 1930.

2599 Wong, Su-ling and Cressy, Earl Herbert. *Daughter of Confucius, a Personal History.* N.Y.: Farrar, Straus and Young, 1952. [Girlhood in a wealthy Guangdong merchant family, 1918-37.]

2600 Yang, Martin C. *A Chinese Village: Taitou, Shantung Province.* N.Y.: Columbia University, 1945. [Sociological description of a north China village during the early 20th century. Includes sections on family and marriage.]

2601 Yang, Simon [Yang, Hsi-meng] and Tao, L. K. [T'ao, Meng-ho], trans. *A Study of the Standard of Living of Working Families in Shanghai.* Institute of Social Research Monographs 3. Peiping: Institute of Social Research, 1931.

2602 Zia, Z. K. "My Viewpoint Regarding Concubinage in China." *China Recorder,* March 1924, pp. 152-55.

FAMILY IN THE PEOPLE'S REPUBLIC OF CHINA (1949-)

2603 Baisinger, Grace and Macy, Virginia. "Family and Community Involvement." *Chinese Education* 11(Winter 1978-1979):97-111.

2604 Briffa, E. M. "Family Policy in Communist China" *Social Action,* Sept. 1959, pp. 366-73.

2605 Broderick, James Lively. "Psychological Significance of the Post-Revolutionary Chinese Family: A Critical-Emancipatory Explanation." Ph.D. dissertation, California School of Professional Psychology, 1976.

2606 *CB* no. 236 (Mar. 1953). "Feudal Marriage Systems and Malpractices Still Found in Most Parts of China," pp. 14–15. [From New China News Agency, Peking, Feb. 1953.]

2607 Chandrasekhar, Sripati; Hinton, Harold Clendenin; Williams, Lea E., et al. *A Decade under Mao Tse-tung*. Hong Kong: Green Pagoda Press, 1959. [See Nils Stefansson, "Youth and the Family," pp. 51–57. Reprinted: *A Decade of Mao's China: A Survey of Life and Thought in China Today*, pp. 50–57. Bombay: Perennial Press, 1960.]

2608 Chao, Paul Kwang-yi. "Analysis of Marxist Doctrine on the Family with Testing Its Validity in Soviet Russia and Communist China." Ph.D. dissertation, New York University, 1963.

2609 Chao, Paul Kwang-yi. "The Marxist Doctrine and the Recent Development of the Chinese Family in Communist China." *J. of Asian and African Studies* 2(July–Oct. 1967):161–73.

2610 Chao, Paul Kwang-yi. *Women under Communism: Family in Russia and China*. Bayside, N.Y.: General Hall, 1977.

2611 Che, Wai-kin. "The Modern Chinese Family, 1959–1975." Ph.D. dissertation, North Texas State University, 1978.

2612 Chen, Edward King-tung. "Communist China's War on the Family." *Southwestern Social Science Quarterly* 33(Sept. 1952):148–55.

2613 Chen, Hsiu-cheng. "A Family in a People's Commune (Yung-feng commune, Hai-ting ch'ü, Peking municipality)." *China Reconstructs* 8(May 1959):14–16.

2614 Chen, Jack. *A Year in Upper Felicity*. N.Y.: Macmillan, 1973. [A rusticated intellectual's report on village life in Henan, 1969–70.]

2615 Chen, Theodore H. E. [Ch'en Hsi-en] and Chen, Wen-hui C. [Ch'en Chung Wen-hui]. "Changing Attitudes towards Parents in Communist China." *Sociology and Social Research* 43(Jan.–Feb. 1959):175–82.

2616 Chen, Wen-hui Chung. *The Family Revolution in Communist China*. Human Resources Research Institute, Research Memorandum 35. Lacklana AFB, San Antonio: AF Personnel and Training Research Center, Air Research and Development Command, 1955.

2617 "A Commune Family." *China Reconstructs* 27(Sept. 1978):9–14, 50.

2618 Das, Man Singh and Bardis, Panos D. *The Family in Asia*. London: Allen & Unwin, 1979. [Contains section on the PRC.]

2619 Davis-Friedmann, Deborah. "Old People and Their Families in the People's Republic of China." Ph.D. dissertation, Boston University, 1979.

2620 *ECMM*, no. 155 (Nov. 16, 1958). Chai, Shang-tung. "How Should We Regard Communist Family Life?" pp. 6–11. [From *Zhongguo qingnian*.]

2621 *ECMM*, no. 157 (Dec. 1, 1958). "The Patriarchal System and the Family." p. 1.

2622 *ECMM*, no. 159 (Dec. 22, 1958). Hu, Sheng. "Concerning the Family—a Letter to a Friend," pp. 14–18. [From *Zhongguo funü*.]

2623 *ECMM*, no. 161 (Dec. 27, 1958). "The People's Communes: Questions and Answers," pp. 38–42. [From *Zhongguo gongren*.]

2624 *ECMM*, no. 167 (Feb. 1959). Shui, Chieh. "How I Managed to Improve My Relations with My Mother-in-Law," p. 7. [From *Zhongguo funü*.]

2625 "A Family Budget." *China Reconstructs* 10(May 1961):35.

2626 Fang, Ying-yang. "Two Days with a Farm Family." *China Reconstructs* 11(June 1962):11.

2627 Fei, Hsiao-tung. "Free and Equal Family." *People's China* 10(May 16, 1955):16–20.

2628 Freedman, Maurice. "The Family under Chinese Communism." *Political Quarterly* 35(July–Sept. 1964):342–50.

2629 Fried, Morton Herbert. "The Family in China: The People's Republic." In *The Family: Its Function and Destiny*, rev. ed., ed. Ruth Nanda Anshen, pp. 146–66. N.Y.: Harper, 1959.

2630 Fried, Morton Herbert. "Trends in Chinese Domestic Organization." In *Symposium on Economic and Social Problems of the Far East*, ed. Edward Franciszek Szczepanik, pp. 405–414. Hong Kong: Hong Kong University, 1962.

2631 Fukutake, Tadashi. *Asian Rural Society: China, India, Japan*. Seattle: University of Washington, 1967. [See chapter 1, "Chinese Village and Japanese Village," pp. 13–25, and part 2, chapter 1, "Village Life in Central China," pp. 79–92.]

2632 Geddes, William R. *Peasant Life in Communist China*. Ithaca, N.Y.: Society for Applied Anthropology, 1963.

2633 Gelder, George Stuart and Gelder, Roma. *Memories for a Chinese Granddaughter*. London: Hutchinson, 1967. [Observations of a British couple in China in the early 1960s.]

2634 Greenblatt, Sidney L., ed. *The People of Taihang: An Anthology of Family Histories*. White Plains, N.Y.: International Arts and Sciences Press, 1972. [Peasant personal oral histories from revolutionary war years. Five are of women: "A Home Given by Chairman Mao," "The Story of Selling Oneself," "A Cave with Two Entrances," "A Woman Farmhand," and "Revolutionary Mother Pao Lien-tzu."]

2635 "A Handbook on Daily Living for Residents of Streets and Neighborhoods (Excerpt): How to Achieve Unity within the Family; Appendix—on Family Agreement." *Chinese Sociology and Anthropology* 8(Summer 1976):3–10. [From *A Handbook of Daily Living*, published in 1951.]

2636 Hellstrom, Inger. "The Chinese Family in the Communist Revolution." *Acta Sociologica* 6(1962):4:156–277.

2637 Hirabayashi, Jo Anne and Tang, Peter S. H. [T'ang Sheng-hao]. "Family." In *A Regional Handbook on Northeast China*, pp. 142–56. Human Relations Area Files Subcontractor's Monographs 61; Washington 9. Comp. Far Eastern and Russian Institute, University of Washington. New Haven: Human Relations Area Files, 1956.

2638 Hsueh, Chih-lan. "Our Family Sets up a Study Class." *China Reconstructs* 17(July 1968):9–11.

2639 Hu, Chih-tao. "A Teacher-Housewife." *China Reconstructs* 2(May–June 1953):10.

2640 Huang, Lucy Jen [Huang, Jen-hua]. "Some Changing Patterns in the Communist Chinese Family." *Marriage and Family Living* 23(May 1961):137–46.

2641 Huang, Lucy Jen [Huang, Jen-hua]. *The Impact of the Commune on the Chinese Family*. Santa Barbara, Calif.: General Electric Co., Technical Military Planning Operation, 1962. [Monograph.]

2642 Huang, Lucy Jen [Huang, Jen-hua]. "The Problem Child and Delinquent Youth in the Communist Chinese Family." *Marriage and Family Living* 25(Nov. 1963):459–65.

2643 Huang, Lucy Jen [Huang, Jen-hua]. "Notes on Official Views with Regard to Mate Selection and Marital Happiness in Family in People's Republic of China." *J. of Comparative Family Studies* 3(Autumn 1972):283–91.

2644 Huang, Lucy Jen [Huang, Jen-hua]. "The Family and the Communes in People's Republic of China: Retrospect and Prospect." *J. of Comparative Family Studies* 7(Spring 1976):97–109.

2645 JPRS, no. 984 D (Mar. 5, 1959). "A Brief Talk about Home," p. 3.
2646 JPRS, no. 2011 (Mar. 5, 1959). "Family and Liberation of Women."
2647 JPRS, no. 8476 (June 19, 1961). Fan, Jo-yu [Fan, Jo-yü]. "Why We Have Abolished the Feudal Patriarchal System," pp. 31–45. [From *Hongqi*.]
2648 JPRS, no. 28105 (Dec. 14, 1964). "How We Think about the Idea of Loving Commune as One's Own Family." [From *Renmin ribao*.]
2649 JPRS, no. 30958 (July 1965). "Family Relationships and Children of Landlords."
2650 JPRS, no. 35120 (Mar. 16, 1966). "Married Women Should Take Part in Activities of Young People." [From *Zhongguo qingnian*, no. 6, pp. 26–27.]
2651 JPRS, no. 39849 (Dec. 8, 1966). "The Worker Families Advance on the Path of Revolutionization." [From *Wenhui bao*.]
2652 Ju, I-hsiung. "The Family Concept in China: Some Comparisons with Thailand." *Solidarity* 5(Nov. 1970):56–65.
2653 Kuo, Chi-hsin. "Peking Housewives Today." *China Pictorial* 1973:3:14–17.
2654 La Dany, Ladislao. "Housewives Problems." *China News Analysis* 121(Feb. 24, 1956):2–7.
2655 [La Dany, Ladislao.] "Drawing the Line: Family Reform." *China News Analysis* 571(July 9, 1965):1–7.
2656 [La Dany, Ladislao.] "The Family." *China News Analysis* 776(Oct. 3, 1969):1–7.
2657 Lal, Amrit. "The Family in Communist China." *Mankind Quarterly* 13(July/Sept. 1972):3–18.
2658 Leopold, Ellen. "The Anomaly of the Housewife." *China Now*, no. 50 (Mar. 1975), pp. 4–6.
2659 Lethbridge, Henry James. "Youth, Society and the Family in China." In *Youth in China*, ed. Edward Stuart Kirby, pp. 31–65. Hong Kong: Dragonfly Books, 1965.
2660 Liu, William Thomas [Liu, Jung] and Yu, Elena S. H. "Variations in Women's Roles and Family Life under the Socialist Regime in China." *J. of Comparative Family Studies* 8(Summer 1977):201–215.
2661 MacDougall, Colina. "Keeping House in China." *Far Eastern Economic Review* 50(Dec. 23, 1965):550–51, 558.
2662 "Maoism and the Family." *Women and Revolution*, no. 7(Autumn 1974):2–7.
2663 Myrdal, Jan and Kessle, Gun. *China: The Revolution Continued*. N.Y.: Random House, 1972. [See pp. 132–38.]
2664 Ni, Ernest. "The Family in China." *Marriage and Family Living* 16(Nov. 1954):315–18.
2665 Parish, William L., Jr. "Socialism and the Chinese Peasant Family." *J. of Asian Studies* 34(May 1975):613–630.
2666 Parish, William L., Jr. and Whyte, Martin King. *Village and Family in Contemporary China*. Chicago: University of Chicago, 1978. [An important recent sociological study, based on refugee interview data. See part 3, "Family Organization and Ritual Life," pp. 131–272.]
2667 "Peasant Family Meetings Repudiate China's Kruschov." *Peking Review* 11(Mar. 8, 1968):16–17.
2668 "The 'Red Family.'" *China Reconstructs* 18(Aug. 1969):13–15.
2669 Salaff, Janet. "The Emerging Conjugal Relationship in the People's Republic of China." *J. of Marriage and the Family* 35(Nov. 1973):705–17.
2670 Schlesinger, Benjamin. "The Family in Communist China." *Social Science* 41(Oct. 1966):221–28.
2671 *SCMM*, no. 264 (May 1, 1961). "Liu Hsiu-lan a Model Dependent of a Miner," p. 28.
2672 *SCMM*, no. 383 (July 28, 1963). "How Can Family Relations Be Handled Properly?" pp. 36–38. [From *Zhongguo qingnian*.]
2673 *SCMM*, no. 390 (Sept. 16, 1963). Yang, Hsiu. "Correctly Deal with Ideological Influence of Families and Relatives," p. 6. [From *Zhongguo Qingnian* 1963:18.]
2674 *SCMM*, no. 394 (Dec. 9, 1963). "Treat the Relationship between Work, Children and Household Chores in a Revolutionary Manner," pp. 23–27. [From *Zhongguo funü*, Nov. 1963.]
2675 *SCMM*, no. 415 (May 4, 1964). "To Understand the Family Correctly Is the Starting Point in Striving for Progress: Reply to a Youth from a Landlord Family," pp. 38–40. [From *Zhongguo funü*, 1964:6.]
2676 *SCMM*, no. 426 (July 20, 1964). "Before and After I Organize My Family to Study Chairman Mao's Works," pp. 18–25. [From *Zhongguo qingnian* 1964:11.]
2677 *SCMM*, no. 448 (Dec. 21, 1964). Fang, Yü. "Break Family Ties, Be a Good Child of the Proletariat," pp. 36-40. [From *Zhongguo qingnian* 1964:21.]
2678 *SCMM*, no. 471 (Mar. 26, 1965). "Be a Good 'Red Housekeeper' for Poor and Lower-Middle Peasants," pp. 16–19. [From *Zhongguo qingnian*.]
2679 *SCMM*, no. 476 (May 16, 1965). Chu, Feng-lan (Tsoch'ang Briagde, Tsoch'ang Commune, Yenchiu *hsien*, Honan). "Can Young Women in the Countryside Still Make Progress after Giving Birth to Children?" p. 18. [From *Zhongguo funü*.]
2680 *SCMM*, no. 490 (June 1, 1965). "Be Revolutionary Parents and Lead Your Children to the Revolutionary Road," p. 26. [From *Zhongguo funü*.]
2681 *SCMM*, no. 490 (June 1, 1965). "A Good Mother Who Cultivates Revolutionary Offspring," p. 20. [From *Zhongguo funü*.]
2682 *SCMM*, no. 493 (May 1, 1965). *Chung-kuo fu-nü* reporters. "The Revolutionary Family Dependents in Tach'ing," p. 1. [From *Zhongguo funü*.]
2683 *SCMM*, no. 501 (Nov. 11, 1965). Sun, Wei-shih. "Newsletter from Tach'ing—Some Commonplace Stories about the Part Played By Workers' Dependents in the Revolution," p. 10. [From *Hongqi*.]
2684 *SCMM*, no. 574 (May 1, 1967). "A Glimpse of the Wicked Family," p. 4.
2685 *SCMP*, no. 115 (May 9, 1951). "A McTyeire Student Denounces Her Own Special Agent Father," pp. 21–22.
2686 *SCMP*, no. 581 (May 27, 1953). "Mrs. Hu Chih-tao's Reply to a British Housewife: Daily Life of a Chinese Housewife," p. 33.
2687 *SCMP*, no. 973 (Dec. 28, 1954). "Filial Piety in Communist China—Tsou Ch'ing-lai and Chao Yu-ch'in Persecute Mother to Suicide," p. 29.
2688 *SCMP*, no. 1009 (Mar. 16, 1955). "Home Life of Senior Chinese Commmunist Cadre: Home of the Vice Minister of Railways," p. 22.
2689 *SCMP*, no. 1309 (June 11, 1956). "Woman Leader Tells Life of Chinese Women, Children," p. 35.
2690 *SCMP*, no. 1547 (June 4, 1957). "Workers' Families Hold National Conference," p. 9.
2691 *SCMP*, no. 1670 (Nov. 29, 1957). "All China Democratic Women's Federation Issues Notification on Extensive Publicity of Home Management with Industry and Thrift," p. 2.
2692 *SCMP*, no. 1821 (July 13, 1958). "The Warmth of the Revolutionary Big Family," p. 3.
2693 *SCMP*, no. 1951 (Jan. 17, 1959). "Promote the Family Life of Democratic Solidarity," p. 8.

2694 *SCMP*, no. 1961 (Jan. 10, 1959). "On the Question of Family," p. 1.

2695 *SCMP*, no. 1977 (Dec. 31, 1958). "The Family Life of Democratic Solidarity Should Be Promoted," p. 3.

2696 *SCMP*, no. 3423 (Feb. 8, 1965). "Is There a Political Relationship between Parents and Children?" p. 12.

2697 *SCMP*, no. 3433 (Mar. 19, 1965). "Families of Workers of Tach'ing Oilfield Take Big Strides Forward along the Road of Revolutionization," p. 8.

2698 *SCMP*, no. 3496 (June 9, 1965). "Can We Give up Ideological Struggle for the Sake of Family Harmony?" p. 6.

2699 *SCMP*, no. 3523 (July 27, 1965). "Yü Shan-ling Gloriously Joins the Communist Party after Reforming Her Thought and Making Fast Progress—She Breaks away from Her Family of the Exploiting Class and Resolutely Follows the Party in Waging Revolution," p. 8. [From *Zhongguo qingnian bao*.]

2700 *SCMP*, no. 4312 (Nov. 29, 1968). "How a Family Runs a Study Class of Mao Tse-tung's Thought," p. 17.

2701 *SCMP*, no. 4354 (Ja. 13, 1969). Hou, Hsueh-chih (poor-peasant commune member of Hsiaoli-chia Brigade, Hsiszu Commune, Haich'eng *hsien*). "Carrying out Struggle between the Two Lines in Family Class for Study of Mao Tse-tung's Thought," p. 9.

2702 *SCMP*, no. 4424 (May 14, 1969). "A Good Method of Running Family Study Class Well," p. 4.

2703 *SCMP*, no. 4760 (Oct. 5, 1970). Pien, Feng-ying. "Apply Mao Tse-tung's Thought to the Proper Management of a Household—How I Run a Family Study Class Well," p. 7.

2704 *SCMP*, no. 5100 (Mar. 14, 1972). "New Life in a Shanghai Workers' Housing Estate," p. 169.

2705 *SCMP*, no. 5426 (July 20, 1973). "Chinese Mine 'Adopts' Three Orphan Sisters," p. 88.

2706 Selden, Mark. "Report from a People's Commune (Ch'eng-kuan Commune, Honan Province)." *Liberation* 17(Jan. 1973):25-35.

2707 Sidel, Ruth. *Families of Fengsheng: Urban Life in China*. Baltimore: Penguin, 1974. [Based on interviews with residents of a city neighborhood in the early 1970s.]

2708 *SPRCP*, no. 5787 (Jan. 24, 1975). "North China Peasants Breaking with Old Conventions," p. 74.

2709 *SPRCP*, no. 6167 (Aug. 19, 1976). "Wuhan Grannies Take Active Part in Social Activities," p. 212.

2710 Stacey, Judith. "When Patriarchy Kowtows: The Significance of the Chinese Family Revolution for Feminist Theory." *Feminist Studies* 2(1975):2-3:64-112.

2711 Stacey, Judith. "Toward a Theory of Family and Revolution: Reflections on the Chinese Case." *Social Problems* 26(June 1979):499-508.

2712 Stacey, Judith. "Toward a Theory of Woman, the Family and Revolution: An Historical and Theoretical Analysis of the Chinese Case." Ph.D. dissertation, Brandeis University, 1979.

2713 Su, Enteh. "Huang-ho and Her New Father." *China Reconstructs* 5(Jan. 1956):28.

2714 Su, Sing Ging. "The Chinese Family System." *Philippine Sociological Review* 2(1954):3:17-26.

2715 Ts'ao, Hsin-hua. "We Apply Chairman Mao's Dialectism to Resolve Family Disputes." In Li, Dun Jen, *Modern China: From Mandarin to Commissar*, pp. 397-405. N.Y.: Scribner, 1978. [Translated from *Renmin ribao*, Oct. 1970.]

2716 Tsui, Hsiu-mei. "A Saleswoman's Home Life." *China Reconstructs* 22(Jan. 1973):32-34.

2717 Tung, Yi-chang. "In the New Society: Helping Mother Fight Selfishness." *China Reconstructs* 18(June 1969):16.

2718 "Two Workers' Families." *China Reconstructs* 27(Dec. 1978):13-15.

2719 Tze, Kang. "Chinese Women and Children." *China Reconstructs* 1(Mar.-Apr. 1952):20-23.

2720 Walstedt, Joyce Jennings. "Reform of Women's Roles and Family Structure in the Recent History of China." *J. of Marriage and the Family* 40(May 1978):379-92.

2721 Wei, Yueh-hsiang. "Mao Tse-tung's Thought is Our Guide in Building a New-Type Family." *Peking Review* 11(Oct. 4, 1968):38-40.

2722 Whyte, Martin King. "The Family." In *China's Developmental Experience*, ed. Michel Oksenberg, pp. 175-92. N.Y.: Praeger, 1973.

2723 Whyte, Martin King. "Family Change in China." *Issues and Studies* 15(July 1979):48-62. [Based on data collected from refugees from China.]

2724 Wong, Alice (Kan). "Changes in Marriage, Family Institutions in China, 1949-1969." In *Selected Seminar Papers on Contemporary China*, 1, ed. Steve Chin and Frank King, pp. 149-78. Hong Kong: University of Hong Kong, 1971.

2725 Yang, C. K. [Yang Ch'ing-k'un]. *Chinese Communist Society: The Family and the Village*. Cambridge, Mass.: M.I.T., 1959.

2726 Yang, Kan-ling. "Family Life—the New Way." *Peking Review* 1(Nov. 18, 1958):9-10.

2727 Yu, Elena S. H. "Family Life and Overseas Remittances in Southeastern China." *J. of Comparative Family Studies* 10(Autumn 1979):445-54. [An observation of Chinese family life in Fujian and Guangdong.]

MARRIAGE AND FAMILY: MINORITIES

2728 Bogan, Mrs. M. L. C. *Manchu Customs and Superstitions*. Tientsin, Peking: China Booksellers, 1928. [See chapter 8, "Seventh Month," pp. 37-45; chapter 13, "The Manchu Wedding Ceremony," pp. 57-65; chapter 14, "The Manchu Funeral Ceremony," pp. 67-95; chapter 15, "The Birth of a Child," pp. 99-109.]

2729 Briggs, Margaret [Liang Yen]. *Daughter of the Khans, by Liang Yen*. N.Y.: W.W. Norton, 1955.

2730 Chan, Kuei-pei. "A Tai Wedding." *China Reconstructs* 11(July 1962):32.

2731 Ch'en, Ch'i-lu. "The Family and Marriage of the Formosan Aborigine." *China Society, Taipei, J.* 4(1964):69-81.

2732 Chen, Ching-ching. "The Population and Family System of the Vata'an Ami." *Bulletin of the Institute of Ethnology, Academia Sinica*, no. 11 (Spring 1961), pp. 182-84. [English abridgement.]

2733 Chen, Chun-chin. "Population and Family System of the Tungho Saisiat." *Bulletin of the Institute of Ethnology, Academia Sinica*, no. 23 (Spring 1967), pp. 163-65. [English abridgement.]

2734 Chiu, Chi-chien. "The Kinship Organization of the Take-Bakha Bunum." *Bulletin of the Institute of Ethnology, Academia Sinica*, no. 13 (Spring 1962), pp. 192-93. [English summary.]

2735 Graham, David Crokett. "The Couvade in Kweichow Province." *West China Border Research Society J.* 7(1935):126-127.

2736 Graham, David Crokett. "Note about the Couvade." *West China Border Research Society J.* 8(1936):180.

2737 Graham, David Crokett. "The Customs of the Chuan Miao." *West China Border Research Society J.* 9(1937):13-115.

2738 Graham, David Crokett. "A Gutner Note on the Couvade." *West China Border Research Society J.* 11(1939):136.

2739 Ko, Siang-feng. "Marriage among the Independent Lolos of Western China." *American J. of Sociology* 54(May 1949):487–96.

2740 Li, Yih-yüan. "The Family Structure of the Western Paiwan Tribe." *Bulletin of the Institute of Ethnology, Academia Sinica*, no. 2 (Sept. 1956), pp. 125–28.

2741 Liu, Pin-hsiung. "Matrilocal Marriage of the Vata'an Ami." *Bulletin of the Institute of Ethnology, Academia Sinica*, no. 9 (Spring 1960), pp. 383–84. [English abridgement.]

2742 Lockhart, James Haldane Stewart. "The Marriage Ceremonies of the Manchus." *Folk-lore* 1(Dec. 1890):481–92.

2743 Mark, Lindy Li. "Patrilateral Cross-Cousin Marriage among the Magpie Miao: Preferential or Prescriptive." *American Anthropologist* 69(Feb. 1967), pp. 55–62.

2744 Rock, Joseph Francis. *The Life and Culture of the Na-khi Tribe of the China Tibet Borderland.* Wiesbaden: Steiner, 1963. [See especially "Marriage and Death," pp. 31–33; "The Status of Women," pp. 33–34; "Dress of the Women," pp. 34–36.]

2745 Serruys, Henry. "Remains of Mongol Customs in China during the Early Ming Period." *Monumenta Serica* 16(1957):137–90. [For discussion of marriage customs, see pp. 171–90.]

2746 Stein, Rolf Alfred. *Tibetan Civilization.* Trans. J. E. Stapleton Driver. Stanford: Stanford University, 1972. [See "The Family," pp. 94–109.]

2747 Tan, Kuei-ying. "A Fishing Family Changes." *China Reconstructs* 18(Jan. 1969):30–31.

2748 Tang, Mei-chun. "The Property System and the Divorce Rate of the Lai-i Paiwan in Taiwan." *Bulletin of the Department of Archaeology and Anthropology*, National Taiwan University, Taipei, no. 28 (Nov. 1966), pp. 45–52.

2749 Taring, Richen Dolma. *Daughter of Tibet.* London: John Murray, 1970.

2750 Thompson, Laurence G. "The Earliest Chinese Eyewitness Accounts of the Formosan Aborigines." *Monumenta Serica* 23(1964):163–204. [Contains accounts of courtship, marriage, and childbirth customs.]

2751 Wei, Hwei-lin. "Ambilateral Lineage and Class System of the Paiwan." *Bulletin of the Institute of Ethnology, Academia Sinica*, no. 9 (Spring 1960), pp. 97–108. [English abridgement.]

2752 Wei, Hwei-lin. "Matri-clan and Lineage System of the Ami." *Bulletin of the Institute of Ethnology, Academia Sinica*, no. 12 (Autumn 1961), pp. 29–40. [English abridgement.]

2753 Wei, Hwei-lin. "Family Types of the Formosan Aboriginal Societies." *National Taiwan University J. of Sociology*, no. 3 (April 1967), pp. 44–46. [Summary.]

2754 Wu, Yen-ho. "Child Training among the Eastern Paiwan." *Bulletin of the Institute of Ethnology, Academia Sinica*, no. 25 (Spring 1968), pp. 104–107.

2755 Zhang, Huaijing and Zhou, Baohua. "Dochhen Drolma's Wedding." *China Reconstructs* 28(1979):9:12–13. [A wedding held in Tibet.]

FAMILY IN HONG KONG, TAIWAN AND OVERSEAS CHINA

2756 Ahern, Emily M. "Affines and the Rituals of Kinship." In *Religion and Ritual in Chinese Society*, ed. Arthur Wolf, pp. 279–307. Stanford: Stanford University Press, 1974. [Based on research in Taiwan.]

2757 Baker, Hugh David Roberts. "Marriage and the Family." In *Aspects of Social Organization in the New Territories*, ed. Hong Kong Branch, Royal Asiatic Society, pp. 27–31. Hong Kong: Cathay Press, 1964.

2758 Barnett, William K. "An Ethnographic Description of San-lei Ts'un, Taiwan, with Emphasis on Women's Roles: Overcoming Research Problems Caused by the Presence of a Great Tradition." Ph.D. dissertation, Michigan State 1970.

2759 Barrett, Richard E. "Short-Term Trends in Bastardy in Taiwan." *J. of Family History* 5(Fall 1980):293–312.

2760 Berliner, Gabriells, et al. "The Chinese Family in San Francisco." Master's thesis (Social Welfare), University of California, Berkeley, 1966–67.

2761 Chang, Shiao-chun. "A Study of Urban House-wife's Role in Modern Society." *Bulletin of the Institute of Ethnology, Academia Sinica*, no. 37 (1974), pp. 39–84. [English abridgement. On the situation in Taiwan.]

2762 Chen, Chi-lu. "The Taiwanese Family." *J. of the China Society* 7(1970):64–79.

2763 Chen, Chiyen [Ch'en, Chi-yen]. "The Foster Daughter-in-Law System in Formosa." *American J. of Comparative Law* 6(Summer 1957):302–314.

2764 Chew, Caroline. "Development of Chinese Family Life in America as Observed in San Francisco 'Chinatown.'" M.A. thesis, Mills College, 1926.

2765 Chiou-kuey. "Family Structure, Marriage and Mortuary Customs of the Hoklo Chinese of Tsau-tun, Nanton." *Bulletin of Department of Archaeology and Anthropology*, National Taiwan University, Taipei, nos. 25–26 (Nov. 1965), pp. 158–68.

2766 Chu, Solomon S. P. "Family Structure and Extended Kinship in a Chinese Community [Taichung, Taiwan]." Ph.D. dissertation, University of Michigan, 1969.

2767 Cohen, Myron Leon. "A Case Study of Chinese Family Economy and Development." *J. of Asian and African Studies* 3(1968):3–4:161–80. [Research undertaken in a south Taiwan Hakka-speaking village.]

2768 Cohen, Myron Leon. "Agnatic Kinship in South Taiwan." *Ethnology* 8(Apr. 1969):167–82.

2769 Cohen, Myron Leon. *House United, House Divided: The Chinese Family in Taiwan.* N.Y.: Studies of the East Asian Institute, Columbia University, 1976. [Anthropological study of the rural joint family in the 1960s.]

2770 Cohen, Myron Leon. "Family Partition as Contractual Procedure in Taiwan: A Case Study from South Taiwan." In *Chinese Family Law and Social Change in Historical and Comparative Perspective*, ed. David C. Buxbaum, pp. 176–204. Seattle: University of Washington, 1978.

2771 Coombs, Lolagene C. and Freedman, Ronald. "Some Roots of Preference: Roles, Activities and Familial Values." *Demography* 16(Aug. 1979):359–76. [Uses data from Taiwan.]

2772 Coombs, Lolagene C. and Sun, Te-hsiung. "Family Composition Preferences in a Developing Culture: The Case of Taiwan, 1973." *Population Studies* 32(Mar. 1978):43–64.

2773 Coombs, Lolagene C. and Sun, Te-hsiung. *Changes in Familial Values in a Developing Society: Taiwan in the Sixties and Seventies.* University of Michigan, Population Studies Center, and Taiwan Provincial Institute of Family Planning, Taiwan Population Studies, Working Papers, no. 42. Ann Arbor, Nov. 1979.

2774 Diamond, Norma. *K'un Shen: A Taiwan Village.* N.Y.: Rhinehart and Winston, 1969. [Anthropological study of a fishing community.]

2775 Diamond, Norma. "The Middle Class Family Model in Taiwan: Woman's Place is in the Home." *Asian Survey* 13(Sept. 1973):853-72.

2776 Freedman, Maurice. *Chinese Family and Marriage in Singapore.* Colonial Research Studies, no. 20. London: H.M. Stationery Office, 1957.

2777 Freedman, Maurice. *The Study of Chinese Society: Essays by Maurice Freedman.* Stanford: Stanford University, 1979. [See "Chinese Kinship and Marriage in Early Singapore," pp. 84-92.]

2778 Gallin, Bernard. "Matrilateral and Affinal Relationships of a Taiwanese Village." *American Anthropologist* 62(Aug. 1960):632-42.

2779 Gallin, Bernard. *Hsin Hsing, Taiwan: A Village in Change.* Berkeley: University of California, 1966.

2780 Green, Blake. "Mystique of the Chinese Woman." *San Francisco Chronicle,* Feb. 11-14, 1970. [A series of four articles on upper and middle class "Americanized" Chinese women—their dress, home life, aspirations for their children.]

2781 Greenfield, D. E. "Marriage by Chinese Law and Customs in Hongkong." *International and Comparative Law Quarterly,* 4th series 7(July 1958):437-51.

2782 Guerin, Gilbert. "The Family in the Chinese Society in Taiwan: General Issues of Family Members." *Annals of Philippine Chinese Historical Association,* June 1975, pp. 179-91.

2783 Haynor, Norman S. and Reynolds, Charles N. "Chinese Family Life in America." *American Sociological Review* 2(Oct. 137):630-37.

2784 Hoe, Bang Seng. "Chinese Canadian Families and the Quality of Life." *Rikka* 3(Aug. 1976):24-28.

2785 Hong, Lawrence K. "The Chinese Family in a Modern Industrial Setting [Hong Kong]: Its Structure and Functions." Ph.D. dissertation, University of Notre Dame, 1970.

2786 Hong, Lawrence K. "A Comparative Analysis of Extended Kin Visitations, Cohabitations, and Anomia in Rural and Urban Hong Kong." *Sociology and Social Research* 57(Oct. 1972):43-54.

2787 Lee, Rose Hum. "The Recent Immigrant Chinese Families of the San Francisco-Oakland Area." *J. of Marriage and Family Living* 18(Feb. 1956):14-24.

2788 Lew, Hilary. "Strangers in Taiwan." *Free China Review* 17(Apr. 1967):29-32. [On Hakka customs.]

2789 Li, Yih-yuan. "Attitudes toward Marriage and the Family among the Overseas Chinese Students in Taiwan." *Bulletin of the Institute of Ethnology, Academia Sinica,* no. 24 (Autumn 1967), pp. 27-34.

2790 Liu, William Thomas [Liu Jung]. "Family Interactions among Local and Refugee Chinese Families in Hong Kong." *J. of Marriage and the Family* 28(Aug. 1966):314-323.

2791 Liu, Yu Chen. "Interaction within Chinese-American Families of Portland." Ph.D. dissertation, Oregon State University, 1951.

2792 Meskill, Johanna Menzel. *A Chinese Pioneer Family, the Lings of Wu-feng, Taiwan.* N.J.: Princeton, 1979. [Historical study of a 19th-century lineage.]

2793 Mitchell, Robert Edward. *Family Life in Urban Hong Kong.* Asian Folklore and Social Life Monographs 24 and 25. Taibei: Orient Cultural Service, 1972.

2794 Mitchell, Robert Edward. *Pupil, Parent and School: A Hong Kong Study.* Asian Folklore and Social Life Monographs 26. Taibei: Orient Cultural Service, 1972.

2795 Mitchell, Robert Edward and Lo, Irene. "Implications of Changes in Family Authority Relations for the Development of Independence and Assertiveness in Hong Kong Children." *Asian Survey* 8(Apr. 1968):309-322.

2796 O'Hara, Albert Richard. "Changing Attitudes toward Marriage and the Family in Free China." *J. of China Society* 2(1962):57-79. [Reprinted in Albert Richard O'Hara, *Research on Changes of Chinese Society,* pp. 9-19.]

2797 O'Hara, Albert Richard. "Some Indications of Changes in Functions of the Family in China." *National Taiwan University J. of Sociology,* no. 3 (April 1967), pp. 59-76.

2798 O'Hara, Albert Richard. *Research on Changes of Chinese Society.* Asian Folklore and Social Life Monographs 20. Taibei: Orient Cultural Service, 1971. [See "Changing Attitudes of University Students toward Marriage and the Family in Taiwan," pp. 21-26.]

2799 O'Hara, Albert Richard. "Adopted Daughters." *J. of the China Society,* vol. 13 (1976). [Discusses reasons for a Taiwanese family to adopt daughters.]

2800 Olsen, Nancy Johnston. "The Effect of Household Composition on the Child Rearing Practices of Taiwanese Families." Ph.D. dissertation, Cornell University, 1971.

2801 Olsen, Nancy Johnston. "Family Structure and Independence Training in a Taiwanese Village." *J. of Marriage and the Family* 35(Aug. 1973):512-19.

2802 Olsen, Nancy Johnston. "Family Structure and Socialization Patterns in Taiwan." *J. of American Sociology* 79(1974):6:1395-1417.

2803 Olsen, Nancy Johnston. "The Role of Grandmothers in Taiwanese Family Socialization." *J. of Marriage and the Family* 38(May 1976):355-72.

2804 Parish, William Lucious, Jr. "Kinship and Modernization in Taiwan." Ph.D. dissertation, Cornell, 1970.

2805 Pasternak, Burton. *Kinship and Community in Two Chinese Villages: Ta-t'ieh, P'ing-tung Hsien, and Chung-she, T'ainan Hsien, Taiwan.* Stanford: Stanford University, 1972.

2806 Robbins, E. V. (Mrs.). *Ten years among the Chinese in California.* Decennial Report of the Occidental Board of the Woman's Foreign Missionary Society. San Francisco, 1883. [Shows the everyday life of the Chinese American woman.]

2807 Rosen, Sherry. "Sibling and In-Law Relationships in Hong Kong: The Emergent Role of Chinese Wives." *J. of Marriage and the Family* 40(Aug. 1978):621-28.

2808 Ruey, Yih-fu [Jui, I-fu]. "Changing Structure of the Chinese Family." *Bulletin of the Department of Archaeology and Anthropology, National Taiwan University* 17/18(Nov. 1961):1-15.

2809 Sa, Sophie. "Family and Community in Urban Taiwan: Social Status and Demographic Strategy among Taipei Households, 1885-1935." Ph.D. dissertation, Harvard University, 1975.

2810 Stanford University China Project. "Family." Human Relations Area Files Subcontractor's Monographs 31; Stanford 5. In *Taiwan (Formosa),* comp. Stanford University China Project, vol. 1, pp. 131-48. New Haven: Human Relations Area Files, 1956.

2811 Stoodley, Bartlet H. "Normative Family Orientations of Chinese College Students in Hong Kong." *J. of Marriage and the Family* 29(Nov. 1967), 773-82.

2812 Tang, Mei-chun. "Life and Family Structure in a Chinese City: Taibei, Taiwan." Ph.D. dissertation, Columbia, 1973.

2813 Tang, Mei-chun. *Urban Chinese Families: An Anthropological Field Study in Taipei City, Taiwan.* Taibei: National Taiwan University Press, 1978. [Reprint: Taibei: Chengwen Publishing Co., 1981.]

2814 Tsung, Shiu-kuen Fan. "Moms, Nuns and Hookers: Extrafamilial Alternatives for Village Women in Taiwan." Ph.D. dissertation, University of California, San Diego, 1978.

2815 Ward, Barbara. *Women in New Asia: The Changing Social Role of Men and Women in South and South-East Asia.* Paris: United Nations Educational, Scientific and Cultural Organization, 1963. [See part 2, "Chinese Women of Singapore," pp. 376-410; and "A Chinese Family in Singapore," pp. 410-421.]

2816 Wei, Hsian-chuen Sharon. "The Impact of Urbanization of the Chinese Family: A Comparative Study of Urban and Rural Families in Contemporary Taiwan." Ph.D. dissertation, University of Southern California, 1980.

2817 Wolf, Margery. *The House of Lim: A Study of a Chinese Farm Family.* N.Y.: Appleton-Century-Crofts, 1968. [Classic study of a Taiwanese farm family based on two years of research in 1959-61.]

2818 Wolf, Margery. "Child Training and the Chinese Family." In *Family and Kinship in Chinese Society*, ed. Maurice Freedman, pp. 37-62. Stanford: Stanford University, 1970. [Also in *Studies in Chinese Society*, ed. Arthur Wolf, pp. 221-246 (Stanford: Stanford University, 1978). Based on field study of a village of Hokkien-speakers in northern Taiwan.]

2819 Wolf, Margery. *Women and the Family in Rural Taiwan.* Stanford: Stanford University, 1972. [Excellent study based on field research in rural Taiwan, 1959-61.]

2820 Wong, Chun-kit [Joseph]. "The Changing Chinese Family." *J. of the China Society* 10(1973):1-136. [On the situation in Taiwan.]

2821 Wong, Chun-kit Joseph. "The Changing Chinese Family Pattern in Taiwan." Ph.D. dissertation, St. John's University, 1980.

2822 Wong, Fai-ming. "Modern Ideology, Industrialization, and the Middle-Class Chinese Family in Hong Kong." Ph.D. dissertation, University of California, Santa Barbara, 1969.

2823 Wong, Fai-ming. "Industrialization and Family Structure in Hong Kong." *J. of Marriage and the Family* 37(Nov. 1975):985-1000.

2824 Wong, Shau-lam. "Social Change and Parent-Child Relations in Hong Kong." In *Families in East and West: Socialization Process and Kinship Ties*, ed. Reuben Hill and René König, pp. 167-74. The Hague: Mouton, 1970.

2825 Wright, Beryl Robina. "Social Aspects of Change in the Chinese Family Pattern in Hong Kong." *J. of Social Psychology* 63(June 1964):31-39.

2826 Yang, Martin M. C. [Yang, Mou-ch'un]. "Changes in Family Life in Rural Taiwan." *J. of the China Society*, 2(1972):68-79.

2827 Yang, Martin M. C. [Yang, Mou-ch'un]. "Child Training and Child Behavior in Varying Family Patterns in a Changing Chinese Society." *National Taiwan University, J. of Sociology* 3(Apr. 1967):82-83. [English summary.]

Politics and the Law

FAMILY AND MARRIAGE LAWS, WOMEN'S LEGAL STATUS: GENERAL AND COMPARATIVE SURVEYS

2828 Buxbaum, David Charles. "Some Aspects of Substantive Family Law and Social Change in Rural China (1896-1967), with a Case Study of a North Taiwan Village." Ph.D. dissertation, University of Washington, 1968.

2829 Buxbaum, David Charles. "From Contract to Status: Trends in Chinese Family Law from 1868-1968." In *Transition and Permanence: Chinese History and Culture*, ed. David Charles Buxbaum and Frederick W. Mote, pp. 203-247. Hong Kong: Cathay Press, 1972.

2830 Buxbaum, David Charles, ed. *Chinese Family Law in Historical and Comparative Perspective.* Asian Law Series, 3. Seattle: University of Washington, Press, 1978.

2831 Chiu, Han-p'ing. "Requisites of Adoption in Roman, Hindu and Chinese Law. The Effect of Adoption in Roman, Hindu and Chinese Law." *China Law Review* 4(July 1930):133-49; 4(Jan. 1931):277-87.

2832 Chiu, Vermier Yantak [Chao, P'ing]. *Marriage Laws and Customs of China.* Hong Kong: Chinese University of Hong Kong, New Asia College, Institute of Advanced Chinese Studies and Research, 1966.

2833 Freedman, Maurice. *The Study of Chinese Society: Essays by Maurice Freedman.* Stanford: Stanford University, 1979. [See "Chinese Family Law in Singapore: The Rout of Custom," pp. 141-60.]

2834 Gales, Robert Robinson. "Marriage and the Family: Chinese Law." *J. of Family Law* (Louisville, Kentucky) 6(1966):36-60.

2835 Luk, Bernard Hung-kay. "Abortion in Chinese Law." *American J. of Comparative Law* 25(Spring 1977):372-92.

2836 McCreery, John L. "Women's Property Rights and Dowry in China and South Asia." *Ethnology* 25(Jan. 1976):163-74.

2837 McGough, James Pierce. "Marriage and Adoption in Chinese Society with Special Reference to Customary Law." Ph.D. dissertation, Michigan State University, 1976.

2838 Parker, Edward Harper. "Comparative Chinese Family Law." *China Review* 8(Sept.-Oct. 1879):67-107.

2839 Tsao, Meng-chun. "The Status of Women in the World Today: China." *Review of Contemporary Law* 7(June 1960):54-60.

2840 Tsao, W. Y. "Chinese Family Law from Customary Law to Positive Law." *Hastings Law J.* 17(May 1966):727-65.

2841 Van der Valk, M. H. "China." In *The Law of Inheritance in Eastern Europe and PRC*, pp. 297-364. Leiden: A. W. Sychoff, 1961.

2842 Woo, Pak Chuen [Wu, Pai-ch'üan]. "A Comparative Study of the Family Law in the Chinese and English Legal Systems." Ph.D. dissertation, University of London [King's College], 1940.

FAMILY AND MARRIAGE LAWS, WOMEN'S LEGAL STATUS: TRADITIONAL AND REPUBLICAN CHINA (TO 1949)

2843 Bryan, Robert Thomas. "Divorce Law of China." *Chinese Social and Political Science Review* 4(June 1919):126-32.

2844 Chang, Tao Hsing. "Inheritance in China." *Iowa Law Review* 20(Jan. 1935):411-415.

2845 Cheung, Steven N. S. "Enforcement of Property Rights in Children, and the Marriage Contract." *Economic J.* 82(June 1972):641-57.

2846 Chiu, Vermier Yantak [Chao, P'ing]. "Some Notes on Chinese Customary Marriage." In *Family Law and Customary Law in Asia: A Contemporary Legal Perspective*, ed. David Charles Buxbaum, pp. 45-49. The Hague: Nijhoff, 1968.

2847 Eitel, Ernest John. "The Law of Testamentary Succession as Popularly Understood and Applied in China." *China Review* 15(Nov.-Dec. 1886):150-55.

2848 Hare, G. T., ed. *Notes on the Family Law and Usages and on the Criminal Code of the Chinese.* Kuala Lumpur: Selangor Government Printing Office, 1904.

2849 Hsia, C. L. "Marriage and Divorce in the Recent Chinese Legislation." *China Quarterly* [Shanghai] 1(Summer 1936):41–45.

2850 Hu, Henry Yu-chieh [Hu, Yu-chieh]. "Marriage and Divorce in Chinese Civil Code, with Reference to the Rules of Conflict of Laws." *Chinese Social and Political Science Review* 22(Jan.–Mar. 1939):400–427.

2851 Huberich, Charles Henry. "The Paternal Power of Chinese Law." *Juridical Review: A Journal of Legal and Political Science* 14(Dec. 1902):378–85.

2852 Jamieson, George. "The History of Adoption and Its Relation to Modern Wills." *China Review* 18(Nov.–Dec. 1889):137–46.

2853 Jamieson, George. *Chinese Family and Commercial Law.* Shanghai: Kelly and Walsh, 1921. [Reprinted: Taibei: Chengwen, 1968.]

2854 Kuo, Yun-kuan. "A Critical Exposition of the Essence of Chinese Family Law." *Chinese Social and Political Science Review* 1(July 1916):21–36.

2855 Lee, Bernice June. "The Change in the Legal Status of Chinese Women in Civil Matters from Traditional Law to the Republican Civil Code." Ph.D. dissertation, Sydney University, 1975.

2856 Levi, Werner. "The Family in Modern Chinese Law." *Far Eastern Quarterly* 4(May 1945):263–73.

2857 McCreery, John L. "Women's Property Rights and Dowry in China and South Asia." *Ethnology* 15(Apr. 1976):163–74. [A study of the Qing code.]

2858 Möllendorff, Paul Georg van. *The Family Law of the Chinese.* Trans. S. M. Broadbent. Rangoon: Superintendent Government Printing and Stationery of Burma, 1925. [From a German-language original of 1895.]

2859 Shiga, Shūzō. "Family Property and the Law of Inheritance in Traditional China." In *Chinese Family Law and Social Change in Historical and Comparative Perspective,* ed. David Buxbaum, pp. 109–150. Seattle: University of Washington, 1978.

2860 Sweeten, Alan R. "Women and Law in Rural China: Vignettes from 'Sectarian Cases' (Chiao-an) in Kiangsi, 1792–1878." *Ch'ing-shih wen-t'i* 3(Dec. 1978):49–68.

2861 Tai, Yen-hui. "Divorce in Traditional Chinese Law." In *Chinese Family Law and Social Change in Historical and Comparative Perspective,* ed. David Buxbaum, pp. 75–108. Seattle: University of Washington, 1978.

2862 "Validity of Common Law Marriage in China." *International Law Quarterly* 1(Spring 1947):71–73.

2863 Van der Valk, Marius Hendrikus. "Freedom of Marriage in Modern Chinese Law." *Monumenta Serica* 3(1938):1–34.

2864 Van der Valk, Marius Hendrikus. *An Outline of Modern Chinese Family Law.* Monumenta Serica Monograph, series 2. Peiping: Henri Vetch, 1939. [Reprinted: Taibei: Chengwen, 1969.]

2865 Van der Valk, Marius Hendrikus. *Conservatism in Modern Chinese Family Law.* Studia et documenta ad iura orientis antiqui pertinentia 4. Leiden: Brill, 1956.

MARRIAGE AND FAMILY LAWS IN THE PEOPLE'S REPUBLIC OF CHINA (1949–)

2866 All China Democratic Women's Federation. *Chinese Women in 1950.* Peking, 1950. [A collection of articles about the effect on women of the 1950 marriage laws.]

2867 "Appendix: The Marriage Law of the People's Republic of China." *Far Eastern Reporter,* Spring 1977, pp. 40–48.

2868 *CB,* no. 136 (Nov. 10, 1951). "Marriage in Communist China," pp. 1–44. [Contains text of the Marriage Law, plus 14 articles on its promulgation and implementation.]

2869 *CB,* no. 236 (Jan. 31, 1953). "Implementation of Marriage Law in Different Parts of the Country Very Uneven," pp. 4–7.

2870 *CB,* no. 236 (Mar. 1953). "Nationwide Campaign to Publicize the Marriage Law in Communist China, Part I," pp. 1–3.

2871 *CB,* no. 243 (May 20, 1953). "Nationwide Campaign to Publicize the Marriage Law in Communist China, Part II," pp. 1–2.

2872 *CB,* no. 741 (Jan. 21, 1964). "Communist Party 6 Ministries Issue Joint Notice for Continued Propaganda on Marriage Law," p. 9.

2873 Cheung, Steven N. S. "The Enforcement of Property Rights in Children, and the Marriage Contract." *Economic J.* 82(June 1972):641–57.

2874 Fu, S. L. [Fu, Shang-lin]. "The New Marriage Law of Communist China." In *Contemporary China,* 1955, ed. Edward Stuart Kirby, pp. 115–138. Hong Kong: Hong Kong University Press, 1956.

2875 Gen, Lewis. "The Marriage Law of New China." *Eastern World,* no. 11 (Nov. 1951), pp. 18–19.

2876 Greene, Felix. *A Divorce Trial in China.* Boston: New England Free Press, n.d. [Pamphlet.]

2877 "A Handbook on Daily Living for Residents of Streets and Neighborhoods (Excerpt): How to Settle Legal Disputes." *Chinese Sociology and Anthropology* 8(Summer 1976):34–53. [Excerpt from *A Handbook of Daily Living* (1951). Contains sections on marriage law.]

2878 Liu, Y. "Reform of Marriage and Family Systems in China." *Peking Review* 11(Mar. 13, 1964):17–19. [About the implementation of the Marriage Law of 1950.]

2879 McAleavy, Henry. "Some Aspects of Marriage and Divorce in Communist China." In *Family Law in Asia and Africa,* ed. James Norman Dalrymple Anderson, pp. 73–89. New York: Praeger, 1968.

2880 Madian, Marcia Dunn. "The Marriage Law of Communist China, 1950–1953: A Means of Disrupting the Traditional Chinese Family System." M.A. thesis, Columbia University, 1962.

2881 "Marriage Law Brings Happiness." *China Reconstructs* 1(July–Aug. 1952):46.

2882 *The Marriage Law of the PRC Together with Other Relevant Articles.* Peking: Foreign Languages Press, 1950. [Relevant articles include Teng Ying-ch'ao, "On the Marriage Law of the PRC" and Chang Chih-jang, "A Much Needed Marriage Law."]

2883 Massell, Gregory J. "Family Law and Social Mobilization in Soviet Central Asia: Some Comparisons with the People's Republic of China." In *Chinese Family Law and Social Change in Historical and Comparative Perspective,* ed. David C. Buxbaum, pp. 400–435. Seattle: University of Washington, 1978.

2884 Meijer, Marinus Johan. "Early Communist Marriage Legislation in China." *Contemporary China* 6(1962/1964) (Pub. 1968):85–102.

2885 Meijer, Marinus Johan. "Problems of Translating the Marriage Law." In *Contemporary Chinese Law: Research Problems and Perspectives,* ed. Jerome Cohen, pp. 210-229. Cambridge, Mass.: Harvard University, 1970.

2886 Meijer, Marinus Johan. *Marriage Law and Policy in the Chinese People's Republic.* Hong Kong: Hong Kong University, 1971. [Contains translations of text of successive laws and policy directives from 1931 to 1964.]

2887 Meijer, Marinus Johan. "Marriage Law and Policy in the People's Republic of China." In *Chinese Family Law and Social Change in Historical and Comparative Perspective,* ed. David C. Buxbaum, pp. 436-483. Seattle: University of Washington, 1978.

2888 Niida, Noboru. "Land Reform and New Marriage Laws in China." *Developing Economics* 2(Mar. 1964):3-15.

2889 *SCMP,* no. 95 (April 17, 1951). "Burmese Women Study New Marriage Law of China," p. 12.

2890 *SCMP,* no. 132 (June 28, 1951). "Women under the New Marriage Law," p. 20.

2891 *SCMP,* no. 535 (Mar. 18, 1953). "National Committee of Campaign for Implementation of Marriage Law Holds 2nd Session," p. 7.

2892 *SCMP,* no. 536 (Mar. 21, 1953). "Liu Ching-fan on Significance of Publicizing Marriage Law," p. 14. [*Renmin ribao,* Mar. 20, 1953.]

2893 *SCMP,* no. 1002 (Mar. 5, 1955). "Present Conditions Relating to Implementation of Marriage Law Stated by Committee Spokesman," p. 2.

2894 *SCMP,* no. 1007 (Mar. 7, 1955). "New Social Atmosphere Appears in Peking after Marriage Law Promotion," p. 30.

2895 *SCMP,* no. 1062 (June 1, 1955). "Ministry of Internal Affairs Promulgates Regulations for Registration of Marriages," p. 32.

2896 *SCMP,* no. 1069 (June 4, 1955). "Make a Good Job of the Registration of Marriages," p. 6. [*Guangming ribao* editorial.]

2897 *SCMP,* no. 1110 (Aug. 12, 1955). "Ministry of Internal Affairs Answers Certain Questions on Registration of Marriages," p. 18.

2898 *SCMP,* no. 1462 (Jan. 4, 1957). "A Word to the Judicial Personnel Who Deal with the Marriage Disputes of the Masses," p. 2.

2899 *SCMP,* no. 1487 (Feb. 5, 1957). "Changchun Mobilizes for Implementation of Marriage Law," p. 20.

2900 *SCMP,* no. 1628 (July 15, 1957). "Disciplinary Penalty Imposed by Nanchang Court on Chu Chi-yen for Beating Women, Violating Law," p. 36.

2901 *SCMP,* no. 2018 (Jan. 31, 1959). "Implement the Marriage Law," p. 15.

2902 *SCMP,* no. 2018 (Jan. 31, 1959). "Temporary Regulations for Marriage Law Are Not Fit for Current Conditions of Sinkiang," p. 15.

2903 Shih, Liang. "The Marriage Law of the People's China." *People's China* 1952:11:9-10, 32.

2904 Tan, Manni. "Why New Marriage Law was Necessary." *China Reconstructs* 30(Mar. 1981):17-21.

2905 Terni, P. V. E. "Chinese Marriage Law of 1949." *International Law Quarterly* 4(1951):420-23.

2906 Van der Valk, Marius Hendrikus. "The Registration of Marriage in Communist China." *Monumenta Serica* 16(1957):347-59.

2907 "Woman Leader on New Marriage Law." *Beijing Review,* Mar. 16, 1981, pp. 21-27.

2908 Woodworth, K. C. "Family Law and Resolution of Domestic Disputes in the PRC." *McGill Law J.* 13(1967):169-77.

2909 Yang, Wen. 'China's Marriage Law in Past and Present." *Women of China* 1980:5:11-13.

2910 Yang, Wen. "The Chinese People Endorse Revised Marriage Law." *Women of China* 1980:12:8-9.

CONSTITUTIONAL LAW: THE PEOPLE'S REPUBLIC OF CHINA (1949-)

2911 Blaustein, Albert P., ed. *Fundamental Legal Documents of Communist China.* Hackensack, New Jersey: F.B. Rothman, 1962. [The laws pertaining to women are the Constitution of the Communist Party, Constitution of the PRC, Electoral Law, Agrarian Reform Law, Labor Insurance Regulations, Constitution of the Trade Unions, Marriage Law of 1950, and Regulations Concerning Retirement of Workers and Staff Members.]

2912 "China's Women at the General Elections." *People's China,* Mar. 16, 1954, pp. 22-23. [Pictorial essay about six women who were elected to office.]

2913 *Fundamental Laws of the Chinese Soviet Republic.* N.Y.: International Publishers, 1934. [Introduction by Bela Kun. Contains a copy of the Regulations Concerning Marriage in the Kiangsi Soviet. See especially pp. 83-88. Also published as *Fundamental Laws of the Chinese Soviet Republic,* ed. Bela Kun. London: Lawrence, 1934.]

2914 Lewis, John Wilson, ed. *Major Doctrines of Communist China.* N.Y.: Norton, 1964. [Includes discussion of women's rights and the law.]

2915 *SCMP,* no. 762 (Mar. 8, 1954). "High Percentage of Women Vote in China," p. 17.

2916 *SCMP,* no. 862 (July 30, 1954). "Draft Constitution Protects Women and Children," p. 24. [*Renmin ribao* editorial.]

2917 *SCMP,* no. 876 (Aug. 23, 1954). "Draft Constitution Provides for Women's Rights," p. 25.

2918 Sun, Chan-ko. "China Steps to Universal Suffrage." *People's China,* Apr. 1, 1953, pp. 5-9.

2919 Xu, Juru. "Women's Rights to Inherit Property Protected." *Women of China* 1980:3:39-40.

MARRIAGE AND FAMILY LAWS: HONG KONG, TAIWAN AND OVERSEAS CHINA

2920 Buxbaum, David C. "A Case Study of the Dynamics of Family Law and Social Change in Rural China." In *Chinese Family Law and Social Change in Historical and Comparative Perspective,* ed. David C. Buxbaum. Seattle: University of Washington, 1978. [Mainly on the situation in a Taiwan village.]

2921 EP. "Matrimonial Property—Wife's Right to Restrain Husband from Disposing of Matrimonial Home: Chan Tsoi Wai-loi v. Chan Kwok-fai." *Hong Kong Law J.* 11(Jan. 1981):100-103.

2922 Freedman, Maurice. "Chinese Family Law in Singapore: The Rout of Custom." In *Family Law in Asia and Africa,* ed. James Norman Dalrymple, pp. 49-72.1 N.Y.: Praeger, 1967.

2923 Lethbridge, Henry. "Rape, Reform and Feminism in Hong Kong." *Hong Kong Law J.* 10(Sept. 1980):260-91.

2924 McGough, James Pierce. "Marriage and Adoption in Chinese Society with Special Reference to Customary Law." Ph.D. dissertation, Michigan State, 1976. [Emphasizing situation in Taiwan.]

2925 Phillips, Elizabeth. "Damages for Adultery." *Hong Kong Law J.* 11(Jan. 1981):54-59.

2926 Phillips, Elizabeth. "Rights in the Matrimonial Home." *Hong Kong Law J.* 11(May 1981):202-213.

2927 Sussex, Elizabeth. "Divorce—Disclosure of Financial Resources, Siu Chow-tong v. Siu Cheng Shui-ying." *Hong Kong Law J.* 9(May 1979):167–69.

2928 Sussex, Elizabeth. "Divorce—Irretrievable Breakdown, Unreasonable Behavior, Lee Mok-ying v. Lee Wing." *Hong Kong Law J.* 9(May 1979):170–71.

2929 Sussex, Elizabeth. "Divorce—Petition within Three Years of Marriage, Kwan Bui Lock v. Isabelle Stamm Lock." *Hong Kong Law J.* 9(Sept. 1979):346–48.

2930 Sussex, Elizabeth. "Divorce—Meaning of 'Living Apart' Grave Financial Hardship, Yuen Nip Yulandna." *Hong Kong Law J.* 10(May 1980):200–203.

WOMEN IN POLITICS: TRADITIONAL CHINA (TO 1911)

2931 Backhouse, Edmund Trelawney and Bland, John Otway Percy. *China under the Empress Dowager: Being the History of the Life and Times of Tz'u Hsi, Compiled from State Papers and the Private Diary of the Comptroller of Her Household.* N.Y.: Houghton Mifflin, 1949. [Reprint of 1910 ed.]

2932 Carl, Katherine Augusta. *With the Empress Dowager.* N.Y.: Century, 1905.

2933 Chun, Jinsie. *I Am Heaven.* Philadelphia: Macrae Smith, 1974. [Portrait of the Empress Wu of the Tang.]

2934 Chung, Sue Fawn. "The Much Maligned Empress Dowager: A Revisionist Study of the Empress Dowager Tz'u-hsi in the Period 1898 to 1900." Ph.D. dissertation, University of California, Berkeley, 1975.

2935 Chung, Sue Fawn. "The Much Maligned Empress Dowager: A Revisionist Study of the Empress Dowager Tz'u-hsi (1835–1908)." *Modern Asian Studies* 13(1979):2:177–96.

2936 Collis, Maurice. *The Motherly and Auspicious.* N.Y.: Putman, 1944. [Biography of Cixi.]

2937 Conger, Sarah Pike. *Letters from China, with Particular Reference to the Empress Dowager and the Women of China.* Chicago: McClurg, 1909.

2938 Der Ling (Princess). *Two Years in the Forbidden City.* N.Y.: Dodd, Mead, 1911. [Memoir of a Manchu noblewoman close to Empress Dowager Cixi.]

2939 Der Ling (Princess). *Old Buddha: A Biography of the Empress Dowager Tz'u Hsi.* N.Y.: Dodd, Mead, 1928.

2940 Dupree, N. H. "T'ang Wu-hou, Empress of China, 625–705: Ten Tombs in Chien County, China." *Archaeology* 32(July 1979):34–44.

2941 Fan, Wen-lan. "Ch'iu Chin: A Woman Revolutionary." *Women of China* 4(Oct.–Dec. 1956):31–33.

2942 Farley, Foster. "The Phoenix-Throne Emperor." *Orientations* 8(Mar. 1977):45–49. [About Empress Wu Zetian.]

2943 Fitzgerald, Charles Palwick. *The Empress Wu.* London: Cresset Press, 1956. [Also published in Melbourne: F.W. Cheshire, 1955.]

2944 Giles, Lionel. "Ch'iu Chin, A Chinese Heroine." *Asiatic Review*, new (4th) series 12(July-Nov. 1917):125–46. pp. 125–146.

2945 Goodrich, Chauncey S. "Two Chapters in the Life of an Empress of the Later Han." *Harvard J. of Asiatic Studies* 25(1964–65):165–77; 26(1966):187–210.

2946 Goodrich, L. Carrington and Fang, Chaoying, ed. *Dictionary of Ming Biography, 1368–1966.* 2 vols. N.Y.: Columbia University, 1976. [8 female entries, including 5 empresses and consorts.]

2947 Guisso, R. W. L. *Wu Tse-t'ien and the Politics of Legitimation in T'ang China.* East Asian Studies Occasional Papers, no. 11. Bellingham: Western Washington University, 1978.

2948 Haldane, Charlotte. *The Last Great Empress of China.* London: Constable, 1965.

2949 Headland, Isaac Taylor. *Court Life in China: The Capital, Its Officials and People.* N.Y.: Revell, 1909.

2950 Hussey, Harry. *Venerable Ancestor: The Life and Times of Tz'u Hsi, 1835–1908, Empress of China.* Garden City, N.Y.: Doubleday, 1949.

2951 Kahn, Harold. "The Politics of Filiality." *J. of Asian Studies* 26(Feb. 1967):197–202. [On the relationship between the Qianlong Emperor and his mother.]

2952 Levy, Howard S. *Harem Favorites of an Illustrious Celestial.* Taizhong, Taiwan: Lin Yunpeng, 1958. [On several outstanding women of the court of the Emperor Xuanzong of the Tang.]

2953 Li, Shih. "Wu Tse-t'ien: A Pro-Legalist, Anti-Confucian Stateswoman of the T'ang Dynasty." *Chinese Studies in History* 11(Summer 1978):26–33.

2954 Lin, Yutang. *Lady Wu, A True Story.* [Historical novel about Empress Wu of the Tang.] London: Heinemann, 1957.

2955 Pan, Ku. "Two Imperial Ladies of Han." Trans. Burton Watson. *Renditions: A Chinese-English Translation Magazine,* no. 1 (Autumn 1973), pp. 7–14.

2956 Rankin, Mary Backus. "The Emergence of Women at the End of the Ch'ing: The Case of Ch'iu Chin." In *Women in Chinese Society,* ed. Margery Wolf and Roxane Witke, pp. 39–66. Stanford: Stanford University, 1975.

2957 Sergeant, Philip Walshingham. *The Great Empress Dowager of China.* N.Y.: Dodd, Mead, 1911.

2958 Shepard, Don, comp. *Women in History.* Los Angeles: Mankind Publishing Co., 1973. [See Philip Finnley's "The Imperial Way of Chinese Women," pp. 77–92; and Angela Stuart's "Tz'u-hsi," pp. 227–52.]

2959 "Twenty-One Hundred-Year-Old Chinese Noble-woman: Han Dynasty Tomb." *Science News* 102(Aug. 12, 1972):103.

2960 Warner, Marina. *The Dragon Empress: Life and Times of Tz'u-hsi, 1835–1908, Empress Dowager of China.* London: Wirdenfeld and Nicolson, 1972.

2961 Wieman, Earl. "Empress of Concubines." 4(Jan. 1973):41–47. [On Yang Guifei, concubine of Emperor Xuanzong.]

2962 Wu, Shu-chiung (Huang) [Mrs. Wu Lien-teh]. *Yang Kueifei: The Most Famous Beauty of China.* Shanghai: Commercial Press, 1923. [Reprints: London: Brentano, 1924; Taibei: Chengwen, 1974. Fictionalized biography of the concubine of Tang Xuanzong traditionally credited with the demoralization of the Tang by paving the way for the rebellion that brought about the collapse of the dynasty.]

2963 Wu, Yung. *The Flight of an Empress.* Trans. Ida Pruitt. London: Faber & Faber, 1937. [On Cixi's flight from Beijing in 1900 during the Boxer disturbance. Written by a court official.]

2964 Yang, Lien-sheng. "Female Rulers in Imperial China." *Harvard J. of Asiatic Studies* 23(1960/61):47–61. [Reprinted in *Studies of Governmental Institutions in Chinese History.* Harvard-Yenching Institute Studies 23, ed. John Lyman Bishop, pp. 153–169. Cambridge: Harvard University Press, 1968.]

2965 Yang, Lien-sheng. *Excursions in Sinology.* Cambridge: Harvard University Press, 1969. [See chapter on female rulers in early and middle periods of Chinese history.]

Note: See also "The Issue of Emancipation before 1911."

WOMEN IN POLITICS: THE CHINESE REPUBLIC (1911-1949)

2966 Ch'en, Yü-ying. "Her Revolutionary Spirit Radiates Like a Great Rainbow." *Chinese Studies in History* 12(Summer 1979):61-72. [In praise of Mao Zedong's first wife, Yang Kaihui, a revolutionary martyr.]

2967 Chiang, Kai-shek, Mme. [Soong, Mayling]. "Conversations with Mikhail Borodin." *Sino-American Relations* 4(Spring 1978):1-26.

2968 Chiang, Mei-ling [Soong, Mayling] [Mme. Chiang Kai-shek]. *Sian: A Coup d'Etat. A Fortnight in Sian; Extracts from a Diary by Chiang Kai-shek.* Shanghai: China Publishing Co., 1937.

2969 Chiang, Mei-ling [Soong, Mayling] [Mme. Chiang Kai-shek]. *This Is Our China.* N.Y. & London: Harper & Bros., 1940.

2970 Chiang, Mei-ling [Soong, Mayling] [Mme. Chiang Kai-shek]. *China Shall Rise Again, Including Ten Official Statements of China's Present Progress.* N.Y. & London: Harper & Bros., 1941.

2971 Chiang, Mei-ling [Soong, Mayling] [Mme. Chiang Kai-shek]. *We Chinese Women: Speeches and Writings during the First United Nations Year.* N.Y.: John Day, 1943.

2972 "Chinese Women and Petticoat Government." *Literary Digest* 64(Jan. 17, 1920):74-78.

2973 "Chinese Women in Politics." *Literary Digest* 62(Sept. 27, 1919):17.

2974 The Criticism Group of the People's Literature Publishing House. "Eternal Glory to Martyr Yang K'ai-hui." *Chinese Studies in History* 12(Spring 1979):44-47.

2975 Eunson, Roby. *The Soong Sisters.* N.Y.: Watts, Franklin, 1975.

2976 Hahn, Emily. *The Soong Sisters.* Garden City, N.Y.: Doubleday, Doran & Co., 1942.

2977 Ho, Hsiang-hing. "When I Learned to Cook." *Chinese Studies in History* 13(Summer 1980):79-87, [Ho records her life during the Tongmenghui period and her views on women's status in modern China. Trans. William A. Wycoff.]

2978 Hsin, Wen-ping. "Martyr Yang K'ai-hui Will Always Live in Our Hearts." *Chinese Studies in History* 12(Summer 1979):54-60.

2979 Hull, Helen. *Mayling Soong Chiang.* N.Y.: Coward-McCann, 1943.

2980 "In Commemoration of the Forty-Sixth Anniversary of the Heroic Martyrdom of Yang K'ai-hui." *Chinese Studies in History* 12(Spring 1979):36-43.

2981 Liang, Hsing. *Liu Hu-lan.* Peking: Foreign Languages Press, 1953. [Biography of a famous young woman guerrilla leader and revolutionary martyr, based on interviews conducted in 1951.]

2982 Liu, Maoshu. "Xiang Jingyu, Champion of the Chinese Women's Movement." *Women of China* 1980:3:33-35; 1980:4:33-35.

2983 Soong, Ching-ling [Mme. Sun Yat-sen]. "The Chinese Woman's Fight for Freedom." *Asia* [Asia and the Americas] 42(July-Aug. 1942):391-93, 470-72.

2984 Soong, Ching-ling [Mme. Sun Yat-sen]. *The Struggle for New China.* Peking: Foreign Languages Press, 1952. [A collection of articles, speeches and statements made between July 1927 and July 1952.]

2985 *SPRCP*, no. 6241 (Dec. 8, 1976). "*Jen-min jih-pao* Features Commemoration of Martyr Yang Kai-hui, Close Comrade-in Arms and Wife of Chairman Mao," p. 155.

2986 *SPRCP*, no. 6242 (Dec. 9, 1976). "Mass Gathering Marks Martyr Yang Kaihui's Death," p. 221.

2987 Teng, Ying-ch'ao. "Remembrances of the May Fourth Movement." *Chinese Studies in History* 14(Fall 1980):93-103.

2988 Ts'ai, Ch'ing-yuan. "Setting the Record Straight [Madame Chiang's Remarks on T. White's 'In Search of History']." *Free China Review* 28(Sept. 1978):19-21.

2989 Tsin, Ching. "Liu Hu-lan." *Chinese Literature* 1972:2:15-43. [Reminiscences about a guerrilla heroine.]

2990 Weigelin, Susanne. "The Martyrdom of Yang Kaihui." *Eastern Horizon* 16(Mar. 1977):12-14.

2991 Witke, Roxane. "Woman as Politician in China of the 1920s." In *Women in China*, ed. M. Young, pp. 33-46. Ann Arbor: University of Michigan, 1973.

2992 "Yang K'ai-hui, Wife and Revolutionary Comrade." *China Reconstructs* 26(Dec. 1977):56-58.

Note: See also "Emancipation Movements: The Chinese Republic (1911-1949)" and "Emancipation Movements in the Communist Revolution, 1921-1949."

WOMEN IN POLITICS; CADRES AND CADRE DEVELOPMENT: THE PEOPLE'S REPUBLIC OF CHINA (1949-)

2993 "Arrest Wang Kuang-mei [Mrs. Liu Shao-ch'i] by Strategy." In Li, Dun Jen, *Modern China: From Mandarin to Commissar*, pp. 330-35. N.Y.: Scribner, 1978. [Translated from *Jinggangshan bao*, Qinghua University, Jan. 1967.]

2994 Berstein, R. "Leader's Rise, a Widow's Fall." *Time* 117(Jan. 12, 1981):27-28. [A report on the trial of Jiang Qing.]

2995 Brittain, Mary Z. "Revolutionary Statesmen." *China Now*, no. 50 (Mar. 1975), pp. 6-7. [Includes leading women Communists.]

2996 *CB*, no. 942 (Nov. 15, 1971). "Pay Attention to the Development of Female Party Members," pp. 9-10.

2997 *CB*, no. 991 (Mar. 14, 1973). "Before and After the Development of a Woman Party Member."

2998 *CB*, no. 991 (Mar. 14, 1973). "Promote Such Responsible Spirit—Postscript," p. 12.

2999 *CB*, no. 991 (Mar. 14, 1973). "She Again Steps Forward in Big Strides," p. 11.

3000 *CB*, no. 995 (May 18, 1973). "Actively and Cautiously Develop Women Party Members with Education in Line as the Key: Anhwei Province," p. 3.

3001 *CB*, no. 995 (May 18, 1973). "The Natural Color of the Laboring People Cannot be Forsaken—About Party Secretary Shen Chi-lan," p. 7.

3002 *CB*, no. 995 (May 18, 1973). T'ang, Sheng-p'ing. "Actively Train Women Party Members and Women Cadres," p. 1.

3003 *CB*, no. 1022 (July 23, 1974). "Female Party Members Vigorously Break into Women's Forbidden Area," p. 6.

3004 *CB*, no. 1022 (Aug. 21, 1974). The Party Committee of Nanchai Commune, Ch'ienyang *hsien*, Shensi. "Promote Outstanding Young Women to the Leading Position," p. 27.

3005 *CB*, no. 1022 (Oct. 15, 1974). "A Female Party Member Fighting As a Vanguard in Criticizing Lin Piao and Confucius," p. 60.

3006 *CB*, no. 1026 (Nov. 30, 1974). "Intensify Training and Education for New Female Party Members," p. 16.

3007 Chen, Gerald. "The Tragic Story of Zhang Zhixin." *Eastern Horizon* 18(Aug. 1979):40–43. [Zhang was a woman Party member accused of being a counter-revolutionary in the early 1970s.]

3008 Ch'en, Kao-hua and T'ien, Jen-lung [of the Institute of History]. "Chiang Ch'ing Is the Spokeswoman of the Exploiting Classes—Refuting the Reactionary Fallacy that 'The Legalists Were the Spokesmen of the Peasants.'" *Chinese Studies in History* 12(Winter 1978/79):86–91. [Translation from *Guangming ribao*, Feb. 3, 1977.]

3009 "Chiang Ch'ing; Chairman Mao's Enigmatic Spouse." *Current Scene* 7(1969):1–14.

3010 "Chiang Ch'ing's Address to Diplomatic Cadres." *Issues and Studies* 11(July 1975):91–96.

3011 "Chiang Ch'ing's Three Counterrevolutionary Performances in the Thirties." *Chinese Studies in History* 12(Spring 1979):48–53.

3012 "Chiang Ch'ing's Wild Dream Shattered." *China Reconstructs* 26(June 1977):2–4.

3013 Chien, T'ieh. "The Chiang Ch'ing Faction and Peiping's Military Forces." *Issues and Studies* 12(Jan. 1976):12–30.

3014 "Chinese Women on Chiang Ch'ing: The Enemy of Women's Liberation." *China Reconstructs* 26(June 1977):8–10.

3015 Chu, Hao-jen. "Mao's Wife—Chiang Ch'ing." *China Quarterly*, no. 31 (July/Sept. 1967), pp. 148–50.

3016 Chung, Hua-min and Miller, Arthur C. *Madame Mao, a Profile of Chiang Ch'ing.* Hong Kong: Union Research Institute, 1968.

3017 Chung-fa. "Document of the Central Committee of the Chinese Communist Party." *Chinese Law and Government* 12(Spring/Summer 1979):134–67. [Evidence of the crimes of the Wang Hongwen, Zhang Chunqiao, Jiang Qing and Yao Wenyuan "anti-Communist Party clique."]

3018 The Criticism Group of the Editorial Department of Chungkuo she-ying. "A Confession of Her Wild Ambitions to Usurp Party and State Power—Critique of Chiang Ch'ing's Sinister Poem on a Photograph." *Chinese Studies in History* 12(Spring 1979):86–91.

3019 The Criticism Group of the United Front Work Department of the Chinese Communist Party's Central Committee. "Why Did Chiang Ch'ing Viciously Attack Sun Yat-sen?" *Chinese Studies in History* 12(Winter 1978/79):80–85. [Translation from *Guangming ribao*, Mar. 13, 1977.]

3020 Davin, Delia. *Woman-Work: Women and the Party in Revolutionary China.* N.Y.: Oxford University Press, 1980.

3021 *ECMM*, no. 83 (Mar. 6, 1957). "Now Many Women Workers, Women APC Members and Women Cadres in China," p. 19.

3022 *ECMM*, no. 125 (feb. 1, 1958). An, Tzu-wen. "A Correct Approach to the Problem of Retirement of Women Cadres," p. 14.

3023 Epstein, Israel. "Soong Ching Ling and Her Times." *China Pictorial* 1981:3:6–11.

3024 Fairfax-Cholmeley. "Peasant Woman Leader." *Eastern Horizon* 4(Nov. 1965):44–48.

3025 Feng, Fei. "Chiang Ch'ing and Her 'Foreign Sister.'" *Chinese Studies in History* 12(Fall 1978):59–62.

3026 "Firm in Conviction, Unceasing in Struggle: An Interview with Deng Yingchao." *China Reconstructs* 30(Aug. 1981):3–7. [Deng, the wife of the late Premier Zhou Enlai, is a member of the political bureau of the Party's Central Committee.]

3027 "Firm in Conviction, Unceasing in Struggle: Deng Yingchao Recalls the Long March." *China Reconstructs* 30(Sept. 1981):28–31. [Part 2 of interview.]

3028 Fu, Hsin. "Behind Chiang Ch'ing's Utmost Dislike of Folk Songs." *Chinese Studies in History* 12(Summer 1979):89–91.

3029 "Good Daughter of the Party." *Chinese Literature*, March 1971, pp. 3–30. [Reportage.]

3030 *A Great Trial in Chinese History.* Beijing: New World Press 1981. [About the trial of Jiang Qing.]

3031 "Growth of a Woman Mine Leader." *China Reconstructs* 24(Nov. 1975):20–21.

3032 Gupta, Krishna P. "Reflections on Witke's Chiang Ch'ing." *China Report* (New Delhi) 14(May-June 1978):69–74.

3033 Han, Suyin. "Interview with Madame Soong Ching-ling." *Eastern Horizon* 5(Nov. 1966):8–11.

3034 History Writing Group of the Chinese Communist Party Kwangtung Provincial Committee. "The Ghost of Empress Lü and Chiang Ch'ing's Empress Dream." *Chinese Studies in History* 12(Fall 1978):37–54.

3035 "A Housewife Deputy to the People's Congress." *People's China*, Mar. 16, 1954, pp. 1–33.

3036 "How Chiang Ch'ing's Tooth Was Lost." *Chinese Studies in History* 12(Spring 1979):54–55.

3037 Hsieh, Chen-ping. "The Rise and Fall of Comrade Chiang Ch'ing." *Asian Affairs* (New York) 5(Jan./Feb. 1978):148–64.

3038 Hsing, Yen-tzu. "Training Women Cadres." *Peking Review* 17(Apr. 5, 1974):18–21.

3039 Hu, Shu-ho. "Chiang Ch'ing's Ignominious Aim in Negating Lu Hsun." *Chinese Studies in History* 12(Spring 1979):62–64.

3040 JPRS, no. 877D (Mar. 1, 1959). Mieh, Chih. "A Discussion on the Study of Political Theory by Women Cadres." [From *Zhongguo funü*, 5 p. 11.]

3041 JPRS, no. 34918 (Mar. 8, 1966). "Stress Politics and Further Develop the Great Power of Women," pp. 1–3. [From *Renmin ribao*.]

3042 JPRS, no. 36983 (May 8, 1966). "Stress Politics and Further Develop the Great Power of Women," [Reprinted from *Communist China Digest* 172, pp. 16–18.]

3043 JPRS, no. 52029 (Dec. 21, 1970). "Chairman Mao's Conversation with His Niece Wang Hai-yung," pp. 34–35.

3044 Klein, Donald W. and Clark, Anne B. *Biographic Dictionary of Chinese Communism, 1921–1965.* Cambridge, Mass.: Harvard University Press, 1971. 2 vols. [Includes biographies of 17 women party leaders. See appendix in vol. 2, p. 1046.]

3045 Ku, Yen. "Chiang Ch'ing's Wolfish Ambition in Publishing 'Matriarchal Society.'" *Chinese Studies in History* 12(Spring 1979):75–79.

3046 Kuo, Feng-lien. "How Chiang Ch'ing Tried to Undermine Tachai." *China Reconstructs* 26(Feb.–Mar. 1977):34–39.

3047 Lan, P'ing [Chiang Ch'ing]. "Chiang Ch'ing's 'Farewell Letter' to T'ang Na." *Chinese Studies in History* 14(1980-81):77–82. [Document of the early love life of Jiang Qing.]

3048 Lan, P'ing [Chiang Ch'ing]. "Why I Have Parted from T'ang Na." *Chinese Studies in History* 14(1980-81):83–91. [Published in Shanghai's *Lianhua huabao*, June 5, 1937.]

3049 Ling, Chia. "Charged Political Status of Chinese Women." *Women of China* 1957:2:8-10.

3050 Liu, Melinda. "Jiang Qing's Curtain Call." *Newsweek* 96(Dec. 1, 1980):52.

3051 Longway, Lynn and Liu, Melinda. "Ganging up on the Gang." *Newsweek* 96(Dec. 8, 1980):57. [On the trial of the "Gang of Four."]

3052 Lu, Ching-wen. "Chiang Ch'ing Cannot Shirk Responsibility for Her Crime in Sabotaging the Revolution in Literature and Art." *Chinese Studies in History* 12(Spring 1979):80-85.

3053 Ly, Singko. *The Fall of Madam Mao*. N.Y.: Vantage Press, 1979.

3054 MacDougall, Colina. "Mrs. Mao's Vocation." *Far Eastern Economic Review* 67(Jan. 29, 1970):27-29.

3055 Maloney, Joan M. "Chinese Women and Party Leadership: Impact of the Cultural Revolution." *Current Scene* 10(Apr. 10, 1972):10-15.

3056 The Mass Criticism Group of the Central Academy of Arts and Crafts. "The Wild Ambition for Usurping State Power Hidden in the 'Chiang Ch'ing Dress.'" *Chinese Studies in History* 12(Summer 1979):92-94.

3057 "More about Mr. and Mrs. Liu Shao-ch'i." *China News Analysis*, no. 663 (June 9, 1967), pp. 1-7.

3058 O'Sullivan, Sue. "Jiang Qing: Who is Really on Trial?" *China Now*, no. 96 (May/June 1981), p. 13.

3059 Ou, Mei. "Chiang Ch'ing and 'Weeding Out Those at the Emperor's Side.'" *Chinese Studies in History* 12(Summer 1979):73-77.

3060 "Pi Ying-lan: Good Daughter of the Communist Party." *Peking Review* 12(Sept. 19, 1969):15-18, 22.

3061 The Propaganda Team of the Ta-chai Production Brigade. "A Major Exposure of Chiang Ch'ing's Features in Worshipping Foreign Things and Restoring Ancient Ways." *Chinese Studies in History* 12(Summer 1979):86-88.

3062 Schell, Orville. "China Encounters the West: The Courtship of Ling Mulan." *Rolling Stone*, Dec. 11, 1980, pp. 42-4. [Story of a Chinese woman who experienced the Cultural Revolution.]

3063 Schell, Orville. "China's Past Is on Trial, Too." *Life* 4(Feb. 1981):103-104. [Report on the trial of the "Gang of Four" and Jiang Qing.]

3064 *SCMM*, no. 261 (Feb. 1, 1961). 'Showing Concern over the Livelihood of the Masses, Consulting Them When Problems Arise," p. 22. [*Zhongguo funü* commentary.]

3065 *SCMM*, no. 277 (Aug. 1, 1961). "She Works Steadily for Eighteen Years—an Account of Comrade Chen Min's Hard-working Spirit," p. 18.

3066 *SCMM*, no. 431 (Aug. 24, 1964). "An Ordinary Woman Party Member," pp. 21-24. [From *Zhongguo funü*.]

3067 *SCMM*, no. 517 (Feb. 27, 1966). Sung, Wen-mei (Vice-chairman of Women's Representative Conference, Pei-hai Hu-t'un Brigade, Machuch'iao Commune, Tunghsien). "From Unwillingness to Work as Cadre to Determination to Make Revolution a Life Career," p. 29. [From *Hongqi*.]

3068 *SCMM*, no. 722 (Jan. 1972). Soong Ching-ling. "The Beginning of a New Era," p. 96. [From *China Reconstructs* 1972:1.]

3069 *SCMM*, no. 739-740 (Oct. 1, 1972). Party Branch of Tunghsing Production Brigade in the Suburbs of Wuchou Municipality, Kwangsi. "Strive to Train Women Cadres," pp. 71-74. [From *Hongqi*.]

3070 *SCMM*, no. 765 (Dec. 1, 1973). Hsia P'ing. "Make Energetic Efforts to Train Women Cadres," p. 17.

3071 *SCMM*, no. 784 (July 1, 1974). The Party Committee of the 2nd Wuchou Municipal Light and Chemical Industries Bureau, Kwangsi. "Pay Attention to Developing Female Membership of the Party," p. 21.

3072 *SCMP*, no. 89 (Mar. 13, 1951). "Soong Ching-ling Sends Greetings to Eugene Dennis."

3073 *SCMP*, no. 1245 (Mar. 7, 1956). "Three Women in Responsible Positions," p. 21.

3074 *SCMP*, no. 1245 (Mar. 7, 1956). "Woman Doctor Becomes People's Deputy," p. 22.

3075 *SCMP*, no. 1276 (Mar. 30, 1956). Teng, Ying-ch'ao. "Follow the Fatherland, Contribute to Socialism," p. 4.

3076 *SCMP*, no. 1378 (Sept. 24, 1956). Ts'ai, Ch'ang. "Speech at September 24th Meeting of Party Congress," p. 9.

3077 *SCMP*, no. 1378 (Sept. 26, 1956). "Yang Chih-hua Speaks on Women Workers at September 26th Meeting of Communist Party Congress," p. 7.

3078 *SCMP*, no. 1556 (June 6, 1957). "Non-Party Leaders in Woman Work Hold Forum," p. 2.

3079 *SCMP*, no. 1617 (Sept. 21, 1957). "New Women's Leaders Elected," p. 1.

3080 *SCMP*, no. 2016 (May 12, 1959). "Ts'ai Ch'ang Receives Tibetan Women's Leaders," p. 11.

3081 *SCMP*, no. 2451 (Mar. 2, 1961). "Energetic Woman Commune Leader in Shansi," p. 14.

3082 *SCMP*, no. 2454 (Mar. 7, 1961). "More Peking Women Join Communist Party," p. 16.

3083 *SCMP*, no. 2689 (Feb. 26, 1962). 'More Shanghai Women Holding Responsible Posts," p. 21.

3084 *SCMP*, no. 2690 (Feb. 27, 1962). "Women Occupy Many Leading Posts in Old Chinese Revolutionary Base," p. 5.

3085 *SCMP*, no. 3175 (Mar. 6, 1964). "Elderly Peasant Woman in Southwest China Becomes Popular Leader," p. 23.

3086 *SCMP*, no. 3409 (Mar. 1, 1965). "East China Women's Deputies," p. 20.

3087 *SCMP*, no. 3412 (Mar. 4, 1965). "Peking Women in Leading Posts," p. 17.

3088 *SCMP*, no. 3413 (Mar. 5, 1965). "Veteran Women Revolutionaries in East China," p. 23.

3089 *SCMP*, no. 4310 (Nov. 14, 1968). Hung, Ping-wen. "Husband and Wife Repudiate Together the Theory of 'Joining the Party to Become Bureaucrats,'" p. 8.

3090 *SCMP*, no. 4359 (Nov. 19, 1969). "Long-time Woman Communist Party member Brimming with Vigour," p. 12. [From New China News Agency, Hangzhou.]

3091 *SCMP*, no. 4375 (Mar. 7, 1969). "Mao Tse-tung's Thought Guides Women Cadres," p. 12. [From New China News Agency, Nanchang.]

3092 *SCMP*, no. 4611 (Mar. 8, 1970). "Woman Party Secretary Nurtured by Mao Tse-tung's Thought," p. 27.

3093 *SCMP*, no. 4613 (Mar. 4, 1970). "A 75-Year Old Woman Communist Full of Revolutionary Vigor," p. 73.

3094 *SCMP*, no. 4697 (July 4, 1970). "A Fine Woman Communist Loyal to Chairman Mao," p. 80.

3095 *SCMP*, no. 4819 (Jan. 8, 1971). "Woman Team Leader Dies Saving Commune Member," p. 96.

3096 *SCMP*, no. 4853 (Feb. 23, 1971). The Communist Youth League Branch of the Women Brigade-Building Team of the Greater Hsingun Region under the Leadership of the Party Organization. "Persevere in Educating China Youth League Members and Youth with Mao Tse-tung's Thought," p. 51.

3097 *SCMP*, no. 4859 (Mar. 6, 1971). "Kuo Shu-chen, Fine Woman Communist Party Member in Northeast China," p. 97.

3098 *SCMP*, no. 4868 (Mar. 16, 1971). "Pay Attention to Training Women Cadres in the Course of Struggle—the Revolutionary Committee of Chien-hu *Hsien*, Kiangsu Province Strengthens Leadership over Work Related to Women," p. 47.

3099 *SCMP*, no. 4931 (June 28, 1971). "Young Woman Party Secretary Takes Lead in Learning from Tachai," p. 85.

3100 *SCMP*, no. 4939 (July 8, 1971). "Woman Communist More Concerned about Others than Herself," p. 18.

3101 *SCMP*, no. 4944 (July 18, 1971). "Central China Woman Communist Firmly Carries Out Chairman Mao's Revolutionary Line," p. 94.

3102 *SCMP*, no. 4953 (July 30, 1971). "Woman Party Branch Secretary Full of Revolutionary Vigor," p. 68.

3103 *SCMP*, no. 4983 (Sept. 13, 1971). Party branch of Taho production brigade, Hsinhsü commune, Chinghsi *hsien*, Kwangtung province. "Pay Attention to the Expansion of the Female Party Membership," p. 8.

3104 *SCMP*, no. 5005 (Oct. 18, 1971). "Chinese Communist Party Committee and Revolutionary Committee of T'ung-ch'eng *Hsien* Steps up Its Work on the Training and Education of Female Cadres," p. 119.

3105 *SCMP*, no. 5016 (Nov. 5, 1971). "Vigorously Foster and Use Women Cadres," p. 99.

3106 *SCMP*, no. 5025 (Nov. 17, 1971). "Lanshan *Hsien*, Hunan Province Vigorously Trains and Uses Women Cadres," p. 128.

3107 *SCMP*, no. 5081 (Feb. 16, 1972). "Vice Chairman Soong Ching Ling Sends Message of Condolence to Mrs. Snow on Death of Mr. Edgar Snow," p. 68.

3108 *SCMP*, no. 5091 (Mar. 1, 1972). "Chinese Women Cadres Make Great Contributions," p. 14.

3109 *SCMP*, no. 5091 (Mar. 2, 1972). "Cultivate and Promote Women Cadres in the Three Major Revolutionary Struggles—the Party Committee of Chinhua District Acts in Accordance with Chairman Mao's Teaching on the Cultivation of Revolutionary Successors," p. 11.

3110 *SCMP*, no. 5094 (Mar. 5, 1972). "Party Committee of Tanch'eng *Hsien*, Honan Province, Seriously Trains and Educates Women Cadres," p. 131.

3111 *SCMP*, no. 5094 (Mar. 6, 1972). "Woman Party Branch Secretary Praised by Poor and Lower-Middle Peasants," p. 141.

3112 *SCMP*, no. 5095 (Mar. 6, 1972). "Cultivate Women Cadres in the Three Major Revolutionary Struggles," p. 175.

3113 *SCMP*, no. 5095 (Mar. 6, 1972). "Woman Communist Devoted to People," p. 184.

3114 *SCMP*, no. 5097 (Mar. 8, 1972). "Party Organizations and Revolutionary Committees in Various Places Strengthen Leadership over Woman Work and Energetically Foster and Use Women Cadres Under the Guidance of Chairman Mao's Proletarian Revolutionary Line," p. 54.

3115 *SCMP*, no. 5100 (Mar. 13, 1972). "Fisherwoman Becomes Good Cadre," p. 167.

3116 *SCMP*, no. 5100 (Mar. 14, 1972). "Northwest China Cotton Mill Trains Women Cadres," p. 166.

3117 *SCMP*, no. 5101 (Mar. 17, 1972). "Conscientiously Train and Use Women Cadres Boldly—The CCP Ch'aoyang *Hsien* Committee Strengthens Line Education on Women and Enables Them to Receive Tempering in the Three Great Struggles," p. 4.

3118 *SCMP*, no. 5101 (Mar. 17, 1972). "Party Committee of Huaiyin Cigarette Factory of Ch'ingchiang City Earnestly Promotes Women Cadres and Gives Full Play to Their Role," p. 6.

3119 *SCMP*, no. 5102 (Mar. 16, 1972). "Woman Party Branch Secretary of North China Production Brigade," p. 62.

3120 *SCMP*, no. 5103 (Mar. 19, 1972). "Cultivate Women Cadres to Reinforce Leadership at Various Levels—the Northwest State No. 1 Cotton Mill Party Committee Holds a Study Class," p. 93.

3121 *SCMP*, no. 5146 (May 23, 1972). "Comrades Chou En-lai, Chiang Ch'ing and Chiao Kuan-hua Meet and Fete Mrs. Snow," p. 192.

3122 *SCMP*, no. 5153 (June 1, 1972). "Soong Ching Ling Fetes New York Times Associate Editor Harrison Salisbury and Wife," p. 77.

3123 *SCMP*, no. 5173 (July 2, 1972). "South China Woman Party Secretary Maintains Close Links with Masses," p. 140.

3124 *SCMP*, no. 5191 (July 28, 1972). "Vice Chairman Soong Ching Ling Meets American Woman Writer Barbara W. Tuchman," p. 90.

3125 *SCMP*, no. 5210 (Aug. 26, 1972). "Train Women Cadres in the Three Great Revolutionary Movements," p. 90.

3126 *SCMP*, no. 5212 (Aug. 28, 1972). "Vice Chairman Soong Ching Ling Meets and Fetes Canadian Professor and Wife," p. 36.

3127 *SCMP*, no. 5227 (Sept. 19, 1972). "Tung Pi-wu, Chou En-lai, Chiang Ch'ing and Li Hsien-nien Meet Her Imperial Majesty Shahbanon of Iran," p. 26.

3128 *SCMP*, no. 5235 (Oct. 2, 1972). "Chou En-lai, Chu Teh, Teng Ying-ch'ao, K'ang K'e-ch'ing Meet and Fete Friendly American Personage Frances Rootes Hadde and Her Husband," p. 241.

3129 *SCMP*, no. 5235 (Oct. 4, 1972). "Teng Ying-ch'ao, K'ang K'e-ch'ing and Ou Tang-liang Give Banquet in Honor of Delegation of Korean Democratic Women's Union," p. 85.

3130 *SCMP*, no. 5247 (Oct. 22, 1972). "Vice Chairman Soong Ching Ling Meets and Fetes American Friendly Personages Maud Russell and Ida Pruitt," p. 181.

3131 *SCMP*, no. 5274 (Dec. 2, 1972). "Teng Ying-ch'ao, K'ang K'e-ch'ing, Ting Hsueh-sung Meet Well Known French Personages," p. 67.

3132 *SCMP*, no. 5283 (Dec. 14, 1972). "Chu Teh, Teng Ying-ch'ao and K'ang K'e-ch'ing Meet American Friendly Personage Nym Wales."

3133 *SCMP*, no. 5311 (Jan. 27, 1973). "Changchiak'ou Municipal Rubber Factory Mindful of Training Women Cadres," p. 109.

3134 *SCMP*, no. 5311 (Jan. 27, 1973). "Peking Textile System Energetically Trains Women Cadres," p. 107.

3135 *SCMP*, no. 5315 (Jan. 24, 1973). "Pay Attention to Training Women Cadres Among Workers Actively—Investigation Report of Changchiak'ou Municipal Rubber Plant in Hopei Province," p. 124.

3136 *SCMP*, no. 5319 (Feb. 8, 1973). "Train Female Cadres and Give Play to Women's Role," p. 92.

3137 *SCMP*, no. 5326 (Feb. 19, 1973). "Chiu Hsiu-ying, Woman Leader of East China Production Team," p. 18.

3138 *SCMP*, no. 5334 (Mar. 4, 1973). "Pay Attention to the Selection of Cadres from Among Young Female Intellectuals," p. 128.

3139 *SCMP*, no. 5336 (Mar. 7, 1973). "East China Rural Women Cadres," p. 21.

3140 *SCMP*, no. 5336 (Mar. 7, 1973). "An Important Matter Worthy of Attention—Report on the Training of Woman Cadres by the Tachai Party Branch," p. 9.

3141 *SCMP,* no. 5337 (Mar. 6, 1973). "Party Organizations at Various Levels in Tinghsien Actively Help Women Cadres to Read and Study Seriously," p. 42.

3142 *SCMP,* no. 5337 (Mar. 6, 1973). "Pay Attention to the Selection of Cadres from Educated Young Women," p. 44.

3143 *SCMP,* no. 5337 (Mar. 6, 1973). "Peking Municipality Actively Brings up Women Party Members," p. 39.

3144 *SCMP,* no. 5338 (Mar. 9, 1973). "East China Village Woman Cadre," p. 99.

3145 *SCMP,* no. 5339 (Mar. 11, 1973). "Women Cadres in Peking's Cotton Textile Industry," p. 144.

3146 *SCMP,* no. 5342 (Mar. 16, 1973). "Women Cadres in Shanghai," p. 58.

3147 *SCMP,* no. 5345 (Mar. 20, 1973). "Woman Party Secretary on East China Islet," p. 173.

3148 *SCMP,* no. 5350 (Mar. 27, 1973). "Good North China *Hsien* Woman Party Secretary," p. 18.

3149 *SCMP,* no. 5362 (Apr. 15, 1973). "Woman Party Secretary of Northwest China Cotton Mill Carries Forward Revolutionary Tradition," p. 184.

3150 *SCMP,* no. 5383 (May 13, 1973). "A *Hsien* in Szechwan Attaches Importance to Training of Women Cadres," p. 15.

3151 *SCMP,* no. 5402 (June 15, 1973). "Tungt'ai *Hsien* Energetically Trains and Develops Women Party Members," p. 48.

3152 *SCMP,* no. 5408 (June 23, 1973). "Teng Ying-ch'ao, Ou Tang-liang, Feng Chiung Meet Guinean Women's Delegation," p. 140.

3153 *SCMP,* no. 5430 (July 26, 1973). "Worker-Cadres in Northeast China Plant," p. 53.

3154 *SCMP,* no. 5441 (Aug. 13, 1973). "More Women Cadres for East China City's Industry," p. 95.

3155 *SCMP,* no. 5452 (Aug. 29, 1973). "Central China Women Communists and Youth League Members Play Exemplary Role," p. 23.

3156 *SCMP,* no. 5453 (Aug. 31, 1973). "Peking Workers in Leading Posts," p. 70.

3157 *SCMP,* no. 5476 (Oct. 4, 1973). "Women Cadres in Former East China Revolutionary Base," p. 193.

3158 *SCMP,* no. 5487 (Oct. 21, 1973). "Noted Chinese Silk Tapestry Factory Trains Worker-Cadres," p. 190.

3159 *SCMP,* no. 5497 (Nov. 7, 1973). "Original Wife of Late Mr. Li Tsung-jen Feted in Peking," p. 206.

3160 *SCMP,* no. 5503 (Nov. 17, 1973). "Teng Ying-ch'ao, Liao Cheng-chih and Lo Ching-chang Meet and Fete Li Hsiu-wen, First Wife of Late Mr. Li Tsung-jen," p. 59.

3161 *SCMP,* no. 5519 (Dec. 12, 1973). "Work Hard to Train Women Cadres," p. 148.

3162 *SCMP,* no. 5524 (Dec. 17, 1973). "Madame Li Hsiu-wen to Settle in Kweilin," p. 90.

3163 *SCMP,* no. 5524 (Dec. 17, 1973). "Woman Deputy Secretary of East China *Hsien* Party Committee," p. 87.

3164 *SCMP,* no. 5565 (Feb. 22, 1974). "Women Alternate Members of Party Central Committee Criticize Lin Piao and Confucius," p. 66. [From *Hongqi*.]

3165 *SCMP,* no. 5574 (Mar. 7, 1974). "Central China Region Actively Trains Women Cadres," p. 21.

3166 *SCMP,* no. 5622 (May 15, 1974). "Li Hsien-nien, Teng Ying-ch'ao, Lin Chia-mei Meet Mexican President Echeverria's Son and Daughter-in-Law," p. 38.

3167 *SCMP,* no. 5654 (July 3, 1974). "A Young Woman Communist," p. 67.

3168 *SCMP,* no. 5726 (Oct. 16, 1974). "Liu Hsiang-ping, Hsieh Ching-i meet Widow of Prominent Black American Scholar Dr. Dubois," p. 120.

3169 Seymour, Joseph. "The Rise and Fall of Chiang Ch'ing." *Women and Revolution,* no. 15 (Summer 1977), pp. 2–5.

3170 Sheridan, Mary. "Young Women Leaders in China." *Signs* 2(Autumn 1976):59–88.

3171 Shih, Yen. "Shattering Chiang Ch'ing's Dream of Becoming Emperor." *Chinese Studies in History* 12(Winter 1978/79):74–79. [Translation from *Renmin ribao,* Nov. 14, 1976.]

3172 Soong, Ching-ling. "The First Five Years." *China Reconstructs* 4(Jan. 1955):2–5.

3173 "Soong Ching Ling." *China Reconstructs* 30(July 1981):3–4. [Article in commemoration of Soong, wife of Sun Yat-sen, who became a member of the Chinese Communist Party and Honorary Chairwoman of the People's Republic of China.]

3174 *SPRCP,* no. 5796 (Dec. 29, 1974). Feng, Shu-min (Standing Committee member, CCP Committee, Haitien *ch'ü* and Vice Chairman of the *ch'ü* Federation of Women). "Fight for the Consolidation and the Strengthening of the Dictatorship of the Proletariat," p. 125.

3175 *SPRCP,* no. 5804 (Feb. 20, 1975). "More Women Becoming Leading Cadres in North China *Hsien,*" p. 99.

3176 *SPRCP,* no. 5813 (Mar. 6, 1975). "Educated Young Girl is Leading Cadre in Northwest China Countryside," p. 61.

3177 *SPRCP,* no. 5813 (Mar. 6, 1975). "Young Woman Pathbreaker," p. 58.

3178 *SPRCP,* no. 5820 (Mar. 17, 1975). "National People's Congress Vice Chairman Li Su-wen Meets Japanese Delegation," p. 195.

3179 *SPRCP,* no. 5862 (May 16, 1975). "National People's Congress Vice Chairman Li Su-wen Meets Mother of Jamaican Prime Minister," p. 108.

3180 *SPRCP,* no. 5886 (June 21, 1975). "Chinese Woman Cadre Leads Peasants in Re-shaping Home Village," p. 101.

3181 *SPRCP,* no. 5891 (June 28, 1975). "How a Young Woman Cadre Matures," p. 158.

3182 *SPRCP,* no. 5895 (July 4, 1975). "Large Numbers of Women Workers Become Cadres in Liaoning," p. 128.

3183 *SPRCP,* no. 5899 (July 10, 1975). "Women Cadres Make Fast Progress in Kwangsi," p. 65.

3184 *SPRCP,* no. 5971 (Oct. 17, 1975). "National People's Congress Vice Chairman Li Su-wen Meets Delegation of American Women for International Understanding," p. 51.

3185 *SPRCP,* no. 5990 (Nov. 26, 1975). "National People's Congress Vice Chairman Li Su-wen Meets Panamanian Women's Delegation," p. 35.

3186 *SPRCP,* no. 6014 (Jan. 2, 1976). "Vice Premier Teng Hsiao-p'ing and National People's Congress Vice Chairman Li Su-wen Meet United States Congress Women's Delegation to China," p. 138.

3187 *SPRCP,* no. 6025 (Jan. 17, 1976). "Condolence Messages to Comrade Teng Ying-ch'ao from Heads of State or Government and Others," p. 251.

3188 *SPRCP,* no. 6054 (Mar. 6, 1976). "Outstanding Rural Woman Cadre in Central China Province," p. 13.

3189 *SPRCP,* no. 6056 (Mar. 9, 1976). "Peking Young Women Cadres Grow Up Rapidly," p. 88.

3190 *SPRCP,* no. 6067 (Mar. 24, 1976). "Young Women Cadres in New Oilfield," p. 164.

3191 *SPRCP,* no. 6126 (June 20, 1976). "Shanghai Girl Red Guard Now Secretary of People's Commune Party Committee," p. 109.

3192 *SPRCP,* no. 6160 (Aug. 9, 1976). "Teng Ying-ch'ao Meets Japanese Professor Araki," p. 129.

3193 *SPRCP,* no. 6170 (Aug. 23, 1976). "Women Party Secretaries in People's Communes in Yenan," p. 106.

3194 *SPRCP,* no. 6194 (Sept. 24, 1976). "State Leaders or Their Wives, Prominent Figures Send Messages of Condolence to Comrade Chiang Ch'ing on Passing of Chairman Mao Tse-tung," p. 203.

3195 *SPRCP,* no. 6195 (Sept. 25, 1976). "More Messages of Condolence Sent to Comrade Chiang Ch'ing on Passing of Chairman Mao Tse-tung," p. 276.

3196 *SPRCP,* no. 6205 (Oct. 12, 1976). "Young Woman Party Secretary of Tachai Brigade Matures through Class Struggle," p. 261.

3197 *SPRCP,* no. 6212 (Oct. 25, 1976). "National People's Congress Vice Chairman Li Su-wen Meets Japanese Guests," p. 179.

3198 *SPRCP,* no. 6226 (Nov. 14, 1976). "Comrade Teng Ying-ch'ao Meets Austrian Journalist," p. 156.

3199 *SPRCP,* no. 6229 (Nov. 19, 1976). "Teng Ying-ch'ao Meets Americans of Chinese Descent," p. 102.

3200 *SPRCP,* no. 6230 (Nov. 14, 1976). Shih Yen. "Shattering Chiang Ch'ing's Dream to Become Empress," p. 109.

3201 *SPRCP,* no. 6230 (Nov. 20, 1976). Hsü Hsün. "Chiang Ch'ing and Empress Lü," p. 104.

3202 *SPRCP,* no. 6230 (Nov. 21, 1976). "*Jen-min jih-pao* Exposes Chiang Ch'ing as Capitulationist in 1930s," p. 113.

3203 *SPRCP,* no. 6232 (Nov. 24, 1976). "Chiang Ch'ing—Political Pickpocket Who Glorified Herself to Hoodwink Public," p. 223.

3204 *SPRCP,* no. 6235 (Nov. 29, 1976). "Tientsin Women Criticize 'Gang of Four,'" p. 125.

3205 *SPRCP,* no. 6236 (Nov. 30, 1976). "Chiang Ch'ing's Dream of Becoming Chinese Empress under Cloak of Elevating Women's Status," p. 176.

3206 *SPRCP,* no. 6238 (Nov. 23, 1976). Ku Yen [of the Institute of Archaeology of the Chinese Academy of Sciences]. "Chiang Ch'ing's Wolfish Design in Publicizing 'Matriarchal Society,'" p. 1.

3207 *SPRCP,* no. 6241 (Dec. 7, 1976). "National People's Congress Vice Chairman Teng Ying-ch'ao Meets Japanese Writers' Delegation," p. 164.

3208 *SPRCP,* no. 6242 (Dec. 3, 1976). Chiang, Yin-nan. "Simplified Characters Are Good Indeed—Bitter Denunciation of Chiang Ch'ing's Vilification of the Simplified Characters," p. 198.

3209 *SPRCP,* no. 6243 (Nov. 23, 1976). Liu, Tsung-ming [of the Peking Bureau of Instrument Industry]. "Evidence of Chiang Ch'ing's Crime in Strangling Revolutionary Literature and Art," p. 8.

3210 *SPRCP,* no. 6243 (Dec. 11, 1976). "National People's Congress Chairman Teng Ying-ch'ao Meets Tanzanian First Vice President Jumbe," P. 44.

3211 *SPRCP,* no. 6244 (Dec. 12, 1976). "Peking Printers Expose Chiang Ch'ing as Fake Friend of Workers," p. 68.

3212 *SPRCP,* no. 6247 (Dec. 16, 1976). "National People's Congress Vice Chairman Teng Ying-ch'ao Meets Venezuelan Youth Delegation," p. 44.

3213 Tai, Dawn. *Chiang Ch'ing; the Emergence of a Revolutionary Political Leader.* Hicksville, N.Y.: Exposition Press, 1974.

3214 "Tearing Down of an Idol." *Time* 117(Jan. 5, 1981):69. [Mao Zedong and his widow under attack.]

3215 "Three Women People's Deputies." *Women of China* 1965:2:13-17.

3216 T'ien-chin jih-pao Editorial Department. "Thoroughly Settle Accounts with Chiang Ch'ing's Monstrous Crimes in Slipping into Tientsin Eight Times." *Chinese Studies in History* 12(Spring 1979):65-74.

3217 Ting, Wang. "Chiang Ch'ing." *Far East Economic Review* 57(Aug. 10, 1967):276-77.

3218 "Training Women Cadres: How the Tachai Party Branch Does It." *Peking Review* 16(Mar. 30, 1973):17-18, 21.

3219 Tso, Sung-fen. "New China's Women in State Affairs." *People's China* 1955:5:15-18.

3220 Tso, Yü-chin. "How the 'Gang of Four' Was Captured." *Chinese Law and Government* 12(Winter 1979/80):67-84.

3221 Wang, Hsin-chen. "Proletarian Revolutionary Woman Fighter." *Peking Review* 11(May 3, 1968):23-25, 33.

3222 Wang, Kung. "What Chiang Ch'ing Did to Culture." *China Reconstructs* 26(May 1977):2-6.

3223 Weiss, Ruth. "Chiang Ch'ing before the People's Tribunal." *Eastern Horizon* 16(Mar. 1977):14-17.

3224 Weiss, Ruth. "Redress and Progress." *Eastern Horizon* 17(Nov. 1978):5-12. [Includes sections on the experiences of women scientists, actresses, etc. who were purged by the Gang of Four.]

3225 Wen, P'ing and Feng, Cheng. "Confession of an Old-Time Capitulationist—Critique of Chiang Ch'ing's Sinister Article 'Our Life.'" *Chinese Studies in History* 12(Spring 179):56-61.

3226 Witke, Roxane Heater. "Chiang Ch'ing's Coming of Age." In *Women in in Chinese Society,* ed. Margery Wolf and Roxane Witke, pp. 169-92. Stanford: Stanford University, 1975.

3227 Witke, Roxane Heater. "Wu Kuei-hsien: Labour Heroine to Vice-Premier." *China Quarterly,* no. 64 (Dec. 1975), pp. 730-40.

3228 Witke, Roxane Heater. *Comrade Chiang Ch'ing.* Boston-Toronto: Little Brown & Co., 1977.

3229 "Women Cadres in Mountain Areas." *China Pictorial* 1973:3:4-7.

3230 "Women Members of Revolutionary Committees." *China Pictorial* 1970:3:26-29

3231 Yang, Yu. "She Serves the People." *People's China,* Dec. 16, 1954, pp. 28-32. [Personal story of Dong Youlan, people's deputy to the National People's Congress.]

3232 Yao, Meng-hsüan. "Chinese Communist Party Power Shift and the Chiang Ch'ing Incident." *Issues and Studies* 13(1977):2:21-37.

3233 Yü, Hsiang. "Chiang Ch'ing's 180-Degree Turn." *Chinese Studies in History* 12(Fall 1978):55-58.

3234 Yüan, Sou. "Bankruptcy of Empress Lü's Dream." *Chinese Studies in History* 12(Winter 1978/79):166-73. [Translation from *Nanking University J.,* Philosophy and Social Sciences Edition, 1976, no. 4.]

Note: See also "Emancipation Movements: The People's Republic of China (1949-)."

WOMEN IN POLITICS: MINORITY AREAS

3235 Ahaidati. "A Chieftain's Daughter." *China Reconstructs* 5(Mar. 1956):25-27. [Biography of a woman of Yi nationality.]

3236 *CB,* no. 995 (May 18, 1973). "A Woman Party Branch Secretary Who Insists on Participation in Labor—about Young Cadre Lu Yü-hsin of Chuang Nationality," p. 9.

3237 *CB,* no. 995 (June 18, 1973). "Life-Long Study, Life-Long Struggle—about Woman Party Member Ts'ui Jung-yu of Korean Nationality," p. 11.

3238 "A Good Leader of the Masses." *China Reconstructs* 19(June 1970):39-41. [About a woman commune chairman in Inner Mongolian Autonomous Region.]

3239 Ho, Chiang-chun. "A Woman Cadre of Yao Nationality." *China Reconstructs* 24(June 1975):19-21.

3240 Hu, Bangxiu. "Women Cadres in Tibet." *Women of China* 1980:3:36-38.

3241 "National Minority Women Cadres in Tibet." *Peking Review* 17(June 7, 1974):30-31.

3242 *SCMP*, no. 3175 (Mar. 4, 1964). "Girl Slave Now Famous Deputy Director of Inner Mongolian People's Commune," p. 24.

3243 *SCMP*, no. 3175 (Mar. 6, 1964). "Southwest China Minority Woman Leader," p. 20.

3244 *SCMP*, no. 3413 (Mar. 5, 1965). "Former Tibetan Herdswoman Elected District Head," p. 28.

3245 *SCMP*, no. 3653 (Mar. 5, 1966). "Young Mongolian Woman Shows Remarkable Initiative and Leadership," p. 22.

3246 *SCMP*, no. 3654 (Mar. 6, 1966). "Outstanding Administrative Leaders Come forward from Multi-National Women in Sinkiang," p. 26.

3247 *SCMP*, no. 4432 (June 2, 1969). "Uighur Woman Propagandist of Mao Tse-tung Thought," p. 14. [From New China News Agency, Urumchi.]

3248 *SCMP*, no. 4622 (Mar. 17, 1970). "Woman Communist of Nahsi Nationality Gives Her Life to Protect People," p. 42.

3249 *SCMP*, no. 4856 (Feb. 27, 1971). "Give Full Play to the Role of Women Cadres of National Minorities, Strengthen Ideological and Political-Line Education," p. 173.

3250 *SCMP*, no. 4860 (Mar. 9, 1971). "Woman Cadre of Uighur Nationality Firmly Defends Chairman Mao's Revolutionary Line," p. 132.

3251 *SCMP*, no. 4936 (July 3, 1971). "Fine Woman Communist Party Member of Chinese Minority Nationality," p. 134.

3252 *SCMP*, no. 5094 (Mar. 5, 1972). "Party Committees of All Levels in Hsianghai, Tuchia and Miao Nationalities Autonomous Chou, Hunan Province, Bring Women Cadres' Active Role into Full Play," p. 129.

3253 *SCMP*, no. 5177 (July 7, 1972). "Women Cadres Trained in South China Multi-National *Hsien*," p. 100.

3254 *SCMP*, no. 5324 (Feb. 18, 1973). "Lichiang Nahsi Autonomous *Hsien* in Yunnan Actively Trains Minority Nationality Women Cadres," p. 137.

3255 *SCMP*, no. 5335 (Mar. 5, 1973). "More Women Cadres of Minority Nationalities," p. 178.

3256 *SCMP*, no. 5335 (Mar. 5, 1973). "Tibetan Commune Woman Leader," p. 174.

3257 *SCMP*, no. 5338 (Mar. 9, 1973). "China's Women Cadres of Minority Nationalities Grow up Quickly," p. 93.

3258 *SCMP*, no. 5339 (Mar. 11, 1973). "Women Cadres of China's Minority Nationalities Make Progress," p. 140.

3259 *SCMP*, no. 5369 (Apr. 25, 1973). 'China Trains Women Cadres of Minority People," p. 71.

3260 *SCMP*, no. 5493 (Oct. 30, 1973). "Women Cadres of China's Small Nationality," p. 23.

3261 *SCMP*, no. 5582 (Mar. 18, 1974). "Large Numbers of Women Cadres in Tibet," p. 126.

3262 *SPRCP*, no. 5822 (Mar. 19, 1975). "Former Tibetan Women Slaves Become Commune Leaders," p. 62.

3263 *SPRCP*, no. 5848 (Apr. 25, 1975). "Women Cadres of Minority People in Southwest China Province," p. 178.

3264 *SPRCP*, no. 6021 (June 12, 1976). "Minority Nationality Women Cadres in Sinkiang," p. 231.

Note: See also "Emancipation Movements: Minorities."

NATIONAL AND REGIONAL WOMEN'S ORGANIZATIONS AND ACTIVITIES: THE PEOPLE'S REPUBLIC OF CHINA (1949-)

3265 All-China Democratic Women's Federation. "The Women's Movement in China." *Chinese Studies in History* 5(Fall 171):88-108.

3266 *CB*, no. 476 (Oct. 15, 1957). "Chinese National Women's Congress, 3d. Peking September 9-20, 1957. Reports and Proceedings."

3267 Chang, Su. "The Women of Chaoshou Ward." *People's China*, Mar. 1, 1955, pp. 18-26. [Ward women's councils are the smallest units of Peking Municipal Democratic Women's Federation.]

3268 Chou, Wei-ling. "Planning the Chinese Communist Trade Union, CYL and Women's Federation Congresses." *Issues and Studies* 11(Aug. 1975):58-71.

3269 *ECMM*, no. 159 (Jan. 1, 1959). "Speech by Comrade Tan Chen-lin at the National Conference of Women Activists in Socialist Construction," p. 19.

3270 "Four Hundred Thousand Women Trade Unionists." *People's China* 1950:8:21.

3271 *Guide to New China*. Peking: Foreign Languages Press, 1952. [See pp. 60-62. Contains the history of the All-China Democratic Women's Federation and brief biographies of important members.]

3272 "International Working Women's Day." *Peking Review* 8(Mar. 12, 1965):19.

3273 "International Working Women's Day." *Beijing Review* 24(Mar. 16, 1981):6-7.

3274 "Introducing the All-China Democratic Women's Federation." *People's China* 1955:5:39.

3275 JPRS, 877D.3 (Mar. 16, 1959). Ts'ai, Ch'ang. "Speech to Representatives of the National Federation of Women." [From *Zhongguo funü* 6, pp. 1-4.]

3276 JPRS, no. 3520 (July 6, 1960). "International Working Women's Day Celebration, Rural and Urban Communes."

3277 JPRS, no. 31119 (Mar. 1965). "International Women's Day," p. 4. [From *Renmin ribao*.]

3278 JPRS, no. 31760 (Aug. 1965). "Text of T'ao Chu's Speech Before Forum of Women's Association." [From *Zhongguo funü* 8:1:1-4.]

3279 JPRS, no. 61588 (Feb. 28, 1974). "Hupeh Directive on Women's Day."

3280 JPRS, no. 66619 (Dec. 28, 1975). "Sinkiang Women's Meeting."

3281 JPRS, no. 66998 (Mar. 8, 1976). "Canton Holds Women's Forum." [Guangdong provincial service in Cantonese (news brief).]

3282 Kirby, E. S., ed. *Contemporary China*. Hong Kong: Hong Kong University Press, 1955. [For the All-China Democratic Federation of Women, see pp. 119, 121, 133, 135n, 242.]

3283 Ku, Ling. "Women Salute March Eight." *People's China*, Aug. 1951, p. 27.

3284 "March 8th Echoes." *Peking Review* 2(Mar. 17, 1959):14.

3285 Min, Zhi. "The Fourth National Women's Congress. *Women of China* 1979:1:14-16.

3286 "Peking Commemorates International Working Women's Day." *Peking Review* 17(Mar 15, 1974):3-4.

3287 *SCMM*, no. 492 (Aug. 1, 1965). "Comrade T'ao Chu's Address at the Kwangtung Forum of the National Federation of Women," p. 25. [From *Zhongguo funü*.]

3288 *SCMM*, no. 522 (Feb. 1, 1966). Chou, Ching-sung [Chairman of Women's Congress of Yinhsi brigade, Fukien province]. "It is Better to Take the Lead in Doing a Thing Once than to Explain It a Thousand Times," p. 1.

3289 *SCMM*, no. 553 (May 10, 1966). Chou, Ching-sung [Chairman of Women's Congress of Yinhsi brigade, Fukien province]. "Ever Onward in the Direction Indicated by Chairman Mao," p. 15. [From *Zhongguo funü*.]

3290 *SCMP*, no. 76 (Mar. 2, 1951). "Slogans for International Women's Day Issued."

3291 *SCMP*, no. 78 (Mar. 5, 1951). "50,000 Women Demonstrate in Tientsin to Celebrate International Women's Day."

3292 *SCMP*, no. 80 (Mar. 7, 1951). "5,000 Women's Representatives in Peking Meet to Celebrate Women's Day."

3293 *SCMP*, no. 80 (Mar. 7, 1951). "Lecture Meeting Held by Women of Peking to Celebrate International Women's Day."

3294 *SCMP*, no. 80 (Mar. 8, 1951). "General Organic Rules Announced by All China Democratic Women's Federation for Women's Representative Conferences."

3295 *SCMP*, no. 81 (Mar. 8, 1951). "Peking and Tientsin Papers Give Prominence to Women's Day."

3296 *SCMP*, no. 81 (Mar. 8, 1951). "Women Throughout China Commemorate International Women's Day."

3297 *SCMP*, no. 81 (Mar. 8, 1951). "Women's Day Marked in Peking with Joyful Program."

3298 *SCMP*, no. 81 (Mar. 10, 1951). "300,000 Shanghai Women Demonstrate on Women's Day; Women of National Minorities in Kweiyang, Lanchow and Tihua Also Demonstrate."

3299 *SCMP*, no. 112 (June 8, 1951). "All China Democratic Women's Federation Holds 30th Meeting of Standing Committee; Donation Drive Launched," p. 3.

3300 *SCMP*, no. 261 (Jan. 22, 1952). "All China Democratic Women's Federation Calls for Release of Lily Waechter," p. 5.

3301 *SCMP*, no. 286 (Mar. 1, 1952). "All China Democratic Women's Federation Notice on Commemoration of International Women's Day," p. 20.

3302 *SCMP*, no. 288 (Mar. 4, 1952). "All China Democratic Women's Federation Issues Slogans for International Women's Day," p. 11.

3303 *SCMP*, no. 291 (Mar. 7, 1952). "Women Medical Workers with CPV to Mark International Women's Day,' p. 20.

3304 *SCMP*, no. 291 (Mar. 8, 1952). "International Women's Day Prominently Featured in Peking Press," p. 19.

3305 *SCMP*, no. 291 (Mar. 8, 1952). "North China Organs Hold Gathering to Mark 'March 8' International Women's Day," p. 20.

3306 *SCMP*, no. 293 (Mar. 10, 1952). "International Women's Day Celebrated in Lhasa for the First Time," p. 28.

3307 *SCMP*, no. 392 (Aug. 9, 1952). "All China Democratic Women's Federation Instructs Subordinate Organizations to Help Government Carry out Decision on Labor Employment" p. 13.

3308 *SCMP*, no. 473 (Dec. 15, 1952). "All China Democratic Women's Federation Decides on Future Tasks," p. 17.

3309 *SCMP*, no. 477 (Dec. 20, 1952). "All China Democratic Women's Federation Decision on Change in Structure and Tasks of Democratic Women's Associations in Administrative Regions," p. 37.

3310 *SCMP*, no. 477 (Dec. 20, 1952). "All China Democratic Women's Federation Holds 4th Executive Meeting," p. 36.

3311 *SCMP*, no. 551 (Apr. 14, 1953). "Second All-China Women's Congress to Open in Peking," p. 17.

3312 *SCMP*, no. 553 (Apr. 15, 1953). "Name List of Presidium of Second All-China Women's Congress," p. 9.

3313 *SCMP*, no. 553 (Apr. 15, 1953). "Second All-China Women's Congress Opened," p. 8.

3314 *SCMP*, no. 558 (Apr. 23, 1953). "Teng Ying-ch'ao Reports to All-Women Congress," p. 33.

3315 *SCMP*, no. 585 (June 8, 1953). "All China Democratic Women's Federation Sends Message of Greeting to World Congress of Women," p. 10.

3316 *SCMP*, no. 643 (Aug. 23, 1953). "All China Democratic Women's Federation Convenes Conference to Discuss Leadership Method and Sum up Keypoint Work Experiences," p. 21.

3317 *SCMP*, no. 643 (Aug. 23, 1953). "Second Standing Committee of All China Democratic Women's Federation Holds First Session," p. 21.

3318 *SCMP*, no. 759 (Mar. 3, 1954). "Peking Plans to Celebrate International Women's Day," p. 22.

3319 *SCMP*, no. 762 (Mar. 7, 1954). "Peking Women Celebrate March 8 Women's Day: Teng Ying-ch'ao Makes Keynote Speech," p. 17.

3320 *SCMP*, no. 762 (Mar. 8, 1954). "Peking Press Marks Women's Day," p. 9.

3321 *SCMP*, no. 762 (Mar. 8, 1954). "Peking Women Celebrate March 8," p. 18.

3322 *SCMP*, no. 764 (Mar. 3, 1954). "All China Democratic Women's Federation Issues Notice on Commemoration of Women's Day," p. 10.

3323 *SCMP*, no. 764 (Mar. 7, 1954). "Peking Women Deputies Meet Women Electors," p. 19.

3324 *SCMP*, no. 764 (Mar. 9, 1954). "Lhasa Patriotic Women's Association Formed," p. 20.

3325 *SCMP*, no. 993 (Feb. 21, 1955). "A Million Women Sign in Peking," p. 36.

3326 *SCMP*, no. 1002 (Mar. 7, 1955). "March 8th Women's Day Celebrated in Peking," p. 1.

3327 *SCMP*, no. 1003 (Mar. 8, 1955). "All China Democratic Women's Federation Gives Reception on Women's Day," p. 14.

3328 *SCMP*, no. 1004 (Mar. 9, 1955). "China Observes International Women's Day," p. 2.

3329 *SCMP*, no. 1006 (Mar. 11, 1955). "Second Anshan Women's Congress Held," p. 38.

3330 *SCMP*, no. 1030 (Apr. 15, 1955). "All China Democratic Women's Federation Establishes Secretariat," p. 44.

3331 *SCMP*, no. 1031 (Apr. 14, 1955). "All China Democratic Women's Federation Decides on 1955 Work Plan," p. 31.

3332 *SCMP*, no. 1048 (May 8, 1955). "All China Democratic Women's Federation Holds First National Urban Women Work Conference," p. 30.

3333 *SCMP*, no. 1065 (June 8, 1955). "Meeting of Young Women's Christian Association National Executive Committee in Peking," p. 20.

3334 *SCMP*, no. 1105 (Aug. 2, 1955). "All China Democratic Women's Federation Holds Second Executive Council Meeting," p. 4.

3335 *SCMP*, no. 1192 (Dec. 11, 1955). "Shanghai Municipal Democratic Women's Federation Strengthens Ideological Education Work of Capitalists' Families," p. 19.

3336 *SCMP*, no. 1229 (Feb. 9, 1956). "Directive on Celebration of Women's Day," p. 11.

3337 *SCMP*, no. 1244 (March 6, 1956). "Peking Women Celebrate International Women's Day," p. 20.

3338 *SCMP*, no. 1245 (Mar. 7, 1956). "International Women's Day Rally in Peking," p. 17.

3339 *SCMP*, no. 1246 (Mar. 8, 1956). "Lively Women's Day Party in Peking," p. 41.

3340 *SCMP*, no. 1246 (Mar. 8, 1956). "Women's Day Celebration in China," p. 41.

3341 *SCMP*, no. 1247 (Mar. 9, 1956). "Christian Women Mark International Women's Day," p. 26.

3342 *SCMP*, no. 1247 (Mar. 11, 1956). "Lhasa Celebrates Women's Day," p. 26.

3343 *SCMP*, no. 1258 (Mar. 9, 1956). Chang Yun. "Speech at Rally Held by Women of All Circles in Peking to Mark the International Women's Day on March 8," p. 20.

3344 *SCMP*, no. 1393 (Oct. 1, 1956). "All China Democratic Women's Federation Notifies Women's Organization to Organize Studies of Documents of Chinese Communist Party 8th National Congress," p. 4.

3345 *SCMP*, no. 1419 (Nov. 23, 1956). "Women's Organization Set up in Tibet," p. 11.

3346 *SCMP*, no. 1446 (Jan. 5, 1957). "National Women's Conference Scheduled for June," p. 12.

3347 *SCMP*, no. 1475 (Feb. 12, 1957). "Joint Notice on Commemoration of International Women's Day," p. 3.

3348 *SCMP*, no. 1487 (Mar. 6, 1957). "All China Democratic Women's Federation Official on 'Five Good' Propaganda Campaign," p. 18.

3349 *SCMP*, no. 1487 (Mar. 7, 1957). "Peking Women Honor Women's Day," p. 17.

3350 *SCMP*, no. 1488 (Mar. 8, 1957). "Women's Day Celebrations in China," p. 10.

3351 *SCMP*, no. 1556 (June 9, 1957). "Third National Women's Congress Postponed to September 1957," p. 9.

3352 *SCMP*, no. 1604 (Aug. 29, 1957). "Women's Congress and Education in Socialism," p. 1.

3353 *SCMP*, no. 1607 (Aug. 29, 1957). "All China Democratic Women's Federation Issues Propaganda Points for Third National Women's Congress," p. 30.

3354 *SCMP*, no. 1611 (Sept. 10, 1957). "Women's Congress Second Day (September 10, 1957)," p. 1.

3355 *SCMP*, no. 1611 (Sept. 11, 1957). "Women's Congress Third Day (September 11, 1957)," p. 15.

3356 *SCMP*, no. 1617 (Sept. 20, 1957). "Women's Congress Closes September 20," p. 1.

3357 *SCMP*, no. 1658 (Sept. 9, 1957). "Women's Federations in Shansi Urge Industrious and Thrifty Home Management and Economization of Food Grains," p. 20.

3358 *SCMP*, no. 1670 (Nov. 29, 1957). "All China Democratic Women's Federation Issues Notification on Extensive Publicity of Home Management with Industry and Thrift," p. 2.

3359 *SCMP*, no. 1708 (Jan. 28, 1958). "All China Democratic Women's Federation Holds Conference of Provincial, Autonomous Region and Municipal Women's Federation," p. 9.

3360 *SCMP*, no. 1718 (Feb. 7, 1958). "All China Democratic Women's Federation Directive on Women's Day," p. 1.

3361 *SCMP*, no. 1723 (Feb. 16, 1958). "Third Shanghai Women's Congress Decides to Launch a 'Five Good' Campaign on Larger Scale," p. 39.

3362 *SCMP*, no. 1729 (Mar. 7, 1958). "International Women's Day Marked," p. 46.

3363 *SCMP*, no. 1729 (Mar. 8, 1958). "Peking Papers on Women's Day," p. 49.

3364 *SCMP*, no. 1729 (Mar. 8, 1958). "Women's Day Party," p. 48.

3365 *SCMP*, no. 1830 (July 31, 1958). "National Conference on Women's Work," p. 3.

3366 *SCMP*, no. 1842 (Aug. 22, 1958). "Women Activists Conference Scheduled," p. 4.

3367 *SCMP*, no. 1848 (Sept. 3, 1958). "Peking Women's Congress Closes," p. 29.

3368 *SCMP*, no. 1879 (Oct. 16, 1958). "Soong Ching-ling Receives Women's Representatives," p. 25.

3369 *SCMP*, no. 1958 (Feb. 15, 1959). "Women Federation Directive on Women's Day," p. 6.

3370 *SCMP*, no. 1971 (Mar. 5, 1959). "Shanghai and Tientsin Women Workers Honor Women's Day," p. 12.

3371 *SCMP*, no. 1971 (Mar. 8, 1959). "Shanghai International Women's Day Gathering," p. 13.

3372 *SCMP*, no. 1973 (Mar. 7, 1959). "China's Cities Mark International Women's Day," p. 6.

3373 *SCMP*, no. 1973 (Mar. 7, 1959). "Peking Women's Rally," p. 7.

3374 *SCMP*, no. 1973 (Mar. 7, 1959). "Production Upsurge to Mark International Women's Day," p. 5.

3375 *SCMP*, no. 1973 (Mar. 7, 1959). "Ts'ai Ch'ang Addresses Peking Women's Rally," p. 8.

3376 *SCMP*, no. 1973 (Mar. 8, 1959). "Chinese Women Celebrate International Women's Day," p. 5.

3377 *SCMP*, no. 1973 (Mar. 8, 1959). "International Women's Day Party in Peking," p. 9.

3378 *SCMP*, no. 2087 (Aug. 20, 1957). "All China Democratic Women's Federation Holds Expanded Conference to Summarize Achievements of Women's Work and Make Arrangements for Present Work," p. 18.

3379 *SCMP*, no. 2200 (Feb. 14, 1960). "Preparatory Committee for Celebration of 50th Anniversary of International Women's Day Formed," p. 5. [Namelist.]

3380 *SCMP*, no. 2200 (Feb. 14, 1960). "Statement of China's People's Organizations on International Women's Day," p. 3.

3381 *SCMP*, no. 2211 (Feb. 24, 1960). "The Second Plenary Meeting of the Third Executive Committee of the National Federation of Women Held in Peking," p. 10.

3382 *SCMP*, no. 2212 (Mar. 3, 1960). "Outstanding Chinese Working Women Elected," p. 1.

3383 *SCMP*, no. 2213 (March 4, 1960). "Broadcast Rally to Be Held on March 5 in Commemoration of International Women's Day," p. 17.

3384 *SCMP*, no. 2213 (Mar. 5, 1960). "'March 8' Awards for Ten Thousand Outstanding Women and Groups," p. 18.

3385 *SCMP*, no. 2214 (Mar. 5, 1960). "Women's Day National Broadcast Meeting in Peking," p. 18.

3386 *SCMP*, no. 2215 (Mar. 7, 1960). "Peking Mass Rally Celebrates Women's Day," p. 1.

3387 *SCMP*, no. 2215 (Mar. 7, 1960). "Shanghai Mass Rally Marks International Women's Day," p. 28.

3388 *SCMP*, no. 2215 (Mar. 8, 1960). "Women's Day Reception in Peking," p. 10.

3389 *SCMP*, no. 2452 (Feb. 22, 1961). "National Federation of Women Issues Message Marking 'March 8,'" p. 1.

3390 *SCMP*, no. 2455 (Mar. 7, 1961). "Peking and Shanghai Women Mark Women's Day," p. 6.

3391 *SCMP*, no. 2455 (Mar. 8, 1961). "China Women Mark International Women's Day," p. 7.

3392 *SCMP*, no. 2455 (Mar. 8, 1961). "*Jen-min jih-pao* Editorial Marks International Women's Day," p. 8.

3393 *SCMP*, no. 2455 (Mar. 8, 1961). "Women's Day Party in Peking," p. 5.

3394 *SCMP*, no. 2685 (Feb. 16, 1962). "National Women's Federation Issues Notification Concerning the Commemoration of the 1962 March 8 International Working Women's Day," p. 1.

3395 *SCMP*, no. 2685 (Feb. 16, 1962). "National Women's Federation Issues Notification Concerning the Commemoration of the 1962 March 8 International Working Women's Day," p. 1.

3396 *SCMP*, no. 2696 (Mar. 7, 1962). "Chinese Women Celebrate International Women's Day," p. 22.

3397 *SCMP*, no. 2696 (Mar. 7, 1962). "International Women's Day Celebrated in Peking," p. 21.

3398 *SCMP*, no. 2696 (Mar. 7, 1962). "New China-Made Train Marks Women's Day," p. 23.

3399 *SCMP*, no. 2720 (Mar. 27, 1962). "Third Kwangtung Provincial Women's Congress Victoriously Concluded," p. 1; "Resolution of Third Kwangtung Provincial Women's Congress," p. 2.

3400 *SCMP*, no. 5326 (July 20, 1973). "Anhwei, Hupeh, Shansi, Kirin and Hopei Hold Women's Congress, Elect Leading Organs for Their Provincial Women's Federation," p. 75.

3401 *SCMP*, no. 5336 (Mar. 6, 1973). "Chinese Stamps for International Women's Day," p. 20.

3402 *SCMP*, no. 5337 (Mar. 8, 1973). "Chinese Foreign Ministry Gives Tea-Party Marking International Working Women's Day," p. 74.

3403 *SCMP*, no. 5337 (Mar. 8, 1973). "Peking Tea Party Honors Foreign Experts and Their Family Members on International Working Women's Day," p. 75.

3404 *SCMP*, no. 5415 (July 5, 1973). "Tientsin Holds 6th Women's Congress, Elects 6th Committee of Its Women's Federation," p. 55.

3405 *SCMP*, no. 5439 (Aug. 6, 1973). "Kwangsi, Kwangtung, Kansu, Tibet, Heilungkiang and Fukien Hold Women's Congresses, Separately Elect Leadership Organs of the Provincial and Regional Women's Federations," p. 1.

3406 *SCMP*, no. 5446 (Aug. 16, 1973). "Kiangsu, Ninghsia and Szechwan Hold Women's Congresses, Separately Elect Leading Bodies of the Provincial and Regional Women's Federations," p. 101.

3407 *SCMP*, no. 5448 (Aug. 19, 1973). "Chekiang Holds Women's Congress, Elects the 5th Committee of the Provincial Women's Federation," p. 1.

3408 *SCMP*, no. 5448 (Aug. 20, 1973). "Liaoning Holds Women's Congress, Elects the Second Committee of the Provincial Women's Federation," p. 4.

3409 *SCMP*, no. 5450 (Aug. 22, 1973). "Yunnan Holds Women's Congress, Elects the 3rd Committee of the Provincial Women's Federation," p. 1.

3410 *SCMP*, no. 5452 (Aug. 25, 1973). "Shensi Holds Women's Congress, Elects the 5th Committee of the Provincial Women's Federation," p. 14.

3411 *SCMP*, no. 5453 (Aug. 27, 1973). "Sinkiang Holds Women's Congress," p. 67.

3412 *SCMP*, no. 5457 (Sept. 4, 1973). "Chinghai Holds Women's Congress, Elects the 4th Committee of the Provincial Women's Federation," p. 93.

3413 *SCMP*, no. 5458 (Sept. 5, 1973). "Kiangsi Holds Women's Congress, Elects the Leading Body of the Provincial Women's Federation," p. 168.

3414 *SCMP*, no. 5462 (Sept. 8, 1973). "Sinkiang Holds Women's Congress and Elects the Leading Body of the Autonomous Region," p. 71.

3415 *SCMP*, no. 5474 (Sept. 24, 1973). "Peking Holds 6th Women's Congress and Elects the 6th Committee of the Peking Women's Federation," p. 1.

3416 *SCMP*, no. 5474 (Sept. 24, 1973). "Shanghai Holds the 6th Women's Congress, and Elects the 6th Committee of the Shanghai Women's Federation," p. 4.

3417 *SCMP*, no. 5479 (Sept. 30, 1973). "Inner Mongolian Autonomous Region Holds the 4th Women's Congress and Elects the Leading Body of the Women's Federation," p. 1.

3418 *SCMP*, no. 5480 (Oct. 1, 1973). "Honan Holds Women's Congress and Elects the Leading Body of the Provincial Women's Federation," p. 51.

3419 *SCMP*, no. 5525 (Dec. 9, 1973). "Kweichow Holds the 3rd Women's Congress and Elects the 3rd Committee of the Provincial Women's Federation," p. 1.

3420 *SCMP*, no. 5575 (Mar. 8, 1974). "Peking Women's Federation Gives Tea Party in Commemoration of International Working Women's Day," p. 54.

3421 *SCMP*, no. 5815 (Mar. 8, 1975). "Peking Tea Party Celebrates International Working Women's Day," p. 130.

3422 *SPRCP*, no. 5823 (Mar. 20, 1975). "Preparatory Meetings for China's Trade Union, Communist Youth League and Women's Congresses," p. 93.

3423 *SPRCP*, no. 5848 (Apr. 26, 1975). "East China Province Holds Women's Congress," p. 172.

3424 *SPRCP*, no. 6055 (Mar. 8, 1976). "Peking Women's Federation Holds Get-together in Celebration of 'March 8' International Working Women's Day," p. 51.

3425 *SPRCP*, no. 6055 (Mar. 8, 1976). "Shanghai Women Workers Greet International Women's Day with Achievement," p. 54.

3426 *SPRCP*, no. 6055 (Mar. 8, 1976). "Women of Various Callings in Peking Meet in Celebration of International Working Women's Day," p. 52.

3427 *SPRCP*, no. 6099 (Mar. 8, 1976). "Women Work Must Doggedly Take Class Struggle as the Key Link—the Peking Municipal Women's Federation," p. 178.

3428 *SPRCP*, no. 6099 (Mar. 9, 1976). "Stand in the Van of the Struggle to Beat Back the Right-Wing to Reverse Verdicts—the Women's Federation of Liaoning Province," p. 182.

3429 "Tientsin Women's Congress." *Peking Review* 16 (July 13, 1973):4.

3430 Wilson, Amy Auerbacher. "Mass Organization Elites in China: The National Leadership of the Women's, Youth, and Trade Union Federations, 1949-1960." Ph.D. dissertation, Princeton, 1979.

3431 "Women to the Fore." *Peking Review* 3 (Feb. 23, 1960):4-5. [Announcement of "red banner" titles to be conferred on outstanding women and groups on Mar. 8.]

3432 "Women's Congresses in Peking and Shanghai." *Peking Review* 16 (Sept. 28, 1973):5, 21.

3433 "Women's Day." *Peking Review* 3 (Mar. 15, 1960):3-4.

3434 "Women's Day." *Peking Review* 7 (Mar. 13, 1964):3.

3435 "Women's Day Celebrations." *Peking Review* 5 (Mar. 16, 1962):3-4.

3436 "Women's Day in Peking." *Peking Review* 16 (Mar. 16, 1973):3.

3437 Wu, Ming. "National Women's Congress." *Women of China* 1957:6:4-7.

3438 Wu, Y. M. "The Second All-China Women's Congress." *Women of China*, June 1953, pp. 1-3.

INTERNATIONAL WOMEN'S ORGANIZATIONS AND ACTIVITIES: THE PEOPLE'S REPUBLIC OF CHINA

3439 "At International Women's Year Conference—Speech by Head of the Chinese Delegation." *Peking Review* 18(July 4, 1975):13–16.

3440 "At the World Congress of Women." *Peking Review* 6(July 5, 1963):8–10.

3441 Bald, Margaret M. "'Women': The Chinese Delegation at Mexico City." *New China* 1(Winter 1976):8–9.

3442 "Chinese Women Fight for Peace." *People's China*, Mar. 1, 1952, p. 10.

3443 Chu, A. W. "Women in the Peace Campaign." *People's China*, 1(1950):6:24.

3444 "Common Task of the Women of the World." *Peking Review* 6(July 5, 1963):10–12.

3445 *ECMM*, no. 1174 (Nov. 20, 1955). "China Committee for World Conference of Working Women," p. 41.

3446 "Peking Acclaims Women Delegates from Asia, Africa and Latin America." *Peking Review* 6(July 19, 1963):17–19.

3447 "Peking Welcomes Home Chinese Women's Delegation." *Peking Review* 6(July 26, 1963):3–4.

3448 "Resolution of Support for Actions of Chinese Women's Delegation Adopted by Peking Rally of Welcome." *Peking Review* 6(July 26, 1963):50.

3449 *SCMP*, no. 40 (Jan. 2, 1951). "Three Members of the All China Democratic Women's Federation Refuse Visas to Indonesia."

3450 *SCMP*, no. 43 (Jan. 6, 1951). "All China Democratic Women's Federation Receives Telegrams of Greeting from Democratic Women's Organizations Abroad."

3451 *SCMP*, no. 52 (Jan. 20, 1951). "Chinese Delegates Leave for Women's International Democratic Federation Meeting."

3452 *SCMP*, no. 60 (Jan. 30, 1951). "40,000 Women in Peking Protest against French Government Fascist Measure."

3453 *SCMP*, no. 60 (Jan. 30, 1951). "Over 40,000 Women in Peking Cable Warning to Yoshida Government."

3454 *SCMP*, no. 62 (Feb. 2, 1951). "Chinese Delegates Attend Women's International Democratic Federation Meeting."

3455 *SCMP*, no. 76 (Mar 2, 1951). "Korean Democratic Women's League Thanks Chairman Mao and Chinese Women for Help."

3456 *SCMP*, no. 80 (Mar. 7, 1951). "Ts'ai Ch'ang Cables Greetings Abroad on Women's Day."

3457 *SCMP*, no. 81 (Mar. 9, 1951). "Chinese Women Receive Greetings from Abroad."

3458 *SCMP*, no. 84 (Mar. 15, 1951). "All China Democratic Women's Federation Receives Women's Day Greeting from Abroad."

3459 *SCMP*, no. 84 (Mar. 16, 1951). "Lu Tsui Reports on Achievement of Women's International Democratic Federation Council Meeting."

3460 *SCMP*, no. 95 (Apr. 17, 1951). "Women's International Democratic Federation Sent Congratulation to Soong Ching-ling," p. 12.

3461 *SCMP*, no. 110 (June 1, 1951). "Women's International Democratic Federation Delegation Investigating United States Atrocities in Korea Arrives in Mukden," p. 16.

3462 *SCMP*, no. 110 (June 4, 1951). "Women's International Democratic Federation Delegates Hold Press Conference in Mukden," p. 16.

3463 *SCMP*, no. 112 (June 8, 1951). "Chinese Delegation to Attend Women's International Democratic Federation Meeting in Sofia Leave Peking," p. 12.

3464 *SCMP*, no. 123 (June 23, 1951). "Women's International Democratic Fact-Finding Commission Reporting to People on United States Atrocities," p. 5.

3465 *SCMP*, no. 220 (Nov. 21, 1951). "Teng Ying-ch'ao to Attend Executive Committee Meeting of Women's International Democratic Federation in Berlin," p. 6.

3466 *SCMP*, no. 224 (Nov. 27, 1951). "Telegram to Women's International Democratic Federation," p. 9.

3467 *SCMP*, no. 290 (Mar. 6, 1952). "All China Democratic Women's Federation Sends Greetings to Japanese Women, 'Let Us Fight Together,'" p. 2.

3468 *SCMP*, no. 291 (Mar. 8, 1952). "Women's International Democratic Federation Sends Greetings to Chinese Women," p. 19.

3469 *SCMP*, no. 436 (Oct. 17, 1952). "A Forum on Question of Rights of Women," p. 18.

3470 *SCMP*, no. 480 (Dec. 26, 1952). "Soong Ching-ling Delivers Speech at Women's International Democratic Federation Council Meeting," p. 21.

3471 *SCMP*, no. 597 (June 21, 1953). "Li Te-ch'uan, Leader of the Chinese Delegation to World Congress of Women (Feature)," p. 20.

3472 *SCMP*, no. 624 (July 29, 1953). "Li Te-ch'uan Gives Report on World Congress of Women to Peking Women," p. 33.

3473 *SCMP*, no. 796 (Apr. 26, 1954). "Chinese Women Denounce United Nations Educational, Scientific and Cultural Organization Resolution in Denying Women's International Democratic Federation Status," p. 10.

3474 *SCMP*, no. 874 (Aug. 12, 1954). "Name-list of Chinese Women's Delegation to Korea," p. 34.

3475 *SCMP*, no. 874 (Aug. 22, 1954). "Chinese Women's Delegation Attends Closing Session of Women's Conference in Korea," p. 35.

3476 *SCMP*, no. 906 (Oct. 11, 1954). "Foreign Women Delegates Give Impression of China," p. 15.

3477 *SCMP*, no. 925 (Nov. 8, 1954). "Chinese Women Support Arrested Greek Women," p. 11.

3478 *SCMP*, no. 926 (Nov. 10, 1954). "Chinese Women Protest against United Nations Economic and Social Council Resolution," p. 11.

3479 *SCMP*, no. 926 (Nov. 10, 1954). "Li Teh-ch'uan Meets Women of Osaka," p. 9.

3480 *SCMP*, no. 935 (Nov. 24, 1954). "Pakistan Woman Leader Begum Hussain Malik Gives Impressions of China," p. 14.

3481 *SCMP*, no. 990 (Feb. 16, 1955). "Workers, Youth, Women Called to Sign Against Atomic Weapons," p. 10.

3482 *SCMP*, no. 1002 (Mar. 7, 1955). "Twelve Million Chinese Women Sign against A-Weapons," p. 14.

3483 *SCMP*, no. 1058 (May 28, 1955). "China Women's Leader Ts'ai Ch'ang Supports World Mothers' Congress," p. 34.

3484 *SCMP*, no. 1062 (June 4, 1955). "Women's Leader Wu Chuan-heng Supports World Congress of Mothers," p. 9.

3485 *SCMP*, no. 1062 (June 7, 1955). "Li Teh-ch'uan Greets World Congress of Mothers," p. 5.

3486 *SCMP*, no. 1084 (July 7, 1955). "Mothers Will Not Allow World to Have War—Says *Kuang-ming jih-pao*," p. 18.

3487 *SCMP*, no. 1085 (July 8, 1955). "Li Teh-ch'uan Speaks at World Mothers' Congress," p. 18.

3488 *SCMP*, no. 1089 (July 14, 1955). "Mothers' Will for Peace is Invincible, Says *Jen-min jih-pao*," p. 28.

3489 *SCMP*, no. 1107 (Aug. 10, 1955). "Li Teh-ch'uan Reports on World Congress of Mothers," p. 2.

3490 *SCMP*, no. 1107 (Aug. 10, 1955). "Peking Women Support Lausanne Decisions," p.3.

3491 *SCMP*, no. 1179 (Nov. 28, 1955). "Peking Women To Mark Women's International Democratic Federation Anniversary," p. 34.
3492 *SCMP*, no. 1181 (Nov. 30, 1955). "Peking Women Celebrate Women's International Democratic Federation Anniversary," p. 14.
3493 *SCMP*, no. 1181 (Nov. 30, 1955). "Soong Ching-ling Greets Women's International Democratic Federation Anniversary," p. 15.
3494 *SCMP*, no. 1181 (Nov. 30, 1955). "Ts'ai Ch'ang Greets Women's International Democratic Federation Anniversary," p. 15.
3495 *SCMP*, no. 1237 (Apr. 27, 1956). Teng Ying-ch'ao. "Speech at Women's International Democratic Federation Meeting," p. 19.
3496 *SCMP*, no. 1245 (Mar. 7, 1956). "Women of Peking Greet Women's International Democratic Federation," p. 18.
3497 *SCMP*, no. 1253 (Mar. 19, 1956). "Chinese Women Mourn the Death of Madame Joliot-Curie," p. 35.
3498 *SCMP*, no. 1259 (Mar. 26, 1956). "Women from Hong-Kong, Macau Coming to Peking," p. 27.
3499 *SCMP*, no. 1269 (Apr. 12, 1956). "International Women's Federation to Meet in Peking," p. 32.
3500 *SCMP*, no. 1290 (May 11, 1956). "Advanced Women Workers Support World Women Meeting," p. 49.
3501 *SCMP*, no. 2215 (Mar. 7, 1960). Teng Ying-ch'ao. "Women Are Important Force for Peace," p. 3.
3502 *SCMP*, no. 4962 (Aug. 14, 1971). "Comrade Chi Teng-kuei, Ts'ai Ch'ang, Teng Ying-ch'ao and Tsao Yu-ou Meet Delegation of Congolese Revolutionary Union of Women," p. 128.
3503 *SCMP*, no. 5249 (Oct. 25, 1972). "Comrades Chou En-lai, Chiang Ch'ing, Chi Teng-kuei, Wang Hung-wen Meet Delegation of Korean Democratic Women's Union," p. 39.
3504 *SCMP*, no. 5271 (Nov. 27, 1972). "Comrades Teng Ying-ch'ao, Lu Yu-lan, K'ang K'e-ch'ing and Ou Tang-liang Meet American Women's Delegation," p. 173.
3505 *SCMP*, no. 5374 (May 4, 1973). "Chinese Women's Delegation Arrives in Pyongyang," p. 86.
3506 *SCMP*, no. 5374 (May 4, 1973). "Chinese Women's Delegation Leaves Peking for Democratic People's Republic of Korea," p. 85.
3507 *SCMP*, no. 5375 (May 5, 1973). "Comrade Kim Song Ae Receives Chinese Women's Delegation," p. 137.
3508 *SCMP*, no. 5376 (May 6, 1973). "Kim Song Ae Gives Banquet in Honor of Chinese Women's Delegation," p. 180.
3509 *SCMP*, no. 5386 (May 22, 1973). "Chinese Women's Delegation Welcomed in Hamhung, Korea," p. 173.
3510 *SCMP*, no. 5391 (May 28, 1973). "Chinese Embassy in Korea Holds Banquet for Chinese Women's Delegation Leaving Pyongyang for Home," p. 32.
3511 *SCMP*, no. 5391 (May 30, 1973). "Chinese Women's Delegation Back in Peking from Korea," p. 34.
3512 *SCMP*, no. 5521 (Dec. 13, 1973). "Peking Women's Meeting Supports South Korean Women's Struggle against Pak Jung Hi Clique,"
3513 *SCMP*, no. 5541 (Jan. 14, 1974). "Li Su-wen Speaks at Session of United Nations Commission on Status of Women," p. 66.
3514 *SCMP*, no. 5556 (Feb. 8, 1974). "Chinese Delegates Back in Peking after Attending Session of United Nations Commission on Status of Women," p. 74.
3515 *SCMP*, no. 5615 (May 6, 1974). "Peking Women Meet to Welcome Delegates of South Vietnam Women's Union for Liberation," p. 203.
3516 *SCMP*, no. 5645 (June 20, 1974). "Lin Li-yun Fetes Japanese Youth Activists Delegation," p. 30.
3517 *SCMP*, no. 5651 (June 29, 1974). "Chinese Workers, Youth and Women Delegation Leaves Peking for Tanzania," p. 193.
3518 *SCMP*, no. 5652 (July 1, 1974). "Chinese Workers, Youth and Women Delegation Arrives in Tanzania," p. 237.
3519 *SCMP*, no. 5661 (July 13, 1974). "Chinese Delegation of Workers, Youth and Women Concludes Visit to Tanzania," p. 178.
3520 *SCMP*, no. 5661 (July 13, 1974). "Kawawa Receives Chinese Delegation of Workers, Youth and Women," p. 179.
3521 *SCMP*, no. 5662 (July 15, 1974). "Chinese Delegation of Workers, Youth and Women Returns to Peking from Tanzania," p. 220.
3522 *SCMP*, no. 5689 (Aug. 21, 1974). "Chinese Women and Youth Delegation Leaves Peking for Congo," p. 69.
3523 *SCMP*, no. 5689 (Aug. 23, 1974). "Chinese Women and Youth Delegation Arrives in Brazzaville," p. 114.
3524 *SCMP*, no. 5697 (Sept. 4, 1974). "Chinese Women and Youth Delegation Concludes Friendly Visit to Congo," p. 70.
3525 *SPRCP*, no. 5777 (Jan. 10, 1975). "Chinese Women's Delegation Arrives in Tokyo," p. 67.
3526 *SPRCP*, no. 5780 (Jan. 14, 1975). "Chinese Women's Delegation Visits Fokushima," p. 153.
3527 *SPRCP*, no. 5782 (Jan. 17, 1975). "Chinese Women's Delegation Visits Kyoto and Aiichi Prefectures," p. 65.
3528 *SPRCP*, no. 5783 (Jan. 19, 1975). "Chinese Women's Delgation Visits Kansai District," p. 112.
3529 *SPRCP*, no. 5787 (Jan. 24, 1975). "Chinese Women's Delegation Returns to Tokyo," p. 86.
3530 *SPRCP*, no. 5790 (Jan. 29, 1975). "Japanese-Chinese Women's Solidarity Meeting Held in Tokyo," p. 203.
3531 *SPRCP*, no. 5954 (Sept. 29, 1975). "Chinese Women's Delegation Leaves Syria for Home," p. 77.
3532 "Statements of the Chinese Women's Delegation." *Peking Review* 6(July 5, 1963):12.
3533 Teng, Ying-ch'ao. *Women of China Build for Peace.* Peking: All-China Democratic Women's Federation, 1952.
3534 Wang, H. "The World Congress of Women." *Peking Review* 6(July 19, 1963):29:14–17.
3535 "Women for Peace." *People's China* 1952:5:4. [Editorial.]
3536 "The World Congress of Women." *Peking Review* 6(July 19, 1963):14–17.
3537 Yang, Yan-yu. "Report on the Moscow World Congress of Women." *Peking Review* 6(July 26, 1963):49–59.

WOMEN'S ORGANIZATIONS AND ACTIVITIES: HONG KONG, TAIWAN AND OVERSEAS CHINA

3538 *The Chinese Women's Anti-Aggression League.* Taibei, 1955.
3539 *SCMP*, no. 1971 (Mar. 8, 1959). "Hong Kong and Macau Women Celebrate Women's Day," p. 15.
3540 *SCMP*, no. 1259 (Mar. 26, 1956). "Women from Hong-Kong, Macau Coming to Peking," p. 27.

Psychology and Religion

PSYCHOLOGY

3541 Abel, Theodora M. and Hsu, Francis L. K. "Some Aspects of Personality of Chinese as Revealed by the Rorschach Test." *J. of Projective Techniques* 13(1949):285-301. [Men and women, Taiwan and American Chinese.]

3542 Broderick, James Lively. "Psychological Significance of the Post-Revolutionary Chinese Family: A Critical Emancipatory Explanation." Ph.D. dissertation, California School of Professional Psychology, 1976.

3543 Christy, Lai Chu Tsui. "Culture and Control Orientation: A Study of Internal-External Locus of Control in Chinese and American Chinese Women." Ph.D. dissertation, University of California, Berkeley, 1977.

3544 Fong, Stanley and Peskin, Harvey. "Sex Role Strain and Personality Adjustment of China-Born Students in America: A Pilot Study." *J. of Abnormal Psychology* 74(1969):563-67.

3545 "Growth of Suicide Problem." *Missionary Review of the World* 58(Oct. 1935):506. [Comparison of male and female suicide rates in several large Chinese cities.]

3546 Hsu, Francis L. K. "Sex Crimes and Personality: A Study in Comparative Cultural Patterns." *American Scholar* 20(Winter 1951/1952):57-66. [Contrasts China and America in terms of family, personality characteristics.]

3547 Huang, Lucy Jen [Huang, Jen-hua]. "The Problem Child and Delinquent Youth in the Chinese Communist Family." *Marriage and Family Living* 25(1963):4:459-65. [About how social structure is altered by working women.]

3548 Keyes, Susan. "Sex Differences in Cognitive Abilities and Sex-Role Stereotypes in Hong Kong Chinese Adolescents: A Developmental Study." Ph.D. dissertation, Harvard, 1980.

3549 Kleinman, Arthur and Lin, Tsung-yi, eds. *Normal and Abnormal Behavior in Chinese Culture.* Hingham, Mass.: D. Reidel Publishing Co., 1980. [Chapters on suicide and the family, deviant marriage patterns, etc.]

3550 Lee, Rose Hum. "Delinquent, Neglected, and Dependent Chinese Boys and Girls of the San Francisco Bay Region." *J. of Social Psychology* 36(Aug. 1952):1.

3551 Mead, Margaret and Métraux, Rhoda. *The Study of Culture at a Distance.* Chicago: University of Chicago Press, 1953. [See Anonymous, "My Inner Self," an autobiographical narrative of childhood by a young woman.]

3552 Olsen, Nancy Johnston. "Family Structure, Child Training, and Achievement Motivation: The Chinese Case." M.A. thesis, Cornell, 1966. [Based on research on Taiwan.]

3553 Olsen, Nancy Johnston. "Sex Differences in Child Training: Antecedents of Achievement Motivation among Chinese Children." *J. of Social Psychology* 83(Apr. 1971):303-304.

3554 Schak, David C. "Determinants of Children's Play Patterns in a Chinese City (Taipei): The Interplay of Space and Value." *Urban Anthropology* 2(Fall 1972):195-204.

3555 Schmeidler, Gertrude and Windholz, George. "Sex Roles and the Subjective: A Cross-Cultural Test." *Signs* 2(Autumn 1976):207-212. [Includes data from Taiwan.]

3556 Tseng, Wen-Shing and Hsu, Jing. "Chinese Culture, Personality Formation and Mental Illness." *International J. of Social Psychiatry* 16(1969-70):1:5-14. [A comparison of psychiatric patients of two different cultures: Chinese in Taiwan and Americans in Massachusetts.]

3557 Vogel, Ezra Feivel. "From Friendship to Comradeship: The Change in Personal Relations in Communist China." *China Quarterly,* no. 21 (Jan.-Mar. 1965), pp. 46-60. [Reprinted in *China Under Mao: Politics Takes Command,* ed. Roderick MacFarquhar, pp. 407-421. Cambridge, Mass.: M.I.T., 1966.]

3558 Vogel, Ezra Feivel. "A Preliminary View of Family and Mental Health in Urban Communist China." In *Mental Health Research in Asia and the Pacific,* ed. William Candill and Tsung-yi Lin, pp. 393-404. Honolulu: East-West Center Press, 1969. [From Conference on Mental Health Research in Asia and the Pacific, East-West Center, 1966.]

3559 Webster, James Benjamin. *Interests of Chinese Students.* Studies in Education and Psychology 1. Shanghai: University of Shanghai, Bureau of Publications, 1932. [Socialization of boys and girls compared.]

3560 Wilson, Richard W. *Learning to Be Chinese: The Political Socialization of Children in Taiwan.* Cambridge, Mass.: M.I.T., 1970.

3561 Wolf, Margery. "Women and Suicide in China." In *Women in Chinese Society,* ed. Margery Wolf and Roxane Witke, pp. 111-142. Stanford: Stanford University, 1975.

3562 Wright, Arthur F. "Sui Yang-ti: Personality and Stereotype." In *The Confucian Persuasion,* ed. Arthur F. Wright, pp. 47-76. Stanford: Stanford University, 1960. [The Oedipus complex in 7th-century China is discussed.]

3563 Wu, Diana Ting Liu. "Beyond the Bamboo Door: A Psychosocial Study of Women and Organizations in Metropolitan China, 1978-1979." Ph.D. dissertation, Wright Institute, 1980.

3564 Wu, Ting-fang. "Chinese and American Women Contrasted." *Harper's Bazaar* 33(July 21, 1900).729-32.

3565 Yap, Pow-meng [Yeh, Pao-ming]. "Koro, a Culture-Bound Depersonalization Syndrome." *British J. of Psychiatry* 111(Jan. 1965):43-50.

SEX AND THE EROTIC

3566 Beurdeley, Michel, et al. *Chinese Erotic Art.* Trans. Diana Imber. Rutland, Vt.: Charles E. Tuttle, 1969. [Translated from the French.]

3567 Bodde, D. "Sexual Sympathetic Magic in Han China." *History of Religions* 3(Winter 1964):292-99.

3568 Brugger, William Christian. "The Male (and Female) in Chinese Society." *Impact of Science on Society* 21(Jan.-Mar. 1971):5-19.

3569 Chang, Ching-sheng. *Sex Histories: China's First Modern Treatise on Sex Education.* Trans. Howard S. Levy. N.Y.: Paragon Book Gallery, 1967.

3570 Chiao, Chien [Ch'iao, Chien]. "Female Chastity in Chinese Culture." *Bulletin of the Institute of Ethnology, Academia Sinica,* vol. 31 (Spring 1971), pp. 205-211.

3571 Chou, Eric. *The Dragon and the Phoenix: Love, Sex and the Chinese.* London: Michael Joseph, 1971. [Also published by Arbor House, 1971.]

3572 Eberhard, Wolfram. *Guilt and Sin in Traditional China.* Berkeley: University of California, 1967. [See "Sexual Sins," pp. 61-65; "Suicide in Short Stories," pp. 94-105.]

3573 Eberhard, Wolfram. *Moral and Social Values of the Chinese: Collected Essays.* Chinese Materials and Research Aids Service Center Occasional Series 6. Taibei: Chinese Materials and Research Aids Service Center, 1971. [See "What Is Beautiful in a Chinese Woman?" pp. 271-304.]

3574 Edwardes, Allen and Masters, R. E. L. *The Cradle of Erotica.* N.Y.: Julian Press, 1962.

3575 Gichner, Lawrence E. *Erotic Aspects of Chinese Culture.* Privately published, 1957.

3576 Hsu, Francis L. K. [Hsü Lang-kuang]. "The Problem of Incest Tabu in a North China Village." *American Anthropologist* new (2nd) series 42(Jan.-Mar. 1940):122-35.

3577 Humana, Charles and Jacobs, Joseph. *The Ying-Yang: The Chinese Way of Love.* London, N.Y.: Wingate, 1971.

3578 J. D. [Dudgeon, John Hepburn?]. "Jottings About the Chinese, No. 1, Summary Revenge for Adultery." *Chinese Recorder* 1(July 1868):49-50.

3579 Levy, Howard S. "Introduction to a Celestial Bedside Manual.'" *Orient/West* 8(July/Aug. 1963):100-102.

3580 Levy, Howard S., ed. & trans. *Warm-Soft Village: Chinese Stories, Sketches and Essays.* Tokyo: Dai Nippon Insatsu, 1964. [About the social life and sex customs of women.]

3581 Needham, Joseph. *Science and Civilization in China,* Vol. 2, *History of Scientific Thought.* Cambridge: Cambridge University, 1956. [Contains description of Taoist sexual hygiene.]

3582 Parrinder, Geoffrey. *Sex in the World's Religions.* N.Y.: Oxford Press, 1980.

3583 Scott, George Ryley. *Far Eastern Sex Life: An Anthropological, Enthnological, and Sociological Study of the Love Relations, Marriage Rites and Homelife of the Oriental Peoples.* London: G.G. Swan, 1943.

3584 Sierksma, F. *Tibet's Terrifying Deities: Sex and Aggression in Acculturation.* Rutland and Tokyo, 1966.

3585 Stafford, Peter. *Sexual Behavior in the Communist World.* N.Y.: Julian Press, 1967. [See "China," pp. 13-57.]

3586 Van Gulik, Robert Hans. *Erotic Color Prints of the Ming Period.* Tokyo, 1951. 3 vols.

3587 Van Gulik, Robert Hans. *Sexual Life in Ancient China.* Leiden: E.J. Brill, 1961. [The standard work.]

3588 Wolf, Arthur Paul. "Childhood Association, Sexual Attraction and the Incest Taboo: A Chinese Case." *American Anthropologist* new (2nd) series 68:4(Aug. 1966):883-98.

3589 Yang, Richard F. S. and Levy, Howard S., trans. & described. *Monks and Nuns in a Sea of Sins.* Sino-Japanese Sexology Classics series, vol. 2. Washington: Warm-soft Village Press, 1971.

RELIGION: BUDDHISM, TAOISM, CONFUCIANISM AND FOLK RELIGIONS

3590 Ahern, Emily. *The Cult of the Dead in a Chinese Village.* Stanford: Stanford University, 1973. [A study of ancestor worship and lineage organization in Jinan, a village in northern Taiwan. Women's roles are discussed in chapters 7 and 8.]

3591 Ahern, Emily. "The Power and Pollution of Chinese Women. In *Women in Chinese Society,* ed. Margery Wolf and Roxane Witke, pp. 193-214. Stanford: Stanford University, 1975.

3592 Buck, Samuel [Pseud.]. "Why Chinese Women Worship Kwan Yin." *Orient* 2(1952):8:18-20+.

3593 Buck, Samuel [Pseud.]. "Gods and Goddesses of Navigation." *Orient* 2(April 1952):25-27.

3594 Chen, Ellen Marie. "Tao as the Great Mother and the Influence of Motherly Love in the Shaping of Chinese Philosophy." *History of Religions* 14(Aug.-Jan. 1974):51-64.

3595 Chen, Ying-chieh. "She Calms the Waves and Cures the Sick." *Free China Review* 22(June 1972):19-22. [The legend of Matsu who has been the guardian deity to seafarers for centuries.]

3596 Chomberlayne, John H. "The Development of Kuan Yin, Chinese Goddess of Mercy." *Numen* 9(Jan. 1962):45-52.

3597 Cissell, Kathryn Ann Adelsperger. "The Pi-ch'iu-ni Chuan: Biographies of Famous Chinese Nuns from 317-516 C.E." Ph.D. dissertation, University of Wisconsin, 1972.

3598 Doré, Henry, S. J. *Researches into Chinese Superstitions.* Trans. M. S. J. Kennelly. Shanghai: T'usewei Printing Press, 1914. 8 vols. [See "Taoist Witches of Hai Chow," vol. 5, pp. 546-62; "Calendar of Gods, Goddesses and Religious Festivals in China," vol. 5, pp. 563-617.]

3599 Jordan, David K. "Supernatural Aspects of Family and Village in Rural Southwestern Taiwan." Ph.D. dissertation, University of Chicago, 1969.

3600 Needham, Joseph. *Science and Civilization in China,* vol. 2, *History of Scientific Thought.* London: Cambridge University, 1956. [In Chapter 10, "The Tao Chia and Taoism," see: "The Water Symbol and the Feminine Symbol," pp. 57-61; "Sexual Techniques," pp. 146-52; "Tantrism and Its Relation with Taoism," pp. 425-30.]

3601 Paul, Diana. *Women in Buddhism.* Berkeley: Asian Humanities Press, 1980.

3602 Potter, Jack. "Cantonese Shamanism." In *Religion and Ritual in Chinese Society,* ed. Arthur Wolf, pp. 207-231. [The shamans in this study are females.]

RELIGION: CHRISTIANS AND CHRISTIANITY

3603 Barnes, Irene H. *Behind the Great Wall, the Story of the Church of England Zenana Missionary Society Work and Workers in China.* London: Marshall Bros., 1896. [See chapter 4, "Chinese Women, Their Own Evangelists."]

3604 Benn, Rachel R. *Ping-Kua; a Girl of Cathay.* Boston: Mass.: Woman's Foreign Missionary Society, Methodist Episcopal Church, 1912. [Story of a Chinese girl who was educated in a Christian girls school.]

3605 Boggs, Lucinda Pearl. *Chinese Womanhood.* N.Y.: Eaton and Mains, 1913.

3606 Brown, Margaret H. *Mrs. Wang's Diary.* Shanghai: Christian Literature Society, 1936.

3607 Burton, Margaret Ernestine. *Notable Women of Modern China.* N.Y.: Fleming H. Revell Co., 1912. [Includes biography of Mary Stone, A Chinese medical missionary.]

3608 Cable, A. M. "The Ministry of Women in the Chinese Church." *Chinese Recorder,* Feb. 1922, pp. 118-120.

3609 Chen, Mrs. C. C. "Chinese Women and Religion." *Missionary Review of the World* 52(Dec. 1929):941-44.

3610 Cheng, Ruth. "Women and the Church." *Chinese Recorder,* Aug. 1922, pp. 538-41.

3611 Chou, Ivy. Oral history, 1976. Midwest China Oral History and Archives Collection. [Interview with Chou, a theological educator in China.]

3612 Dixon, Esther MacCracken. *Problems of the Chinese Home and Some Aspects of the Contribution of the Church toward Their Solution.* Madison, N.J., 1944.

3613 Evans, Kathleen B. "Itineration among Women." *Chinese Recorder,* Mar. 1925, pp. 171-75.

3614 F., M. M. "A Tribute of Love." *Chinese Recorder,* Dec. 1916, pp. 830-42.

3615 Fung, Raymond. "Case Studies from China." *International Review of Missions* 70(Apr. 1981):5-24. [A Chinese woman recalls her Christian experience in the People's Republic of China, including the years without the church.]

3616 Gamewell, Mrs. M. N. "Memorable Visit to Some Tribespeople in Yunnan." *Chinese Recorder,* Dec. 1919, pp. 803-815.

3617 Gibson, Otis. *Chinese in America.* Cincinnati: Hitchcock & Walden, 1877. [See chapter on "Missionary Work among Chinese Women in California."]

3618 Hollister, Mary Brewster. *Lady Fourth Daughter of China.* The Central Committee on the United Study of Foreign Missions, 1932.

3619 Horning, Emma and Royer, B. Mary. *Twice Born Women, a Sketch of the Evangelistic Work of the Church of the Brethren as Conducted among Women in India and China.* Elgin, Ill.: General Mission Board, n.d.

3620 Hunter, Edward. *The Story of Mary Liu.* N.Y.: Farrar, Straus and Cudahy, 1957. [Experiences of a Chinese girl, a member of the Christian Literature Society and Methodist Church in Nanking, Shanghai and America.]

3621 Innocent, Mrs. *China for Christ. The Women and Children of the Flowery Land.* London: J.C. Watts, 1888.

3622 Kahn, Ida. "The Place of Chinese Christian Women in the Development of China." *Chinese Recorder,* Oct. 1919, pp. 659-62.

3623 Lü, Mrs. Ch'ang-chu (Tu). *Everlasting Pearl: One of China's Women;* by A. M. Johannsen, 1913.

3624 Lutheran World Federation. "Women in the Life of the Churches. *Lutheran World* 23(1976):2:141-43. [Reports from Hong Kong, etc.]

3625 MacDiarmid, D. N. *Tse Koo, a Heroine of China, the Story of Annie James.* Presbyterian Church of New Zealand, 1945.

3626 Mei, Mrs. H. C. "Making the Home Christian." *Chinese Recorder,* July 1922, pp. 472-76.

3627 *SCMP,* no. 1065 (June 8, 1955). "Meeting of Young Women's Christian Association National Executive Committee in Peking," p. 20.

3628 *SCMP,* no. 1247 (Mar. 9, 1956). "Christian Women Mark International Women's Day," p. 26.

3629 Seton, Grace (Gallatin) Thompson. Papers, 1903-1940. Smith College, Sophia Smith Collection. [Contains information on Mary Stone, a Chinese medical missionary in China.]

3630 "A Study of the Young Women's Christian Association of China: 1890-1930." *Chinese Studies in History* 10(Spring 1977):73-88 (Part 1); 11(Fall 1977):18-63 (Part 2); 11(Summer 1978):48-71 (Part 3).

3631 Ward, J. S. "The Place of Women in the Church." *Chinese Recorder,* Jan. 1922, pp. 37-43; Feb. 1922, pp. 121-25.

3632 White, Mary Culler. *Meet Mrs. Yu.* N.Y.: Abingdon-Cokesbury Press, 1948.

3633 *Women Leaders of Present Day China: Chinese Christians Worth Knowing.* Boston: Women's Board of Missions, n.d.

3634 "Women of China and the Gospel." *Hinds Missionary Review* 27(Mar. 1904):216-19.

3635 Wong, Molly. *They Changed My China.* Nashville, Tenn.: Broadman Press, 1970.

3636 Woodsmall, Ruth Frances. *Eastern Women Today and Tomorrow.* Boston: Central Committee on the United Study of Foreign Missions, 1933.

3637 Yin, Hsiang. "Protestant Women in Shanghai." *Women of China* 1957:6:29-31.

3638 "The Young Women's Christian Association in China." In *The Christian Occupation of China,* ed. Milton Theobald Stauffer, pp. 375-77. Shanghai: China Continuation Committee, 1922.

3639 Yuan, Y. Y. "Chinese Women and the Chinese Christian Church." *Chinese Recorder,* Oct. 1919, p. 665.

3640 The YWCA of China. Records, 1912-1952. Young Women's Christian Association, Archives of the National Board.

Note: See also "Western Women Missionaries in China."

Science, Technology and the Military

WOMEN AND THE MILITARY: TRADITIONAL AND REPUBLICAN CHINA (TO 1949)

3641 "Chinese Women at War." *Current History* 51(Mar. 1940):52-53.

3642 "Chinese Women at War: Work of Relief Associations." *China at War* 10(Apr. 1943):26-28.

3643 Haass, Lily K. "Chinese Women's Organizations." In *Wartime China, as Seen by Westerners,* pp. 83-94. Chungking: China Publishing Co., 1942.

3644 Hinton, Joan. "Story of a Red Army Woman." *China Reconstructs* 12(Nov. 1963):33-36 (Part 1); 12(Dec. 1963):38-41 (Part 2).

3645 Kwei, Helen Huie. "Chinese Women in War Work." *China Forum* (Hankow) 1(Mar. 12, 1938):103-105.

3646 Soong, Mayling [Mme. Chiang Kai-shek]. "The Mobilization of China's Women." *People's Tribune,* new series 23(1938):29-32.

3647 Spicer, Eva Dykes. "Chinese Women and the War." *China Quarterly* (Shanghai) 5(1939-1940):799-823. [Another edition: Chungking: China Information Committee, 1940(?), 27 pp.]

3648 Tseng, P. S. "Chinese Women and the National Crisis." *Asiatic Review* 35(1939):515-520.

3649 "Wartime Work of Chinese Women." *Monthly Labor Review* 58(Mar. 1944):571-72.

Note: See also "Emancipation Movements in the Communist Revolution, 1921-1949."

WOMEN AND THE MILITARY: THE PEOPLE'S REPUBLIC OF CHINA (1949-)

3650 "Advanced Women Fliers." *China Reconstructs* 19(Mar. 1970):32-34.

3651 "China's Women Pilots Develop." *Peking Review* 17(Apr. 26, 1974):30.

3652 Ch'iu, Shih-tung. "The Role of Women in Chinese Communist Armed Units." *Issues and Studies* 10(Sept. 1974):554-61.

3653 Chu, Hui-fen. "Shouldering Heavy Duties for the Revolution." *Peking Review* 16(Aug. 17, 1973):7-8. [Story of a woman pilot.]

3654 *ECMM,* no. 186 (June 16, 1959). "Actively Nurture Woman Warriors on the Front," p. 38.

3655 "Island Militia Women." *China Reconstructs* 23(May 1974):29-34.

3656 *JPRS,* no. 34670 (Feb. 27, 1966). "Have Weapons, Not Make-up." [From *Hongqi.*]

3657 Liu, Yiu-chu. "She Flew King Birenda to Tibet." *Eastern Horizon* 15(1976):4:37-39.

3658 "Mistress of the Sky: Wu Xiumei, China's First Woman Pilot." *China Pictorial* 393(Mar. 1981):34-35.

3659 *SCMM,* no. 474 (May 1, 1965). Hsin, Yao-lu and Wang, Chin-ling. "When Dawn Breaks on Tournament Grounds—An Account of the Military Tournament of Women Militia Squads on the Fukien Front," p. 1. [From *Zhongguo funü.*]

3660 *SCMM*, 517 (Feb. 27, 1966). Yang Tso-hung [Deputy leader of militiawomen company, Taomitou Brigade, Huangchang Commune, Wuch'ing *hsien*, Hopei province]. "I Prefer an Army Uniform to a Girl's Dress," p. 12. [From *Hongqi*.]

3661 *SCMP*, no. 290 (Mar. 6, 1952). "Women Fighters of People's Air Force Fly to Peking to Attend International Women's Day Rally," p. 3.

3662 *SCMP*, no. 291 (Mar. 7, 1952). "New China's Pilots to Give an Air Show in Peking," pp. 18-19. [A celebration on International Women's Day—an airshow staged by China's first air women.]

3663 *SCMP*, no. 291 (Mar. 8, 1952). "March 8 Rally in Peking: New China Women Master Science of Aviation," p. 18.

3664 *SCMP*, no. 557 (Apr. 22, 1953). "Women Members of Chinese People's Volunteers," p. 14.

3665 *SCMP*, no. 2704 (Mar. 8, 1962). "Armed Forces Units on Fukien Front Commend a Number of Woman Officers, Woman Employees, and Wives of Army Officers," p. 3.

3666 *SCMP*, no. 4546 (Nov. 7, 1969). "Flying with Extended Wings over the Course Opened by Chairman Mao—a Report on the Growth of Female Pilots in a Certain Unit of the People's Liberation Army Air Force," p. 6.

3667 *SCMP*, no. 4611 (Mar. 8, 1970). "Outstanding Chinese Woman Air Pilot," p. 3.

3668 *SCMP*, no. 4648 (Apr. 25, 1970). "Woman Army Doctor Who Serves the People Whole-heartedly," p. 21.

3669 *SCMP*, 4853 (Feb. 24, 1971). "Fight for the Consolidation of the Proletarian Dictatorship—a Story of Several Communist Party Members of Youthful Vigor in the Region of Tsinghai," p. 54. [Among model Communists discussed was Che Guangmei, a woman revolutionary fighter responding to Mao's call.]

3670 *SCMP*, no. 4860 (Mar. 8, 1971). "Outstanding Chinese Woman Pilot," p. 133.

3671 *SCMP*, no. 4883 (Apr. 13, 1971). "Woman Army Surgeon Firmly Carries out Chairman Mao's Proletarian Revolutionary Line in Medical and Health Work," p. 140.

3672 *SCMP*, no. 4965 (Aug. 17, 1971). "Militiawomen on South China Island," p. 15.

3673 *SCMP*, no. 5095 (Mar. 5, 1972). "The 'Lei Feng Women Militia Squad,'" p. 169.

3674 *SCMP*, no. 5098 (Mar. 9, 1972). "Women Fighters of the People's Liberation Army," p. 83.

3675 *SCMP*, no. 5099 (Mar. 12, 1972). "Militiawomen in Southeast China Coastal Areas," p. 138.

3676 *SCMP*, no. 5156 (June 7, 1972). "Outstanding People's Liberation Army Woman Technician," p. 22.

3677 *SCMP*, no. 5163 (June 15, 1972). "The Militiawomen of Hsitao Island Are Forging Ahead," p. 82.

3678 *SCMP*, no. 5189 (July 25, 1972). "Militiawomen on South China Sea Coast," p. 100.

3679 *SCMP*, no. 5336 (Mar. 7, 1973). "Militiawomen on South China Coast," p. 20.

3680 *SCMP*, no. 5338 (Mar. 10, 1973). "Follow Lei Feng's Road of Growth and Be a Good Fighter of Lei Feng Type—Female Fighters of a Certain Regiment of the People's Liberation Army Signal Corps," p. 85.

3681 *SCMP*, no. 5338 (Mar. 10, 1973). "Make an Energetic Contribution to Borderland Defense and Borderland Construction—Female Fighters Stationed in Tibet," p. 88.

3682 *SCMP*, no. 5339 (Mar. 12, 1973). "Women Fighters Battling at Their Stations to Defend the Motherland," p. 123.

3683 *SCMP*, no. 5415 (July 1, 1973). Chu Hui-fen [Deputy Political Commissar of the China Civil Aviation General Administration]. "I Must Live up to the Higher Expectation of the Party," p. 13. [An account of a woman pilot's life.]

3684 *SCMP*, no. 5433 (Aug. 1, 1973). "Woman Militia Platoon on South China Sea Coast," p. 205.

3685 *SCMP*, no. 5593 (Mar. 8, 1974). "Under the Solicitude of Chairman Mao and the Party, Women Pilots of the Air Force Unit are Sturdily Growing to Maturity," p. 12.

3686 *SCMP*, no. 5744 (Nov. 12, 1974). "Militia Men and Women of Kazakh Region—Third of the Series of the Ili Kazakh Autonomous Region," p. 18.

3687 *SCMP*, no. 5814 (Mar. 7, 1975). "Women Pilots in New China," p. 95.

3688 *SPRCP*, no. 5879 (Apr. 28, 1975). "Cavalrywomen on the Tableland," p. 8.

3689 *SPRCP*, no. 5886 (June 20, 1975). "Chinese Girl Fights Leopard Barehanded," p. 108. [Story of how a militiawoman fought a leopard barehanded in Hubei province.]

3690 *SPRCP*, no. 6113 (June 1, 1976). "A Woman Captain," p. 277.

3691 "They Call Themselves Mu Kuei-ying." *China Reconstructs* 9(Oct. 1960):38. [Mu Guiying, the name of a woman general of the Song dynasty, is adopted as a title of honor for outstanding women.]

3692 "Women Fliers." *Peking Review* 8(Mar. 12, 1965):27.

3693 "Women Gunners on the South China Sea Front." *China Reconstructs* 18(June 1969):32-36.

3694 "Women Pilots to the Rescue." *Peking Review* 2(June 30, 1959):5.

3695 Wu, Hsiu-mei. "Breaking Down Male Supremacy: Taking to the Skies." *China Reconstructs* 24(Mar. 1975):10-11.

SCIENCE AND SCIENTISTS: THE PEOPLE'S REPUBLIC OF CHINA (1949-)

3696 Bian, Bian. "Women Scientists Make a Pledge." *Women of China* 1979:1:7-9.

3697 Chen, Chiang. "Women in a Research Institute." *China Pictorial* 1973:3:18-21.

3698 Fang, Ling. "China's First Woman Harbour Engineer." *China Reconstructs* 14(June 1965):36-39.

3699 Hu, Yao-ting. "An Interview with a Woman Scientist." *Women of China* 1964:3:1-2, 16.

3700 "I Am Part of the World Now: Tsou Yi-hsin, Research Worker at the Purple Mt. Observatory, Nanking." *Women of China* 3(July-Sept. 1956):28-30.

3701 Li, Zhong. "A Woman Engineer in an Oil Refinery." *Women of China* 1979:10:2-4.

3702 Lu, Zhong. "A Woman Chemical Engineer." *Women of China* 1980:7:17-21.

3703 Quan, Yingqian. "The Rocky Road to Science." *China Reconstructs* 28(May 1979):72-74.

3704 *SCMM*, no. 237 (Aug. 16, 1960). "Woman Agronomist of a Mountainous Region—Chang Ying-hang," p. 26.

3705 *SCMP*, no. 1285 (May 4, 1956). "Women Surveyors Leave for Huai River Tributary," p. 18.

3706 *SCMP*, no. 1971 (Mar. 8, 1959). "Women Design, Make and Film Tugboat in Shanghai," p. 14.

3707 *SCMP*, no. 2136 (Nov. 7, 1959). "Young Girl Fulfills Geological Prospecting Task by Several Times," p. 8.

3708 *SCMP*, no. 2215 (Mar. 8, 1960). "Peking Women Contribute to Science, Engineering and Medicine," p. 24.

3709 *SCMP*, no. 2695 (Mar. 6, 1962). "China Provides Opportunities for Women in Scientific Work," p. 34.

3710 *SCMP*, no. 3175 (Mar. 5, 1964). "Young Peasant Woman Cited for Scientific Experimentation," p. 21.
3711 *SCMP*, no. 3653 (Mar. 5, 1966). "Young North China Woman Leads Work in Wiping out Insect Pests," p. 21.
3712 *SCMP*, no. 3653 (Mar. 5, 1966). "Young Mongolian Woman Shows Remarkable Initiative and Leadership," p. 22. [In the work of sand control, afforestation and water conservation.]
3713 *SCMP*, no. 3808 (Oct. 22, 1966). "Woman Worker Engineer Yu Feng-ying Reports on Her Creative Study and Application of Chairman Mao's Works," p. 19.
3714 *SCMP*, no. 4858 (Mar. 5, 1971). "Chinese Women Active in Geological Prospecting," p. 54.
3715 *SCMP*, no. 4859 (Mar. 7, 1971). "Outstanding Chinese Woman Technician," p. 95.
3716 *SCMP*, no. 5095 (Mar. 7, 1972). "Outstanding Chinese Woman Surveyor," p. 181.
3717 *SCMP*, no. 5339 (Mar. 12, 1973). "Women Meteorological Fighters on a South China Sea Outpost," p. 124.
3718 *SCMP*, no. 5367 (Apr. 23, 1973). "Central China Woman Worker—Capable Technical Innovator," p. 215.
3719 *SCMP*, no. 5425 (July 19, 1973). "How a Woman Shipbuilding Engineer Introduces Innovation," p. 53.
3720 *SCMP*, no. 5574 (Mar. 7, 1974). "Liu Hsiang-ping, Hsieh Ching-yi, Chien Cheng-ying, Chen Hu-hua, Lin Li-yun Meet and Fete Japanese Women Scientists' Delegation," p. 29.
3721 *SCMP*, no. 5729 (Oct. 21, 1974). "Women's Active Role in Agricultural Scientific Experiments," p. 252.
3722 *SPRCP*, no. 5821 (Mar. 18, 1975). "Woman Engineer at China's New Oilfield," p. 26.
3723 *SPRCP*, no. 5882 (June 15, 1975). "East China Women Make Agricultural Scientific Experiment," p. 164.
3724 *SPRCP*, no. 5888 (June 24, 1975). "Chinese Women Technicians Help Design Railways," p. 18.
3725 *SPRCP*, no. 5968 (Oct. 22, 1975). "Woman Meteorologist in Tibet," p. 145.
3726 *SPRCP*, no. 6053 (Mar. 4, 1976). "Peasant Women's Scientific Groups Contribute to Research," p. 167.
3727 *SPRCP*, no. 6055 (Mar. 7, 1976). "Women Chemical Engineers in China," p. 58.
3728 Sun, Kuei-chin. "Woman Engineer Li Ya-yun." *China Pictorial* 1973:3:26–27.
3729 "Women Railway Construction Technicians." *Peking Review* 18(Aug. 29, 1975):21.
3730 Zengbian. "Guardian of the Forest—Shen Momei, Forestry Specialist." *Women of China* 1980:9:3–5.

SCIENCE AND SCIENTISTS: HONG KONG, TAIWAN AND OVERSEAS CHINA

3731 Wu, Tze-wo. "The Most Outstanding Woman Physicist." *West and East* (Taipei) 10(Sept. 1965).

Sports and Fashion

SPORTS

3732 Anstice, E. H. "Footloose and Free: Sports and the Young Women of Modern China." *Travel* 65(Oct. 1935):34–35.
3733 "Athletes Going to the 8th Asian Games." *China Reconstructs* 27(Dec. 1978):5–9.
3734 "Back to the Homeland." *China Reconstructs* 27(May 1978):2–9. [Includes information about women's single badminton championship.]
3735 "Chinese Expedition Again Ascends World's Highest Peak: The Women Who Made the Final Ascent." *China Reconstructs* 24(Sept. 1975):34–36.
3736 *ECMM*, no. 1154 (Oct. 20, 1955). "New Record for Women's Javelin Throw," p. 12.
3737 Li, Shu-lan. "Athletes in China: Past and Present (2): The Training of Archers." *China Reconstructs* 24(Dec. 1975):12–14.
3738 Lin, Wenbin. "'Women Skin Divers,' A Color Documentary." *China Reconstructs* 28(Mar. 1979):12–14.
3739 Liu, Ya-chun. "Athletes in China: Past and Present (3): I Love Gymnastics." *China Reconstructs* 24(Dec. 1975):14–15.
3740 "A Master Woman Archer." *China Reconstructs* 10(Oct. 1961):10–34.
3741 "Mothers' Basketball Team in a Mountain Village." *China Reconstructs* 23(Apr. 1974):30.
3742 *SCMP*, no. 2698 (Mar. 8, 1962). "China Has 600 Women Masters of Sports," p. 22.
3743 *SCMP*, no. 4874 (Mar. 29, 1971). "Chinese and Korean Women's Basketball Volleyball Players Play Last Friendly Exhibition Matches in Peking," p. 154.
3744 *SCMP*, no. 4884 (Apr. 14, 1971). "Chinese Women's Basketball Team Leaves Peking for Cuba on Friendly Visit," p. 31.
3745 *SCMP*, no. 4886 (Apr. 16, 1971). "Chinese Women's Basketball Team Arrives in Cuba," p. 115.
3746 *SCMP*, no. 4890 (Apr. 22, 1971). "Opening Ceremony in Cuba for Friendly Matches between Chinese and Cuban Women's Basketball Teams," p. 66.
3747 *SCMP*, no. 4898 (May 3, 1971). "Chinese Women Basket-Ballers End Friendship Matches in Cuba," p. 254.
3748 *SCMP*, no. 4901 (May 8, 1971). "Peking Woman High Jumper Wu Fu-Sha," p. 128.
3749 *SCMP*, no. 4913 (May 26, 1971). "Chinese Women's Basketball Team Arrives in Chile," p. 93.
3750 *SCMP*, no. 4920 (June 8, 1971). "Chinese Women Basketball Team on Friendly Tour in Chile," p. 175.
3751 *SCMP*, no. 4923 (June 12, 1971). "Chinese Charge d'Affaires Ad Interim in Chile Gives Cocktail Party on Occasion of Chinese Women's Basketball Team's Visit," p. 117.
3752 *SCMP*, no. 4926 (June 18, 1971). "Chinese Women's Basketball Team Arrive in Conakry for Friendly Visit," p. 98.
3753 *SCMP*, no. 4927 (June 20, 1971). "Opening Ceremony for Friendly Guinean-Chinese Women's Basketball Matches Held in Conakry," p. 141.
3754 *SCMP*, no. 4928 (June 20, 1971). "Feature Story: Chinese Women's Basketball Team in Chile," p. 177.
3755 *SCMP*, no. 4932 (June 28, 1971). "Chinese Women Basketball Team Warm Welcomed While Touring Guinea," p. 154.
3756 *SCMP*, no. 4934 (June 30, 1971). "Chinese Ambassador to Guinea Gives Farewell Reception for Chinese Women's Basketball Team," p. 43.
3757 *SCMP*, no. 4936 (July 2, 1971). "Chinese Women's Basketball Team Leaves Guinea for Home," p. 165.
3758 *SCMP*, no. 4984 (Sept. 17, 1971). "Chinese Men's Basketball and Women's Volleyball Teams Arrive in Pyongyang," p. 99.
3759 *SCMP*, no. 4985 (Sept. 16, 1971). "Chinese Men's Basketball and Women's Volleyball Teams Leave Peking for Korea," p. 42.

3760 *SCMP*, no. 5043 (Dec. 18, 1971). "Chinese Women's Basketball Team and Men's Volleyball Team Arrive in Bucharest," p. 141.

3761 *SCMP*, no. 5052 (Jan. 1, 1972). "Chinese Women's Basketball Team and Men's Volleyball Team Return to Peking," p. 153.

3762 *SCMP*, no. 5071 (Jan. 27, 1972). "Friendly Exhibition Matches Between Albanian, Peking Men's and Women's Volleyball Teams," p. 69.

3763 *SCMP*, no. 5079 (Feb. 10, 1972). "Chinese Women Skater and Swimmer Break National Records," p. 110.

3764 *SCMP*, no. 5082 (Feb. 16, 1972). "Chinese Women's Speed-Skating Team Leaves Peking for Europe," p. 125.

3765 *SCMP*, no. 5098 (Mar. 11, 1972). "Chinese Women's Speed-Skating Team Back in Peking," p. 118.

3766 *SCMP*, no. 5207 (Aug. 21, 1972). "Chinese PLA Women's Basketball Delegation Leaves Peking for Korea," p. 178.

3767 *SCMP*, no. 5208 (Aug. 22, 1972). "Chinese PLA Women's Basketball Delegation Arrives in Pyongyang," p. 33.

3768 *SCMP*, no. 5209 (Aug. 24, 1972). "DPRK Ministry of National Defense Fetes Chinese PLA Women's Basketball Delegation," p. 76.

3769 *SCMP*, no. 5223 (Sept. 13, 1972). "Chinese PLA Women's Basketball Delegation Leaves Pyongyang for Home," p. 87.

3770 *SCMP*, no. 5223 (Sept. 14, 1972). "Chinese PLA Women's Basketball Delegation Back in Peking," p. 88.

3771 *SCMP*, no. 5251 (Oct. 28, 1972). "Chinese Women's Volleyball Delegation Back in Peking After Visit to Cuba, Peru, Chile and Mexico," p. 138.

3772 *SCMP*, no. 5272 (Nov. 28, 1972). "Chinese Women's Volleyball Team Back from Burma," p. 220.

3773 *SCMP*, no. 5332 (Mar. 1, 1973). "Chinese Men's and Women's Volleyball Teams Leave Peking for Korea," p. 65.

3774 *SCMP*, no. 5334 (Mar. 3, 1973). "Chinese Women's Speedskating Team Returns to Peking," p. 154.

3775 *SCMP*, no. 5337 (Mar. 8, 1973). "Peking Round-City Race Marks International Women's Day," p. 62.

3776 *SCMP*, no. 5338 (Mar. 9, 1973). "Chinese Women's Basketball Team Arrives in Cuba," p. 110.

3777 *SCMP*, no. 5342 (Mar. 16, 1973). "Profile of Chinese Table Tennis Champion Lin Hui-ching," p. 60.

3778 *SCMP*, no. 5348 (Mar. 25, 1973). "Chinese Men's and Women's Volleyball Teams Return to Peking," p. 121.

3779 *SCMP*, no. 5363 (Apr. 17, 1973). "Chinese Men's and Women's Basketball Teams Conclude Friendly Visit to Albania," p. 20.

3780 *SCMP*, no. 5405 (June 19, 1973). "Peking Men's and Women's Volleyball Team Leaves Peking for Syria, Italy, and Lebanon," p. 246.

3781 *SCMP*, no. 5418 (July 8, 1973). "Chinese Women's Basketball Team Leaves Peking for Italy," p. 192.

3782 *SCMP*, no. 5420 (July 10, 1973). "Chinese Women's Basketball Team Arrives in Italy," p. 73.

3783 *SCMP*, no. 5430 (July 25, 1973). "Chinese Women Basketball Players Leave Rome for Home," p. 75.

3784 *SCMP*, no. 5478 (Oct. 7, 1973). "Chinese Women Athletes Break National Record," p. 355.

3785 *SCMP*, no. 5631 (May 29, 1974). "Chinese Women's Basketball Delegation Leaves Peking for Korea," p. 35.

3786 *SCMP*, no. 5633 (June 1, 1974). "Chinese and Albanian Women's Volleyball Teams Hold Friendly Match in Peking," p. 118.

3787 *SCMP*, no. 5647 (June 21, 1974). "Chinese Women's Volleyball Team Visits Canada," p. 117.

3788 *SCMP*, no. 5651 (June 29, 1974). "Chinese Women's Basketball Team Concludes Visit to Korea," p. 189.

3789 *SCMP*, no. 5655 (July 4, 1974). "Chinese Women's Volleyball Team Concludes Visit to Canada," p. 136.

3790 *SCMP*, no. 5659 (July 11, 1974). "Chinese Teenage Girl Cracks World Archery Record," p. 72.

3791 *SCMP*, no. 5661 (July 13, 1974). "How Chinese Girl Scales World Peak in Archery," p. 167.

3792 *SCMP*, no. 5662 (July 16, 1974). "Chinese Malagasy Women Basketballers Play Friendly Match in Peking," p. 216.

3793 *SCMP*, no. 5696 (Sept. 3, 1974). "China Wins Men's and Women's Gymnastic Team Titles at 7th Asian Games," p. 45.

3794 *SCMP*, no. 5697 (Sept. 3, 1974). "Chinese Men and Women Gymnasts Win Team Competition at Asian Games," p. 85.

3795 *SCMP*, no. 5697 (Sept. 4, 1974). "Chinese Gymnasts Finish 1, 2, 3 in Women's Individual Competition," p. 90.

3796 *SCMP*, no. 5697 (Sept. 4, 1974). "Results of Women's Gymnastics and Springboard Diving at Asian Games," p. 88.

3797 *SCMP*, no. 5697 (Sept. 5, 1974). "Chinese Woman Shooter Becomes First World Record Breaker at the Asian Games," p. 93.

3798 *SCMP*, no. 5697 (Sept. 5, 1974). "Chinese Woman Shooter Breaks World Record at Asian Games," p. 92.

3799 *SCMP*, no. 5699 (Sept. 6, 1974). "Chinese Women Win First and Third Places in Platform Diving at Asian Games," p. 186.

3800 *SCMP*, no. 5700 (Sept. 8, 1974). "Chinese Girl Sets New World Archery Record," p. 255.

3801 *SCMP*, no. 5700 (Sept. 9, 1974). "China Beats Indonesia in Women's Badminton Finals at Asian Games," p. 256.

3802 *SCMP*, no. 5700 (Sept. 9, 1974). "China Becomes Group Winner in Women Table Tennis Team Event at Asian Games," p. 257.

3803 *SCMP*, no. 5700 (Sept. 9, 1974). "China Wins First Two Places in Women's 1,500 m. Race at Asian Games," p. 255.

3804 *SCMP*, no. 5700 (Sept. 9, 1974). "Peking Women's Volleyball Team Leaves for Romania," p. 246.

3805 *SCMP*, no. 5701 (Sept. 9, 1974). "China Wins Asian Games Men's, Women's Badminton Team Titles from Indonesia," p. 54.

3806 *SCMP*, no. 5701 (Sept. 10, 1974). "China Beats Japan in Semi-Final Run of Women's Table Tennis Team Event at Asian Games," p. 56.

3807 *SCMP*, no. 5701 (Sept. 10, 1974). "China Wins First Two Places in Women's Long Jump at Asian Games," p. 57.

3808 *SCMP*, no. 5702 (Sept. 10, 1974). "Women's Long Jump and Shot Put Finals at Asian Games," p. 106.

3809 *SCMP*, no. 5702 (Sept. 11, 1974). "China Wins Women's Table Tennis Team Event at Asian Games," p. 113.

3810 *SCMP*, no. 5702 (Sept. 11, 1974). "Chinese Woman High Jumper Wins Third Place at Asian Games," p. 112.

3811 *SCMP*, no. 5702 (Sept. 12, 1974). "Chinese Woman Wins Javelin Event at Tehran Games," p. 114.

3812 *SCMP*, no. 5703 (Sept. 13, 1974). "Chinese Girl Breaks World Archery Record," p. 164.

3813 *SCMP*, no. 5704 (Sept. 14, 1974). "China Wins Badminton Gold, Silver Medals in Men's, Women's Singles, Women's Doubles," p. 29.

3814 *SCMP*, no. 5704 (Sept. 14, 1974). "China Wins Women's Discus Title at 7th Asian Games," p. 206.

3815 *SCMP*, no. 5704 (Sept. 15, 1974). "China Wins Women's Table Tennis Singles Championships at Asian Games," p. 211.

3816 *SCMP*, no. 5708 (Sept. 19, 1974). "Peking Women's Volleyball Team Leaves Bucharest for Rome," p. 146.

3817 *SCMP*, no. 5735 (Nov. 1, 1974). "Chinese Women Volleyballers Leave Mexico for Cuba," p. 49.

3818 *SCMP*, no. 5742 (Oct. 12, 1974). "Chinese Women Shooters Shatter World Record in Standard Pistol Team Event," p. 141.

3819 *SCMP*, no. 5743 (Nov. 13, 1974). "Chinese Women's Volleyball Team Ends Visit to Cuba," p. 176.

3820 *SCMP*, no. 5744 (Nov. 16, 1974). "Peking Women's Basketball Team to African Countries," p. 35.

3821 *SCMP*, no. 5748 (Nov. 22, 1974). "Peking Women's Basketball Team Concludes Visit to Ghana," p. 225.

3822 *SCMP*, no. 5748 (Nov. 24, 1974). "Peking Women's Basketball Team Hold First Match in Bamako," p. 226.

3823 *SCMP*, no. 5752 (Nov. 29, 1974). "Peking Women's Basketball Team Concludes Visit to Mali," p. 202.

3824 *SCMP*, no. 5754 (Dec. 2, 1974). "Peking Women's Basketball Team Plays First Match in Dakar," p. 39.

3825 *SCMP*, no. 5759 (Dec. 11, 1974). "Peking Women's Basketball Team Concludes Visit to Senegal," p. 35.

3826 "Shanghai Teenage Girls Break World Archery Record." *China Reconstructs* 23(June 1974):48.

3827 *SPRCP*, no. 5763 (Dec. 18, 1974). "Peking Women's Basketball Team Concludes Visit to Nigeria," p. 82.

3828 *SPRCP*, no. 5781 (Jan. 15, 1975). "Peking Women Volleyball Team Leaves for Kuwait," p. 34.

3829 *SPRCP*, no. 5784 (Jan. 18, 1975). "Peking Women's Volleyball Team Plays First Match in Kuwait," p. 149.

3830 *SPRCP*, no. 5788 (Jan. 25, 1975). "Peking Women's Volleyball Team Leaves Kuwait for Home," p. 124.

3831 *SPRCP*, no. 5795 (Feb. 5, 1975). "Chinese Men's and Women's Speed-Skating Team Leave Peking for World Championships."

3832 *SPRCP*, no. 5798 (Feb. 10, 1975). "Chinese Women's Table Tennis Team Wins World Title," p. 94.

3833 *SPRCP*, no. 5798 (Feb. 10, 1975). "Team Events Conclude at 33rd WTTC with China Winning Men's, Women's Team Titles," p. 95.

3834 *SPRCP*, no. 5815 (Mar. 8, 1975). "Women's Day Relay Race Held in Peking," p. 132.

3835 *SPRCP*, no. 5843 (Apr. 19, 1975). "Tientsin Women's Volleyball Team Leaves for Tour of Somalea and Togo," p. 194.

3836 *SPRCP*, no. 5879 (Jan. 10, 1975). "Chinese Women's Volleyball Team Leaves for Japan," p. 9.

3837 *SPRCP*, no. 5883 (June 16, 1975). "Noted Woman Acrobat Contrasts Old and New Societies," p. 218.

3838 *SPRCP*, no. 5948 (Sept. 22, 1975). "Chinese Schoolgirl Cracks World Record in Women's Small-Bore Standard Rifle Event," p. 206.

3839 *SPRCP*, no. 5977 (Nov. 5, 1975). "Chinese Men's and Women's Basketball Teams Leave for Peru," p. 72.

3840 *SPRCP*, no. 5985 (Nov. 16, 1975). "Chinese Women's Basketball Team Arrives in Los Angeles," p. 44.

3841 *SPRCP*, no. 5988 (Nov. 20, 1975). "Chinese Women's Basketball Team Visits U.S.," p. 178.

3842 *SPRCP*, no. 5989 (Nov. 23, 1975). "Chinese Women's Basketball Team Visits Rochester, N. Y.," p. 219.

3843 *SPRCP*, no. 5992 (Nov. 27, 1975). "Chinese Women's Basketball Team Ends Visit to New York City," p. 134.

3844 *SPRCP*, no. 5992 (Nov. 28, 1975). "China Wins Men's and Women's Team Titles at Scandinavian Table Tennis Championships," p. 128.

3845 *SPRCP*, no. 5992 (Nov. 28, 1975). "US President Receives Chinese Women's Basketball Team," p. 134.

3846 *SPRCP*, no. 5993 (Nov. 30, 1975). "Chinese Women's Basketball Team Leaves Washington for Home," p. 182.

3847 *SPRCP*, no. 5993 (Dec. 29, 1975). "Chinese Women's Basketball Team Hold Last Match in US," p. 181.

3848 *SPRCP*, no. 6029 (Jan. 24, 1976). "China Wins Men's, Women's Team Titles at Romanian Table Tennis Championship," p. 124.

3849 *SPRCP*, no. 6067 (Mar. 25, 1976). "Wang Wen-chuan Breaks World Record in Women's Archery," p. 168.

3850 *SPRCP*, no. 6068 (Mar. 26, 1976). "Three Chinese Girls Break World Archery Record," p. 215.

3851 *SPRCP*, no. 6164 (Aug. 15, 1976). "1976 Peking International Friendship Invitational Women's Basketball Tournament Opens in Shanghai," p. 97.

3852 *SPRCP*, no. 6166 (Aug. 18, 1976). "Friendly Get-Together Among Players in 1976 International Women's Basketball Tournament," p. 182.

3853 *SPRCP*, no. 6168 (Aug. 20, 1976). "First Round Matches Completed at International Friendship Invitational Women's Basketball Tournament in Shanghai," p. 6168.

3854 *SPRCP*, no. 6168 (Aug. 21, 1976). "Second Round Matches Begin at International Friendship Invitational Women's Basketball Tournament in Shanghai," p. 47.

3855 *SPRCP*, no. 6170 (Aug. 24, 1976). "Second Round Matches Continue at International Friendship Invitational Women's Basketball Tournament in Shanghai," p. 125.

3856 *SPRCP*, no. 6170 (Aug. 24, 1976). "Shantung Women's Basketball Team Leaves Peking for Mauritius and Madagascar," p. 123.

3857 *SPRCP*, no. 6171 (Aug. 25, 1976). "Peking International Women's Basketball Invitational Tournament Promotes Friendship and Unity," p. 157.

3858 *SPRCP*, no. 6172 (Aug. 26, 1976). "1976 Peking International Women's Basketball Friendship Invitational Tournament Closes," p. 193.

3859 *SPRCP*, no. 6180 (Sept. 7, 1976). "Chinese Women's Basketball Team Leaves Mauritius for Madagascar," p. 205.

3860 *SPRCP*, no. 6194 (Sept. 24, 1976). "Chinese Women's Basketball Team Leaves for Yugoslavia," p. 202.

3861 *SPRCP*, no. 6196 (Sept. 28, 1976). "Chinese Women's Basketball Team Plays First Match in Yugoslavia," p. 202.

3862 *SPRCP*, no. 6203 (Oct. 8, 1976). "Chinese Women's Basketball Team Leaves Yugoslavia for Home," p. 171.

3863 *SPRCP*, no. 6203 (Oct. 9, 1976). "China's Shantung Women's Basketball Team Concludes Visit to Madagascar," p. 159.

3864 *SPRCP*, no. 6211 (Oct. 23, 1976). "Sian Friendship Delegation and Women's Volleyball Team Leave for Japan," p. 110.

3865 *SPRCP*, no. 6213 (Oct. 26, 1976). "Chinese Women's Basketball Delegation Leaves Peking," p. 251.

3866 *SPRCP*, no. 6215 (Oct. 29, 1976). "1976 National Women's Athletic Meet Held in Shanghai," p. 109.

3867 *SPRCP*, no. 6241 (Dec. 8, 1976). "Chinese Women's Basketball Delegation Leaves Hongkong for Home," p. 172.

3868 *SPRCP*, no. 6241 (Dec. 8, 1976). "Chinese Women's Volleyball Team Leaves for Peru," p. 168.

3869 *SPRCP*, no. 6245 (Dec. 12, 1976). "Chinese Women's Volleyball Team Plays First Match in Peru," p. 138.

3870 Tan, Aiqing. "Career and Family" A Sports Couple." *China Reconstructs* 28(Aug. 1979):62–63, 65.

3871 Tao, Peng-fei. "Send-off of Yatung Girls' Basketball Team Bringing Honors Back to Homeland." *West and East Monthly* 17:4:2–5. [Girls basketball team in Taiwan.]

3872 "They Are Champions—At China's 4th National Games." *Women of China* 1980:1:24–25.

3873 "Women's Volleyball—a Higher Standard." *China Reconstructs* 27(Mar. 1978):42–43.

3874 Yen, Nai-Hua. "Outstanding Young Athletes." *China Reconstructs* 24(Jan. 1975):36–37.

3875 Yuan, Weimin. "Asian Champions—China's Women's Volleyball Coach Tells How." *Women of China* 1980:4:24–25, 14.

FASHION

3876 Arlington, Lewis C. "Chinese Women's Coiffures." *China J.* 2(1929):4–10, 69–76, 119–126.

3877 Chambers, William. *Designs of Chinese Buildings, Furniture, Dresses, Machines and Utensils.* London: privately published, 1957.

3878 Chen, Jui-ho. "Clothing Attitudes of Chinese and American College Women." Ph.D. dissertation, Pennsylvania State University, 1970.

3879 "Chinese Dress through the Ages." *Free China Review* 20(Feb. 1970):35–42.

3880 *ECMM*, no. 32 (Mar. 16, 1956). "Let Us Make Our Dress Look Pretty," p. 41. [From *China's Youth*.]

3881 Nan, Lai. "Women's Dress in China." *Women of China*. 1980:5:18–25.

3882 Priest, Alan. *Costumes from the Forbidden City.* N.Y.: Arno Press, 1974.

3883 *SCMP*, no. 1224 (Feb. 2, 1956). "Peking Discussion on Style and Color of Clothes," p. 9.

3884 *SCMP*, no. 1237 (Feb. 24, 1956). "First Designs Chosen for Peking Fashion Show," p. 17.

3885 *SCMP*, no. 1243 (Feb. 12, 1956). "Minutes of the Forum Held on Fashion on February 1," p. 8.

3886 *SCMP*, no. 1243 (Feb. 12, 1956). "New Styles Designed for Fashion Show in Peking," p. 8.

3887 *SCMP*, no. 1243 (Feb. 25, 1956). "Fashion Show to be Opened in Shanghai," p. 12.

3888 *SCMP*, no. 1243 (Mar. 4, 1956). "300 Different Dresses to be Shown in Shanghai Fashion Show," p. 12.

3889 *SCMP*, no. 1247 (Mar. 10, 1956). "Too Many Entries for Peking Fashion Show," p. 9.

3890 *SCMP*, no. 1251 (Mar. 15, 1956). "New Style Dresses for Women and Children," p. 11.

3891 *SCMP*, no. 1258 (Mar. 26, 1956). "Spring Dress for Shanghai," p. 34.

3892 *SCMP*, no. 1261 (Apr. 2, 1956). "Fashion Show Opens in Shanghai," p. 29.

3893 *SCMP*, no. 1262 (Mar. 20, 1956). "Beautify Fashions in Dress," p. 9. [*Guangming ribao* editorial.]

3894 *SCMP*, no. 1262 (Mar. 31, 1956). "New China's First Fashion Exhibition," p. 8.

3895 *SCMP*, no. 1266 (Apr. 9, 1956). "Orders for New Fashions in Clothing," p. 17.

3896 *SCMP*, no. 1270 (Apr. 15, 1956). "Fashion Show in Urumchi," p. 23.

3897 *SCMP*, no. 1368 (Sept. 9, 1956). "Clothes Designing Group in Shenyang," p. 14.

3898 *SCMP*, no. 1904 (Nov. 10, 1958). "Miao and Tang Women in Southeast Kweichow Improve Their Dress," p. 39.

3899 Scott, Adolphe Clarence. "Chinese Hair Styles." *Orient*, Feb. 1951, pp. 28–30. [On Chinese women in Hong Kong.]

3900 Scott, Adolphe Clarence. *Chinese Costume in Transition.* Singapore: Moore, 1958. [Reprint: N.Y.: Theatre Arts Books, 1960.]

Western Women in China

WESTERN WOMEN (OTHER THAN MISSIONARIES) IN TRADITIONAL AND REPUBLICAN CHINA (TO 1949)

3901 Alsop, G. F. *My Chinese Days.* Boston: Little, 1918.

3902 Angell, Sarah (Caswell). Papers, 1746–1903. University of Michigan, Bentley Historical Library, Michigan Historical Collections." [Includes diaries describing author's life in China during her husband's diplomatic mission there.]

3903 Bowen, Katharine Giltinan. Oral History tapes, Minnesota Historical Society, Audio-visual Library. [Bowen reminisces about her experience in China during World War II.]

3904 Buck, Pearl. "In Memoriam: Sketch of Dr. Sydenstricker." *Presbyterian Survey* 23(Sept. 1932):567–68; 23(Oct. 1932):408–609; 23(Nov. 1932):675–76.

3905 Buck, Pearl. *My Several Worlds, a Personal Record.* N.Y.: John Day, 1954.

3906 Burt, Reynolds J. Papers, 1896–1935. United States Army Military History Institute. [Includes letters by Burt's wife about her experience in China as wife of the senior U.S. Army officer stationed there.]

3907 Calhoun, William James, and Calhoun, Lucy (Monroe). Papers, 1909–1913. Newberry Library. [Lucy Calhoun, the wife of an American envoy to China from 1909 to 1913, describes the final days of the Qing dynasty and the formation of the Republic.]

3908 Churchill, Sarah J. Papers, 1900. Library of Congress, Manuscript Division. [On Churchill's journey to China, including comments on the Boxer Rebellion, which broke out during her trip.]

3909 Claassen, Evelyn. Oral history, 1962. Cornell University, Department of Manuscripts and University Archives. [About Claassen's impression of China when she accompanied her husband, an entomologist, to China during 1924–25.]

3910 Dahlin, Helen (DePass). Oral history, 1976. Midwest China Oral History and Archives Collection. [Concerns Dahlin's childhood in Tianjin from 1923 to 1931 when her father, a U.S. military officer, served in China.]

3911 Hahn, Emily. *China to Me, a Partial Autobiography.* Garden City, N.Y.: Doubleday, Doran & Co., 1944.

3912 Hahn. Papers, 1917– . Indiana University, Lilly Library. [Hahn, a writer, describes her experience in China during the Japanese occupation prior to World War II.]

3913 Hughes, C. Elizabeth. Oral history, 1977. Midwest China Oral History and Archives Collection. [A nurse's experience in China.]

3914 King-Salmon, Frances W. *House of a Thousand Babies: Experiences of an American Woman Physician in China (1922–1940).* N.Y: Exposition Press, 1968.

3915 Ma, Haide, Dr. [George Hatem]. "On Agnes Smedley." *Women of China* 1980:10:18–19.

3916 McKinnon, Jan and McKinnon, Steve. "Agnes Smedley: A Working Introduction." *Bulletin of Concerned Asian Scholars* 7(Jan./Mar. 1975):6–11.

3917 McKinnon, Stephan R. "Researching Agnes Smedley in China." *China Quarterly*, no. 77 (Mar. 1979), pp. 122–25.

3918 Mateer, A. H. *Siege Days: Personal experiences of American Women and Children during the Peking Siege.* Taibei: Chengwen, 1976. [Reprint of 1903 edition.]

3919 Middleton, Dorothy. *Victorian Lady Travellers.* N.Y.: Dutton, 1965.

3920 Nevius, Mrs. Helen S. *Our Life in China.* N.Y.: R. Carter and Bros., 1869.

3921 Pruitt, Ida. *A Childhood.* Asian Library Series, no. 10. San Francisco: Chinese Materials Center, 1978.

3922 Smedley, Agnes. Papers, 1894-1950. Arizona State University Archives. [Papers of Smedley, who lived in China from 1928 to 1940.]

3923 Smedley, Agnes. *China's Red Army Marches.* London: Lawrence and Wishart, 1936.

3924 Smedley, Agnes. *Battle Hymn of China.* London: Gollancz, 1944.

3925 Smedley, Agnes. *China Fights Back: An American Woman with the Eighth Route Army.* Westport, Conn.: Hyperion, 1977. [Reprint of 1938 edition.]

3926 Smith, Mabel Waln. *Springtime in Shanghai.* London: Harrap, 1957.

3927 Spinney, Anna G. Papers, 1885-1902. Essex Institute. [Letters from Peking, Canton, and Shanghai.]

3928 Stone, Grace (Zaring). Papers, 1927-1971. Boston University, Mugar Memorial Library, Special Collections. [Information about residence in China.]

3929 Strong, Anna Louise. *China's Millions.* N.Y.: Coward-McCann, 1928.

3930 Sword Family. Papers, 1750-1863. Historical Society of Pennsylvania. [Contains letters by Mary Sword, who lived in Macao and Canton.]

3931 Tesdell, Margaret Stanley. Oral history, 1977. Midwest China Oral History and Archives Collection. [Interviews concerning Tesdell's nursing activity in China during 1946-48.]

3932 Walsh, Richard John. *A Biographical Sketch of Pearl S. Buck.* N.Y.: John Day, Reynal and Hitchcock, 1936.

3933 Wheelhouse, Frances. *Eleanor Mary Hinder: An Australian Woman's Social Welfare Work in China between the Wars.* Sydney: Wentworth Books, 1978.

3934 Women Authors. Collection, n.d. Downers Grove Historical Society. [Includes Alice Tisdale Hobart, a resident of China from 1908 to 1921.]

3935 Yaukey, Grace [Cornelia Spencer]. *The Exile's Daughter, a Biography of Pearl S. Buck.* New York: Coward-McCann, 1944.

3936 Yü, Yü-cha. "Pearl Buck and the Chinese Peasant." *Sino-American Relations* 4(Winter 1978):49-64. [Reprint from *Asian Culture Quarterly* 4(Autumn 1978).]

WESTERN WOMEN (OTHER THAN MISSIONARIES) IN THE PEOPLE'S REPUBLIC OF CHINA (1949-)

3937 Gelder, George Stuart and Gelder Roma. *Memories for a Chinese Granddaughter.* London: Hutchinson, 1967. [British in China in the 1960s.]

3938 Hicks, Cherrill. "English Feminist in China, Part I." *China Now*, no. 82 (Jan.-Feb. 1979), pp. 14-15.

3939 Hicks, Cherrill. "English Feminist in China, Part II." *China Now* 83(Mar.-Apr. 1979).

3940 Kramer, Ione. "Life on East Wind Road; an American in a Chinese Village." *Eastern Horizon* 6(Aug. 1967):12-23; 6(Sept. 1967):55-63.

3941 MacLaine Shirley. *You Can Get There from Here.* N.Y.: W. W. Norton, 1975. [Account of MacLaine's journey to the PRC as head of a women's delegation.]

3942 Sandroff, Ronni. "Shirley MacLaine: Is the Human Race Gonna Make It?" *New China* 1(Summer 1975):39-40. [About MacLaine's trip to the PRC.]

3943 Schu, Mark J. "Friendship Has a History: Anna Louise Strong." *New China* 3(Fall 1979):43-46.

3944 Sibley, Jean. "Living with Chinese Workers: An Exchange Student's Experience in China." *Far Eastern Reporter*, Oct. 1978, pp. 3-29.

3945 Strong, Anna Louise. *Tibetan Interviews.* Peking: New World Press, 1959.

3946 Strong, Anna Louise. *When Serfs Stood up in Tibet: Report.* Peking: New World Press, 1960.

3947 Strong, Anna Louise. *Letters from China.* Peking: New World Press, 1963.

3948 Strong, Anna Louise. "Why I Like to Live in Peking at the Age of 80: Letter Sent to My College Class Reunion, Oberlin College, June 1965." *Women of China* 1966:2:20-21, 24.

3949 Tesdell, Margaret Stanley. Oral history, 1977. Midwest China Oral History and Archives Collection. [Includes Tesdell's description of a visit in 1972 to the PRC as part of the American Friends Service Committee delegation.]

3950 Wood, Leili. "Letters from Leili." *China Now*, no. 75 (Nov./Dec. 1977), pp. 19-22.

3951 Wood, Shirley. *A Street in China.* London: Michael Joseph, 1958.

3952 Zhao, Fengfeng. "In Memory of Anna Louise Strong." *Women of China* 1980:2:36-38.

WESTERN WOMEN MISSIONARIES IN CHINA

3953 Adams, Marie. Papers. N.d. Archives of DePauw University and Indiana United Methodism.

3954 Akins, Ethel M. Oral history, 1976. Midwest China Oral History and Archives Collections.

3955 Allen, Arthur J. Papers, 1938-1954. Columbia University, Rare Book and Manuscript Library. [Correspondence of Allen and his wife who were Episcopal missionaries in China from the 1930s to 1951.]

3956 Allen, Netta Powell. Oral history, 1970-1971. University of California, Berkeley, The Bancroft Library, Manuscripts Division.

3957 Anderson, Alice K. Oral history, 1976. Midwest China Oral History and Archives Collection.

3958 Anderson, Colena. Oral history, 1977. Midwest China Oral History and Archives Collection.

3959 Atwood, Hazel M. Papers, 1933-1950. University of Oregon Library, Special Collections.

3960 Board of Foreign Missions, Evangelical Lutheran Church and its Antecedents. Records, 1893-1960s. Luther Theological Seminary, Archives of the American Church. [Includes letters from women missionaries and wives of missionaries serving in China.]

3961 Board of Global Ministries, Division of World Missions. Records, 19th and 20th centuries. United Methodist Church, Commission on Archives and History. [Includes Mrs. Lyman Hale, who was a missionary to China with her clergyman husband from 1915-1939.]

3962 Bonafield, Julia A. Papers, 1888-1943. West Virginia University, West Virginia Collection.

3963 Bost, Ethel W. Papers, 1925. East Carolina University, East Carolina Manuscript Collection.

3964 Boucher, Mae. Papers, 1926-49. University of Oregon Library, Special Collections.

3965 Boynton, Grace Morrison. Papers, 1925-51. Schlesinger Library.

3966 Brethren. Collection, ca. 1890– . McPherson College Library, Brethren Room. [Includes pamphlets with biographical sketches of female Brethren missionaries who served in China.]

3967 Bright, Carrie Lena McMullen. Oral history, 1976. Midwest China Oral History and Archives Collections.

3968 Brooks, Rachel. Papers, n.d. The New York Public Library, Manuscripts and Archives.

3969 Buck, Pearl S. *The Exile: Portrait of an American Mother in China*. N.Y.: Reynal & Hitchcock, 1936. [Biography of the author's mother, a missionary in late imperial and early Republican China.]

3970 Burgess, Alan. *The Small Woman*. N.Y.: Dutton, 1957. [Story of Gladys Aylward. Also published in London: Evans Bros. 2nd ed., 1959.]

3971 Cable, Mildred. *A Woman Who Laughed; Henrietta Soltau, Who Laughed at Impossibilities and Cried: "It Shall Be Done."* London: China Inland Missions, 1934.

3972 Caterer, Helen. *Foreigner in Kweilin: The Story of Rhoda Watkins, S. Australian Nursing Missionary*. London: Epworth, 1966.

3973 Cheney, Monona L. Papers, 1918–30. University of Oregon Library, Special Collection.

3974 Cherry Hill. Collection, ca. 1700–1960. New York State Library, Manuscripts and Special Collections. [Includes materials of Catherine Visscher (Van Rensselaer) Bonney, who served as a missionary to China in the 1850s and 1860s.]

3975 China Missionaries. Oral history, 1969–71. Columbia University, Oral History Collection. [Women interviewed on the influence of the missionary movement in China between 1900 and 1950.]

3976 China Missionaries Oral History Project. Oral history, ca. 1969–72. University of California, Berkeley, Bancroft Library, Manuscripts Division. [Includes interviews with Mary Lee Latimer, who describes her experiences in China as the daughter of missionaries and as a teacher in mission and non-mission schools; and Margaret (Garrett) Smythe, who discusses her childhood in China as the daughter of missionaries, her return to China in 1928 and service in a mission hospital.]

3977 China. Records, 1927–49. Sisters of Charity of Cincinnati, Motherhouse. [Records pertaining to the missions in China of the Sisters of Charity.]

3978 China Records Project: Brown, Velva V. Papers, 1920–71. Yale Divinity School Library.

3979 China Records Project: Carr, Ruth M. (White). Papers, 1917–26. Yale Divinity School Library.

3980 China Records Project: Dawson, Mary E. S. Papers, 1921–31. Yale Divinity School Library.

3981 China Records Project: Hartwell, Emily Susan. Papers, 1875–1949. Yale Divinity School Library.

3982 China Records Project: Hinman, Kate (Bailey). Papers, 1908–61. Yale Divinity School Library.

3983 China Records Project: Perkins, Elizabeth S. Papers, 1907–27. Yale Divinity School Library.

3984 China Records Project: Personal Papers. Collection, 1834–1973. Yale Divinity School Library. [Includes papers concerning women missionaries in China.]

3985 Clarke, Eric and Clarke, Ruth Johnson. Papers, ca. 1904–49. Stanford University Libraries, Manuscripts Division. [The Clarkes were missionaries in China.]

3986 Codrington, Florence I. *Hot-Hearted; Some Women Builders of the Chinese Church*. London: Church of England Zenana Missionary Society, n.d.

3987 Conche, Edith. "The Biola Preaching Bands and Women's Work." *Chinese Recorder*, Nov. 1922, pp. 710–714..

3988 Cox, Venetia. Papers, 1917–58. East Carolina University Manuscripts Collection.

3989 Cranston, Mildred (Welch). Oral History, 1971. University of California, Berkeley, Bancroft Library, Manuscripts Division.

3990 Darley, M. E. *Light of the Morning: The Story of the Church of England Zenana Missionary Society Work in the Kienning Prefecture of the Fuh-kien Province, China*. London: Church of England Zenana Missionary Society.

3991 Daughters of the Revolution. Records, 1919–1973. Suffolk County Historical Society. [Includes material on women missionaries in China.]

3992 Davis, Lydia (Lord). Papers, 1862–1944. Oberlin College Archives.

3993 Dawson, Edwin Collas. *Heroines of Missionary Adventure*. London: Seeley, Service & Co., 1930.

3994 Dixon, Esther MacCracken. *Problems of the Chinese Home and Some Aspects of the Contribution of the Church toward Their Solution*. Madison, N.J., 1944.

3995 Dudley, Marion. Papers, 1927–66. University of North Carolina Library, Southern Historical Collection.

3996 Endicott, Mary Austin. *Five Stars over China: The Story of Our Return to New China*. Toronto, 1953.

3997 F., M. M. "A Tribute of Love." *Chinese Recorder*, Dec. 1916, pp. 830–42. [A tribute to an American woman missionary, Miss Cornelia Leavenworth Bonnell in Shanghai.]

3998 Farmer, Wilmoth Alexander (Rev.). *Ada Besson Farmer, a Missionary Heroine of Kuang Si, South China*. Atlanta: Foote & Davis, 1912.

3999 Farnham, J. M. W. *A Devoted Life: Mary Jane (Scott) Farnham*. Shanghai: Commercial Press, 1913.

4000 Fielde, Adele Marion. Papers, 1884–1919. Academy of Natural Sciences. [Letters of Fielde, a naturalist and missionary. They contain information about the Academy, of which she was a member.]

4001 Fisher, Frederick and Fisher, Welthy. Papers, 1902– . Boston University, Mugar Memorial Library Special Collections. [Papers of Frederick Bohn Fisher (1882–1938), a bishop of the Methodist Episcopal Church and missionary to India, and of his wife, Welthy Blakesley (Honsinger) Fisher (1879–), an author and teacher in China and India.]

4002 Fitch, Janet. *Foreign Devil: Reminiscences of a China Missionary Daughter, 1909–1935*. Taibei: China Materials Center, Taipei Liaison Office.

4003 Foster Family. Papers, 1851–1951. Yale Divinity School Library. [Clara (Hess) Foster (1859–1945) and her husband John Marshall Foster were Baptist missionaries in China from 1888 to 1894 and 1898 to 1900.]

4004 Frantz, Marie J. (Regier). Papers, n.d. Bethel College, Mennonite Library and Archives.

4005 Fremont, NE, First Congregational Church, UCC. Records, 1880–1945. Nebraska State Historical Society. [Includes manuscript material regarding the work of a member, Miss Ruth Mulliken, who was a missionary to China from 1910 until 1942.]

4006 Garlick, Phyllis L. *Destiny at the Door; China Faces the Future*. London: Chun Church Missionary Society, 1945.

4007 Garst, Mrs. Laura (Delany). *In the Shadow of the Drum Tower*. Cincinnati: Foreign Christian Missionary Society, 1911.

4008 Goforth, Mrs. Rosalind (Bellsmith). *Goforth of China*. Grand Rapids, Mich.: Zondervan Publishing House, 1937.

4009 Granskou, Ella Odland. Oral history, 1977. Midwest China Oral History and Archives Collection.

4010 Gray, Cammie. "Some Practical Problems in Evangelistic Work." *China Recorder*, Mar. 1922, pp. 190-93.

4011 Gress, Ruth A. Papers, 1939-58. University of Oregon Library, Special Collections.

4012 Guinness, Joy. *Mrs. Howard Taylor, Her Web of Time*. London: China Inland Mission, 1950.

4013 Hamilton, Horace Ernst. *China Two Generations Ago; a Family Sketch of Guy and Ernst Hamilton, Presbyterian Medical Missionaries in the Interior of North China*. Denver: Big Mountain Press, 1957.

4014 Hamlin, Huybertie Lansing (Pruyn). Papers, 1878-1957. Albany Institute of History and Art Library.

4015 Hanson, Constance Twedt. Oral history, 1976. Midwest China Oral History and Archives Collection.

4016 Hartwell Family. Papers, 1849-1969. Yale Divinity School Library. [Includes papers of Eliza H. (Jewett) (Mrs. Jesse) Hartwell (1837-70) and her daughter Anna Burton Hartwell (1870-1961), both of whom were Baptist missionaries in China.]

4017 Hawker, George. *Open the Window Eastward; Glimpses of Women's Missionary Work in India and China*. London: Carez Press, 1917.

4018 Hayes, Helen. Oral history, 1977. Midwest China Oral History and Archives Collection.

4019 Haygood, Atticus Greene. Papers, 1861-1952. Emory University, Robert W. Woodruff Library, Special Collections Department.

4020 Hemenway, Ruth V. Papers, 1924-42. Smith College, Sophia Smith Collection.

4021 Hobart, Emily. Papers, 1884-1928. University of Oregon Library, Special Collections.

4022 Hodges, John M. and Hodges, Ruth. Papers, 1735-1966. North Carolina Division of Archives and History. [Contain a 1910 letter in the Hodges family papers from "Cousin Cattie," a Presbyterian missionary to China.]

4023 Holkeboer, Tena. Papers, 1920-63. Western Theological Seminary Library.

4024 Holway, Amy Richardson. Papers, 1917-49. Schlesinger Library.

4025 Honsinger, Welthy. *Beyond the Moon Gate, Being a Diary of Ten Years in the Interior of the Middle Kingdom*. N.Y., Cincinnati: Abingdon Press, 1924.

4026 Houston, Lyda Suydam. Oral history, 1970-71. University of California, Berkeley, Bancroft Library, Manuscripts Division.

4027 Hyde, Agnes Holstad. Oral history, 1923-76. Midwest China Oral History and Archives Collection.

4028 Hylbert, Ethel (Lacey). Oral history, 1970. University of California, Berkeley, Bancroft Library, Manuscripts Division.

4029 Jacquet, Myra Anna. Papers, 1913-43. University of Oregon Library, Special Collections.

4030 Jarvis, Anna Moffet. Papers, 1920-77. Midwest China Oral History and Archives Collection.

4031 Jarvis, Bruce W. Papers, 1927-28. University of Oregon Library, Special Collections. [Jarvis (1885-1970) was a physician in China from 1923-1949. Correspondence, personal narratives, manuscript reports, documents, photos, clippings and publications contain material about the experiences of Anna Moffet, a missionary administrator in China from 1920 to 1945.]

4032 Jeter, Jeremiah Bell. *An American Woman in China, and Her Missionary Work There*. Boston: Lothrop, 1874.

4033 Jeter, Jeremiah Bell. *A Memoir of Mrs. Henrietta Shuck*. Boston: Gould, Kendall & Lincoln, 1846. [The first female American missionary sent to China.]

4034 Jones, Clara J. Oral history, 1976. Midwest China Oral History and Archives Collection.

4035 Jones, Lucile (Williams). Oral history, 1970. University of California, Berkeley, Bancroft Library, Manuscripts Division.

4036 Kallen, Horace M. Papers, 1902-1975. American Jewish Archives.

4037 Kemp, E. G. *Reminiscences of a Sister: S. Florence Edwards of Taiyuanfu*. London: Carey Press, 1919.

4038 Kennedy, Alice Carey (Traver) Libby. Papers, 1903-59. Washington State University Library. [Includes papers of Kennedy's sister Edith G. Traver (1881-), a Baptist missionary to China.]

4039 Kirk, Hazel M. Papers, 19th c.-1961. Bridgeport Public Library, Historical Collections. [Includes letters from Elizabeth C. Wright, a missionary at the Presbyterian mission in Beijing.]

4040 Lacy, Henry Veere. Papers, 1909-50. University of Oregon Library, Special Collections. [Papers of Lacy and his wife, both missionaries in China.]

4041 Lanneau, Sophie Stephens. Papers, 1907-1950. Wake Forest University Library, North Carolina Baptist Historical Collection.

4042 Loomis, Augustus Ward, Family. Papers, 1803-97. Cornell University, Department of Manuscripts and University Archives. [Letters by Loomis and his wife, Mary Ann Loomis, Presbyterian missionaries in Zhejiang.]

4043 Lord, Lucy T. *Memoirs of Mrs. Lucy T. Lord, of the Chinese Baptist Mission*. Philadelphia: American Baptist Publishing Society, 1854.

4044 McCormick, Sister Mary Colmcille. Oral history, 1971. University of California, Berkeley, Bancroft Library, Manuscripts Division.

4045 Main, Ida Belle (Lewis). Papers, 1910-49. University of Oregon Library, Special Collections.

4046 Marcelline, Sister M. O. P. *Sisters Carry the Gospel*. World Horizon Reports, no. 15. Maryknoll, N.Y.: Maryknoll Publications, 1956.

4047 Martinson, Cora. Oral history, 1977. Midwest China Oral History and Archives Collection.

4048 Mead, Lucy Irene. Papers, 1901-1925. Essex Institute.

4049 Methodist Missionaries. Papers, n.d. Baker University Library, United Methodist Historical Collection and Library. [Contains papers of women missionaries, including Irma Highbaugh (?-1973), a 1915 Baker graduate who served in China before World War II.]

4050 Mickey, M. Partia. Papers, 1914-1940. Oberlin College Archives.

4051 Minor, Louella. Papers, 1884-1935. University of Washington Libraries, Archives and Manuscripts Division.

4052 Morse, Esther. Papers, 1929-63. University of Oregon Library, Special Collections.

4053 Murray, Katie. Papers, 1927-63. East Carolina University, East Carolina Manuscript Collection. [Miss Murray was a missionary to China from 1927 to 1950 and in Taiwan from 1954 to 1959.]

4054 National Board. Records, 1876-1964. Young Women's Christian Association, Archives of the National Board. [Includes material concerning fieldwork in China.]

4055 Nelsen, Frida R. Oral history, 1976. Midwest China Oral History and Archives Collection.

4056 Ohlinger, Franklin. Papers, 1862–1919. Rutherford B. Hayes Library. [Ohlinger (1845–1919) and his wife Bertha (Schweinfurth) Ohlinger (1856–1934) were missionaries to China from 1876 to 1886.]

4057 Olson, Lillian A. Oral history, 1977. Midwest China Oral History and Archives Collection.

4058 Palmborg, Rosa W. *China Letters, Written by Rosa W. Palmborg, Seventh Day Baptist Medical Missionary to China, 1894–1940.* Plainfield, N.J.: Recorder Press, 1943.

4059 Pedersen, Thyra E. Papers, 1923–74. Schlesinger Library.

4060 Pierce, Florence. Papers, 1926–62. Young Women's Christian Association, Archives of the National Board.

4061 Platt, H. L. *Story of the Years; a History of the Woman's Missionary Society of the Methodist Church, Canada, from 1881 to 1906.*

4062 Platt, W. J. *Three Women: Mildred Cable, Francesca French, Evangeline French.* London: Hodder & Stoughton, 1964. [Three missionaries who lived among the Chinese from Gansu corridor to the Golir.]

4063 Price, P. F. "In Memoriam. Mrs. Ella Davidson Little." *Chinese Recorder,* Sept. 1916, pp. 634–36.

4064 Reed, Alice Clara. Oral history, 1969. University of California, Berkeley, Bancroft Library, Manuscripts Division.

4065 Reik, Elsie I. Papers, 1922–27. University of Oregon Library, Special Collections.

4066 Root, Helen I., ed. *Our China Mission.* Chicago: Woman's Missionary Society, Free Methodist Church, 1932.

4067 Rosalia, Sister Mary. *One Inch of Splendor.* N.Y.: Field Afar Press, 1941.

4068 Sallee, Annie (Jenkins). Papers, 1897–1967. Baylor University, Texas Collection.

4069 Schintz, Mary Ann. *An Investigation of the Modernizing Role of the Maryknoll Sisters in China.* Ph.D. dissertation, University of Wisconsin, 1978.

4070 Scott, Mrs. Grace (Ciggie). *Twenty-Six Years of Missionary Work in China.* 2nd ed. N.Y.: American Tract Society, 1897.

4071 Simester, Edith Winifred. Papers, 1945–46. University of Oregon Library, Special Collections.

4072 Simkin, Margaret (Timberlake). Oral history, 1970–71. University of California, Berkeley, Bancroft Library, Manuscripts Division.

4073 Skinner, James Edwards. Papers, 1889–1956. University of Oregon Library, Special Collections. [Skinner and his wife were medical missionaries in China.]

4074 Smith Family. Papers, 1894–1971. Yale Divinity School Library. [Includes correspondence and writings of Helen Huntington Smith (1902–1971), appointed a missionary to China in 1929.]

4075 Smith, Myrtle A. Papers, 1921–47. University of Oregon Library, Special Collections.

4076 Smythe, Margaret Garret. Oral history, 1977. Midwest China Oral History and Archives Collection.

4077 Snow, Myra L. Papers, 1928–44. University of Oregon Library, Special Collections.

4078 Sovik, Gertrude. Oral history, 1976. Midwest China Oral History and Archives Collection.

4079 Stanley, Louise (Hathaway). Oral history, 1971. University of California, Berkeley, Bancroft Library, Manuscripts Division.

4080 Stevens, Mrs. Helen [Norton]. *Memorial Biography of Adele M. Fielde, Humanitarian.* N.Y.: Fielde Memorial Committee, 1918.

4081 Stuart, Mary Horton. Papers, n.d. Museums of the City of Mobile, Alabama.

4082 Syrdal, Borghild Roe. Oral history, 1977. Midwest China Oral History and Archives Collection.

4083 Tack, Minnie. Oral history, 1977. Midwest China Oral History and Archives Collection.

4084 Taylor, Mrs. Mary Geraldine (Guiness). *Guiness of Honan, by his Sister, Mrs. Howard Taylor*

4085 Taynton, Susan (Herring) Jeffries. Papers, 1896–1964. East Carolina University, East Carolina Manuscript Collection.

4086 Teagarden, Lyrel G. Papers, 1921–56. University of Oregon Library, Special Collections.

4087 Thode, Frieda Oelschiaeger. Papers, n.d. Concordia Historical Institute.

4088 Tinling, Christine I. *Memories of the Mission Field.* London: Morgan and Scott, 1926.

4089 Traver, Edith Grace. Papers, 1910–30. American Baptist Historical Society.

4090 Victoria, Sister Mary. *Nun in Red China.* N.Y.: McGraw-Hill, 1953.

4091 Ward, Katherine Bertha Boege. Oral history, 1970–71. University of California, Berkeley, Bancroft Library, Manuscripts Division.

4092 Ward, Katherine Bertha Boege. Oral history, 1977. Midwest China Oral History and Archives Collection.

4093 Wallis, Gertrude (Steel-Brooke). Papers, 1917–53. San Diego Public Library, California Room.

4094 Wheeler, Laura Maude. Papers, 1903–48. University of Oregon Library, Special Collections.

4095 White, E. Aldersey, ed. *A Woman Pioneer in China: The Life of Mary Ann Aldersey, from Materials Supplied and Edited by E. Aldersey White.* London: Livingstone Press, 1932.

4096 Wiley, Martha. Papers, ca. 1900–50. Yakima Calley Museum and Historical Association.

4097 Wiley, Martha. Oral history, 1969. University of California, Berkeley, Bancroft Library, Manuscripts Division.

4098 Wilkinson, Leila Fayssoux Davidson. Papers, 1920–50. South Carolina Historical Society.

4099 Williams, George L. and Williams, Mary Alice Moon. Papers, 1890–1912. Oberlin College Archives.

4100 Wilson, Emma Webber. Papers, ca. 1950–70. Kansas West Conference of the United Methodist Church, Commission on History and Archives.

4101 Winans, Pearl (Fosnot). Oral history, 1970. University of California, Berkeley, Bancroft Library, Manuscripts Division.

4102 Winslow, Carolyn V. *Tomorrow.* Winona Lake, Ind.: Young People's Missionary Society, 1945.

4103 *With Our Missionaries in China, by Mrs. Emma Anderson and Other Missionaries in the Field.* Mountain View, Calif., Kansas City, Mo.: Pacific Press Publishing Association, 1920.

4104 Wolcott, Jessie L. Papers 1939–50. East Carolina University, East Carolina Manuscript Collection.

4105 Woman's Foreign Missionary Society, Nebraska Conference, Methodist Episcopal Church. Records, 1899–1919. Nebraska Wesleyan University, United Methodist Church Archives.

4106 Young, Mildred Test. Oral history, 1977. Midwest China Oral History and Archives Collection.

4107 Young Women's Christian Association. Records, 1884–1961. University of Nebraska-Lincoln Archives.

Index of Authors

A. C. D. 0777
Abbott, Elizabeth Lee 0082
Abel, Theodora M. and Hsu, Francis L. K. 3541
Adams, Marie 3953
Ah-mei 1841
Ahaidati 3235
Ahern, Emily M. 2756, 3590, 3591
Ai, Nan 2321
Ai, Wu 1823, 1842
Aird, John Shields 0793-0796, 0842
Akins, Ethel M. 3954
Allen, Arthur J. 3955
Allen, Netta Powell 3956
Alley, Rewi 1290
Alsop, G. F. 3901
An, Tzu-wen 3022
Anderson, Alice K. 3957
Anderson, Colena M. 2120, 3958
Anderson, Emma 4103
Anderson, Eugene N., Jr. 1652, 2509
Anderson, John Ellis 0952
Anderson, Mary Raleigh 0018
Anderson, Paul 0116
Andors, Phyllis 0336, 0337, 1056, 1057
Andrews, Y. B., Mrs. 0189
Angell, Sarah (Caswell) 3902
Anson, Robert Sam 2172
Anstice, E. H. 3732
Applegarth, Margaret Tyson 2173
Arlington, Lewis C. 0780, 0781, 1645, 3876
Armbruster, W. 0633, 1620
Arnold, Fred Sidney 0953
Arrigo, Linda Gail 1621
Atherton, Gertrude 2174
Attwood, J. and Garavente, Jean 0338
Atwood, Hazel M. 3959
Austen, N. 0190
Avery, Roger Christopher 0797
Ayscough, Florence Wheelock 0191

Backhouse, Edmund Trelawney and Bland, John Otway Percy 2931
Bacon, Margaret 0339, 0340
Baisinger, Grace and Macy, Virginia 2603
Baker, Hugh D. R. 2470, 2510-2512, 2757
Bald, Margaret M. 3441
Bao, Wenqing 2121
Barclay, George Watson 2424
Barnes, Irene H. 3603
Barnett, William K. 0634, 2758
Barrett, Jane 0341
Barrett, Richard E. 2759
Bashford, James Whitford 0192
Beahan, Charlotte 0165, 0166
Beattie, Hilary J. 2513
Bedwany, Theresa Labib 0954
Beedham, B. 0844
Belden, Jack 0282
Bendel, Jean-Pierre and Hua, Chang-i 0798
Bender, Paul 2307
Benn, Rachel R. 3604
Berelson, Fernand and Freedman, Ronald 0955
Berliner, Gabriells, et al. 2760
Bernard, Suzanne 2122
Bernstein, Thomas 1457
Berstein, R. 2994

Best, A. E. 0645
Beurdeley, Michel, et al. 3566
Bian, Bian 3696
Bianco, Lucien 0845
Birch, Cyril 1692
Birch, Cyril, ed. 1693
Bismark, Karl 2243
Bjorge, Gray J. 1928
Blake, E. 0193
Blake, Fred C. 1655, 2308
Blaustein, Albert P., ed. 2911
Blitsten, Dorothy R. 2530
Bodard, Lucien 0342
Bodde, D. 3567
Bogan, Mrs. M. L. C. 2728
Boggs, Lucinda Pearl 0194, 3605
Bohlmeyer, Jeannine 2236
Bonafield, Julia A. 3962
Bone, C. 0195
Boserup, Ester 1058
Bost, Ethel W. 3963
Boucher, Mae 3964
Boušková, Marcela 1929, 1930
Bowden-Smith, A. G. 0196
Bowen, Katharine Giltinan 3903
Boyd, C. T., Mrs. 0019
Boynton, Grace Morrison 3965
Braga, Anthony 2089
Brandauer, Frederick P. 0167, 1779
Brethren 3948
Bridgman, Mrs. Eliza Jane (Gillet) 2531
Briffa, E. M. 2604
Briggs, Margaret [Liang Yen] 2729
Bright, Carrie Lena McCullen 3967
Brittain, Mary Z. 0343, 2995
Broderick, James Lively 2605, 3542
Brooks, Rachel 3968
Brown, Carrie Chu 2532
Brown, Karen 2175
Brown, M. 0611
Brown, Margaret H. 3606
Brown, Velva V. 3978
Browne, Vivian E. 0344
Broyelle, Claudie 0095
Brugger, Florence 2425
Brugger, William Christian 3568
Bryan, Robert Thomas 2278, 2843
Bryson, Mary Isabella 2533, 2534
Buck, Pearl S. 0197, 0283, 0345, 2176-2184, 2279, 2567, 2568, 3904, 3905, 3969
Buck, Samuel [pseud.] 0117, 3592, 3593
Budd, Josephine E. 0020
Bunch-Weeks, Charlotte 0096
Burchett, Wilred, C. 0284
Burgess, Alan 3970
Burr, John S. 1060
Burt, Reynolds J. 3906
Burton, E. D. et al. 0706
Burton, Margaret Ernestine 0021, 0022, 0168, 0707, 1061, 3607
Butters, H. R. 1622
Buxbaum, David C. 2828, 2829, 2920
Buxbaum, David C., ed. 2244, 2830
Buxton, Rose and Langton, Patricia 0346

Cable, A. M. 3608

Cable, Emma R. 1543
Cable, Mildred 3971
Calhoun, William James and Calhoun, Lucy (Monroe) 3907
Callis, Maud Eva 0097
Cameron, J. 0347
Camp, Sharon L., ed. 0849
Campbell, N. M. 0198
Carl, Katherine Augusta 2932
Carpenter, Frances 1656
Carr, Ruth M. (White) 3979
Carscallen, H. M. 0199
Casterline, John Bernt 2426
Caterer, Helen 3972
Cather, Helen Virginia 1623
Cernada, George Peter 0956
Cernada, George Peter and Chow, L.P. [Chou Lien-pin] 0957
Cernada, George Peter and Lu, Laura P. 0958
Chai, Ch'u and Chai, Winberg, trans. and eds. 1694
Chai, Shang-tung 2620
Chakravarti, Tripurari 0349
Chalakahu 1940
Chambers, William 3877
Chan, Anita 1328
Chan, Hok-lam 0118, 0119
Chan, Itty 0043
Chan, K. C. 0959, 0960
Chan, Kuei-pei 2730
Chan, Lily M. 0782
Chandrasekhar, Sripati 0350
Chandrasekhar, Sripati; Hinton, Harold Clendenin; Williams, Lea E., et al. 2607
Chang, Chi 1941, 2372
Chang, Chih-jang 2882
Chang, Ching-hsi 1624
Chang, Ching-sheng 3569
Chang, Ching-wen 2309
Chang, Chun 1942
Chang, Denis K. L. 2427
Chang, E. 1062
Chang, Eileen 1828, 2216, 2217, 2218, 2219
Chang, Feng-ju; Li Chih-k'uan; and Liu Chung 0286
Chang, H. C., trans. 1695
Chang, H. M. 0351
Chang, Hsi-ch'eng 2280
Chang, Hsiang-yu [Chang, Hsiang-yü] 1114
Chang, Hsiao-mei 0406, 1291
Chang, Hwei-lan 0023
Chang, Jun-mei 2123
Chang, Ke and Yang, Ching-hsiang 1458
Chang, Kuei-mei 0352
Chang, Kung-kong 0961
Chang, Li-han [Chang Lihan] 1943, 2310
Chang, M. C.; Cernada, George Peter; and Sun, T. H. [Sun Te-hsiung] 0962
Chang, Ming-cheng 0799
Chang, Mo-yuan 1944
Chang, Shao-wei 0200, 2281
Chang, Shiao-chun 2761
Chang, Su 3267
Chang, Tao Hsing 2844
Chang, Tsu 1718
Chang, Yu 1490
Chang, Yu-san 1341
Chang, Yu-teh 1945
Chang, Yü-fa 0169
Chang, Yun 3343
Chang, Yung-mei 1946

Chao, Buwei Yang [Chao, Pu-wei] 0201, 2124
Chao, Cheng-min 1947
Chao, Chi-chen 2282
Chao, Ngo-ni 1367
Chao, Pao-chi 1948
Chao, Paul Kwang-yi 2608-2610
Chao, Shu-li 1824
Chao, Wen 1949
Chao, Y. R. [Chao, Yuan-jen] 1646
Chau, Virginia Chi-tin 0783
Che, Wai-kin 2611
Chen, Chi-lu 2762
Ch'en, Ch'i-lu 2731
Chen, Chiang 3697
Chen, Ching-ching 2732
Chen, Chiyen [Ch'en Chi-yen] 2428, 2763
Chen, Chun-chin 2733
Chen, Chung-hsien 0720
Chen, Edward King-tung 2612
Chen, Ellen Marie 3594
Ch'en En-nü 1427
Chen, F. L. et al. 0963
Chen, Fang 1158
Chen, Gerald 3007
Chen, Han-seng 1159-1161
Chen, Hsiu-cheng 2613
Chen, Hsu 2311
Chen, Hui 1950
Chen, I-fu 2471
Chen, J. 0353
Chen, Jack 2614
Chen, Jo-hsi [Chen Ruoxi]* 1833, 2220
Chen, Jui-ho 3878
Chen, K. Y. 0657
Ch'en, Kao-hua and T'ien, Jen-lung 3008
Chen, Kuan-chin 0098
Chen, May Ying 0083
Ch'en, Mei-ying 2367
Chen, Mrs. C. C. 3609
Chen, Muhua 0856
Chen, Pei 1951
Chen, Pi 0721, 1952
Chen, Pi-chao 0857, 0858
Chen, Pi-chao and Miller, Ann 0859
Chen, Shao-hsing [Ch'en Shao-hsing]; Wang Yao-tung; and Foley, Frederick Joseph 0964
Chen, Ta [Ch'en, Ta] 0800, 1063, 1064
Chen, Ta [Ch'en Ta] and Shyrock, John Knight 1647
Ch'en, Teng-k'e 1953
Chen, Theodore H. E. [Ch'en Hsi-en] and Chen, Wen-hui C. [Ch'en Chung Wen-hui] 2615
Ch'en, Toyoko Yoshida 1780
Ch'en, Wen-chen 0658
Chen, Wen-hui Chung 2616
Chen, Ying-chieh 2221, 3595
Chen, Yuan-tsung* 1954
Ch'en, Yü-ying 0287, 2966
Cheney, Monona L. 3973
Cheng, C. K. 2569
Cheng, Ch'eng K'un 2472
Cheng, Fan and Chuan, Yeh 1955
Cheng, Hawthorne [Cheng, Chün] 2283
Cheng, Hsuan 1956
Cheng, Irene [Cheng Ho Ai-ling] 0084
Cheng, Ruth 3610
Cheng, Stephen H. L. 1781, 1782
Cherry Hill 3974

Cheung, Steven N. S. 2845, 2873
Chew, Caroline 2764
Chhodnam, Drolma 1544
Chi, Feng 2329
Chi, I. C. [Ch'i I-cheng] and Mao, W. P. [Mao Wen-ping] 0965
Chi, I. C. [Ch'i I-cheng]; Chow, L. P. [Chou Lien-pin]; and Rider, Rowland V. 0695, 0966
Chi, Pang-yuan, et al., eds. 2222
Chi, Wei-wen 1234
Chi, Wen 1957
Chia, La-hsiang 1329
Chiang, An-hui 0722
Chiang, Ch'ing 3047, 3048
Chiang, J. P. 0085
Chiang, Kui-ching 2237
Chiang, Mei-ling. *See* Soong, Mayling
Chiang, Tzu-lung 1958
Chiang, Yee [Chiang, I] 2570
Chiang, Yin-nan 3208
Chiang, Yung-ching 0202
Chiao, Chi-ming 0801
Chiao, Chien [Ch'iao, Chien] 2245, 3570
Ch'i-chun 2125
Ch'ien, Chung-shu 1843
Chien, Pei-heng 1959
Ch'ien Shih-lung 2411
Chien, T'ieh 3013
Chien, Tze 0723
Chin, Ai-li Sung [Ch'en, Ch'en Ai-li] 1931, 2090, 2238, 2284
Chin, Chao-yang 1960
Chin, Chi-tsu and Hung, Sung 0354, 1371
Chin, Chin-chih 1162
Chin, Hsin-ju 0120
Chin, James J. 2429
Chin, Yueh-ying 0724
Ching, Chih 1961
Ching, Chung Shou and Bagwell, May 1066
Ch'ing, Fu-wen 0526
Ching, Hung 1163
Ching, Lin 1962
Ching, T. S. and Vaughn, K. E. 0208
Chiou-kuey 2765
Chiu, Chi-chien 2734
Chiu, Han-p'ing 2831
Ch'iu, Shih-tung 3652
Chiu, Vermier Yantak [Chao P'ing] 2246, 2832, 2846
Cho, Lee-jay and Kobayashi, Kazumasa, eds. 0804
Choi, Jai-seuk 2473
Chomberlayne, John H. 3596
Chong, Lily Pao-hu 2126
Chou, Ching-sung 3288, 3289
Chou, Eric 3571
Chou, Hung-hsiang 0122
Chou, Ivy 3611
Chou, Ke-chin 1963
Chou, Keh-chou 1331
Chou, K'e-hsien 2317
Chou, M. J. 1118
Chou, Ngo-fen 0861
Chou, Pien 1332
Chou, Tse-tsung 0209
Chou, Tsung-chi 1964
Chou, Wei-ling 3268
Chou, Yung-chuang 1965
Chow, C. F. 0210
Chow, Ching Lie 2127
Chow, Chung-cheng 2128

Chow, Fan 1119
Chow, L. P. [Chou, Lien-pin] 0968–0974
Chow, L. P. [Chou, Lien-pin] and Hsu, S. C. [Hsü, Shih-chü] 0976
Chow, L. P. [Chou, Lien-pin], et al. 0967, 0975
Chow, Tse-tsung 0646
Christy, Lai Chu Tsui 3543
Chu, A. W. 3443
Chu, Cheng-ping 0696
Chu, Feng-lan 2679
Chu, Fu-t'ang 0659
Chu, Godwin C. and Hsu, Francis L. K., eds. 2312
Chu, Hao-jen 3015
Chu, Hui-fen 3653, 3683
Chu, Leonard L. 0862
Chu, Po-lu 2535
Chu, Shih-ming (Mrs.) 2571
Chu, Solomon Shu-ping 2515, 2766
Chu, T. C., Mrs. 0211
Chu, Teh 0123
Ch'ü, T'ung-tsu 0124, 2247, 2536
Chu, Yu-yuan 1966
Chuan, Nung-tiao 1491
Chuang, Hsin-cheng 1783
Chuang, Shen 1784
Chun, Daphne [Ch'in Hui-chen] 0977, 0978
Chun, Jinsie 2933
Chun, Ying-mei 2242
Chung, Hua-min and Miller, Arthur C. 3016
Chung, Hui-lan 0851
Chung, Sue Fawn 2934, 2935
Chung, Wen 1932
Chung-fa 3017
Churchill, Sarah J. 3908
Cissell, Kathryn Ann Adelsperger 3597
Claassen, Evelyn 3909
Clarke, Eric and Clarke, Ruth Johnson 3985
Clinton, J. Jarrett and Baker, Jean, eds. 0979
Close, U. 0212, 2286
Codrington, Florence I. 3986
Cohen, Charlotte Bonny 0099, 0359
Cohen, Myron L. 2474, 2475, 2767–2770
Colby, Venetta 2129
Collins, Leslie E. 0100, 2248
Collis, Maurice 2185, 2936
Collver, Alden Speare, Jr. and Liu, Paul K. C. [Liu K'o-chih] 0980
Conche, Edith 3987
Conger, Darius J. and Luan, David C. 0805
Conger, Sarah Pike 2937
Coombs, Lolagene C. 0981, 0982
Coombs, Lolagene C. and Chang, Ming Cheng 0983
Coombs, Lolagene C. and Freedman, Ronald 2771
Coombs, Lolagene C. and Sun, Te-hsiung 2772, 2773
Cooper, Elizabeth 0125, 0126
Cormack, Mrs. J. G. 2287
Cornaby, William Arthur 1696, 2538
Coughlin, Richard James 0806
Coughlin, Richard James and Coughlin, Margaret Morgan 0984
Cousins, Norman 0863
Cox, Venetia 3988
Cranston, Mildred (Welch) 3989
Crawford, William Bruce 1785
Creel, H. G. 0127
Croizier, Ralph 2092
Croll, Elisabeth Joan 0360–0366, 1165, 1334, 1335, 2313, 2314
Crook, David 2315

Crook, David and Isabel 1336
Crook, Isabel and David 0367
Culliton, Barbara J. 0864
Cummins, H. W. 0101
Curtin, Katie 0289, 0368, 0369
Cusack, Dymphna 0370

Daggett, Mary (Stewart) [Mrs.] 2186
Dahlin, Helen (DePass) 3910
Darley, M. E. 3990
Das, Man Singh and Bardis, Panos D. 2618
Davies, Derek 2130
Davies, H. 0170
Davin, Delia 0290-0292, 0371, 1166, 1337, 3020
Davis, John A. (Rev.) 1545
Davis, Lydia (Lord) 3992
Davis-Friedmann, Deborah 2619
Dawson, Edwin Collas 3993
Dawson, Mary E. S. 3980
De Beauvoir, Simone 0293
De Groot, Jan Jakob Maria 2249-2251
De Mendoza, Juan G. 0128
Delmar, Rosalind 0372
Der Ling, Princess [Derling] 1844-1847, 2131, 2572, 2938, 2939
Deza, Alfonso B. 0374
Diamond, Norma 0375, 0635, 0636, 1338, 1626, 2774, 2775
Dillon, Richard H. 1546
Ding Ling. *See* Ting Ling
Dixon, Esther MacCracken 3612, 3994
Djang, Hsiang-lan 0214
Djerassi, Carl 0865
Donnelly, Jannete C. 1339
Doolittle, Justus 0129
Doré, Henry, S.J. 2252, 3598
Dorros, Sybilla Green 0376, 2316
Douglas, Sir Robert Kennaway 2539
Dreijmanis, John 0866
Drucker, A. R. 0171
Drunken Whiskers [Pseud.] 1571
Dudgeon, John Hepburn 0785
Dudley, Marion 3995
Duffield, Anne 2187
Dull, Jack L. 2253
Dupree, N. H. 2940

E. E. [Entwistle] 1068
Eber, Irene 2093
Eberhard, Wolfram 0130, 0172, 0985, 1660-1663, 1786, 2254, 2430, 2476, 2517, 2540, 3572, 3573
Eberhard, Wolfram, ed. 1661
Eberstade, N. 0044
Edwardes, Allen and Masters, R. E. L. 3574
Edwards, E. D. 1699
Ehrlich, P. R. and Holdren, J. P. 0808
Eitel, Ernest John 2847
Ellithorpe, H. 0868
Eloesser, Leo 0725
Emerson, John Philip 1169
Endicott, Mary Austin 3996
Epstein, Israel 0045, 1069, 3023
Eskelund, Karl 2289
Eunson, Roby 2975
Evans, David Meurig Emrys 2431
Evans, Kathleen B. 3613
Evans, Nancy Jane Frances 0173, 1787

F., M. M. 3614, 3997
Faber, Ernst 0131, 0132
Fairfax-Cholmeley, Elsie 1342, 1343, 3024

Falkenheim, Victor Carl 0809
Fan, Fang-chün 0294
Fan, Jo-yu [Fan, Jo-yü] 2647
Fan, Wen-lan 0174, 2941
Fang, Chi 1170
Fang, Fu-an 1071
Fang, Hao 2223
Fang, Jufen 2134
Fang, Kuei-mei 1171
Fang, Ling 3698
Fang, Nan 1967
Fang, Wen-jen 2135
Fang, Ying-yang 2626
Fang, Yü 2677
Far, Sui Seen 2432
Farley, Foster 2942
Farmer, Wilmoth Alexander (Rev.) 3998
Farnham, J. M. W. 3999
Faundes, Anibal and Luukkainen, Tapani 0870
Faurot, Jeannette L. 2239
Faust, Ernest Caroll 0708
Fei, Chih 2332
Fei, Hsiao-t'ung [Fei, Hsiao-t'ung] 1106, 2518, 2573, 2627
Feifel, Eugene 2255
Feng, Ch'i-yung 0461
Feng, Chang 1968
Feng, Cheng-hai 1073
Feng, Fei 3025
Feng, Han-yi [Feng, Han-chi] 2519
Feng, Han-yi and Shryock, J. K. 2290
Feng, Menglong [Feng, Meng-lung] 1700, 1743-1749
Feng, Shu-min 3174
Feng, Teh-ying 1969
Feng, Wenbing 1839
Feng, Xiaxiong 2136
Fenn, William P. 1572
Fessler, Loren 0637, 0871, 0986
Feuerwerker, Yi-tsi Mei 1933, 1934, 2137, 2094
Fielde, Adele M. 0133, 2256, 4000
Finnigan, O- D- and Keeny, Spurgeon Milton 0987
Fish, Michael B. 1788
Fisher, Frederick and Fisher, Welthy 4001
Fisher, Welthy, Mrs. (Honsinger) 1701, 1848
Fitch, Janet 4002
Fitzgerald, Charles Palwick 2943
Flax, Michael Howard 0663
Fong, H. D. [Fang Hsien-t'ing] 1074
Fong, Patricia M. 1627
Fong, Stanley and Peskin, Harvey 3544
Forsythe, Irene 2188
Foster Family 4003
Foster, Arnold, Mrs. (Amy) 0024
Foster, J. 1719
Frantz, Marie J. (Regier) 4004
Fraser, S. E. 0872
Freeberne, John Derek Michael 0873
Freedman, Deborah Selin 0988
Freedman, Maurice 2257, 2258, 2477-2479, 2520, 2628, 2776, 2777, 2833, 2922
Freedman, Maurice, ed. 2480
Freedman, Ronald 0989-0991
Freedman, Ronald and Adlakha, A. L. 0993
Freedman, Ronald, et al. 0992
Freedman, Ronald; Hermalin, Albert; and Chang, Ming-cheng 0994
Freedman, Ronald; Moots, Baron; and Wei, Sou-pen 0810
Freedman, Ronald and Sun, T. H. [Sun Te-hsiung] 0995

Freedman, Ronald and Takeshita Yuzuru John 0996, 0997
Freedman, Ronald; Takeshita, Y. John; and Sun, T. H. 0998
Frenier, Mariam D. 0102, 0295
Frey, W. 2291
Fried, Morton H. 2481, 2482, 2521, 2629, 2630
Fu, Chou 1970
Fu, Hsin 3028
Fu, James S. 1789
Fu, Mao-chi 1648
Fu, S. L. [Fu, Shang-lin] 2874
Fu, Tse 1840, 1971
Fu, Wen 0380
Fukutake, Tadashi 2631
Fung, Raymond 3615

Galbraith, Winifred 0217
Gales, Robert Robinson 2834
Gallin, Bernard 2433, 2778, 2779
Gamarekian, E. 1628
Gamble, Sidney 0218, 0786, 1107, 1849, 2574-2576
Gamewell, M. N., Mrs. 0219, 3616
Gardner, M. 2189
Garlick, Phyllis L. 4006
Garst, Mrs. Laura (Delany) 4007
Geddes, William R. 2632
Gelder, George Stuart and Gelder, Roma 2633, 3937
Gen, Lewis 2875
Gentry, Curt 1573
Gernet, Jacques 0134
Gibson, Otis 3617
Gichner, Lawrence E. 3575
Gigliesi, Primerose 2138
Giles, H. A. 1790, 1791
Giles, Lionel 0176, 2944
Gillespie, Robert W. 0999
Glenn, W. 1574
Goforth, Mrs. Rosalind (Bellsmith) 4008
Gola, H. R. 1548
Goldblatt, Howard Charles 2139
Goldman, Merle 2140
Goldwasser, Janet and Dowty, Stuart 0381, 1172
Goldwater, Janet and Doughty, Stuart [sic]. See Goldwasser and Dowty
Goode, William Josiah 2483
Goodman, R. 2577
Goodrich, Chauncey S. 2945
Goodrich, L. Carrington 2541
Goodrich, L. Carrington and Fang, Chaoying, ed. 2946
Goodstadt, Leo F. 0811
Gordon, Linda 0382
Gould-Martin, Katherine 0697
Graham, David Crokett 2735-2738
Graham, Dorothy and Bennet, James W. 2190
Granskou, Ella Odland 4009
Grantham, Alexandra Ethelred 2191
Gray, Cammie 4010
Gray, John H. 0135
Green, Blake 2780
Green, K. R. 0220
Greenblatt, Sidney L., ed. 2634
Greene, Felix 2876
Greene, R. S. 0709
Greenfield, D. E. 2434, 2781
Greenhalgh, Susan 0787
Greenwood, Sylvia 0384
Gress, Ruth A. 4011
Grieder, Jerome B. 1792
Grya, Noel 0385

Guan, Zaihan 0874
Guerin, Gilbert 2782
Guinness, Joy 4012
Guisso, R. W. L. 2947
Guisso, R. W. L., ed. 0103
Guo, Linxiang 2141
Gupta, Krishna P. 3032
Guy, R. A. 0647

Haass, Lily K. 3643
Haden, Allen 2192
Hahn 3912
Hahn, Emily 2976, 3911
Hai, Mo 1827, 1972, 1973
Haldane, Charlotte 2948
Hamilton, Horace Ernst 4013
Hamilton, Pauline Ernst 2578
Hamlin, Huybertie Lansing (Pruyn) 4014
Han, Suyin [Chow, Elizabeth K.] 0595, 0875-0878, 1293, 1850-1855, 2334, 3033
Han, Tzu 0046
Han, Tzu* 1974
Han, Wen 0478
Han, Wen-chou and Yao, Lung-chang 1549
Hanan, Patrick 1793
Hand, Mildred 0221
Handlin, Joanna F. 0009
Hannin, Ethel Edith 0222
Hanson, Constance Twedt 4015
Hao Jan 1975-1979
Harding, Gardner Ludwig 0223
Hare, G. T., ed. 2848
Harley, Ann 0386
Harris, J. H. 1550
Hartwell Family 4016
Hartwell, Emily Susan 3981
Haslewood, Hugh Lyttleton 1551
Hawker, George 4017
Hawkes, David 1794
Hayes, Helen 4018
Haygood, Atticus Greene 4019
Haynor, Norman S. and Reynolds, Charles N. 2783
Headland, Isaac Taylor 0136, 2542-2546, 2579, 2949
Heath, F. J. 1575
Heenan, Brian 0879
Hegel, Robert E. 1795
Heidt, Sarajane 1000
Hellstrom, Inger 2636
Hemenway, Ruth V. 4020
Henderson, Edward 1576
Henriques, Fernando 1577
Hensman, Bertha and Mack, Kwok-Ping, trans. 1664
Hensman, Bertha, trans. 1665
Herdan, Innes 2142
Hermalin, Albert I. 1001
Hermalin, Albert I.; Freedman, Ronald; Sun Te-hsiung; and Chang Ming-cheng 1002
Hermalin, Albert I.; Seltzer, Judith A.; and Lin, Chin-hsing 0086, 1003
Hessney, Richard Charles 1796
Heyer, Virginia 1797
Hibbert, Eloise Talcott 0137, 2193
Hickey, Margaret 1123
Hicks, Cherrill 0728, 3938, 3939
Highbaugh, Irma 2580, 2581
Hightower, James R. 1798
Himes, Norman E. 0838
Hinder, Eleanor M. 1075

Hinman, Kate (Bailey) 3982
Hinton, Carma 0387
Hinton, Joan 3644
Hinton, William 0388, 1345
Hirabayashi, Jo Anne and Tang, Peter S. H. [T'ang Sheng-hao] 2582, 2637
Hirata, Lucie Cheng 1578, 1629
Ho, Chiang-chun 3239
Ho, Ching-chih 1981
Ho, Hsiang-hing 2977
Ho, Kuo Cheng 0296
Ho, Ping-ti 2484
Ho, Ro-se* 1856
Ho, Shu-yu 1982
Ho, Wei 1983
Hobart, Emily 4021
Hobbs, Lisa 0389
Hodges, John M. and Hodges, Ruth 4022
Hoe, Bang Seng 2784
Hoffman, Charles 1493
Holder, C. F. 1552
Holkeboer, Tena 4023
Hollister, Mary Brewster 3618
Holmgren, Jennifer 0138
Holway, Amy Richardson 4024
Hommel, Rudolf P. 1108
Hong, Lawrence K. 0390, 2785, 2786
Honsinger, Welthy 4025
Hopkins, Keith 1631
Horn, Joshua S. 0729
Horning, Emma and Royer, B. Mary 3619
Hosie, Dorothea (Lady) [Soothill] 0025, 0224, 2547, 2583
Hou, Hsueh-chih 2701
Hou, Yu-chen 1537
Houghton, Ross C. 0139
Houston, Lyda Suydam 4026
Howell, E. Butts, trans. 1702
Hsi, Yung. 1984
Hsia, C. L. 2849
Hsia, C. T. [Hsia, Chih-ch'ing] 1799-1802, 2095
Hsia, C. T., ed. 1828
Hsia, P'ing 3070
Hsiao Hung [Chang, Nai-ying]* 1857-1862
Hsiao, Kan 1579
Hsiao, Kuan-hung 1985
Hsiao, Kung-ch'üan 2548
Hsiao, Wen 1580
Hsiao, Yu-hsuan 1986
Hsiao, Yun-peng 2096
Hsieh, Chen-ping 3037
Hsieh, Frances Mei-huei Yang [Hsieh, Yang Mei-hui] 2097
Hsieh, Ping-ying 0225, 0226, 2143-2145
Hsieh, Wan-ying. See Ping Hsin
Hsin, Wen-ping 0297, 2978
Hsin, Yao-lu and Wang, Chin-ling 3659
Hsing, Yen-tzu 3038
Hsiung, Shih-i 1865
Hsiung, Shih-i, trans. 1864
Hsiung, Yana 2584
Hsu, C. 1174
Hsu, Francis L. K. [Hsü, Lang-kuang] 1649, 2259, 2485-2487, 2522, 2549, 2585, 2586, 3546, 3576
Hsü, Hsün 3201
Hsu, Huai-chung 1987
Hsu, Kai-yu 1935
Hsu, Kuang 0298, 0299, 0393, 0394
Hsu, Kwang. See Hsu Kuang

Hsü, Lin 0880
Hsu, Meng-hsiung 0227
Hsu, Ming-chiang 2381
Hsu, Pang-ta 2146
Hsü, Pao-ch'eng 0881
Hsu, S. C. [Hsü, Shih-chü] 0882, 1004-1008
Hsu, S. C. [Hsü, Shih-chü]; Wei H. Y. and Niu L. C. 1011
Hsu, Shou Shang; Ou-yang, Hsiao Lan; and Yoehngoo Tsohsang Wu Lew 0026
Hsu, T. C. [Hsü, Shih-chü] and Chow, L. P. [Chou, Lien-pin] 1009, 1010
Hsu, Ti-shan 1866
Hsu, Vivian Ling, ed. 1829
Hsu, Yu 1666, 2224
Hsueh, Chih-lan 2638
Hsueh, Yen 1988
Hu, Bangxiu 3240
Hu, Chi-hsi 0300
Hu, Chih-tao 0047, 2639
Hu, Chin 1175
Hu, Fa-lien 1187
Hu, Henry Yu-chieh [Hu, Yu-chieh] 2850
Hu, Hsi-mei 0228
Hu, Hsien-chin 2523
Hu, Pin-ching 2147, 2148
Hu, Pingsa [Mrs. T. C. Chu] 0229
Hu, Sheng 1496, 2622
Hu, Shih 0140, 0141, 1803, 1804, 2550
Hu, Shu-ho 3039
Hu, Yao-ting 3699
Hua, To 1346
Huang, Chao-yen 2098
Huang, Chunming 1833
Huang, H. H. and Wang, T.H. 0648
Huang, Jen L. 2337
Huang, L. J. 0395
Huang, Lin 1347
Huang, Lu-yin* 1867
Huang, Lucy Jen [Huang, Jen-hua] 2338, 2439, 2640-2644, 3547
Huang, Min-chang 0087
Huang, Ying 1494
Huberich, Charles Henry 2851
Huggins, Alice Margaret 2194, 2195
Huggins, Alice Margaret and Robinson, Hugh 2196
Hughee-Hallett, F. 0230
Hughes, C. Elizabeth 3913
Hughes, R. 0396, 0883
Hull, Helen 2979
Humana, Charles and Jacobs, Joseph 3577
Hummel, Siegbert 1667
Hung, Ping-wen 3089
Hung, Sheng 1751, 1752
Hung, Ying 1124
Hunter, Edward 3620
Hussey, Harry 2950
Hutchinson, Paul 0231
Hyde, Agnes Holstad 4027
Hylbert, Ethel (Lacey) 4028

Ikeda, Toshio 0698
Imahari, Seiji 0649
Ingalls, Jeremy 1805
Innocent, Mrs. 3621
Isaacs, Harold Robert, ed. 1830
Ishida, Euchiro 1668

J. D. [Dudgeon, John Hepburn?] 3578
Jackal, Patricia Stranahan 0302
Jacobs, Fang-chih Huang 2551
Jacobs, Sue Ellen 0002

Jacquet, Myra Anna 4029
Jade [Pseud. (Refugee from Mainland China)] 0399
Jain, Anrudh Kumar 1012-1016
Jamieson, George 2852, 2853
Jancar, Barbara Wolfe 0400
Jarvie, Ian C., ed. 2440
Jarvis, Anna Moffet 4030
Jarvis, Bruce W. 4031
Jen, Hsi-lien 2331, 2382
Jen, T'ai 0232
Jenner, Delia 0233
Jenner, W. F., ed. 1831
Jernigan, Muriel M. 2197
Jeter, Jeremiah Bell 4032, 4033
Johnson, Elizabeth 0699
Johnson, Kay Ann 0104, 0401, 2489
Johnson, Kinchen, trans. 1669
Johnson, W. O. 0402
Johnston, Reginald Fleming 0142, 0650
Jones, Clara J. 4034
Jones, Lucile (Williams) 4035
Jones, M. I. 0027
Jordan, David K. 2441, 3599
Jou Shih [Chao, P'ing-fu; Rou Shi] 1868-1870
Ju, Chih-chüan* 1989-1997
Ju, I-hsiung 2652
Jui, Wan 0504

Kahn, Harold 2951
Kahn, Ida 2293, 3622
Kallen, Horace M. 4036
Kan, Aline 2349
Kan, Chia-ming 0028
Kane, Penny 0887, 0888
K'ang, K'e-ch'ing 0303-0305
K'ang, Yu-wei 0143
Kang-Wang, J. F. 0700
Kao, Feng; Chang, Tso-pin; and Lang, Ch'eng-hsin 1554
Kao, Hsiao-sheng 1998
Kao, Hung 1999
Kao, Ming 1720
Kao, Shou-ch'eng 2373
Kao, Ta-kuan 2489
Kao, Yin 2000
Kaplan, Edward H. 0003
Kashiwagi, Toshio 1704
Katagiri, T. and Terao, Takuma 0889
Katz, Naomi and Milton, Nancy, eds. 1832
Keeny, Spurgeon Milton 1017
Keeny, Spurgeon Milton and Cernada, George Peter 1018
Kehl, Dorothy 0413
Kemp, E. G. 4037
Kennedy, Alice Carey (Traver) Libby 4038
Keyes, Susan 3548
Keyte, John Charles 2198
Kiang, Kang-hu 2490
K'in, Sin 2260
Kin, Y. 0234
Kindermann, Charles Robert 1019
King-Salmon, Frances W. 3914
Kingston, Maxine Hong 0414, 2225
Kinnosuke, A. 0235
Kirby, E. S., ed. 3282
Kirk, Hazel M. 4039
Klein, Donald W. and Clark, Anne B. 3044
Kleinman, Arthur and Lin, Tsung-yi, eds. 3549
Knoerle, Jeanne 1806
Ko, Chih-li 1477

Ko, Siang-feng 2739
Kobayashi, T. 1936
Komor, M. 2294
Kong, Jiesheng 2350
Koo, D. Y. 1076
Koo, Helen Ping-ching [Mrs. Richard Billsborrow] 1020
Koo, Ping Yuan 1077
Koo, W. K. Wellington 0236
Kräuter, Uwe 1355
Kräuter, Uwe and Wilson, Patricia 2150
Kraft, Joseph 0415
Kramer, Ione 3940
Krichmar, Albert; Smith, Virginia Carlson; and Wiederrecht, Ann E. 0004
Kriger, Sara F. 0701
Kristeva, Julia 0105, 0416, 0417
Kroeber, Alfred Louis 2524
Ku, Ling 3283
Ku, Yen 3045, 3206
Ku, Yü 2001
Kulp, Daniel H. 2587
K'ung, Chueh and Yuan, Ching* 2002, 2003
Kung, Li 0468
Kung, Lydia 1632, 1633
Kung, Mao 1499
Kung, Shien-Woo 1634
Kuo, Chi-hsin 2653
Kuo, Chung-yi 1538
Kuo, Feng-lien 3046
Kuo, Helena (Ching-ch'iu) 0237
Kuo, Mo-jo 1871
Kuo, Ning 2004
Kuo, Ping-wen 1078
Kuo, Po 2005
Kuo, Yun-kuan 2854
Kwan, Rebecca S. 0418
Kwei, Helen Huie 3645
Kyong, Bae-tsung 1079

L. C. C. 0238
L. V. 0667
La Dany, Ladislao 0890, 2654-2656
Lacy, Henry Veere 4040
Laidlaw, Karen A. and Stockwell, Edward G. 0891, 1021
Lake, Douglas; Kramer Ione; and Epstein, Israel 1356
Lal, Amrit 0892, 2657
Lam, Peggy 1022, 1023
Lam, Peggy and Smith, Doreen 0812
Lamson, Herbert Day 0710, 0813, 0814, 0839, 0840, 1582
Lan, Dean 1635
Lan, P'ing. See Chiang Ch'ing
Lancing, George 2199
Landy, Laurie 0306
Lane, Kenneth Westmacott [Keith West] 2200
Lang, Olga 2491
Lanneau, Sophie Stephens 4041
Lao She 1834, 1839
Lau, Joseph S. M., ed. 1833, 2226
Laufer, Berthold 0651
Leader, Shelah Gilbert 0419, 0420
Leaf, E. H. 2151
Leavelle, Elizabeth 2201
Lee, B. E. 1583
Lee, Bernice June 2855
Lee, Rose Hum 2787, 3550
Lee, Shu-ching [Li, Shu-ch'ing] 2492
Lee, T. M. [Li, Tung-ming] and Chow L. P. [Chou, Lien-pin] 1024
Lee, T. Y. 1025
Lee, Tsung-ying 1357

Lee, Yu-hua* 2227
Lee, Yu-hwa 2006
Legge, James, trans. 0144
Leopold, Ellen 2658
Leslie, Gerald R. 2493
Lethbridge, Henry 1584, 2659, 2923
Levi, Werner 2856
Levy, Howard S. 0145, 0788, 1807, 2952, 3579
Levy, Howard S., ed. & trans. 3580
Levy, Marion Joseph, Jr. 2494
Lew, Hilary 2788
Lewis, Elizabeth F. 2202
Lewis, Ida Belle 0010, 0029, 0030, 0031
Lewis, John Wilson, ed. 2914
Li, Ch'ing-chao* 1721, 1722
Li, Chang-chih 1808
Li, Chao-wei 1670
Li, Chen 1126
Li, Chi 2007
Li, Chien-sheng 0852
Li, Chun 1840, 2008–2010
Li, Chun-chao 2023
Li, Dun J. 0146
Li, He 2228
Li, Hsing-tao 1723, 1724
Li, Hui-hsin 2011
Li, Ju-chen 1754–1757
Li, Ju-ching 2012
Li, Shen 0668
Li, Shih 2953
Li, Shu-lan 3737
Li, Teh-chuan 0853
Li, Tung-ch'ing 1113
Li, Wen-yuan 1827
Li, Yih-yüan 2740, 2789
Li, Yü 1758, 1759
Li, Zhong 3701
Liang, Hsing 0307, 2981
Liang, Shih-chiu 2240
Liang, Yen 1188
Liao, Chengzhi 2152
Liao, Su-hua 0460
Lieh-Mak, F.; Tam, Y. K.; and Ng, S. 1026
Lihan, Chang 2351
Lim, Kha-ti 2328
Lin, Adet 1872
Lin, Adet* and Lin, Anor* 1873
Lin, Anor [Lin, Tai-yi]* 1874, 1875
Lin, Chi 2013
Lin, Chin-lan 2014
Lin, Fan 1358
Lin, Hua 2380
Lin, Huaimin 1833
Lin, Lieh-hui 2340
Lin, Robert 2442
Lin, Rui-sui 0815
Lin, Wei-hung 0177
Lin, Wenbin 3738
Lin, Yin-ko 2015
Lin, Yueh-hwa [Lin, Yüeh-hua] 2495
Lin, Yutang 1706 1760, 1809, 1876–1879, 2954
Lin, Yü-t'ang [Lin Yutang], trans. 1705, 1880
Ling, Cheng 1462
Ling, Chia 0422, 3049
Ling, Hsu-hua. See Ling, Shu-hua
Ling, M. L. 2352
Ling, Shu-hua* 1881–1886

Ling, T. See Ting Ling
Liu, Bingqi and Zhang, Tianlai 0734
Liu, Chao 0423
Liu, Chen* 2017
Liu, Ching-an 1671
Liu, Chun-jo 1937
Liu, Francis S. F. [Liu, Shih-fang] 2261
Liu, Hongfa 2353
Liu, Hsi-chun 1520
Liu, Hsiang 0011
Liu, Hui-chen (Wang) 2525
Liu, James J. Y. 1810
Liu, Jung-en, trans. 1707
Liu, K. C. and Sun, T. H. 0816
Liu, Kuang-p'u and Ch'en Fu-t'ung 0309
Liu, Li-wen 0409, 0466
Liu, Liang-ch'ung 0894
Liu, Lo-ch'un 2318
Liu, M. 2354
Liu, Maoshu 0310, 2982
Liu, Melinda 3050
Liu, P. T. and Chow, L. P. [Chou, Lien-pin] 1027
Liu, Pin-hsiung 2741
Liu, T'ieh-yün 1761
Liu, Teh-chang 2018
Liu, Ts'un-yan 2229
Liu, Tsung-ming 3209
Liu, William Thomas [Liu Jung] 2790
Liu, William Thomas [Liu Jung] and Yu, Elena S. H. 2660
Liu, Xinwu 2019
Liu, Y. 2878
Liu, Ya-chun 3739
Liu, Yiu-chu 3657
Liu, Yu Chen 2791
Lo, Kuang-pin 2020
Lo, Pin-chi [Chang, P'u-chün] [Luo, Binji] 2021
Lo, Rong-rong 2443
Lo, Shu 2022
Lo, Shu Hua 0032
Lo, Tung Fan [Lo, Tung-hsün] 2262
Lockhart, James Haldane Stewart 2742
Logan, Lorna E. 1585
Longstreet, Stephen 1586
Longway, Lynn and Liu, Melinda 3051
Loomis, Augustus Ward 1636
Loomis, Augustus Ward, Family 4042
Loraine, J. A. 0895
Lord, Lucy T. 4043
Lowe, Chuan-hua 0005
Lu, Ching-wen 3052
Lu, Fei* 2024, 2025
Lu Hsün [Lu Xun; Chou, Shu-jen] 0239–0241, 0311, 1811, 1831, 1838, 1887–1900
Lu, Laura P.; Chen, H. C.; and Chow, L. P. [Chou, Lien-pin] 1028
Lü, Mrs. Ch'ang-chu (Tu) 3623
Lu Xun. See Lu Hsün
Lu, Y. L. 0424
Lu, Zhong 3702
Lu, Zilan 0896
Lucas, Christopher 0425
Luk, Bernard Hung-kay 2835
Lund, Caroline 0426
Luo, Binji 1835, 1840, 2153
Luo, Qiong 0605
Ly, Singko 3053
Lyle, Katherine Ch'iu 0897–0899
Lyman, Stanford M. 2444

M. F. C. 2552
Ma, Feng 2026, 2027
Ma, Haide, Dr. [George Hatem] 3915
Ma, Hsin-teh 0427
Ma, K. C., trans. 1080
Ma, Ke 2028
Ma, Y. W. and Lau, Joseph S. M. 1708
MacCreery, J. 2263
MacCunn, Ruthann Lum 2230
MacDiarmid, D. N. 3625
MacDougall, Colina 2661, 3054
MacFarquhar, E. 0430
MacKinnon, Catherine 2295
MacKinnon, Jan and MacKinnon, Steve 3916
MacKinnon, Stephan R. 3917
MacLaine Shirley 3941
Macciocchi, Maria Antonietta 0428, 0429
Mace, David and Vera 2264
Macgowan, Rev. John 0178, 2553
Mackay, Margaret 2203, 2204
Madian, Marcia Dunn 2880
Mai, Hui-ting 2496
Main, Ida Belle (Lewis) 4045
Malchinhu 2029, 2030
Maloney, Joan M. 3055
Man, Mu-ch'un 0463
Mao, Nathan K. 1813
Mao, Tse-tung 0312
Mao Tun [Shen, Yen-ping] 2154
Marcelline, Sister M. O. P. 4046
Mariya, Mitsuo 2554
Mark, Lindy Li 2743
Marsh, Robert M. and O'Hara, Albert R. 2445
Martin, Bernard 0148
Martin, Diana 0006
Martinson, Cora 4047
Marvin, Joyce 0431
Mason, Richard L. 2205
Massell, Gregory J. 2883
Mateer, A. H. 3918
Mauldin, Wayman Parker 0900
Mauldin, Wayman Parker; Nortman, Dorothy; and Stephen, Frederick F. 1029
May, Alfred J. 2555
Mayers, William Frederick 2556
McAleavey, Henry 1587, 1812, 2355, 2879
McCormick, Sister Mary Colmcille. 4044
McCreery, John L. 2836, 2857
McDougall, Colin 0789
McGough, James Pierce 2837, 2924
McLeod, Alexander 1555
McNabb, Robert Leroy 0147
Mead, Lucy Irene 4048
Mead, Margaret and Métraux, Rhoda 3551
Medhurst, Walter Henry 2265
Mei, Anna Kong 0242
Mei, Lan-fang 2099
Mei, Mrs. H. C. 3626
Meijer, Marinus Johan 2884-2887
Mels, E. 0149
Mercer, M. 0432
Meskill, Johanna Menzel 2792
Michael, Franz 0179
Mickey, M. Partia 4050
Middleton, Dorothy 3919
Mieh, Chih 3040
Miller, I. L. 1588
Miller, Lucien M. 1814

Miller, Ronald Dean 1589
Miln, Louise 2206, 2207
Milton, Nancy 0433
Min Tzu 0807
Min, Zhi 3285
Minkowski, Alexandre 0669
Minor, Louella 4051
Mitchell, Robert Edward 0088, 1030-1032, 2793, 2794
Mitchell, Robert Edward and Lo, Irene 2795
Mo, Shih-lung 1763
Mo, Ying-feng 2031
Mode, Charles J. and Soyka, Michael G. 1033
Mohapatra, Partha Sarathi 1034
Möllendorff, Paul Georg van 2858
Monroe, Harriet 2557
Moos, Elizabeth 1298
Morris, M. C. 1590
Morrison, Elizabeth 0033
Morrison, Raymond L. and Salmon, Jack D. 0817, 0901
Morse, Esther 4052
Mosher, Steven W. 0818
Mossman, Mereb E. 2297
Moudud, Hasna J. 0434
Mu, Cheng 0670, 0736
Mu, Lan-ying 0464
Mueller, E. 1035
Munro, Stanley R., trans. 1834
Murray, Katie 4053
Mututantri, Barbara 0435
Myrdal, Jan 0436, 1360
Myrdal, Jan and Kessle, G. 0437, 2663

N., Y. I. 0243
Nai, Chi-chang 2032
Nair, N. K. and Chow, L. P. [Chou, Lien-pin] 1036
Nan, Lai 3881
Nan, Ts'ai-ying 1349
Nee, Victor 2497
Nee, P. 1081
Needham, Joseph 3581, 3600
Nelsen, Frida R. 4055
Nelson, Howard George Horatio 2558
Nevius, Mrs. Helen S. 3920
Newcomb, Holly Ellen 0106
Newell, Jane I. 2589
Ng, Pedro Pak-tao 0902
Ni, Ernest In-hsin [Ni, In-hsin, Ni, Yin-hsin] 0819, 0820, 2590, 2591, 2664
Nicholson, Susan 0441
Nieh, Hua-ling* 1828 2232
Nieh, Hua-ling*, ed. 1836
Nieh, Kan-nu 1901
Nien, Chi 1299
Niida, Noboru 2888
Nishio, Yvonne Wong 0442
Nossal, Frederick 0903
Nuckols, Margaret Lynn 0049

O'Callaghan, Sean 1557, 1591
O'Hara, Albert Richard 0012, 0107, 0113, 0150-0152, 0443, 0638, 2446-2448, 2796-2799
O'Sullivan, Sue 0445, 0446, 3058
Ohlinger, Franklin 4056
Oldt, Frank 0711
Olsen, Nancy Johnston 2800-2803, 3552, 3553
Olson, Lillian A. 4057
Opper, Michael 1181, 1182
Orleans, Leo A. 0050, 0821-0825, 0904-0906
Orleans, Leo A., ed. 0907

Osgood, E. I. 2559
Ostrofsky, Diane Betty 1082
Ou, Mei 3059
Owen, Frank 2208

P. R. 0314
Pa Chin [Li, Fei-kan] 1902, 1903, 1938
Paddock, A. E. 1083
Pai, Hsing-chien 1725
Pajet, J. 0244
Palandri, Angela Jung 1815
Palmborg, Rosa W. 4058
Pan, Chia-lin 0826
Pan, Ku 2955
P'an, Kuang-tan 2498
Pan, Margaret Tai-li 1592
P'an, Mei-ying 1374
Pang, Yong-pil 0790
Pao, Chia-lin 0180
Parish, William L., Jr. 2665, 2804
Parish, William L., Jr. and Whyte, Martin King 2666
Parker, Edward Harper 2838
Parrinder, Geoffrey 3582
Partington, T. B. 1816
Pasternak, Burton 2356, 2805
Paterson, I. 0246
Paul, Diana 3601
Pearson, Margaret Jean 0247
Pedersen, Thyra E. 4059
Pegg, Leonard 2449
Pei, Kuo-hung 1606
P'ei, Hsing 1726
Peng, J. Y.; Chow, L. P. [Chou, Lien-pin]; and Corsa, Leslie 1037
Penn, Colin 1183
Perkins, Elizabeth S. 3983
Pettit, Charles 2209
Phillips, Elizabeth 2925, 2926
Pickens, Gary; and Soyka, Michael 1038
Pien, Feng-hao 2034
Pien, Feng-ying 2703
Pierce, Florence 4060
Pillsbury, Barbara L. K. 0652
Ping Hsin [Hsieh, Wan-ying]* 1863, 1904
Platt, H. L. 4061
Platt, W. J. 4062
Po, Chü-i 1727
Po, Hsing-chien 1728
Podmore, D. and Chaney, D. 2450
Pollard, Edward B. 0153
Pollard, R. S. 2357
Poston, Martha Lee 2210
Potter, Jack 3602
Potter, R. G. 1039
Potter, R. G., et al. 1040
Poulter, Mabel C. 0653
Powell, Charles A. 0712
Pratt, Jean 2451
Price, Jane 0315
Price, M. 0248
Price, O. 1559
Price, P. F. 4063
Priest, Alan 3882
Pruitt, Ida 1560, 2592, 3921
Prybyla, Jan 1501
P'u, Sung-ling 1709, 1764, 1765
Purwin, L. and Block, R. H. 0713
Pye, Edith M-. 0249

Quan, Yingqian 3703
Queen, Stuart Alfred; Habenstein, Robert Wesley; and Adams, John B. 2499
Quong, Rose, trans. 1710

Radin, Paul 1677
Rankin, Mary 0181, 0182, 2956
Rawski, Evelyn Sakakida 0013
Reber, Calvin H., Jr. 2299
Record, J. C. and Record, W. 0451
Reed, Alice Clara 4064
Reik, Elsie I. 4065
Rexroth, Kenneth and Chung, Ling, trans. 1711, 2241
Ridehalgh, A. and McDouall, J. C. 2452
Rietveld, Harriet 1084
Ris, H. W. 0452
Rishi, W. R. 2453
Ritzman, M. E. 0154
Robbins, E. V. (Mrs.) 2806
Rock, Joseph Francis 2744
Rogers, Charles 0089
Roman, A. 1085
Root, Helen I., ed. 4066
Ropp, Paul S. 0183
Rosalia, Sister Mary 4067
Rosen, Sherry 2454, 2807
Ross, E. A. 0250
Ross, John. A. and Koh, Kap-suk 1041
Rou Shi [Jou Shih] 1831, 1838
Rousseau, A. M. 0454
Rowbotham, Sheila 0108
Rowe, Elizabeth et al. 0090
Ruben, Sanchez 0317
Ruey, Yih-fu [Jui, I-fu] 2808
Russell, Flo 0614
Russell, J. 1561
Russell, Maud 0455
Rutstein, Shea Oscar 1042
Ryan, E. 2455

Sa, Sophie 2809
Salaff, Janet W. 0738, 0909, 1639, 1640, 2359, 2456, 2457, 2669
Salaff, Janet Wietzner and Merkle, Judith 0456
Sallee, Annie (Jenkins) 4068
Sampson, Theos 0184
Sandroff, Ronni 3942
Sanford, Agnes Mary (White) 2211
Sang, Hu 2101
Sankar, Andrea Patrice 0639
Sansan* 2233
Sarker, Subhash Chandra 0827
Satoh, May Miki 1678
Scarborough, William 1650
Schaffer, Edward H. 1679, 1680, 1681
Schak, David C. 2458, 3554
Schell, Orville 2360, 3062, 3063
Schintz, Mary Ann 4069
Schlegel, Gustaaf 1593
Schlesinger, Benjamin 2670
Schmeidler, Gertrude and Windholz, George 3555
Schran, Peter 1363
Schu, Mark J. 3943
Schultz, T. Paul 1043
Schuman, J. 0457
Schurmann, H. F. 1817
Schwarcz, Vera 0251
Scott, Adolphe Clarence 3899, 3900
Scott, George Ryley 3583

Scott, Mrs. Grace (Ciggie) 4070
Seesholtz, Ann G. 0034, 0253
Selden, Mark 0539, 2706
Seligmann, J. 0703
Sergeant, Philip Walshingham 2957
Serruys, Henry 2745
Serruys, Paul 2300
Seton, Grace (Gallatin) Thompson 0254, 3629
Seward, George 1595
Seymour, Joseph 3169
Sha, Hung-ping 2037
Shan, Lingyi; Wang, Chuanfeng; and Zhang, Wenyu 0077
Shao, Li-tzu 0850, 0854
Shapiro-Perl, Nina 2412
Shen, Fu 0155
Shen, Hsiu-chin 1470
Shen, Lien-ting 2403
Shen, Ts'ung-wen [Shen, Tseng-wen] 1905-1907
Sheng, Chiang 1683
Shepard, Don, comp. 2958
Shephard, Esther 1684
Shepherd, Charles R. 1596
Sheridan, Mary 3170
Sheth, Ketaki 1151
Shiga, Shūzō 2859
Shih, Chung-wen 1730
Shih, Liang 2903
Shih, Lu 2377
Shih, Min 2038
Shih, Vincent Y. C. 0185
Shih, Yen 3171, 3200
Shimer, Dorothy Blair, ed. 0109
Shui, Chieh 2624
Shun, Chung-wen 1908
Sibley, Jean 3944
Siddiqui, Mohammed K. 1044
Sidel, Ruth 0110, 0686, 0739, 2707
Sierksma, F. 3584
Simester, Edith Winifred 4071
Simkin, Margaret (Timberlake) 4072
Simon, G. E. 2560
Simpson, Bertram Lenox [Putnam Weale] 2212
Sinanian, Natalie J.R. 0640
Siu, Bobby 0255, 0256
Skinner, G. William, ed. 2526
Skinner, James Edwards 4073
Sladetien, Joseleyne 0541
Sleeman, John H. 0156
Smedley, Agnes 0318, 0542, 0624, 2301, 3922-3925
Smith, Arthur 0157
Smith Family 4074
Smith, Mabel Waln 3926
Smith, Myrtle A. 4075
Smith, Peter C. 2459
Smythe, Lewis Strong Casey 2593, 2594
Smythe, Margaret Garret 4076
Snow, Edgar 0829
Snow, Edgar, comp. and ed. 1838
Snow, Helen Foster [Nym Wales] 0111, 0319, 0543
Snow, Myra L. 4077
Solidum, Estella D. 1059
Soo, Annie 1641
Soong, Ching Ling [Soong Ching-ling, Mme. Sun Yat-sen] 0257, 0548, 0549, 1527, 2983, 2984, 3068, 3172
Soong, Mayling [Chiang, Mei-ling; Mme. Chiang Kai-shek] 1686, 2967-2971, 3646
Souile, Charles George, comp. and trans. 1712

Sovik, Gertrude 4078
Spade, Beatrice 0014
Speare, A.; Speare Mary; and Lin, Hui-sheng 1045
Spence, Jonathan 0158
Spencer, C. 1109
Spencer, Robert F. and Barnett, S. A. 2302
Spicer, Eva Dykes 3647
Spinney, Anna G. 3927
Srikantan, Kodaganallur Sivaswamy 1046
Stacey, Judith 0571, 0572, 2500, 2501, 2710-2712
Stafford, A. C. 0160
Stafford, Peter 3585
Stanford, Sally 1597
Stanley, Louise (Hathaway) 4079
Stein, Guenther 0322
Stein, Rolf Alfred 2746
Stevens, Mrs. Helen [Norton] 4080
Stone, Grace (Zaring) 3928
Stoodley, Bartlett H. 0091, 2811
Strong, Anna Louise 0259, 0260, 1087, 1442, 3929, 3945-3948
Stuart, Mary Horton 4081
Su, Enteh 2713
Su, Feng 2416
Su, Huei 0573
Su, M. 1273, 1443
Su, Ru-chiang 0841
Su, Sing Ging [Hsü, Sheng-chin]. 2502, 2714
Su, Yu-fu 0774
Suh-ho 0792
Sun, Chan-ko 2918
Sun, Ching-jui 2039
Sun, Hsiao-chu 1274
Sun, Kuei-chin 3728
Sun, Lai-chin 2040
Sun, Li 2041-2045
Sun, Phillip S. Y. 1818
Sun, T.H. [Sun, Te-hsiung] 1047, 1048
Sun, Tan-wei 1531
Sun, Tsai-hua 0932
Sun, Wei-shih 2046, 2683
Sun, Y. 2047
Sun, Yung 2048
Sung, An-na 2049
Sung, Betty Lee 1642
Sung, Hsin-ju 0574
Sung, Hung-hua 2102
Sung, Kuei-sheng and Lang, Chih-jen 1562
Sung, Wen-mei 3067
Sung, Yüh 1731
Sussex, Elizabeth 2927-2930
Swann, Nancy Lee 0015, 2160
Sweeten, Alan R. 2860
Sword Family 3930
Syrdal, Borghild Roe 4082
Sze, Mai-mai* 1909, 1910

T. H. 0324
Tack, Minnie 4083
Taeuber, Irene Barnes 0830, 2595
Taeuber, Irene Barnes and Orleans, Leo A. 0933
Tai, Dawn 3213
Tai, Yen-hui 2861
Takeshita, John Yuzuru; Reng, J. Y.; and Liu, Paul K. C. [Liu K'o-chih] 0704
Takeshita, John Yuzuru 1050
Tamney, Joseph B. 2503
Tan, Aiqing 3870
Tan, Kuei-ying 2747
Tan, Manni 2904

Tan, Wen-chen 1444
Tang, Chindon Yiu 0035
T'ang, Hsien-tsu 1768
Tang, Mei-chun 2748, 2812, 2813
T'ang, Sheng-p'ing 3002
Tang, Tao 1939
Tang, Tien-yüan 2050
Tannenbaum, Gerald 2111
Tao, L. K. [Tao, Meng-ho] 2504
Tao, Li-kung 2596
T'ao, Ling and Johnson, Lydia 1088
Tao, P. L. K. 2505
Tao, Peng-fei 3871
Tao, S. M. 0714
Taring, Richen Dolma 2749
Tavris, Carol 0575
Tayler, John Bernard and Zung, W. T. 1089
Taylor, Mrs. Mary Geraldine (Guiness) 4084
Taynton, Susan (Herring) Jeffries 4085
Tcheng, Soumay 0262
Teagarden, Lyrel G. 4086
Teh, Yung 2161
Teng, Ying-ch'ao 0576-0580, 2882, 2987, 3075, 3495, 3501, 3533
Teng, Yuan-ying 0628, 1617
Terni, P. V. E. 2905
Terrill, R. 0934
Tesdell, Margaret Stanley 3931, 3949
Thode, Frieda Oelschiaeger 4087
Thompson, Laurence G. 2750
Thorborg, Marina 1277, 1445
Thurston, John Lawrence, Mrs.; and Chester, Ruth M. 0036
Tie, Yun 1278
Tien, Chien 2052
Tien, H. Y. 0581
Tien, H. Yuan [T'ien Hsin-yüan] 0935-0942
Tien, H. Yuan, ed. 0831
Tien, Han 2053
Tien, J. S. 0582
T'ien, Ju-k'ang 1090
Tien, Kuei-ying 1279
Tien, Leng 2054
Tien, Lin 1446
Ting Ling [Ding Ling; Chiang, Ping-chih]* 0308, 1911-1923, 2056, 2057, 2132, 2162, 2163
Ting, Nai-tung 1687
Ting, Tzu-ping 2058
Ting, Wang 3217
Ting, Yao-k'ang 1769
Ting, Yi and Ho, Ching-chih 2055
Tinling, Christine I. 4088
Titiev, Mischa and Tien, Hsing-chih [T'ien Hsing-chih] 2561
Tjan, Tjoe-som 2267
Topley, Marjorie 0654, 2268, 2460-2462
Traver, Edith Grace 4089
Tretiak, L. D. 0584
Treudley, Mary B. 2597
Triviere, Leon 0943
Ts'ai, Ch'ang 0285, 0379, 0405, 0499, 0503, 1112, 3076, 3275
Ts'ai, Ch'ing-yuan 0642, 2988
Tsai, Yung-mei 0643
Ts'ao, Hsin-hua 2715
Ts'ao, Hsüeh-ch'in [Cao Xueqin] 1770-1775
Tsao, Kuan-chun 1140
Tsao, Lady [Pan Chao] 0016
Tsao, Li Yieni 0186, 2242, 2562
Tsao, M. Ch. 0585
Tsao, Meng-chun 2839

Ts'ao, Ming [Lo, Ts'ao-ming]* 2059-2062
Tsao, W. Y. 2840
Tsay, Queenie 0655
Tseng, Lily 0715
Tseng, P. S. (Pao-sun) 0263, 3648
Tseng, Wen-shing and Hsu, Jing 3556
Tsha, T. Y. [Ts'ai Cheng-ya] 1091, 1092
Tsin, Ching 0325, 2063, 2989
Tsin, Yu 1110
Tso, An-hua 0944
Tso, S. K. Sheldon [Chu, Shih-k'ang] 1093
Tso, S. W. 2269
Tso, Sung-fen 3219
Tso, Yü-chin 3220
Tsou Yi-hsin 3700
Tsui, Ching-tai 0692
Tsui, Hsiu-mei 2716
Tsui, Yu-lan 0586
Tsung, Pu 2064
Tsung, Shiu-kuen Fan 2814
Tsung, T. 2463
Tu, G. L. T. 1051
Tu, P'eng-ch'eng* 2065
Tuan, Chi-hsien 1052
Tuan, Ti-wei 0775
Tung, Chun-lun and Chiang, Yuan 2066
Tung, Feng-wen 1413, 2112
Tung, Mei 1280
Tung, Yi-chang 2717
Turner, H. F. 0037
Twanmoh, Chien-ming. 0264
Tze, Kang 2719

Una, Lady Troubridge, trans. 2213

Van Gulik, Robert Hans 3586, 3587
Van Vorst, Bessie (McGinnis) 0265
Van Wettum, B. A. J. 2270
Van der Valk, Marius Hendrikus 2841, 2863-2865, 2906
Varma, Asha 0946
Veneris, Jim 2417
Victoria, Sister Mary 4090
Vogel, Ezra Feivel 3557, 3558

Wagner, Augusta Bertha 1097
Wales, Nym [Helen Foster Snow] 0326, 0327, 1098
Waley, Arthur 1688, 1713, 1819, 1820
Walker, Kathy LeMons. 0328
Wallace, L. Ethel 0038
Wallis, Gertrude (Steel-Brooke) 4093
Walls, Jan Wilson 2164
Waln, N. 2303
Walsh, Richard John 3932
Walshe, William Gilbert 2271
Walstedt, Joyce Jennings 2507, 2720
Walton, Cara May 0039, 1099
Wan, Shan-hung and Hung Tieh-shan 1281
Wang, Ai-chu 0403
Wang, An-yu 2067
Wang, C. M. and Sun, T. H. 0833
Wang, Cheng 2598
Wang, Chiao 1448
Wang, Chi-chen, trans. 1839
Wang, Elizabeth Te-chen 1714
Wang, H. 3534
Wang, Hai-p'o 1293
Wang, Ho-ho 2068
Wang, Hsi-t'ang; Lien, Pu-wang; and Yao, I-shan 0329
Wang, Hsin-chen 1282, 3221

Wang, Janet F. 1053
Wang, Jen-ying 0705, 2527
Wang, Kai-hsi 0716
Wang, Kung 3222
Wang, Shan-hung and Hung, Tieh-shan 2069
Wang, Shih-fu 1776-1778
Wang, Shu-yuan, et al. 2070
Wang, Tung-ching 1283
Wang, Wen-hsing 2235
Wang, Yi-chang 1054
Wang, Yi-chih 0330
Wang, Yu Jung 0092
Wang, Yüan-chien 2071, 2072
Wang, Yun-ch'ang; Li, Yueh-ling; and T'ien, Shen-yuan 1366
Ward, Arthur Sarsfield 2214
Ward, Barbara 2815
Ward, J. S. 3631
Ward, Katherine Bertha Boege 4091, 4092
Warner, Marina 2960
Watson, James L. 1563, 2528
Weakland, John H. 2113
Webster, James Benjamin 3559
Wei, Cheng Yu-hsia [Mme. Wei Tao-ming] 0266
Wei, Chin-chih 0187, 2073
Wei, Hsian-chuen Sharon 2816
Wei, Hwei-lin 2751-2753
Wei, T. F. 2304
Wei, W. L. 0267, 1598
Wei, Wen 0693
Wei, Wilson Shih-sheng 0040
Wei, Yueh-hsiang 2721
Weigelin, Susanne 0331, 2990
Weinbaum, Batya 0588
Weiss, Ruth 0589, 0590, 3223, 3224
Wen, Chieh 2074
Wen, Chun-chuan and Shan, Fu 1284
Wen, P'ing and Feng, Cheng 3225
Wen, Tzu-pien 1487
Wertheim, W. F. 0834
West, Anthony 1821
Westland, A. B. 2464
Wheeler, Jane E. 1449
Wheeler, Laura Maude 4094
Wheelhouse, Frances 3933
White, E. Aldersey, ed. 4095
White, F. J. 0041
White, J. 0268
White, Lynn T. III 0947
White, Mary Culler 3632
Whitehead, Raymond L. 0591
Whitehead, Rhea 0592, 0593
Whyte, Martin King 2419, 2420, 2722, 2723
Whyte, Robert O. and Whyte, Pauline 1450
Wicher, Edward Arthur 1599
Wieman, Earl 2563, 2961
Wikander, Ingeborg 1100
Wilbur, Clarence Martin 1564
Wiley, James Hundley 1600
Wiley, Martha 4096, 4097
Wilhelm, Helmut 2116
Wilhelm, Richard 2272
Wilkinson, Hiram Pardes 2564
Wilkinson, Leila Fayssoux Davidson 4098
Wilkinson, William Henry 2273
Williams, F. T. 0269
Williams, George L. and Williams, Mary Alice Moon 4099
Williams, Samuel Wells 0017, 0161

Willis, Donald S. 1822
Wilson, Amy Auerbacher 3430
Wilson, Emma Webber 4100
Wilson, Richard W. 3560
Wimsatt, Genevieve 2165, 2215
Winans, Pearl (Fosnot) 4101
Winnington, Alan 0630, 1565
Winslow, Carolyn V. 4102
Witke, Roxane Heater 0270, 0271, 2991, 3226-3228
Wittfogel, Karl A. 0162
Wolcott, Jessie L. 4104
Wolf, Arthur Paul 0835, 2465-2467, 3588
Wolf, Arthur Paul and Huang, C. T. 2468
Wolf, Arthur Paul and Huang, Chieh-shan 2274
Wolf, Margery 0163, 2817-2819, 3561
Wolf, Margery and Witke, Roxanne, eds. 0164
Wong, Alice (Kan) 2421, 2724
Wong, Aline K. 0644, 1643
Wong, C. M [Wang, Mei-ch'ih] 2275
Wong, Chun-kit Joseph 2820, 2821
Wong, Dorothy T. 0273
Wong, Fai-ming 1644, 2822, 2823
Wong, Jade Snow 2234
Wong, Jayce Mende 1601
Wong, K. Chimin [Wang Chi-min] 0717
Wong, K. and Wu, L. 0656
Wong, Molly 3635
Wong, Shau-lam 2824
Wong, Su-ling and Cressy, Earl Herbert 2599
Wong, Sun-ming 2276
Woo, Pak Chuen [Wu, Pai-ch'üan] 2842
Woo, Sun-pei 1102
Wood, Edith Elmer 2565
Wood, Leili 3950
Wood, S. 0606
Wood, Shirley 0776
Wood, Shirley 3951
Woodsmall, Ruth Frances 0274, 3636
Woodworth, K. C. 2908
Wright, Arthur F. 3562
Wright, Beryl Robina 2825
Wu, Ching-chao [Wu, Ching-ch'ao] 1651
Wu, Diana Ting Liu 3563
Wu, Hsiao-ming 1618
Wu, Hsiu-mei 3695
Wu, Ming 3437
Wu, Pei-yi 1690
Wu, Shu-chiung (Huang) [Mrs. Wu Lien-teh] 2962
Wu, Ting Fang [Wu Ting-fang] 0275, 3564
Wu, Tze-wo 3731
Wu, Y. M. 3438
Wu, Yang 2166
Wu, Yen-ho 2754
Wu, Yen-ko 2076
Wu, Yung 2963

Xu, Juru 2919

Yan, Kuo-shu; Ko, Yun-ho; and Yang, Pen-hua 0093
Yan, Qing 2422
Yang, Ai-wen 1288
Yang, C. H. 1157
Yang, C. K. [Yang, Ch'ing-k'un] 2508, 2725
Yang, Chen-sheng 1924
Yang, Chih-hua 1186
Yang, Ching 1535
Yang, Chingchu [Yang, Ch'ing-ch'u] 1833, 2227
Yang, Gladys 2167

Yang, H. C. 1289
Yang, Hsien-yi and Yang, Gladys 1715
Yang, Hsiu 2673
Yang, Kan-ling 2726
Yang, Kuei-fang 0616, 0631
Yang, Lien-sheng 2964, 2965
Yang, Liu 2423
Yang, Martin C. 1111, 2600
Yang, Martin M. C. [Yang, Mou-ch'un] 2826, 2827
Yang, Mei-ching 1691
Yang, Minru 2168
Yang, Mo* 2077
Yang, Pi-wang 2277
Yang, Richard F. S. and Levy, Howard S., trans. 3589
Yang, Simon [Yang, Hsi-meng] and Tao, L. K. [T'ao, Meng-ho], trans. 2601
Yang, Tse-feng 1619
Yang, Tso-hung 3660
Yang, Wen 2909, 2910
Yang, Y. 1455
Yang, Yan-yu 3537
Yang, Yang 2118
Yang, Yu 3231
Yang, Yun-shen 2078
Yao, Hsin-nung 1925, 1926, 2169
Yao, Keh-ming 2079
Yao, Li-kung 2366
Yao, Meng-hsüan 3232
Yao, R. 1602
Yap, Pow-meng [Yeh, Pao-ming] 3565
Yaukey, Grace [Cornelia Spencer] 3935
Yeh, Ch'an-chen 2170
Yeh, Lin 2119
Yeh, Mien 2080
Yen, Chih-t'ui 2566
Yen, Han-wen Edwin 0094
Yen, Nai-Hua 3874
Yen, W. W., trans. 1716
Yi, Chun 0632
Yi, Ke 0694
Yin Fu [Hsü, Yin-fu] 1927
Yin, Hsiang 3637
Yin, Yi-ping 2081
Ying, Kuei-fang 0609, 0948
Young, Ludvig J-. 0276
Young, Marilyn Blatt 0115
Young, Mildred Test 4106
Young, T. S. 2306
Yu, Elena S. H. 2529, 2727
Yu, H. 0610, 0949
Yü, Hsiang 3233
Yu, Jen 2082
Yu, Li 2319
Yu, Lihua* 1833
Yu, Tsung-hsin 2083
Yu, Y. C. 0836, 0837
Yu, Yu 2084
Yü, Yü-cha 3936
Yu, Yun-chuan 2085
Yüan, Ch'en 1732
Yüan, D. Y. 2469
Yüan, Sou 3234
Yuan, Tzu-jen 2363
Yuan, Weimin 3875
Yuan, Y. Y. 3639
Yueh, Wen 2086
Yüen, Feng and Wang, Tien-ch'i 1566
Yule, E. S. 0278

Yusuf, Alieas 2087
Zen, Sophia H. Chen [Mrs. Hong-che] 0279
Zengbian 3730
Zhang, Hu 0334
Zhang, Huaijing and Zhou, Baohua 2755
Zhang, Pei-Zhu 0951
Zhao, Fengfeng 3952
Zhao, Shuili 1831
Zhou, Yixing 2171
Zia, Z. K. 2602
Zung, Wei-tsung 1105

Index of Chinese Women as Subjects

Ah Toy 1573
Aijiguli 2089

Ban Zhao 0015, 0016, 0116, 2160
Bao Lianzi 0286, 0329
Bemis, Polly 2230
Bi Yinglan 1362, 3060
Bing Xin [Xie Wanying] 1929, 1930, 2120

Cai Chang 0285, 0303, 3044, 3080, 3375, 3456, 3483, 3494, 3502
Cai Dingli 0326
Cao Mengjun 3044
Chang Chieh. *See* Zhang Jie
Chang Chih-hsin. *See* Zhang Zhixin
Chang Ch'in-ch'iu. *See* Zhang Qinqiu
Chang, Eileen 2236
Chang Jui-fang. *See* Zhang Ruifang
Chang Ying-hang. *See* Zhang Yinghang
Chang Yun. *See* Zhang Yun
Chao Chin. *See* Zhao Jin
Che Guangmei 3669
Ch'e Kuang-mei. *See* Che Guangmei
Chen Chong 2171
Ch'en Ch'ung. *See* Chen Chong
Chen Ennü 1427
Chen Min 3065
Chen Shaomin 0305, 3044
Chen Yuanji 2158
Chen Yuanyuan 1739
Chung, Margaret 2174
Chhodnam, Drolma 1544
Chi Chih-i. *See* Ji Zhiyi
Chiang Ch'ing. *See* Jiang Qing
Ch'ien Ying. *See* Qian Ying
Chin Yueh-ling. *See* Jin Yueling
Ch'iu Chin. *See* Qiu Jin
Ch'iu Hsiu-ying. *See* Qiu Xiuying
Cho Wen-chün. *See* Zhuo Wenjun
Chou Ching-sung. *See* Zhou Jingsong
Chou, Ivy 3611
Chu Ying-t'ai. *See* Zhu Yingtai
Cixi, Empress Dowager 1926, 2184, 2185, 2931, 2932, 2934-2939, 2950, 2957, 2958, 2960, 2963
Cui Rongyou 3237
Cui Yingying 1732, 1776-1778, 1798

De Ling [Der Ling, Princess] 1844-1847, 2131, 2572, 2938, 2939
Deng Yingchao 0490, 2987, 3026, 3027, 3044, 3075, 3128, 3129, 3131, 3132, 3152, 3160, 3166, 3187, 3192, 3198, 3199, 3207, 3210, 3212, 3314, 3465, 3502, 3504
Ding Ling [Jiang Bingzhi] 0308, 1922, 1933, 1934, 2056, 2057, 2094, 2120, 2123, 2132, 2133, 2136, 2151, 2154, 2162, 2163, 3044
Dong Youlan 3231
Dou E 1730

Fang Ju-fen. *See* Fang Rufen
Fang Rufen 2134

Gan Jiaming 0028
Guan Yin 3592, 3596
Guo Fenglian 1355
Guo Shuzhen 3097

Han Suyin 0595, 2129, 2130
He Lianzhi 0303
He Xiangning 2152, 2977

Ho Hsiang-ning. *See* He Xiangning
Ho Lien-chih. *See* He Lianzhi
Hongxian 1810
Hsiang Ching-yü. *See* Xiang Jingyu
Hsiao Hung. *See* Xiao Hong
Hsieh Ping-ying. *See* Xie Bingying
Hsieh Wan-ying. *See* Bing Xin
Hsüeh T'ao. *See* Xue Tao
Hu King-Eng, Dr. 0082

I Hsiao-li. *See* Yi Xiaoli

Hung-hsien. *See* Hongxian

Ji Zhiyi 0032
Jiang Bingzhi. *See* Ding Ling
Jiang Qing 2092, 2994, 3008-3019, 3025, 3028, 3030, 3032, 3034, 3036, 3037, 3039, 3045-3048, 3050-3054, 3056, 3058, 3063, 3121, 3127, 3169, 3171, 3194, 3195, 3200-3206, 3208, 3209, 3211, 3213, 3214, 3216, 3217, 3220, 3222, 3223, 3225, 3226, 3228, 3232-3234, 3503
Jin Yueling 2149
Ju Chih-chuan. *See* Ru Zhijuan
Jung Kuang-hsiu. *See* Rong Guangxiu

Kan Chiaming. *See* Gan Jiaming
Kang Keqing 0303-0305, 0326, 3128, 3129, 3131, 3132, 3504
K'ang K'o-ch'ing. *See* Kang Keqing
Kuan-yin. *See* Guan Yin
Kuo Feng-lien. *See* Guo Fenglian
Kuo Shu-chen. *See* Guo Shuzhen

Lan Ping. *See* Jiang Qing
Li Chen. *See* Li Zhen
Li Chien-chen. *See* Li Jianzhen
Li Ch'ing-chao. *See* Li Qingzhao
Li Dechuan 0494, 3044, 3471, 3472, 3479, 3485, 3487, 3489
Li Fenglan 2142
Li Hsiu-wen. *See* Li Xiuwen
Li I-an. *See* Li Yian
Li Jianzhen 3044
Li Qingzhao 1721, 1722, 2147
Li Shuangshuang 2009
Li Suwen 3178, 3179, 3184, 3185, 3197, 3513
Li Teh-ch'uan. *See* Li Dechuan
Li Xiuwen 3159, 3160, 3162
Li Yayun 3728
Li Yian 2126
Li Zhen 0303
Li Zongren, Mrs. *See* Li Xiuwen
Lin, Adet 1873
Lin, Anor [Lin Taiyi] 1873
Lin Hui-ching. *See* Lin Huijing
Lin Huijing 3777
Ling Mulan 3062
Liu Hsiu-lan. *See* Liu Xiulan
Liu Hulan 0307, 0317, 0323, 0325, 2063, 2118, 2981, 2989
Liu Laolao 1789
Liu, Mary 3620
Liu Xiulan 2671
Lü, Empress 3034, 3201, 3234
Luo Ch'iung. *See* Luo Qiong
Luo Qiong 3044

Meng Chiang-nü. *See* Meng Jiangnü
Meng Jiangnü 1654, 1674
Mu Guiying 3691

Mu Kui-ying. *See* Mu Guiying

Nie Yinniang 1726, 1810
Nieh Yin-niang. *See* Nie Yinniang

Ou Meng-chüeh. *See* Ou Mengjue
Ou Mengjue 3044
Ou Tangliang 3044, 3129, 3152

Pan Chao. *See* Ban Zhao
Pao Lien-tzu. *See* Bao Lianzi
Pi Ying-lan. *See* Bi Yinglan
Ping Hsin. *See* Bing Xin

Qian Ying 3044
Qiu Jin 0174, 0176, 0181, 0182, 2941, 2944
Qiu Xiuying 3137

Rong Guangxiu 0304
Ru Zhijuan 2122, 2135

Sai Chin-hua. *See* Sai Jinhua
Sai Jinhua 1571, 1587, 1812, 1822
Shen Hsiu-chin. *See* Shen Xiujin
Shen Rong 2167
Shen Xiujin 1487
Shi Liang 0484, 2903, 3044
Shuai Meng-chi. *See* Shuai Mengqi
Shuai Mengqi 3044
Si Xia 0051
Song Meiling [Soong Mayling] 2967, 2975, 2976, 2979, 2988
Song Qingling [Soong Ching Ling] 2975, 2976, 3023, 3033, 3044, 3072, 3107, 3122, 3124, 3126, 3130, 3173, 3368, 3460, 3470, 3493
Ssu Hsia. *See* Si Xia
Stone, Mary 3607, 3629
Sung Ch'ing-ling. *See* Song Qingling
Sung Mei-ling. *See* Song Meiling

Teling. *See* De Ling
Teng Ying-ch'ao. *See* Deng Yingchao
Ting Ling. *See* Ding Ling
Tou O. *See* Dou E
Ts'ai Ch'ang. *See* Cai Chang
Ts'ai Ting-li. *See* Cai Dingli
Tsou Yi-hsin. *See* Zou Yixin
Ts'ui Jung-yu. *See* Cui Rongyou
Ts'ui Ying-ying. *See* Cui Yingying
Tung Yu-lan. *See* Dong Youlan
Tz'u-hsi. *See* Cixi, Empress Dowager

Wang Baochuan 1864, 1865
Wang Guangmei 2993, 3057
Wang Hai-jung. *See* Wang Hairong
Wang Hairong 3043
Wang Kuang-mei. *See* Wang Guangmei
Wang Pao-ch'uan. *See* Wang Baochuan
Wencheng, Princess 2053
Wen-chi, Lady. *See* Wenji, Lady
Wenji, Lady 1742
Wong, Jade Snow, 2234
Wu, Empress. *See* Wu Zetian
Wu Fusha 3748
Wu Guixian 3227
Wu Hsiu-mei. *See* Wu Xiumei
Wu Kuei-hsien. *See* Wu Guixian
Wu Xiumei 3658
Wu Zetian 1754, 2933, 2940, 2942, 2943, 2947, 2953, 2954

Xiang Jingyu 0303, 0310, 0330, 2982, 3044
Xiao Hong [Zhang Naiying] 2139, 2153
Xiao Shufang 2138

Xie Bingying 0225, 0226, 0247 2143-2145
Xie Wanying. *See* Bing Xin
Xue Tao 2148, 2168

Yang Buwei 0201, 2124
Yang Guifei 1719, 1727, 1751, 1752, 1788, 2191, 2200, 2961, 2962
Yang Kaihui 0287, 0288, 0297, 0301, 0320, 0321, 0331, 0333, 2117, 2966, 2974, 2980, 2985, 2986, 2990, 2992
Yang Kuei-fei. *See* Yang Guifei
Yang Mo 2098, 2166
Yang Pu-wei. *See* Yang Buwei
Ye Chanzhen 2170
Yeh Ch'an-chen. *See* Ye Chanzhen
Yi Xiaoli 2172
Yu Fengying 1229-1231, 3713
Yu Lan 2150
Yü Hsuan-chi. *See* Yu Xuanji
Yu Xuanji 2164, 2165

Zhang Ailing. *See* Chang, Eileen
Zhang Jie 2141
Zhang Qinqiu 3044
Zhang Naiying. *See* Xiao Hong
Zhang Ruifang 2150
Zhang Yinghang 3704
Zhang Yun 3044
Zhang Zhixin 3007
Zhao Buwei. *See* Yang Buwei
Zhao Jin 0488
Zhou Jingsong 3288, 3289
Zhu Yingtai 1672
Zhuo Wenjun 1871
Zou Yixin 3700

HQ 1767 .C45 copy 2

Cheng, Lucie.

Women in China